GUIDE TO
THE CINEMA(S) OF
CANADA

Reference Guides to the World's Cinema

Guide to the Cinema of Spain
Marvin D'Lugo

Guide to American Cinema, 1965–1995
Daniel Curran

Guide to African Cinema
Sharon A. Russell

Guide to American Cinema, 1930–1965
Thomas Whissen

Guide to the Silent Years of American Cinema
Donald W. McCaffrey and Christopher P. Jacobs

Guide to the Cinema of Sweden and Finland
Per Olov Qvist and Peter von Bagh

GUIDE TO THE CINEMA(S) OF CANADA

EDITED BY PETER HARRY RIST

Reference Guides to the World's Cinema
Pierre L. Horn, Series Adviser

GREENWOOD PRESS
Westport, Connecticut • London

Library of Congress Cataloging-in-Publication Data

Guide to the cinema(s) of Canada / edited by Peter Harry Rist.
     p. cm.—(Reference guides to the world's cinema, ISSN 1090–8234)
    Includes bibliographical references and index.
    ISBN 0–313–29931–5 (alk. paper)
    1. Motion pictures—Canada—History. I. Rist, Peter. II. Series.
  PN1993.5.C2 G85   2001
  791.43'0971—dc21   00–049072

British Library Cataloguing in Publication Data is available.

Library of Congress Catalog Card Number: 00–049072
ISBN: 0–313–29931–5
ISSN: 1090–8234

First published in 2001

Greenwood Press, 88 Post Road West, Westport, CT 06881
An imprint of Greenwood Publishing Group, Inc.
www.greenwood.com

Printed in the United States of America

The paper used in this book complies with the
Permanent Paper Standard issued by the National
Information Standards Organization (Z39.48–1984).

10 9 8 7 6 5 4 3 2 1

In loving memory of my mentor, Bill Everson

CONTENTS

SERIES FOREWORD

For the first time, on December 28, 1895, at the Grand Café in Paris, France, the inventors of the *Cinématographe*, Auguste and Louis Lumière, showed a series of eleven two-minute silent shorts to a public of thirty-five people each paying the high entry fee of one gold franc. From that moment, a new era had begun, for the Lumière brothers were not only successful in their commercial venture, but they also unknowingly created a new visual medium quickly to become, throughout the world, the half-popular entertainment, half-sophisticated art of the cinema. Eventually, the contribution of each member of the profession, especially that of the director and the performers, took on enormous importance. A century later, the situation remains very much the same.

The purpose of Greenwood's *Reference Guides to the World's Cinema* is to give a representative idea of what each country or region has to offer to the evolution, development, and richness of film. At the same time, because each volume seeks to present a balance between the interests of the general public and those of students and scholars of the medium, the choices are by necessity selective (although as comprehensive as possible) and often reflect the author's own idiosyncrasies.

André Malraux, the French novelist and essayist, wrote about the cinema and filmmakers: "The desire to build up a world apart and self-contained, existing in its own right . . . represents humanization in the deepest, certainly the most enigmatic, sense of the word." On the one hand, then, every *Guide* explores this observation by offering discussions, written in a jargon-free style, of the motion-picture art and its practitioners, and on the other provides much-needed information, seldom available in English, including filmographies, awards and honors, and ad hoc bibliographies.

Pierre L. Horn
Wright State University

PREFACE AND INTRODUCTION

This book is, first and foremost, a work of the film studies program of Concordia University's Cinema Department. This is not to say that anyone in the program who was not involved in this project should be held accountable for its shortcomings. But so many ex-students were involved, myself included, that the book has clearly taken on characteristics of the program's general approach to film studies within the context of a fine arts faculty. Simply stated, many of us are interested in "film style" for its own sake, and in all the many ways it relates to "content." Indeed, I am deeply indebted for my own formation as a film scholar to my first two film teachers, Vlada Petric (a visiting professor in film history) and John Locke (film aesthetics). It is fair to say that had I not studied cinema initially at Concordia, I might not have pursued the discipline at all. Both professors, who had graduated from New York University in cinema studies, insisted on viewing films closely, often using an analytical projector. I was amazed at how much fascinating cinematic detail could be discovered in the most sophisticated films, and, by extension, at how many mistakes would consistently be made by so-called film critics of the period (mid-1970s), who were rarely concerned with style. After becoming a graduate student myself at NYU, I learned that, even at the home of close visual film analysis, they had virtually given up the struggle to keep their Athena frame-by-frame projectors going. I have subsequently learned that Cinema Concordia is virtually the only educational institution to maintain the now-extinct technology. As much as we are keeping up with advances in the video domain, in our determination to screen films on celluloid where possible, we have become "dinosaurs" in a very good sense, I believe.

I was also encouraged to have more respect for Canadian films than heretofore through John Locke's classes. I had seen Allan King's *A Married Couple* when it was first released in Montreal, but before I studied film aesthetics I had no idea that it was so important a film in its addressing the question of difference between fiction and documentary film modes. Furthermore, I was unaware of the important Canadian tradition of experimental filmmaking until John Locke (as Vlada's guest) introduced Michael Snow's *Wavelength* in the summer of 1976. After completing my studies in New York, where, unfortunately, Canadian film seemed virtually nonexistent, I was able to deepen my knowledge of our homegrown cinema at the University of Western Ontario. When I arrived in 1981, Seth Feldman was teaching a survey course on Canadian film. He allowed me to sit in and watch some early classics such as Nell and Ernie Shipman's *Back to God's Country* and the amazing Newfoundland epic, *The Viking*. At the same time I was able to read Peter Morris' landmark history of Canadian film before World War II (and the formation of the National Film Board), *Embattled Shadows*. This remains, arguably, the finest single book on Canadian cinema and is, undoubtedly, the essential work on the subject. In it Morris argues that Canadians have traditionally been overly modest about their own films, and always deferred to Hollywood, avoiding commercial competition. Morris makes it clear that even before John Grierson and the NFB, the short film form was far more prominent in Canada than the feature. Thus, when I began to teach Canadian film at Western in the mid-1980s I showed as many short films as features and I emphasized that the documentary, experimental, and animation modes are at least as important to the overall history of Canadian, English-language film as features. Needless to say, this book reflects these tendencies.

Deciding who and what to include in a guide to a national cinema is, of course, difficult. First of all, I asked the editors at Greenwood Press if I could entitle this work "A Guide to Canadian *Cinemas*" rather than ". . . Cinema." This slight difference from other volumes in the same series is necessary in order to recognize that there are at least two distinct societies in Canada, the anglophone majority, spread throughout the country, and the francophone minority, concentrated in the province of Quebec. The nationalist movement in Quebec is represented by the Parti Québécois in provincial politics and the Bloc Québécois on the federal level. The former first came to power in 1976, and currently controls the legislature, while the latter were, until recently, the official opposition in Ottawa. It is quite possible that Quebec will separate from the rest of Canada in the not-too-distant future, but, in any event, Quebec can be understood as being a culturally distinct "nation" in many ways. Although a great many English-language films have been made in Quebec, and although its major city, Montreal, was the home of both English and French (ONF) units of the National Film Board for most of its history, films made in the French language in Quebec, as a group, share characteristics that tend to be very different from other "Canadian" films. Indeed, most of the literature on Quebec filmmaking, written in French, refers to *le cinéma québécois* as a distinct entity. A third distinct society is the collective of diverse First Nations people, who have yet to really establish their own film culture outside of the NFB. Nevertheless, many Canadian native people (actors in particular) have been far more successful at breaking down the barriers of the mainstream film and television industries than their counterparts in the United States. Other regions of Canada, especially the western provinces of British Columbia and Alberta, have also been asserting their differences in recent years, and so it is appropriate that we give prominence at the beginning of each entry to the place of birth for individuals and the province of production for films.

In deciding which films should appear in the guide, I relied very heavily on the poll of film critics and filmmakers conducted by the Canadian film magazine, *Take One*, in 1993 (see Appendix C). I've also paid attention to the Canadian Film Awards, currently called the Genies (a name which works in both official languages—it means "genius" in French). Remarkably, these awards, and the nominations for them by the members of the Academy of Canadian Cinema and Television, have become a very accurate indicator of artistic quality, unlike their Oscar equivalents (see Appendix B). Invariably, the most artistically challenging Canadian feature films from the previous twelve months receive Genie nominations and often win. But it wasn't always this way. In the early years of the Canadian Film Awards, films had to be entered into the competition, and often there were no eligible feature films. The emphasis was on short films in general and those made at the NFB in particular, and a precedent was set of ignoring the best French-language films. Quebecois film people persist in being suspicious of the "Canadian" film awards to this day, and, in February of each year, the Rendez-vous du cinéma québécois is now held to honor the best in Quebec cinema. I have also taken some account of these results as well as the prominence of certain films at international events, like the Oscars and the Cannes International Film Festival. And, as I've suggested above, I've included many shorts, including a number of experimental films which are significant in bridging the gap between film and other fine arts areas, and which tend to have a very high profile in Canada's university film programs. In fact, given that Canadian film production is continually marginalized and dwarfed by its southern neighbor, independent and experimental filmmaking occupy a position of greater importance here than in virtually any other country in the world. To ignore such cinematic practice is to ignore the best of our cinema(s). A final consideration for inclusion has been the performance of Canadian films at the box office; for example, Canada's top three money makers of all time, *Porky's, Meatballs,* and *Heavy Metal,* are included. However, the main focus in the book has been placed on what most Canadians and Quebecois would consider to be the best of home-grown filmmaking, the Canadian "art" cinema (for want of a better phrase).

One of the most crucial decisions I made was to include only films made by a production company incorporated in Canada, that is, Canadian-made films, rather than films made in Canada or films made by Canadians. I have included a few co-productions with other countries. *Quest for Fire* isn't generally discussed as a "Canadian" film, but it is a good example of the successful exploitation of the tax shelter law that existed in the late 1970s and early 1980s, encouraging investment from outside of Canada's borders and setting the stage for Hollywood's large slate of productions in Canada in the 1990s. Of course, rules are made to be broken, and so I have included three early feature films shot in Canada by American filmmakers, that very clearly have Canada and Canadians as their subjects: Robert Flaherty's *Nanook of the North*, H. P. Carver's *The Silent Enemy*, and Varick Frissell's *The Viking*. Perhaps these three films, all of them landmarks of documentary practice, reflect the lack of interest that Canadians had in their own wilderness and indigenous cultures. But they also certainly reflect the dominance of U.S. film practice over Canadian, even outside the Hollywood mainstream, which persisted until the production boom of the mid-1970s.

In deciding which filmmakers and actors should be represented in the book, I followed my focus on "Canadian-made" films by selecting only people who have worked primarily in Canada (or, at least, who have done a significant amount of film work in Canada). Strangely, this has meant eliding most of the Canadian filmmakers and actors who are best known elsewhere (and who, most often, are not known to be Canadians at all). Not wanting to disappoint the reader who might wonder who these famous Canadians are, I have produced a brief synopsis of 100 Canadian film people who have been successful elsewhere, (see Appendix A). For the main text I chose to include all of the most notable home-based figures, obviously, but when it became apparent that entries on persons would invariably be longer than those on films, I concluded that it would be more efficient to represent some filmmakers by an entry on a single film, rather than by a personal entry. I had originally wanted to include key cinematographers, screenwriters, editors, composers, and art directors as well as directors, but eventually I abandoned this idea, including only those cinematographers who had also become important film directors, for example, Michel Brault and Peter Mettler. Unfortunately, I had to omit figures like Georges Dufaux, Guy Borremans, Martin Duckworth, and Richard Leiterman, all of whom have made significant contributions to the development of Canadian film style. Furthermore, I failed to include entries on the great film composers Howard Shore and Maurice Blackburn as well as other stalwarts of the NFB/ONF sound departments such as Marcel Carrière and Eldon Rathburn. In fact, the only non-directors to have been included as "filmmakers" are a few entrepreneurs and producers as well as the first NFB film commissioner, John Grierson.

I was helped greatly in making the difficult decisions on who and what to omit by a core group of collaborators. After making my initial list of films, I invited Donato Totaro to compile a list of filmmakers, and Stacey Abbott and Simon Brown to compile a list of actors. I made my own list of actors to compare with Stacey and Simon's, and between the three of us we established a basic list. They then proceeded to write most of the actor entries. Meanwhile, I held a series of meetings with Donato, Dave Douglas, Mitch Parry, Johanne Larue, Louis Goyette, and Alain Dubeau in order to modify the films and filmmakers lists, and to divide up much of the work. They also helped me in decisions on format. It is fair to say that without their help, I wouldn't have been able to complete this project in less than five years, and I would have lacked some confidence in my choices. On a work of this scale, there is safety in numbers, I feel. Johanne and Louis, both of whom teach Quebecois cinema at Concordia, were instrumental in decisions made on Quebecois films and film-makers, and Dave (who teaches English Canadian film) drew attention to un-derappreciated anglophone actors and filmmakers. We couldn't include everyone Dave suggested, but I'm sure that the final choices are much more balanced than they would have been had I tried to complete this project on my own. Of the major contributors, only Simon Brown would consider himself to be an expert on film acting, and thus our work in this area is, perhaps, less rigorous and scholarly than in others. Nevertheless, in recognizing that Canadian actors are mostly much better known to the general public than Canadian filmmakers, the inclu-sion of actors in the guide should encourage a wider readership for it. This is also one aspect of the project that separates it from Peter Morris' indispensable *The Film Companion* (1984), the other being that we are relatively up-to-date.

Morris' "comprehensive guide to more than 650 Canadian films and film-makers" is one of the absolutely key research sources we called upon in pre-paring our volume. Others include the two *Dictionnaire du cinéma québécois*, various NFB catalogues, and the *Canadian Feature Film Index: 1913–1985*, which D. J. Turner and Micheline Morisset painstakingly researched for the Public Archives of Canada. We relied on this book in particular for accurate credits, running times, and dates of production and release. Unfortunately, ex-tensive credits, which we had planned to include, and on which so much ad-ditional research was done, have been cut, for reasons of length. Fortunately, we have still been able to represent 175 films and 125 people in the 298 entries here. Nevertheless, I regret so many of the omissions that inevitably occur. We had intended to include the international co-production *Atlantic City* (Louis Malle, France/Canada, 1980), and the television mini-series *The Boys of St. Vincent* (John N. Smith, 1993), which was released theatrically outside of Can-ada. But we decided that international co-productions and films made for tele-vision were luxuries we couldn't afford. We extended the latter policy to exclude any work made on video rather than film. No doubt this decision will prove to be controversial with some readers, especially because it meant excluding the Inuit videaste Zacharius Kannuk, who works in relatively conventional narrative ways, and who could be regarded as a "filmmaker" who just happens to work in video. In an attempt to do justice to the overall history of Canadian film, some contemporary filmmakers, actors, and their work have been elided. Inev-itably, this means that what makes the Canadian cinema(s) of today so excit-ing—their diversity of interests and styles, through the work of First Nations people, gay and lesbian filmmakers, and people of color—is, perhaps, not as strongly represented here as it should be. Clearly, also, the field of animation is underrepresented, possibly because of a lack of expertise in our core group of writers. In any event, we have tried to cover the ground as widely as we could, and hope that readers will be able to appreciate more fully the people and works that constitute the history of the Canadian cinemas.

ABBREVIATIONS AND ACRONYMS USED IN THE TEXT

ABC	American Broadcasting Corporation
ACPAV	Association coopérative de productions audio-visuelles
act.	actor
ACTRA	Alliance of Canadian Cinema, Television and Radio Artists
AFCOOP	Atlantic Filmmakers Co-op
AFI	American Film Institute
anim.	animator
APFQ	Association des producteurs de film du Québec
ARRFQ	Association des réalisateurs et réalisatrices de films du Québec
ASN	Associated Screen News
CBC	Canadian Broadcasting Corporation
CFA	Canadian Film Artists
CFDC	Canadian Film Development Corporation
CFMDC	Canadian Film Makers Distribution Centre
CGI	Computer graphics imaging
cin.	cinematographer
CN	Canadian National [Railroad]
CPR	Canadian Pacific Railroad
dir.	director
d.o.p.	director of photography
ed.	editor
F.L.Q.	Front de Libération du Québec
f.p.s	frames per second
GPO	General Post Office [UK]
LIFT	Liaison of Independent Filmmakers of Toronto
narr.	narrator
NASCAD	Nova Scotia College of Art and Design
NBC	National Broadcasting Corporation [US]
NFB	The National Film Board of Canada
NIFCO	Newfoundland Independent Filmmakers Co-op
ONF	Office National du Film
pov	point-of-view
POW	prisoner of war
prod.	producer
rel.	released; year of release

scr.	screenplay [writer]
SCTV	Second City Television
SRC	Société Radio Canada
UCLA	University of California at Los Angeles

NOTES ON ENTRY FORMAT

For entries on films, the title of the film in bold and italics is the original Canadian title. If it was released under alternative titles these follow the entry title, in italics and in brackets. Where the original title was in French, the Canadian English release title is shown in italics, with alternative release titles, in italics and in brackets.* If the English release title is not a direct translation, then this translation from the original French title is also provided (but not in italics). This information is followed by the director(s), province of production (or Toronto or Montreal), year of first public screening, and running time in minutes (min.). If the film was not originally made in the 35mm gauge (the standard for theatrical release) then this is indicated, as well as whether the film stock was in color or b+w (black and white). If there was no dialogue or if the film was silent, this is also indicated. The place of production is usually the location of the principal production company rather than where the film was shot, but if the film was made by a key Canadian institution (e.g., the NFB), then this is indicated as well as the main production location, in parentheses. It is assumed that "NFB" indicates Ottawa production until the end of World War II, and Montreal (also for "ONF") thereafter. When it took three years or more to make the film, or when there were three or more years from the start of production to the first public screening, then this is indicated: for example, 1963–65, or 1963–67 (rel. 1971).

For entries on persons, his or her name is followed by year of birth and birthplace (if known). Where the individual is deceased, the year of death is provided (and where possible, the place of death). The tasks that the individual has performed in his or her film career follow, in roughly descending order of importance.

The names of films and persons containing separate entries in this book are cross-referenced. Within the written text of individual entries, when a film title or person with a separate entry is referred to for the first time, the name will appear in capital and small capital letters (e.g., CLAUDE JUTRA, MOUVEMENT PERPÉTUEL.

The filmographies include all feature-length Canadian films and selected shorts. International co-productions are included, but not foreign (including U.S.) films. Films made for Canadian television are included, but not television programs. The same above-mentioned procedures have been used for dating

*Note, however, that the film 24 HEURES OU PLUS . . . is alphabetized as VINGT QUATRE HEURES OU PLUS . . . and is found in the V section of this book.

works, and the listings show film titles (in italics) for each year of first exhibition, separated by semicolons. French titles have not been translated, and this
applies to titles mentioned in the text. Only French-language films included as
entries are translated in their respective credits. We experienced a problem in
choosing a consistent format for French titles. Except for proper names, capital
letters are only used for the first word in the title even where it is the article
Le, La, or *Les.* Hence a familiar title, such as *The Decline of the American
Empire* is written here as *Le déclin de l'empire américain,* rather than *Le Déclin
de l'empire Américain,* which at least one of our francophone contributors prefers.

The bibliography for text entries are cited in chronological order with earlier
dates preceding later dates.

POSTSCRIPT: DECEMBER 1999

We had to stop somewhere, and I made the cutoff point for all references and
entries the end of 1997. Much has happened since then. Sadly, Joyce Wieland,
Kathleen Shannon, Eve Lambart, Pierre Perrault, Yvan Patry, and others have
died. The Quebec industry has finally broken ranks with the rest of Canada and
started its own awards, the Jutras, to rival the Genies, but, ironically, the same
film, *The Red Violin/Le violin rouge,* won the bulk of the Jutras and the Genies
for films released in Canada in 1998. In addition to this international co-
production, directed by François Girard, a number of remarkable films have been
made and many new books and key articles have appeared. And we have finally
given up trying to use 16mm analyzer projectors at Concordia University.

ACKNOWLEDGMENTS

Clearly, many people should be thanked for helping me produce this book.
First, I am grateful to all of the contributors, especially Stacey, Simon, and
Donato who were closely involved from the beginning, and the core group of
Johanne, Louis, Mitch and Dave, who, like the other three, helped to shape its
contents. Many contributors volunteered to help with the editing process, and I
wish I could have found ways to take greater advantage of these offers. Donato,
in particular has been terrifically helpful, and Mitch's contributions have been
invaluable. I jumped right in to using computer hardware and software without
ever taking the time to understand what I was doing, and Mitch has been my
computing "rock" throughout. He has devoted countless hours to the production
of this book. I also want to thank two supervising editors at Greenwood Press
for their patient tolerance, Pamela St. Clair and Pierre L. Horn, as well as Nicole
Cournoyer, Barbara Goodhouse, and Arlene Belzer who have done an amazing
job of paying attention to the details. No doubt every contributor would like to
thank many individuals and institutions, and I apologize for not including their

names here. I didn't solicit them. I am sure that many would wish to thank the staff of La Cinémathèque québécoise, which is still the single most useful film research library in Montreal, perhaps in Canada.

At Concordia University, I have always had tremendous support from the staff of the Audio Visual Department (now part of Instructional and Information Technology Services, IITS), giving me access to films and videos, especially Oksana Dykyj, Danielle Carter, Pina Splendorio, Max Di Bitonto; Cindy Canavan and her great student projectionists, Vivien Dang-Tran and Tammy Smith; Luis Nasim and his student assistants at the Learning Labs including Vesselina Stoeva and François Primeau. Staff at the university libraries have been helpful, and I would particularly like to thank Lauren Lerner (who is now Chair of the Art History Department). Also, the staff of our Mel Hoppenheim School of Cinema (formerly Department of Cinema) have always been on hand to assist me: Barbara Rousse and Cheryl Williams have been incredibly supportive over the years, and more recently Shirley McLeod, Lyne DesLauriers, and Heather Meehan have carried on the tradition. As for the Cinema Full-Time Faculty, I must thank them all for putting up with me as chair for so long and allowing me the scope to work on my own research. All of the film studies professors could have made valuable contributions to this book: John Locke, Tom Waugh, Mario Falsetto, Carole Zucker, Katie Russell, and Martin Lefebvre are all scholars of Canadian Cinema(s). Undoubtedly, the book would have been stronger with their involvement, but, I just didn't want to bother them. As for film production and animation; eventually I decided to not include work produced by our Full-Time Faculty (e.g., Chris Hinton, Marilú Mallet, Marielle Nitoslawska) for fear of being accused of too much nepotism. (We hired Richard Kerr after the book was finished.) I would also like to thank Fine Arts dean Christopher Jackson, his associate deans and staff who have been very gracious to me while I have been working on this book. Additionally, I should say that I am always learning from our students. So many students registered in Canadian film courses that I have taught at Concordia and Western have contributed to my understanding of the subject. They are too numerous to mention, but, at least, I can't go without mentioning two of our extraordinary M.A. students, Kris Moen and Scott Preston, and a couple of former Western students, Teresa Tarasevitch and Eric Dinsmore. I consider myself fortunate to be able to teach because students keep us in touch with the changing world outside our walls and help to counteract the aging process. Finally, and most important, I thank my longtime companion, Shelley Coleman who, for some reason, continues to believe that what I do is worthwhile and who has given me the courage to get through the difficult "bits" of life.

CHRONOLOGY OF CANADIAN FILMS

Note: Feature films are capitalized.

1914	*EVANGELINE* (lost)
1919	*BACK TO GOD'S COUNTRY*
1922	*NANOOK OF THE NORTH* (United States/France)
1928	*CARRY ON, SERGEANT!*
1930	*THE SILENT ENEMY* (United States)
1931	*THE VIKING* (United States)
1932	*Grey Owl's Little Brother*
1934	*Rhapsody in Two Languages*
1936	*FROM NINE TO NINE*
1934–37	*EN PAYS NEUFS*
1937	*WOMAN AGAINST THE WORLD*
1941	*Churchill's Island*
1942	*Action Stations* *Women Are Warriors*
1944	*Our Northern Neighbour*
1945	*Listen to the Prairies*
1947	*LA FORTERESSE/WHISPERING CITY* *La poulette grise*
1948	*The Loon's Necklace*
1949	*Begone Dull Care/Caprice en couleurs* *Mouvement perpétuel*
1951	*LA PETITE AURORE L'ENFANT MARTYRE*
1952	*Neighbours/Voisins*

	Seeing in the Rain TICKET TO HEAVEN
1982	LA BÊTE LUMINEUSE LES FLEURS SAUVAGE THE GREY FOX *If You Love This Planet* *Sifted Evidence* *So Is This* *Transitions*
1972–83	AMERIKA
1983	VIDEODROME
1982–84	SONATINE
1984	LA FEMME DE L'HÔTEL
1981–85	ELVIS GRATTON: LE KING DES KINGS
1985	*The Big Snit* CRIME WAVE MY AMERICAN COUSIN *Parallax: Ten Cents a Dance*
1986	THE ADVENTURE OF FAUSTUS BIDGOOD ANNE TRISTER DANCING IN THE DARK LE DÉCLIN DE L'EMPIRE AMÉRICAIN *?O, Zoo! (The Making of a Fiction Film)* POUVOIR INTIME
1987	FAMILY VIEWING I'VE HEARD THE MERMAIDS SINGING LIFE CLASSES A WINTER TAN UN ZOO LA NUIT
1988	DEAD RINGERS TALES FROM THE GIMLI HOSPITAL
1989	BYE BYE BLUES COLD COMFORT JÉSUS DE MONTRÉAL ROADKILL *You Take Care Now*
1990	THE COMPANY OF STRANGERS UNE HISTOIRE INVENTÉE LA LIBERTÉ D'UN STATUE PERFECTLY NORMAL SAM AND ME
1991	BLACK ROBE (co-prod., Australia) MASALA NAKED LUNCH

1985–92   *MANUFACTURING CONSENT:*
                   NOAM CHOMSKY AND THE MEDIA

1992   *CAREFUL*
                   THE FALLS: A CAUTIONARY TALE
                   FORBIDDEN LOVE: THE UNASHAMED STORIES OF
                   LESBIAN LIVES
                   LÉOLO (co-prod., France)
                   REQUIEM POUR UN BEAU SANS-COEUR

1993   *CALENDAR* (co-prod., Germany and Armenia)
                   I LOVE A MAN IN UNIFORM
                   KANEHSATAKE: 270 YEARS OF RESISTANCE
                   THIRTY-TWO SHORT FILMS ABOUT GLENN GOULD

1994   *DOUBLE HAPPINESS*
                   EXOTICA

1995   *LE CONFESSIONAL* (co-prod., UK)
                   MARGARET'S MUSEUM (co-prod., UK)
                   RUDE
                   SCREAMERS (co-prod., United States and Japan)
                   SOUL SURVIVOR
                   ZIGRAIL

1996   *CRASH*
                   HARD CORE LOGO
                   KISSED
                   LILIES

1997   *THE SWEET HEREAFTER*

GUIDE TO
THE CINEMA(S) OF
CANADA

A

À TOUT PRENDRE *Take It All* [*The Way It Goes*]. Claude Jutra, Montreal, 1963, 99 min., 16mm, b+w. *À tout prendre* is a wonderfully audacious, inventive first feature that molds the liberating formal qualities of the 1940s and 1950s American avant-garde and later cinéma vérité into a jazzy, free-form narrative. *À tout prendre* is a veritable cornucopia of filmic chicanery: jump cuts, freeze frames, superimpositions, looping, direct audience address, stock footage, and extraneous interludes. However, the film's honest, mature approach to the themes of identity (including sexual and moral identity) and middle-class angst cuts through its playful formal experimentation. The film is largely autobiographical, with CLAUDE JUTRA replaying his real life relationship with Johanne Harrelle, an African American fashion model. Their relationship is soon challenged by Jutra's bohemian lifestyle and his latent homosexuality. The latter, perhaps a first in Quebec cinema, is subtly played out in two brief scenes. Jutra's confused sexuality may also be implicitly expressed in the many subjective fantasy sequences where he has violent encounters with men (recalling Jutra's short *MOUVEMENT PERPÉTUEL*). While *À tout prendre* is consumed by this sense of art-as-catharsis, it also has social and political resonance (for example, the voice-over of a bank manager speaking to Claude in English; the "Québec Libre" graffiti; the satirical representation of the clergy). The film's energy and freedom, while expressing the personal, is also a product of Quebec's intellectual and cultural history. Independently produced on a $60,000 budget, *À tout prendre* won prizes as the top Canadian film at the 1963 Montreal Film Festival and the Best Feature Film at the 1964 Canadian Film Awards.

BIBLIOGRAPHY: Colin Young, *"À tout prendre,"* in Feldman and Nelson, 153–156.

Donato Totaro

ACTION STATIONS! Joris Ivens, NFB, 1942, 42 min., b+w. *Action Stations!*, abridged as *Corvette Port Arthur*, in the "World in Action" series, was arguably the best wartime documentary made by the NFB. The director, Joris Ivens, was a celebrated advocacy documentarist who had made films all over the world, from his native Netherlands, to Belgium—supporting mineworkers in *Misère au Borinage* (1933)—to Spain and China fighting fascism—with *Spanish Earth* (1937) and *The Four Hundred Million* (1941), respectively—and working for the U.S. Department of Agriculture—*Power and the Land* (1940). JOHN GRIERSON admired Ivens' politically motivated work and specifically brought him to the NFB to make a wartime "information" film which would personalize the efforts of the Royal Canadian Navy, while using the prestigious director to help train filmmaking apprentices. According to Ivens scholar Thomas Waugh, two members of the corvette *Port Arthur*'s crew would be the focus, "a young recruit from the prairies" and an "older more seasoned sailor," and direct sound recording would be employed in some scenes. As it happened, the structuring device was abandoned, leaving most of the film's action to be collective, and very little sync sound was used. It differs from other NFB documentaries in being only partially a compilation, employing original footage for its last two thirds. Although it feels like an observational documentary in following the maneuvers of the *Port Arthur*, it does in fact contain a great deal of material staged for the camera, including an attack on a U-boat where Canadians play the parts of Germans! Ivens was angered that his film was cut down to the two-reel "World in Action" version for theatrical release, in July 1943. His own five-reel version, which had been completed in 1942, was officially premiered in Port Arthur, Ontario, on May 3, 1943, and was finally released nontheatrically in 1944 to the NFB's industrial, rural, and trade-union circuits, where it would probably have been seen by over half a million Canadians.

BIBLIOGRAPHY: Thomas Waugh, *"Action Stations!* Joris Ivens and the National Film Board," in Walz, 37–62.

Peter Rist

THE ADVENTURE OF FAUSTUS BIDGOOD. Michael Jones, Newfoundland, 1986, 110 min., 16mm (blown up to 35mm), color. The brainchild of brothers Michael and Andy Jones, *The Adventure of Faustus Bidgood* was hailed upon its release as the "first" feature film from Newfoundland (if one considers Peter Carter's *The Rowdyman* [1972] an import). The difficulty of producing an independent feature in Newfoundland posed significant challenges for Jones, who was forced to rely on the existing facilities of NIFCO, the talent pool of his fellow CODCO troupe, and various government grants to finance the film. The result of this process meant that *Bidgood* took some ten years from its inception to finally make it to screen. Described by actor Robert Joy as "if Ingmar Bergman had directed Monty Python," *Bidgood* follows the dual existence of its lead character, Faustus Peebles Bidgood, who in one reality is a minor civil clerk in the Newfoundland government. Faced with constant taunts by his fellow workers, he dreams that he is the president of a free Newfoundland. In a second reality, President Bidgood, on his last day in office, must cope with throngs of people, while he himself dreams of being nothing more than a filing clerk. Both characters are counseled by shadowy Mephistophelean figures: Faustus by an imaginary friend named Bogue, while President Bidgood debates the legacy of his political ideals with his longtime confidant, Vasily Bogdonavitch Shagoff. The schizophrenic nature of the film is further supported by additional subplots, which variously range from the mysterious absence of the "poet premiere" of the province, to a series of child murders which may have a connection to a famed child educator, Uncle Henny Penny, and the production of an annual Crippled Children's Benefit show which features the celebration of Newfoundland culture through the rendition of "Billy's Boots."

BIBLIOGRAPHY: Joan Sullivan, "The Advent of Faustus Bidgood," *Cinema Canada*, no. 135 (November 1986); Peter Wintonick, "The Adventure of Faustus Bidgood," *Cinema Canada*, no. 135 (November 1986).

Dave Douglas

ALLIGATOR SHOES. Clay Borris, Ontario, 1981, 99 min., 16mm, color. Clay Borris' second film, like his first, *Rose's House* (1977), is a labor of love. Independently produced on a shoestring budget after the CFDC turned the film down for finance, *Alligator Shoes* features mostly amateur actors (many of whom are Borris' family members) in a drama about the Cabbagetown (Toronto) life of one working-class family. Clay Borris and his brother Gary portray two brothers (Mike and Bin) whose lives revolve around the Cabbagetown taverns. An aunt (Ronalda Jones) with a history of mental illness comes to visit the family, causing some friction in the brothers' close relationship. Bin tries to bring Aunt Danielle out of her shell, but is unprepared when she makes a sexual advance at him. His rejection leads to her subsequent suicide, an event that initially prompts a confrontation between the two brothers, but ultimately reconfirms their relationship. The autobiographical nature of Borris' films offers a unique vision within Canadian cinema, one that critics at the Cannes Film Festival applauded, but sadly not one that has attracted a large audience at home. *Alligator Shoes* received minimal release, mostly on CBC television.

Dave Douglas

PAUL ALMOND. Born 1931, Montreal. Director, writer, and producer. Paul Almond is best known for the trilogy of films *ISABEL* (1968), *Act of the Heart* (1970), and *Journey* (1972), for which he served as both director and screenwriter, and which all featured GENEVIÈVE BUJOLD as the main actor. Despite the groundbreaking presence in these films of elements more usually associated with European art cinema (an emphasis on the interiority of characters, the eschewing of traditional narrative structures, complex visual symbolism), they garnered mixed critical reviews, especially the last two films in the trilogy. Almond's work reflects the strong influence of Gaspé spirituality (both his father and his uncle were Anglican clergymen) and the theater (his mother and aunt ran an acting school, and Almond himself was heavily involved in theater productions while at Oxford). Working at the CBC from 1954 to 1967, Almond was the creative force behind numerous award-winning television productions in such series as "Festival," "Quest," "Playdate," and "Folio." Most of these were dramas, and often foregrounded Almond's skill in working with actors. Almond met Bujold in 1965. They married in 1967, and Almond wrote all of the films in his trilogy with her in mind. As a group, the trilogy explores the themes of sexual repression and crises of faith, making stunning use of Quebec locations. For many critics, Paul Almond's relative obscurity and the critical and commercial failure of his trilogy are a tragic comment on the fate of Canadian feature filmmakers who attempt to move beyond the confines of the documentary impulse.

FEATURE FILMS AS DIRECTOR: *Isabel*, 1968; *Act of the Heart*, 1970; *Journey*, 1972; *Final Assignment*, 1980; *Ups & Downs*, 1983; *Captive Hearts*, 1987; *The Dance Goes On*, 1991.

BIBLIOGRAPHY: Janet Edsforth; James Leach, "Paul Almond's Fantastic Trilogy," in Feldman, 58–68.

Helen and Paul Salmon

AMERIKA. Al Razutis, British Columbia, 1972–83, 170 min., 16mm, color. This feature-length experimental film is one of the two major works of Al Razutis. An ambitious attempt to express "the various sensations, myths, landscapes of the industrialized Western culture" (Tony Reif, CFMDC catalogue, 1993), the film consists of a series of shorter films, all made between 1972 and 1983, which were then reworked and re-edited into the feature-length form. The fifteen films, some of which have been released separately—*98.3 KHz (Bridge at Electrical Storm)*, 1973; *The Wasteland and Other Stories*, 1976; *A Message from Our Sponsor*, 1979; *The Wildwest Show*, 1980; *Exiles*, 1983—document the artistic and political transitions of Razutis' career, beginning with his early 1970s "visual alchemy" inspired cinema (*Vortex*, 1972), through his "structural film" phase (*The Wasteland*), to his later works (*Fin, The Lonesome Death of Leroy Brown*), which mark the artist's increasingly agitated stance toward the larger questions of the project of avant-garde cinema. Events such as Razutis' 1982 trial in Ontario on charges of obscenity—stemming from a 1981 screening of *A Message From Our Sponsor* in Peterborough, Ontario—undoubtedly influenced the final section of the film. Here, Razutis brings focus to the theme of state encroachment on artistic expression. The tone of the later films expresses Razutis' growing identity with an "outlaw" status, evincing an openly anarchistic political perspective. From the early 1970s through the 1980s Razutis was a central figure in the avant-garde circles of Vancouver, involved with such organizations as Intermedia Co-op, CFMDC West, and Cineworks, as well as publishing a magazine of the avant-garde, *Opsis*, all the while teaching at Simon

Fraser University. In the late 1980s Razutis left Vancouver for the B.C. coastal islands, and subsequently curtailed his filmmaking activities in favor of working in other artistic mediums.

BIBLIOGRAPHY: Al Razutis, "Recovering Lost History: Vancouver Avant-Garde Cinema 1960–69," in Rombout, 160–73.

Dave Douglas

ANNE TRISTER. Léa Pool, ONF, 1986, 102 min., color. Filmed on location in Israel, Switzerland, and Montreal, *Anne Trister* is a film about grief and the process of coming to terms with loss. Following her father's funeral in Israel, Anne Trister (Albane Guilhe) abandons her family, her lover, and her education in order to fly to Montreal, where she seeks comfort from her friend Alix (Louise Marleau), a psychologist working with children. Simon Lévy (Nuvit Ozdogru), a restaurateur and family friend, gives Anne a huge abandoned warehouse, which she transforms into a studio. At the same time, the renovations give her an idea for an environmental piece, and she begins to paint a fantasy interior on the scarred and badly damaged walls—a brilliant metaphor for her own internal state. As Anne tries to come to terms with her own pain, Alix works with Sarah (Lucie Laurier), a young girl traumatized by sexual abuse; the child's transformation parallels the reawakening of Anne. When Anne confesses her love for Alix, the two become temporarily estranged, but finally—though briefly—become lovers following an accident in the studio. LÉA POOL's second feature displays an impressive use of color: during Anne's bleakest moments the sets are almost entirely a muted blue (especially during a particularly moving sequence when Anne, paralyzed with depression, passes an entire day sitting in the same spot on the floor). Scenes with Alix tend to be stylistically straightforward, while those featuring Anne alone are often much more lyrical; the difference in style perfectly reflects the motions of grief, which is, after all, a result of the confrontation between intensely painful emotions and the flatness of the quotidian. Particularly impressive is the treatment of the "painting environment" in Anne's studio; the artwork, by Geneviève Desgagnés and Daniel Sirdey, functions not only as a trompe l'oeil but also as a new environment created from the ruins of the old. Ultimately, the film is about women's friendships—their joys, their complexity, their strength.

BIBLIOGRAPHY: David Clandfield, 81–82.

Mitch Parry

THE APPRENTICESHIP OF DUDDY KRAVITZ. Ted Kotcheff, Montreal, 1974, 121 min., color. One of the biggest commercial successes in Canadian cinema, *The Apprenticeship of Duddy Kravitz* was widely praised upon its release, and was the first Canadian film to win top prize (the Golden Bear) at the Berlin Film Festival. Wonderfully evocative of Jewish life in Montreal in the 1940s, this film recounts the attempts of an unscrupulous anti-hero (Duddy:

Richard Dreyfuss) to achieve material success at the cost of personal relationships and human compassion. Using a strong ensemble cast, the film evokes the
unique vitality of its period, and does justice to Mordecai Richler's novel's
memorable gallery of distinctive characters and picaresque situations. Duddy's
combination of zest for life and moral cynicism is powerfully evoked by his
relationship with and exploitation of his lover Yvette (MICHELINE LANCTÔT)
and an epileptic innocent (Randy Quaid) whom Duddy swindles. Despite its
commercial and critical success, *The Apprenticeship of Duddy Kravitz* constitutes a powerful reminder of the problematic nature of the "Canadianness" of
Canadian cinema. It was a breakthrough film in its ambitious attempt to depict
a dynamic and previously underrepresented strata of Montreal society, and to
bring a Canadian literary classic to the screen. However, *Duddy Kravitz* was
also a very cosmopolitan production, featuring an international cast and production crew (with an American actor in the central role), and a "Hollywood
North" style which gave a generically neutral rather than specifically Canadian
feel to the film. The film's Canadian-born director, Ted Kotcheff, subsequently
had a successful career in Hollywood (*First Blood*, 1982, the first "Rambo"
film) and returned to direct the rather less successful *Duddy Kravitz* sequel,
Joshua, Then and Now (1985), the most expensive Canadian film up to that
time.

BIBLIOGRAPHY: Martin Knelman, "You See, Daddy, You See?," in Knelman (1977),
115–34.

Helen and Paul Salmon

DENYS ARCAND. Born 1941, Deschambault, Quebec. Director, writer, actor.
While still a history student at Université de Montréal, Denys Arcand co-directed
a feature film, *Seul ou avec d'autres* (1962). The film's title, a phrase commonly
heard in Catholic confessionals, translates into "alone or with others," and refers
to a priest's response to a parishioner's usual opening ("Forgive me, Father, for
I have sinned"). Thus, Arcand was making historical and social aspects of Quebec—namely, religion, somewhat freshly diminished by the Quiet Revolution—
part of his discourse very early in his career, while providing a charming New
Wave–like depiction of student life. After graduation, Arcand joined the ONF,
where he worked on a historical trilogy of short documentaries. His work went
rather unnoticed until he directed the controversial feature *ON EST AU COTON*
(1970), a documentary that propelled him into the spotlight. A very successful
documentary feature (*Québec: Duplessis et après . . .*) followed shortly after-
wards, but not before the young filmmaker had tried his hand at fiction, with
La maudite galette (1971). This initial foray not only marks Arcand's debut at
the Cannes Film Festival (where it was shown in La Semaine de la Critique),
but also the beginning of a long-lasting love story between the director and local
critics, who saw in *Galette* an extension of Arcand's contribution to documentary. In 1973 came *RÉJEANNE PADOVANI*, an operatic drama that intelligently

mixes the political with the personal, daringly shaping some of its characters on real-life personalities. *Gina* appeared in 1975, and still stands as Arcand's most genre-oriented film. Reflecting on his own experience shooting *On est au coton*, Arcand shows the coexistence in a small-town hotel of a film crew, there to shoot a documentary about the labor conditions of employees working in the textile industry, and a striptease dancer. Courageously played by Céline Lomez, Gina reveals a fascinating complexity: a vulnerable sex-toy in the hands of a ruthless manager/pimp, she is also a strong-headed, self-affirming woman. Although *Gina* was well received, it was too often dismissed as an attempt to copy the "American way." In 1986, LE DÉCLIN DE L'EMPIRE AMÉRICAIN brought international recognition and tremendous success to Arcand, both of which were confirmed and increased with his following effort, JÉSUS DE MONTRÉAL. After a hiatus of nearly five years (during which he nevertheless directed one sketch for *Montréal vu par . . .*), the "hero" of Quebecois cinema then released his first English feature, *Love and Human Remains*, based on Brad Fraser's play. For the first time in years, Quebec audiences and film critics alike responded indifferently, as though they were reacting to Arcand's decision to make a "Canadian" film as a betrayal. And then, with everyone expecting a film about the fashion industry and supermodels, Arcand revealed *Joyeux calvaire*, a low budget and simple fable focusing on the lives of homeless people. The critical reaction was quiet, as was its commercial performance. Despite the recent ups and downs of his films' reception, Denys Arcand not only remains the most successful Quebecois filmmaker, but also occupies a central position in Canadian film history.

FILMS AS DIRECTOR: *À l'est d'Eaton* (short, co-dir., S. Venne), 1959; *Seul ou avec d'autres* (co-dir., D. Héroux and S. Venne, also co-scr. with Venne), 1962; *Champlain* (short), 1964; *Les Montréalistes; La route de l'Ouest; Montréal un jour d'été* (shorts), 1965; *Volleyball* (short), 1966; *Atlantic Parks* (short), 1967; *La maudite galette* (also act.); *Québec: Duplessis et après . . .* (also ed.), 1972; *Réjeanne Padovani* (also scr., ed., and act.), 1973; *Gina* (also scr. and ed.), 1975; *On est au coton*, 1968–76; *La lutte des travailleurs d'hôpitaux* (short), 1976; *Le confort et l'indifférence*, 1977–82; *Le crime d'Ovide Plouffe*, 1984; *Le déclin de l'empire américain*, 1986; *Jésus de Montréal*, 1989; *Montréal vu par . . .* (co-dir., M. Brault, A. Egoyan, J. Leduc, L. Pool, P. Rozema), 1991; *Love and Human Remains*, 1994; *Joyeux calvaire*, 1997.

BIBLIOGRAPHY: Michel Coulombe (1993).

Alain Dubeau

GABRIEL ARCAND. Born 1949, Deschambault, Quebec. Actor. After completing his philosophy degree at McGill University in Montreal, Arcand studied drama in Marseilles, France. He had already appeared in his first feature film, his brother DENYS ARCAND's *La maudite galette* (1971), where he was noticed by Jean-Guy Noël, who wrote, with Gabriel in mind, the role of a fireman who allows his village to burn as a passive protest against authority. The film, *Tu brûles . . . tu brûles*, gave Arcand his first leading role, which he then followed with a smaller part in *RÉJEANNE PADOVANI*, again directed by his brother. It was as the shy idealist in *Suzanne* (1980) that Arcand began to hit his stride, playing a character of deep and hidden emotions, struggling with internal conflicts. This was followed by *Les Plouffe*, where Arcand was mesmerizing as the shy and sensitive Ovide. *Variety* described his performance as "one of the best ever filmed in Quebec" (4/29/81, p. 18), and Arcand's exploration of the character was so full and impressive that he became the center of the sequel, *Le crime d'Ovide Plouffe* (1984). Here Ovide struggles with an unhappy marriage and an ill-timed love affair. Arcand's training under Jerzy Grotowski in Poland had reached beyond dialogue to explore character interiority through sound and gesture, and his role in *LE DÉCLIN DE L'EMPIRE AMÉRICAIN* displays this most obviously. As the shady lover/possible drug dealer, Arcand had few lines, spending much of the time with his eyes hidden behind dark glasses, yet his character is revealed in every gesture. He won Genie Awards for both *Le déclin* and *Ovide Plouffe*. In the late eighties, Arcand gave two outstanding performances in family dramas. In *La ligne de chaleur* he played a father who becomes gradually more haunted by his own father's death and his increasing inability to relate to his own son, while in *Les portes tournantes* he was the brooding painter son of Monique Spaziani's Celeste. One of the most respected actors in Quebec, Arcand has been seen less frequently on the big screen in the 1990s, although he returned to prominence as the detective in *Le fabrication d'un meutrier* (1996).

FILMS AS ACTOR: *La maudite galette* (also music), 1971; *Tu brûles . . . tu brûles; Réjeanne Padovani*, 1973; *Pauline* (part 1 of *Deux contes de la rue Berrie*), 1974; *Gina; Les vautours*, 1975; *Ti-cul Tougas*, 1976; *Parlez nous d'amour; Panique*, 1977; *L'Âge de la machine*, 1978; *Au revoir . . . à Lundi*, 1979; *L'affaire Coffin; Suzanne*, 1980; *Les Plouffe*, 1981; *Le toasteur* (short), 1982; *Mémoire battante*, 1983; *Le crime d'Ovide Plouffe*, 1984; *Agnes of God; Metallo blues* (short), 1985; *Le déclin de l'empire américain*, 1986; *La ligne de chaleur*, 1987; *Les portes tournantes; L'air de rien*, 1988; *Nelligan*, 1991; *Blood of the Hunter*, 1995; *Le fabrication d'un meutrier*, 1996.

BIBLIOGRAPHY: Pierre Jutras, "Entrevue avec Gabriel Arcand," *Copie Zero*, no. 22 (October 1984): 16–17.

Simon Brown

ROBERT AWAD. Born 1949, Beirut, Lebanon. Director, animator, producer. Robert Awad is one of the leading filmmakers from the NFB's Atlantic region division (Newfoundland and the Maritime provinces). In 1951 Awad's family moved to New Brunswick, where he would later receive a bachelor's degree in fine arts. He moved to Montreal in 1970 to study architecture at McGill University, though he became increasingly interested in film animation. He returned to New Brunswick, where he would earn an apprenticeship with the NFB. Awad's films are marked by a characteristically Acadian sensibility that finds humor in all aspects of life; a humor, however, which is always accompanied by satirical observation. In *Truck* and *Automania*, for example, Awad lampoons the 20th century obsession with and dependence on the automotive vehicle. Awad is best remembered for his two minor masterpieces, *L'affaire Bronswik* (1978) and *La fièvre du castor* (1980). With *Bronswik* Awad pioneered the Canadian "mockumentary," a parody of the traditional NFB documentary form using live action and animation. It poses as a documentary exposé of a multi-national conspiracy to encode Bronswik television sets with subliminal waves that turn viewers into mindless consumer zombies (a premise that foreshadows the horror satire *Dawn of the Dead* [dir. George Romero, 1979], *Halloween 3: Season of the Witch* [1983], *VIDEODROME* [1983], and *The Stuff* [dir. Larry Cohen, 1985]). *L'affaire Bronswik* was a product of the 1970s, which included Brian Wilson Key's best-selling exposé of subliminal messages in advertising, *Subliminal Seduction*. Equally topical was *La fièvre du castor*, a film that poked fun at Canadian nationalism and identity during the impending 1980 Quebec sovereignty referendum. *La fièvre du castor* also uses the mockumentary style, in a sublimely ridiculous scenario where the disappearance of Canada's closely guarded national symbol, the beaver, leads to a national identity crisis!

CANADIAN THEATRICAL SHORTS, AS DIRECTOR: *Truck*, 1975; *L'affaire Bronswik* (co-dir., André Leduc), 1978; *La fièvre du castor* (English version, *The National Scream*) (co-dir., David Verrall), 1980; *Amuse-gueule*, 1984; *Rencontre de certains types*, 1989; *Question de rire*, 1993; *Automania*, 1994.

BIBLIOGRAPHY: Gary Evans (1991), 241, 265.

Donato Totaro

B

BACK TO GOD'S COUNTRY. David M. Hartford, Alberta, 1919, 79 min., b+w (tinted), silent. *Back to God's Country* is the finest extant Canadian silent film and the only one produced by "Ten Percent" ERNIE SHIPMAN (the most successful Canadian feature filmmaker before the 1960s) to have survived intact. It is most remarkable for the involvement of Ernie's then-current (fourth) wife, NELL SHIPMAN, who adapted popular writer James Curwood's story to the screen and starred in the resulting film. Her adaptation reduced the role of the dog, Wapi (played by two Great Dane siblings), and increased her own, Dolores LeBeau, displeasing Curwood. Dolores lives in harmony with her wildlife friends in a remote wilderness, looking after her father (Ray Laidlaw). A criminal, Rydal (Wellington Playter), attempts to rape her while disguised as a Mountie, and she dives into the rapids in an unsuccessful attempt to save her father's life. Nell marries a writer, Peter (Wheeler Oakman), and Rydal reappears captaining a ship carrying the couple on an arctic voyage. After Rydal injures Peter, Nell saves him by leading a dogsled across the frozen tundra (Lesser Slave Lake, Alberta). She has befriended the wild Wapi and sics him on Rydal's team. Over fifty years ahead of its time, *Back to God's Country* featured a woman in the central action role, who saves her disabled husband and threatens the villain's life with a gun; thinking and acting her way out of trouble. The film was also an auteurist work for Nell Shipman, featuring her menagerie of beloved animals, and reflecting the cruel oppression of aboriginal people by the white man, even suggesting through Rydal's disguises that male authority itself is corrupt. Partially shot in California, *God's Country* was otherwise very much a Canadian production, wherein the harsh winter conditions took the life of Australian actor Ronald Byram (who had been playing the lead) and gave the company manager, Bert Van Tuyle, severe frostbite in one foot. Nell was especially effusive about Joseph Walker's cinematography in her autobiography, *The Silent Screen and My Talking Heart*, claiming that he made twenty-nine passes through the camera to make one complex superimposition of her and her animals at the Kern Lake, California, location, where she also swam naked for one infamous scene, engendering the poster caption "Is the Nude Rude?" *Back to God's Country* was restored to its original color tints in the mid-1980s by D. J. Turner of Canada's national film archives.

BIBLIOGRAPHY: Kay Armatage, "Dog and Woman, Together at Last: Animals in the Films of Nell Shipman," *CineACTION*, nos. 24/25 (1981): 38–44; D. J. Turner.

Peter Rist

THE BACK-BREAKING LEAF. Terence Macartney-Filgate, (Ontario) NFB, 1959, 29 min., b+w. Filmed on tobacco farms in Delhi, Southwestern Ontario, *The Back-Breaking Leaf* was the last of the "Candid Eye" series of films directed by Terence Macartney-Filgate. The first of the thirteen-film series, made for Canadian television, *Days Before Christmas/Bientôt Noël* (1958), set the pattern for Macartney-Filgate's other six works with its emphasis on the quotidian (inspired by the British Free Cinema movement) and its objective, observational, but revelatory style (inspired by Henri Cartier-Bresson's photography and writing). Born in England in 1924, the director/cinematographer joined the NFB as a scriptwriter in 1954. Less of a romantic than other members of Unit B, Macartney-Filgate's voice can be heard off-screen in *Leaf* asking the tobacco harvesters how they feel when they get up in the morning and when they finish work at night. Visually as well, his hand-held camera relentlessly probes the back-breaking work. Indeed, executive producer TOM DALY complained of *Leaf*'s monotonous footage of work, managing to encourage editor John Spotton to structure the material into one main task per apparent day of activity. Yet, the film's strength (read Macartney-Filgate's strength) is its (his) refusal to shy away from the travails of the migrant workers, both on the sound and image tracks. On the other hand, although not effusive or bombastic, Stanley Jackson's voice does tend to dominate the first half of *Leaf*, necessary though it is to explain the unusual details of tobacco harvesting within such a short running time.

BIBLIOGRAPHY: Charlotte Gobeil.

Peter Rist

PAULE BAILLARGEON. Born 1945, Rouyn-Noranda, Quebec. Actor, writer, director. In 1969, Paule Baillargeon was one of a number of students who left L'École Nationale de Théâtre in protest against its traditional approach. Shortly after, she was one of the founder members of the Grand Cirque Ordinaire, a progressive drama group. Her first important film role came in 1970 in *Entre tu et vous*, a part she won when the scheduled actress dropped out because of the nudity involved. Baillargeon then appeared in *Le grand film ordinaire*, a documentary about Le Grand Cirque, and *Montréal Blues* (1972), which grew out of the Cirque's work. An actress who does not shy away from controversial material, and with a strong sense of social and feminist politics, she developed her skills during the 1970s in a variety of challenging projects. These included small roles in two films by DENYS ARCAND, *RÉJEANNE PADOVANI* and *Gina*, as well as *Le temps de l'avant* (ANNE-CLAIRE POIRIER). Her next film, which she co-wrote with director Pierre Harel, was *Vie d'ange* (rel. 1979), in which she played Star Morgan, a singer who gets literally stuck *en flagrante* with a young stud. Baillargeon is an accomplished comedienne, as she shows in this film and also, memorably, as the religious fanatic in Arcand's *JÉSUS DE MONT-RÉAL*. She is also a fine dramatic actress, as illustrated in LÉA POOL's *LA FEMME DE L'HÔTEL* and as the doubting, haunted Sister Gertrude in *La dame en couleurs* (CLAUDE JUTRA, 1985). Although she continues to act, most notably as the object of Sheila McCarthy's affections in *I'VE HEARD THE MERMAIDS SINGING*, Baillargeon has become an accomplished director. Her first major work was *LA CUISINE ROUGE* (1979), co-directed and written with Frédérique Collin. It is a highly theatrical, dialogue-heavy, and stylized film. Nevertheless, it is an audacious piece, drawing some excellent performances from a strong cast. Her next film as director, *Sonia* (1986), in which she also stars, deals with the subject of Alzheimer's disease. It is sensitive and moving without being sentimental. Baillargeon concentrates on the truth of the performances, and draws an outstanding one from Kim Yaroshevskaya. Her latest fiction film as director is *La sexe des étoiles* (1995), which she also scripted, and which deals openly and honestly with the subject of a transsexual.

FILMS AS ACTOR: *Et pourquoi pas?*, 1969; *Entre tu et vous*, 1970; *Le grand film ordinaire*, 1971; *Et du fils; Montréal Blues*, 1972; *Réjeanne Padovani*, 1973; *Ô ou l'invisible enfant*, 1971–74; *Gina; Les vautours; Le temps de l'avant; L'amour blessé* (voice only), 1975; *La piastre; East End Hustle*, 1976; *Langes bleus* (short); *Le soleil se lève en retard; Panique*, 1977; *Décembre* (TV), 1978; *Vie d'ange* (also co-scr.), 1974–79; *Albédo* (short), 1982; *La femme de l'hôtel*, 1984; *Passion: A Letter in 16mm* (short); *La dame en couleurs*, 1985; *Sonia* (also dir.), 1986; *I've Heard the Mermaids Singing; Les voisins*, 1987; *Jésus de Montréal; Trois pommes à côté du sommeil; Les heures précieuses* (TV), 1989; *Love-moi*, 1990; *L'assassin jouait du trombone; Montréal vu par . . .* (also co-scr.), 1991.

FILMS AS DIRECTOR: *Anastasie oh ma chérie* (short), 1977; *La cuisine rouge* (co-dir; also scr.), 1980; *Sonia* (short), 1986; *Le complexe d'Edith; Solo* (shorts), 1991; *La sexe des étoiles* (also scr.), 1995.

BIBLIOGRAPHY: Pierre Jutras, "Table ronde avec Raymond Cloutier, Paule Baillargeon, Luce Guilbeault, Marcel Sabourin," *Copie Zero*, no. 22 (October 1984): 4–9; Carole Zucker, "Les oeuvres récentes d'Anne-Claire Poirier et Paule Baillargeon," *Copie Zero*, no. 11 (1981): 52–55.

Simon Brown

BAR SALON. Marc-André Forcier, Montreal, 1972–74, 84 min., 16mm, b+w. MARC-ANDRÉ FORCIER's second feature established the concerns he would follow in later films. Charles (GUY L'ÉCUYER) runs a small, miserable bar in

Montreal; his daughter Michèle (Madeleine Chartrand) works at the bar while preparing for her marriage to Robert (Jacques Marcotte). The regular customers at the bar include a group of aging alcoholics whose façade of old-world respectability collapses nightly, a gang of young toughs who routinely break into violent fights which are forgotten the next morning, and François (Forcier), a mute young man. The opening sequence encapsulates Forcier's technique throughout the rest of the film: a close-up of Michèle applying makeup as she looks into a mirror (as though preparing for a big night out) is immediately followed by a reverse-angle long shot, revealing that she is simply looking into the bar mirror before leaving at closing time. Filmed in 16mm, *Bar salon* depicts a terribly dispirited and broken society, characterized by the exhausted resignation of a bar's last customers stumbling out into the night. Even the most intimate moments can be crushed by violence and drunken despair. At one point, Michèle and Robert dance after the bar closes; at that moment, the young thugs—who have continued drinking out on the street—hurl a bottle through the bar's window, shattering the intimacy inside. In one of the film's most powerful and stylistically mature moments, Michèle, disturbed by Robert's increasing drunkenness, puts on her wedding dress and stares into the mirror; a near-silent series of fades to white brilliantly captures the hopelessness of her impending marriage without completely eradicating the necessity of hope. *Bar salon* won special mention for the Critics' Prize from the Association québécoise des critiques du cinéma and the Silver Mermaid at the Sorrenta Film Festival in Italy (both 1974).

BIBLIOGRAPHY: James Leach, "Second Images: Reflections on the Canadian Cinema(s) in the Seventies," in Feldman, 100–110.

Mitch Parry

JEAN BEAUDIN. Born 1939, Montreal. Director, editor, writer. Jean Beaudin earned a diploma from the École des Beaux-Arts in Quebec City and then moved to Zurich, Switzerland, where he studied design. In 1964 he joined the ONF, first working on animated films and then directing some educational films. His first fictional films were not well received. These were four shorts made between 1972 and 1975 (beginning with *Les indrogables*) which reflect the best of the style of the later features. Jean Beaudin's great illustrative talent, his image compositional style and careful lighting, together with enchanting natural landscapes filmed on location, emerge from all the shots of *J. A. MARTIN, PHOTOGRAPHE* (1977), *Cordélia*, and *Mario* (1984), the first two of which were historical reconstructions. *J. A. Martin* was set at the beginning of the century. *Cordélia* was based on the true story of a woman condemned to death in the 19th century. A year after *Mario*, which followed the relationship between an adolescent boy and his autistic brother, Beaudin directed *Le matou*, based on the novel by Yves Beauchemin, a superproduction which marked a departure from his personal style. After making a number of commercials, Beaudin made some television series, which were very successful. "L'or et le papier" (1989) won him the Prix Gémeaux for best director, and then "Les filles de Caleb" (1990–91), adapted from a best seller by Arlette Cousture, garnered thirteen Gémeaux in 1991. During the same year, his adaptation of the play by René-Daniel Dubois, *Being at Home with Claude*, marked his return to filmmaking.

FILMS AS DIRECTOR: *Vertige; Et pourquoi pas?* (shorts), 1969; *Stop*, 1971; *Le diable est parmi nous; Les indrogables* (short), 1972; *Trois fois passera . . .* (short), 1973; *Par une belle nuit d'hiver* (short), 1974; *Cher Théo* (short), 1975; *J. A. Martin, photographe* (also scr. and ed.); *Jeux de la XXIe Olympiade* (co-dir., M. Carrière, G. Dufaux, and J.-C. Labrecque), 1977; *Cordélia* (also scr. and ed.), 1980; *Mario* (also scr.), 1984; *Le matou*, 1985; *La bioéthique: Une question de choix—L'homme à la traîne* (short), 1986; *Being at Home with Claude*, 1991; *Craque la vie!* (TV film), 1994.

BIBLIOGRAPHY: Dominique Benjamin, "Jean Beaudin au début du siècle," *24 Images*, no. 5 (May 1980): 28–34, 72–74; Claude Lavoie, " 'Je fais un métier mal équilibré qui ne me permet guère de mener une vie normale': Entretien avec Jean Beaudin," *Cine-Bulles* 4, no. 6 (April–May 1985): 4–8.

Isabelle Morissette

BEGONE DULL CARE/CAPRICE EN COULEURS. Norman McLaren and Evelyn Lambart, NFB, 1949, 8 min., color, no dialogue. *Begone Dull Care* represents the extreme experimental pole of NORMAN MCLAREN's work at the NFB and is one of the most remarkable fusions of film and music ever achieved. McLaren and his underappreciated co-worker EVELYN LAMBART took a piece of music composed by Canadian jazz pianist Oscar Peterson entitled "Begone Dull Care" and produced a purely graphic and rhythmic visual equivalent. McLaren was inspired by New Zealander Len Lye's painting directly on film techniques to produce perhaps the most widely seen cameraless film ever made. *Begone Dull Care* consists of three movements: two fast (fortissimo) with a slow (pianissimo) in between. Whereas the mainly monochromatic mid-section emphasizes line (in partial imitation of bass strings) through the delicate scratching of black emulsion, the opening and closing fugues contain spectacular, rapidly changing designs and colors. Indeed, the 35mm filmstrip can be viewed in itself as an artwork, unraveled and held up to the light to observe a sometimes smooth, flowing design with no regard for the individual frames which are normally observed on the screen intermittently, one frame at a time. McLaren considered that it was primarily the "movement" which connected the music and film, rather than "instrumentation or coloration or harmony" and claimed that he and Lambart worked on the basis of "shots" equivalent to "musical phrase lengths," producing five or six versions of each, some of which were "painted as the movieola was running." *Begone Dull Care* won six international awards between 1949 and 1954. A "documentary" award at Berlin (1951) and an "art" film award at Venice (1950) demonstrate the difficulty of categorizing such a breakthrough, experimental film.

BIBLIOGRAPHY: Derek Elley, "Rhythm 'n' Truths," *Films and Filming* 20, no. 9 (June 1974): 30–36.

Peter Rist

THE BEST DAMN FIDDLER FROM CALABOGIE TO KALADAR. Peter Pearson, (Ontario) NFB, 1968 (CBC telecast, March 1969), 49 min., 16mm, b+w. Originally intended as the pilot program for the "Challenge for Change" series, PETER PEARSON's depiction of the rural life of a busher* in the Ottawa valley outgrew the designed mandate and was released separately. To present the case for social assistance, Pearson focused on the fictional story of Emery Prometer (Chris Wiggins) and that of his family. Facing the birth of their tenth child, Emery adamantly refuses to allow his family to accept social assistance when prompted to by a social aid worker. He is equally opposed to allowing his wife Glad (KATE REID) to use birth control. Seeing the endemic poverty of her parents, and knowing the life her mother leads, Emery's eldest daughter Rosie (MARGOT KIDDER) sneaks away to the city to work as a telephone operator and get an education. Pearson's film is energized by stellar performances from his principal cast, as well as superb cinematography. Tony Ianzelo utilized the dominant trends of *cinéma vérité* to represent the social world of the Prometers and to poignantly expose the bleak future that the world holds for all, save the independently minded Emery. At the Canadian Film Awards that year the film won eight Etrogs.

Dave Douglas

LA BÊTE LUMINEUSE The Shimmering Beast. Pierre Perrault, (Quebec) NFB, 1982, 127 min., color. More than just a simple film about moose-hunting, *La bête lumineuse* is the fascinating portrait of a group of hunters brought together in a Maniwaki log cabin for a few days in the fall of 1980 who abandoned themselves to the most excessive overflowing of alcohol, food, and words. It has often been said that PIERRE PERRAULT's documentaries "fictionalize" reality by means of catalyzing elements which serve to create a form of suspense over the course of the depicted events. Here, the catalyzing element is the poet Stéphane-Albert Boulais, who ceaselessly poeticizes moose-hunting. The presence of the poet among the hunters considerably transforms the dynamic of the group. Boulais establishes a sensibility clearly unknown to the hunters, which, furthermore, generates a number of tensions. Thus, when the poet reads the homage he has written for his friend Bernard (a true declaration of love), it is as though he has committed a dangerous betrayal of the hunter's virility. An unflinching exploration of male rituals, *La bête lumineuse* is profoundly disturbing because of the rawness of the situations it exposes and because it demonstrates how promiscuity among men can tear off all masks. Perrault often uses

*A local term for a low-subsistence worker who clears land and attempts to live off it; not a "lumberjack."

an associational montage which allows him to comment in a humorous and sometimes ironic manner on the events experienced by the hunters. In this film, it is not so much the moose but the men hunting them who capture all the attention of the spectators.

BIBLIOGRAPHY: Stéphane-Albert Boulais.

Louis Goyette

BETWEEN FRIENDS [*Get Back*]. Don Shebib, Ontario, 1973, 91 min., color. The third feature film of DON SHEBIB was his first without WILLIAM FRUET as scriptwriter. Though regarded with a lesser prominence than *GOIN' DOWN THE ROAD*, this film marks a maturing direction for Shebib. Its tale of a botched payroll heist by two surfing friends contains many elements and themes common to the director's oeuvre, presented here in a more sombre manner. The story features Toby (Michael Parks), a small-time crook and surfer, who leaves California after a drug deal goes sour. He travels to Toronto to meet up with an old surfing friend, Chino (Chuck Shamata), and Chino's girlfriend, Ellie (Bonnie Bedelia). Chino has an idea to rob a northern mining company payroll office and talks the reluctant Toby into the scheme. Before the heist can occur Toby has a brief affair with the malaise-wrought Ellie. When Chino discovers this betrayal, his idolization of Toby and dreams of the good old days are shattered. Distracted during the robbery, Chino causes the plan to fail, resulting in a shooting spree in which he is mortally wounded. As Chino dies in a barren field Toby reflects on what was in California. Richard Leiterman's documentary realist style of cinematography combines with the bleak wintry landscape to amplify the pathos of the characters' lives. Where Shebib had earlier lionized aspects of "guy-culture" in a Hawksian sense, he here laments their passage.

BIBLIOGRAPHY: Piers Handling (1978).

Dave Douglas

THE BIG SNIT. Richard Condie, (Manitoba) NFB, 1985, 10 min., color. This Oscar-nominated animated short is one of the NFB's most prized (seventeen awards) and frequently viewed films. In *The Big Snit* a neurotic, middle-aged couple engage in a heated domestic squabble during a game of Scrabble, oblivious to the nuclear war raging outside their window. Condie's subtle drawings and characterizations are part of a comic style that is best described as "surreal comedy of frustration" (also hilariously manifested in his ode to procrastination, *Getting Started* [1979]). The film is laced with absurdist touches that exploit the animator's creative license on the natural world, yet speak straight to a heart of truth. Scrabble can be a frustrating game, but has anyone ever backed themselves into a tray with seven E tiles, or tried to use "carrost"? Communion between two souls requires an acceptance of mutual idiosyncrasies and obsessions, even if they include periodic sawings of household furniture (the husband) or taking one's eyes out and shaking them back into place (the wife). In the end the film reaffirms the couple's need and love for each other. It ends paradisaically for all, except the frazzled cat that finally packs it in and leaves domesticity behind.

BIBLIOGRAPHY: Giannalberto Bendazzi, 264–65.

Donato Totaro

THE BITTER ASH. Larry Kent, British Columbia, 1963, 80 min., 16mm, b+w. Working with rudimentary film equipment, a volunteer cast of University of British Columbia theater majors, and a $5,000 budget, LARRY KENT's first feature film burst onto an unsuspecting Canadian film scene. Unlike many of Canada's other filmmakers of his generation, Larry Kent possessed neither a background in film nor the support of the film establishment. Kent's portrait of young adults on the margins of society rejects the image of an affluent society of the sixties. Over the course of a couple of days, the lives of three individuals become intertwined as they each search for an escape from their own existence. Des (Alan Scarfe), a disaffected working-class man, must decide what to do about his girlfriend's pregnancy when he meets Laurie (Lynn Stewart), whose marriage to Colin (Philip Brown) is equally fragile. Des and Laurie have a brief affair, but soon realize this offers no escape from their banal lives. Filmed in a semi-improvisational manner, *The Bitter Ash*'s portrait of the early 1960s evokes an ethos similar to that of *Pull My Daisy* (Robert Frank/Alfred Leslie, United States, 1959). Richard Bellamy's hand-held camera work combined with a restless editing style gave the film a rawness that shocked audiences. With its provocative subject material, the film acquired a reputation quickly, as did its director. Subsequent release across the country through university film societies influenced other directors to move into cinema, leading to a boom in university-based production by the middle of the 1960s.

BIBLIOGRAPHY: Dave Douglas, "Exile on Hastings and Main Street," *Canadian Journal of Film Studies* 5, no. 2 (Fall 1996).

Dave Douglas

BLACK ROBE. Bruce Beresford, Australia/Canada (Quebec), 1991, 93 min., color. A strange object in Canadian cinema, as most co-productions are, *Black Robe* was directed by an Australian and primarily shot in English in Quebec's Saguenay/Lac St.-Jean region. Fresh from winning the Best Picture Oscar in 1990 for *Driving Miss Daisy*, Beresford had wanted to make a film of Brian Moore's book from the day it was published. In this first collaboration between Canada and Australia, we follow the ordeal of Father Paul Laforgue (LOTHAIRE BLUTEAU), recently arrived in Quebec (then called Nouvelle-France) from France, whose mission is to reach a desolate Jesuit outpost, take it over, and pursue saving the souls of the local "savages." Guided by a group of Algonquin Indians throughout his journey, Laforgue faces bitter cold, difficult living conditions, and violent attacks from other tribes. He ultimately questions his faith, almost to relinquish it, but realizes too late the damage done by colonization, as the closing images of him so eloquently illustrate: baptizing "natives," who thus hope to be saved from a murderous fever. Set in 1634, this historical saga had the potential to be a wonderful film, perhaps a Canadian equivalent of Roland Joffé's *The Mission* (United States/UK, 1986). As it is, Beresford's effort is not entirely convincing. The construction of Laforgue's character and his psychological transformation (doubting his religious fervor) are brought about far too abruptly, in the last moments of the film. Bluteau's detached and some-what anemic performance can also be faulted. Otherwise, *Black Robe* does ex-hibit some undeniably positive qualities, one of them being the honest depiction of the First Nations peoples' customs. Carrying a strong anthropological dis-course, *Black Robe* provides a refreshing alternative to the Hollywood image of "Indians." Also, the significant role of dreams and the realm of the imaginary in the indigenous peoples' lives is superbly integrated into the narrative. Func-tioning as action catalysts as well as premonitory announcements of Algonquin destiny, the dream sequences are magnificently rendered in stop motion, and momentarily display what the film ought to have been. *Black Robe* won six Genies, including Best Film and Best Director.

Alain Dubeau

BLINKITY BLANK. Norman McLaren, NFB, 1955, 5 min., color, no dialogue. One of NORMAN MCLAREN's most innovative films, *Blinkity Blank* predated American and European "experiments" with the "flicker effect" in the 1960s. In it, the director/animator played with the audience's ability to see, sometimes giving the viewer a virtually subliminal image for less than 1/24th of a second: that is, a single frame of film. Scratching on black leader, McLaren continued to work with comic bird images and actually constructed a minimal narrative within an ostensibly abstract work: two apparent birds scratch and fight, but eventually come together to produce an egg. The film's title is an onomatopoeic representation of the film's image track and soundtrack and gives an indication of the viewer's struggle to see. Working with the remarkable experimental com-poser Maurice Blackburn, McLaren built a soundtrack of improvisational jazz mixed with scratches which coincided with the occasional scratched and painted lights in the dark. Indeed, this film appears to contain more action on the (op-tical) soundtrack than on the film's image track. This is one of many elements in the film which are reflexive; where we are led to think about filmmaking and projection processes. Brilliantly, McLaren (and Blackburn) constructed a short piece of delightful entertainment that simultaneously provides a metaphor on vision.

BIBLIOGRAPHY: Donald McWilliams, 88–90.

Peter Rist

BLOOD AND FIRE. Terence Macartney-Filgate, (Montreal) NFB, "Candid Eye" series, 1958, 29 min., b+w. Although it is not the best known of the NFB

"Candid Eye" films, *Blood and Fire* is probably the best example of observational, "candid" style in the series, and is, as such, a quintessential Terence Macartney-Filgate work. In Canadian film historian Peter Morris' words, *Blood and Fire* epitomizes TOM DALY's Unit B "direct cinema approach" with its "attempt to capture the essence of an ordinary situation while remaining at an ironic distance." The film begins rather conventionally with a Montreal Salvation Army parade and some interviews with officers in the corps. However, once the film settles on a scene of a prayer meeting, the "candid" approach takes over. A number of apparently derelict men are in attendance, and their blank stares delimit interpretation. But one man eventually comes to the rail, in penitence and with tears in his eyes, to "make peace with god in order to ease his turmoil." Stanley Jackson's downbeat commentary subsides so that there is no way of knowing who these men are, where they come from, and why they are there. As an audience we are free to make of the scene what we will. No doubt Macartney-Filgate's ironic touch can be found in his allowing the pathetic scene to unfold, and his decision to end the film on another parade, now in the rain, with high angle shots looking down on the participants' feet, only adds to the depressive mood. Some observers found the director's decision to film the prayer meeting to be exploitative, and, indeed, the film stands as a model of the problematic observational documentary which attempts to represent people just as they are.

BIBLIOGRAPHY: Peter Morris (1984), 35, 187.

Peter Rist

LOTHAIRE BLUTEAU. Born 1958, Montreal. Actor. Lothaire Bluteau was a student at the Conservatory of Dramatic Arts in Montreal and has since established himself as one of Canada's leading actors on both stage and screen. Serious and intense, Bluteau often portrays troubled characters undergoing internal conflict. In the early eighties, he gained recognition in plays such as *Gotcha* and *L'impromptu d'Outremont* and made his stage directorial debut. Simultaneously, he was gradually moving into film with small roles in *Bleue brume, Rien qu'un jeu* and *Sonia*, among others. Bluteau's critical acclaim in 1985 for his performance in the original stage version of *Being at Home with Claude* was finally repeated on screen in Yves Simoneau's *Les fous de bassan* (1987), where Bluteau played his most demanding film role to date as Perceval Brown, the mentally handicapped brother of the lead character. His intensity and air of mystery made him an ideal choice for DENYS ARCAND's modern-day Messiah in *JÉSUS DE MONTRÉAL*. As Daniel, an actor whose performance of Jesus in a controversial Passion play begins to merge with his own identity, Bluteau is passionate and driven while simultaneously appearing to be caught in a series of events beyond his own control. This performance, for which he won the Best Actor Genie in 1989, brought Bluteau international recognition and was followed by numerous film roles as tortured young men driven by their

own demons, from the deeply religious missionary in Bruce Beresford's BLACK
ROBE to a refreshingly comic role as a sultan in Sally Potter's *Orlando* (1993,
UK) and his most recent Canadian appearance in Robert Lepage's LE CONFES-
SIONAL. Here, Bluteau sensitively portrays a man attempting to redefine his own
identity through the reexamination of his family history.

FILMS AS ACTOR: *Bleue brume* (short), 1982; *Rien qu'un jeu*, 1983; *Les années de
rêves*, 1984; *Sonia*, 1986; *Les fous de Bassan*, 1987; *La nuit avec Hortense; Mourir*
(short), 1988; *Bonjour Monsieur Gauguin; Jésus de Montréal*, 1989; *Black Robe* (Can/
Australia), 1991; *Being at Home with Claude*, 1992; *Le confessional*, 1995.

Stacey Abbott

LES BONS DÉBARRAS *Good Riddance*. Francis Mankiewicz, Quebec, 1980,
114 min., color. In *Les bons débarras*, an unwed mother, Michelle (MARIE
TIFO), lives with her overly possessive eleven-year-old daughter Manon (Charlotte Laurier) and her dim-witted, alcoholic brother Guy (GERMAIN HOUDE). To
survive, the threesome chop and sell firewood to local customers. This simple
narrative is overwhelmed by a subtext ripe with psychosocial reverberations,
generated mainly by Manon. Manon is fiercely jealous of anyone who vies for
her mother's attention and will stop at nothing to "steal" her back. When this
occurs her dark eyes turn angry and she is capable of manic-like mood changes.
For example, Manon eliminates her mother's policeman lover Maurice (Roger
Lebel) by concocting a story about his molesting her; when the emotionally
dependent brother Guy gets drunk at the wheel, Manon goads him to drive to
his death. At moments like these Manon recalls the "evil child" figure from
films such as *The Bad Seed* (United States, 1956) and *The Other* (United States,
1972). But she also exudes a tenderness and childlike vulnerability that make
her painfully human. It is a performance perched between *id*-like greed and
genuine emotional trauma. However, as in *Wuthering Heights*, the novel that
holds sway over Manon's girl-woman psyche, there is little violence or obvious
horror in *Les bon débarras*, but instead a brooding sense of obsessive passion.
MICHEL BRAULT's understated cinematography of the rural landscape provides
an atmospheric background to the overcharged emotions. In the end this perfect
fusion of evocative imagery and dialogue gives *Les bon débarras* its haunting
beauty. It won eight Genie Awards in 1981, including Best Feature Film, Best
Direction, Best Lead Actress (Tifo), and Best Cinematography.

BIBLIOGRAPHY: Joan Irving, "Francis Mankiewicz: To Berlin with Love," *Cinema
Canada*, no. 63 (March 1980): 11–15; Marshal Delaney, "Artists in the Shadows: Some
Notable Canadian Movies," in Feldman, 9–11.

Donato Totaro

PHILLIP BORSOS. Born 1953, Hobart, Tasmania; died 1995, Vancouver, B.C.
Director. Though his career was tragically cut short at the age of forty-one, by
acute myoblastic leukemia, Phillip Borsos was widely respected as one of the

most important filmmakers to emerge in Canadian cinema during the mid-to-late seventies. His early documentary works, *Cooperage, Spartree*, and *Nails* (1975–79), all garnered critical acclaim and awards (the first two, CFA Awards, with *Nails* winning a Genie). Each film celebrated an earlier period of Canadian history through the skills and crafts of the day presented through a lyrical documentary style that was both visually impressive and emotionally evocative. *Nails* remains one of Borsos' finest achievements and quite simply the best damn film ever made on the subject of nails. The success of his documentary work enabled Borsos to switch to feature films, which he accomplished with THE GREY FOX in 1982. The film was a phenomenal success both in Canada, where it won seven Genies, and abroad, especially among American film critics and filmmakers. Following the success of this film Borsos flirted with Hollywood, directing *The Mean Season*, but decided that his future lay in a model of film-making not unlike that of DAVID CRONENBERG, financing and directing world-class films from his home base in Vancouver. The undertaking of the bio-epic of Dr. Norman Bethune was to be one of Borsos' great Canadian works, but the international co-production was soon mired in difficulties, ranging from artistic differences among cast members and writer Ted Allen, to location difficulties and ideological differences among the film's national financiers. In the middle of one of the production delays a documentary film (*The Making of Bethune*, Peter Raymont) emerged on the difficulties Borsos was encountering. When *Bethune* was eventually released in 1990 the luster had long gone away. Borsos resurrected himself from the project with *Far from Home: The Adventures of Yellow Dog* (1995), all the while struggling with his leukemia. His premature death at the age of forty-one shocked many in Canadian cinema.

FILMS AS DIRECTOR: *The Barking Dog*, 1973; *Cadillac*, 1974; *Cooperage*, 1975; *Spartree*, 1977; *Nails*, 1979; *The Grey Fox* (feature), 1982; *The Mean Season* (US, feature, 1984); *One Magic Christmas* (feature), 1985; *Bethune* (feature and TV mini-series), 1990; *Far from Home: The Adventures of Yellow Dog* (feature), 1995.

BIBLIOGRAPHY: Blaine Allan, "Canada's Sweethearts, or Our American Cousins," *Canadian Journal of Film Studies* 2, nos. 2–3 (1993).

Dave Douglas

MICHEL BRAULT. Born 1928, Montreal. Cinematographer, director, producer, scriptwriter. Before being officially employed by the Office National du Film in 1956, Michel Brault became CLAUDE JUTRA's close friend, collaborating on all of his early films. A leading figure of *cinéma direct*, Brault played a key role in the birth of the Quebecois cinema and its blossoming on the international stage. As a cinematographer, Brault liberated the camera from its fixed tripod, thus making it a participant in the action and, at the same time, creating a closer relationship between the camera and the filmed subjects. LES RAQUETTEURS (1958), which Brault co-directed with GILLES GROULX, exemplifies this new documentary approach. This spirit of authenticity combines with a great visual beauty in *POUR LA SUITE DU MONDE* (1963), co-directed by PIERRE PERRAULT. This film remains a remarkable work of ethnography about the inhabitants of Ile-aux-Coudres, who behave with freshness and spontaneity. Brault left the ONF in 1965. In 1967 he directed *Entre la mer et l'eau douce*, his first fiction feature, starring Claude Gauthier and GENEVIÈVE BUJOLD. Closely related to documentary, and suffused with the aesthetic of *cinéma direct*, the film records the ascent of Claude, a young popular singer, together with the breakup of his relationship with his girlfriend Geneviève. With *LES ORDRES* (1974), which relates the events of the October Crisis in 1970, Brault authored a magnificent work of *fiction documentée* (Gilles Marsolais' term for this special kind of docu-drama). In addition to the films that he directed, Brault worked as cinematographer on several of the most beautiful works of Quebec cinema, including *À TOUT PRENDRE, MON ONCLE ANTOINE*, and *Kamouraska* (1973) by Claude Jutra, *Le temps d'une chasse* (1972) and *LES BONS DÉBARRAS* by FRANCIS MANKIEW-ICZ, and *MOURIR À TUE-TÊTE* by ANNE-CLAIRE POIRIER. Brault was less visible during the 1980s and 1990s. Nevertheless, in 1989 he directed *Les noces de papier*, a telefilm which was marked by the moving return of actress Bujold, then *Mon amie Max* in 1994. He was awarded the Prix Albert-Tessier in 1986.

FILMS AS DIRECTOR INCLUDE: *Les raquetteurs* (co-dir., Gilles Groulx), 1958; *La lutte* (co-dir., Claude Fournier, Claude Jutra, Marcel Carrière), 1961; *Pour la suite du monde* (co-dir., Pierre Perrault), 1963; *La fleur de l'âge: Geneviève*, 1965; *Entre la mer et l'eau douce*, 1967; *Les enfants de néant* (co-dir., Annie Tresgot), 1968; *L'Acadie, L'Acadie?!?* (co-dir., Perrault), 1971; *Les ordres*, 1974; *L'emprise* (co-dir., Suzanne Guy), 1988; *Les noces de papier*, 1989; *Montréal vu par . . .* (co-dir.), 1991; *Mon amie Max*, 1994.

BIBLIOGRAPHY: Gilles Marsolais (1974); Marsolais (1972); "Michel Brault," *Copie Zéro*, no. 5 (1980).

Louis Goyette

DONALD BRITTAIN. Born 1928, Ottawa; died 1989, Montreal. Director, writer, producer. Donald Brittain is a monumental figure in the history of Canadian cinema and an equally important figure in the documentary tradition of the NFB. Born in Ottawa, Brittain studied at Queen's University before working as a police reporter for the *Ottawa Journal* from 1951 to 1954. He then left Canada to travel in Mexico, Europe, and Africa (travel which had a significant influence on his later film work); he also worked briefly as a foreign correspondent in Tangier and as an interpreter in a Cote d'Azur bordello, and finally returned to Canada after winding up broke in the Russian sector of Vienna. Brittain began working at the NFB in 1954, serving as location manager on *Canadian Pacific* and *Salt Cod*. After several unsuccesful attempts as a scriptwriter, Brittain's script for *Royal Canadian Corps of Signals* (1956) was accepted, and his first film as director, *Sight Unseen*, was released in 1958. Brittain's big break came in 1960, when he was assigned the roles of writer and director for "Canada at War", a massive thirteen-part series about the Canadian war effort in World War

II. "Canada at War" marks a definitive moment in Brittain's career and is in many ways indicative of the stylistic avenues he would follow in his later work. Compiled from hours of war footage, the series is a carefully assembled retelling of history, characterized by Brittain's increasingly precise writing and impeccable editing. With *Fields of Sacrifice* (1964) Brittain began the production of some of his most important work, including *Bethune* (1964), for which he wrote the story of the legendary Canadian hero of the Chinese Revolution, and *Memorandum* (1966), a scathing depiction of the Nazis and their legacy. Brittain made *Tiger Child*, the first IMAX film, for Expo '70 in Osaka, and then returned to the NFB. After the tremendous achievement of VOLCANO: AN INQUIRY INTO THE LIFE AND DEATH OF MALCOLM LOWRY, for which he received an Oscar nomination, Brittain began to make increasing forays away from the NFB, directing and writing a number of documentaries and docudramas. Brittain's approach to filmmaking was characterized by the accumulation of footage, which he would then assemble while writing the voice-over narration; he opposed the idea of documentaries based on pre-prepared scripts, choosing instead to allow the narration to develop out of the visuals. Above all, perhaps Brittain will be most remembered as a brilliant writer whose laconic lyricism was perfectly matched with a passionate devotion to social justice.

FILMS AS DIRECTOR INCLUDE: *Sight Unseen; Setting Fires for Science,* 1958; *A Day in the Life of Jonathan Mole,* 1959; *Everybody's Prejudiced,* 1961; "Canada at War," 1962; *Fields of Sacrifice; Bethune,* 1964; *Memorandum,* 1966; *Saul Alinsky Went to War,* 1968; *Tiger Child,* 1970; *Cavendish Country,* 1973; *Dreamland: A History of Early Canadian Movies 1895–1939* (feature; also scr.); *King of the Hill,* 1974; *His Worship, Mr. Montreal,* 1975; *Volcano: An Inquiry into the Life and Death of Malcolm Lowry* (feature; also scr., prod.), 1976; *The Champions* (feature; also narr., prod.), 1977; *The Dionne Quintuplets* (feature; also prod.), 1978; *The Accident at Memorial Station* (feature, TV), 1983; *Canada's Sweetheart: The Saga of Hal. C. Banks* (feature, TV; also scr., prod.), 1985; *The King Chronicle* (3 TV features), 1988; *Family: A Loving Look at CBC Radio,* 1989.

BIBLIOGRAPHY: Terry Kolomeychuk.

Mitch Parry

BÛCHERONS DE LA MANOUANE. Arthur Lamothe, (Quebec) ONF, "Temps présent" series, 1962, 28 min., b+w. ARTHUR LAMOTHE's first film, *Bûcherons de la Manouane,* is one of the beacons of Quebecois *cinéma direct*. Before shooting it, Lamothe worked in an Abitibi lumberjack camp, as a result of which he made a denunciatory documentary, marking the "debut of the socially engaged cinema" in Quebec (according to Normand Ouellet). Humanist that he is, Lamothe presents a touching look at the men isolated in the Haute-Maurice region, at odds with their lamentable working conditions: inappropriate wages, deficient diet, and so on. Guy Borremans and Bernard Gosselin's images place the emphasis on the extreme rigor of the climate. The chiaroscuro photography of dimly lit camp interiors testifies to the profound solitude in which the lumberjacks live. The soundtrack alternates direct sound, folksongs, and voice-over commentary in a fashion that offers a vision of the world of the lumberjacks that is at the same time realist, poetic, and rhetorical. One can already notice in this, his first short film, Lamothe's interest in Canada's First Nations, which becomes a central problematic at the heart of the cineaste's work. Further, Lamothe adopts the figure of a visionary in demonstrating an environmental conscience which was surprising at this time. *Bûcherons de la Manouane* won a number of prizes both in Canada and elsewhere, including the Voile d'argent at the Locarno Festival in Switzerland and the Grand Prix for the best short film at the Festival du cinéma canadien (both in 1963).

BIBLIOGRAPHY: Yvan Patry and Robert Daudelin.

Louis Goyette

GENEVIÈVE BUJOLD. Born 1942, Montreal. Actor. Geneviève Bujold was educated in a convent and later went on to study acting for three years (1958–1961) at the Montreal Conservatory of Drama. Three months before she was due to graduate, she was offered the role of Rosine in a stage production of *The Barber of Seville*. As students were not allowed to act professionally, she quit in order to accept the role. This proved to be the right choice for Bujold, as she joined the Théâtre de Rideau Vert directly following the production's completion. For the next three years, she toured Europe with the company, performing in plays by Molière, Shakespeare, and Ibsen. While not touring she found time to act in over sixty TV and radio programs. In 1962 she made her first film appearance in both the English and French versions of *Amanita Pestilens* in a supporting role. In 1964 she played the title character in the "Geneviève" episode of the Canadian/French co-production of *La fleur de l'âge* directed by MICHEL BRAULT. This collaboration was to be the first of many for these two notable Quebecois artists. One of Bujold's biggest and most unusual breaks came in 1965 while on tour in France. Alain Resnais' mother was so impressed with the young actress' stage presence that she urged her son to meet Bujold. Resnais cast her in *La guerre est finie* two months after the meeting. With Resnais, Bujold began her education in acting for the camera. From this point onward, Bujold's career became more focused on film, gradually moving away from the stage. She made a notable impact on Hollywood playing such doomed heroines as the Queen in *Anne of a Thousand Days*, for which she received an Oscar nomination. Unlike so many Canadian actors who achieve fame in the United States, however, she did not abandon her native country but chose to shuttle among Canada, France, and Hollywood, making films in both English and French. Throughout her career, she has worked with some of the most distinctive contemporary filmmakers, including CLAUDE JUTRA, Brian De Palma, and DAVID CRONENBERG. Her film career, however, has been marked by three particularly intense creative collaborations with directors Michel Brault, Alan Rudolph, and PAUL ALMOND, resulting in some of her most outstanding performances. Bujold is an instinctive actress, often playing mature, intelligent women who temper their strength with an air of vulnerability. She has won the Genie Award for Best Actress on no less than four occasions: three times for a performance in a leading role—*ISABEL* (1968), *The Act of the Heart* (1970), and *Kamouraska* (1973)—and once as Best Supporting Actress, for *Murder by Decree* in 1980.

FILMS AS ACTOR: *Amanita Pestilens* (French & English versions), 1962; *La fin des étés* (short); *La fleur de l'age; La terre de boire*, 1964; *Entre la mer et l'eau douce*, 1967; *Isabel*, 1968; *The Act of the Heart; Marie-Christine* (short), 1970; *Journey*, 1972; *Kamouraska*, 1973; *Murder by Decree* (Can/UK), 1979; *Final Assignment*, 1980; *Dead Ringers; Les noces de papier* (TV), 1988; *And the Dance Goes On*, 1990; *Oh, What a Night*, 1992; *Mon amie Max*, 1994; *Dead Innocent*, 1996.

BIBLIOGRAPHY: Daniele Parra, "Un leçon de beauté," *Revue de Cinéma/Image et Son*, no. 470 (April 1991): 47–53.

Stacey Abbott

JACKIE BURROUGHS. Born 1942, UK. Actor, director. Jackie Burroughs is one of Canada's most political and outspoken actresses, with an acting style as distinct as her own personality. She made minor headway in the film industry in the late sixties by appearing in DONALD OWEN's *The Ernie Game* and, although she appeared sporadically in films throughout the 1970s, she spent most of this period performing at Stratford (Ontario), as well as gaining critical praise for her work in television, winning awards for the CBC productions of "12 1/2 cents" and "Vicky." It was in the 1980s, however, that she began to make an impact on the big screen. She received a Genie for her performance as the feminist photographer/love interest of Richard Farnsworth in *THE GREY FOX* and won a further Genie for her work in *The Wars*. Furthermore, she became familiar to Canadian audiences by appearing regularly in the CBC TV series "The Road to Avonlea." In 1987, Burroughs found a character that would enable her to escape the confines of traditional drama, Maryse Holder in *A WINTER TAN*. Burroughs was drawn to Holder's book of her letters, *Give Sorrow Words*, and collaborated on its screen adaptation. So personal a project was this that Burroughs undertook to co-direct the film, but it is Burroughs' fiery performance that carries it. Not hesitating to use direct address, Burroughs faces the camera, unashamedly recounting sexual exploits with young Mexican men, disillusionment with modern feminism, and disgust with the aging process. It is a tour de force performance. Despite her many skillful performances before and after *A Winter Tan*, Burroughs has never demonstrated greater confidence and attachment to a role.

FILMS AS ACTOR: *The Ernie Game*, 1967; *Eat Anything*, 1971; *A Fan's Notes; Running Time*, 1972; *Monkeys in the Attic; 125 Rooms of Comfort*, 1974; *My Pleasure Is My Business* (Can/Ger), 1975; *Partners*, 1976; *The Kidnapping of the President*, 1980; *The Intruder; Heavy Metal* (voice only), 1981; *The Grey Fox*, 1982; *The Wars* (Can/Ger);

Quebec/Canada 1995 (TV), 1983; *Gentle Sinners* (TV); *Overdrawn at the Moneybank* (Can/US); *The Surrogate*, 1984; *The Undergrads; The Care Bears Movie* (voice only); *All the Years*, 1985; *The Housekeeper; John and the Missus*, 1986; *A Winter Tan* (also co-dir.), 1987; *The Midday Sun; Whispers* (Can/US); *Food of the Gods II*, 1989; *Distress Signals* (narr.), 1990; *Careful*, 1992; *How Dinosaurs Learned to Fly* (short, voice only), 1995; *Platinum* (TV), 1997.

BIBLIOGRAPHY: "Jackie Burroughs: A Career of Deep Shame," *Cinema Canada*, no. 145 (October 1987).

Stacey Abbott

PASCALE BUSSIÈRES. Born 1968, Montreal. Actor. Pascale Bussières is one of the rising stars of Quebec cinema. Since her debut feature, SONATINE (1984), she has increasingly tackled complex and challenging roles, and has been nominated for a clutch of awards. Her first was a Genie nomination for *Sonatine*, in which she played a young girl who enters into a suicide pact with a friend. Bussières has an easy, effortless acting style, inhabiting her characters totally and bringing them to life with great subtlety. She continued to work in films for the ONF and on television while studying film production at Concordia University, before returning to the big screen in *La vie fantôme* (1992), for which she was voted Best Actress at Montreal's Festival des Films du Monde. She followed this by being reunited with MICHELINE LANCTÔT for *Deux actrices* (1993), not only playing a fictional character, but also appearing as herself, discussing her own life and her approach to the role. Since then she has gone from strength to strength, showing her versatility in 1994 when she appeared both in *Eldorado* and *When Night Is Falling*. In the first, she plays a bratty street punk and petty thief. The film is a Generation-X drama, filmed with a hand-held style and with a script that was improvised by the cast with director Charles Biname. It contrasts sharply with *When Night Is Falling*, a lyrical, symbolic, and romantic tale of lesbian love in which Bussières plays a teacher at a theological college who falls for a circus performer. Director PATRICIA ROZEMA draws performances of great passion from her cast, with Bussières at the emotional center of the film and the linking stream between both worlds. She received separate Genie nominations for the two films. The success of these films has brought Bussières to the attention of international filmmakers, and recently she went to New Zealand to appear in the children's drama *Whole of the Moon*, 1996.

FILMS AS ACTOR: *Sonatine*, 1984; *Le peau et les os; Le chemin de Damas* (TV) 1988; *Femme de Pierre*, 1990; *Moise*, 1991; *La vie fantôme*, 1992; *Deux actrices*, 1993; *When Night Is Falling; Eldorado*, 1994; *Windsor Protocol* (TV, Can/UK); *The Whole of the Moon* (TV, Can/NZ); *Thunder Point* (TV, Can/UK); *Honeymoon; Les milles merveilles de l'univers*, 1996; *L'âge de brâise* (Fr/Can); *Twilight of the Ice Nymphs; Platinum* (TV), 1997.

BIBLIOGRAPHY: Marcel Jean, "Portrait: Pascale Bussières," *24 Images*, no. 64 (December 1992–January 1993): 24–25.

Simon Brown

BYE BYE BLUES. Anne Wheeler, Alberta, 1989, 117 min., color. One of the largest productions to come out of the Canadian West, *Bye Bye Blues* was writer/ director ANNE WHEELER's second feature film. It won three Genie awards, for Best Actress (Rebecca Jenkins), Best Supporting Actress (Robyn Stevan), and Best Original Song (Bill Henderson). The film chronicles the struggle of a young wife and mother forced to make a life for herself in rural Alberta after her husband is taken prisoner in World War II. Frustrated by the lack of freedom in her parents' home, Daisy earns her own living by playing in a local swing band. As the band's success grows, so does her uncertainty about her husband's return. She is torn between her new life of travel and fame, personified by Max, the attentive American trombone player in the group, and the security and love of her family. When a telegram arrives announcing her husband's safe return Daisy must choose between two worlds. Anne Wheeler's screenplay was loosely based on the wartime experiences of her own mother, Nell Homer. Wheeler and cinematographer Vic Sarin, shooting on location in India and Alberta, used natural lighting to create a soft, nostalgic mise-en-scène that evokes this period in Canadian history. Wheeler has commented that her goal was to explore the idea that despite the tragedy and heartache associated with this era, "the war revealed all sorts of possibilities." The film tenderly captures a fragile balance between independence and responsibility, as well as the pain and suffering women on the home front were confronted with.

Alice Black

C

CALENDAR. Atom Egoyan, (Toronto) Canada/Germany/Armenia, 1993, 75 min., 16mm, color. Arguably director ATOM EGOYAN's finest film, *Calendar* is also the quintessential Canadian feature film of the 1990s: an independently made, multicultural, international co-production which in its structure is deeply informed by the Canadian traditions of documentary and experimental filmmaking. But it almost didn't get made at all. Egoyan had been promised funding by Soviet Armenia to make a film in his ancestral homeland, but with the precipitous decline of the post-communist ruble he needed support from elsewhere, and got it from German television. The film was shot in 1992. *Calendar*'s skeletal narrative finds a photographer (Egoyan) and his wife (Arsinée Khanjian) on assignment in Armenia to shoot churches for a calendar. We see her in the static frame of the camera, directed by Egoyan's off-screen voice, while she translates their Armenian guide's (Ashot Adamian) advice and historical information. The twelve calendar episodes are shown to be flashbacks from scenes in the photographer's apartment in Toronto where he entertains a young woman of a different ethnicity each month, each of whom makes a phone call in her own "foreign" language after dinner. It is gradually revealed that he is pining over losing his wife (presumably to the guide), as he repeatedly watches videotapes that they made in Armenia. Like Egoyan's earlier *FAMILY VIEWING*, there is a marked visual difference between film and video, but unlike its predecessor, the crude monochrome video seems here to have a positive, emotional association, as the dynamic, moving video images are contrasted with the photographer's distanced, albeit beautiful, static framings. The stylistic implications are that the wife's warm openness is conveyed through the tactile, sensuous intimacy of video in contrast to the husband's cold aestheticism. Appropriately enough, given its German funding, *Calendar* was premiered at the Berlin Film Festival in February 1993, where it won the first prize in the Forum of Young Cinema.

BIBLIOGRAPHY: Ron Burnett, "Between the Borders of Cultural Identity: Atom Egoyan's *Calendar*," *CineACTION*, no. 32 (Fall 1993): 30–34.

Peter Rist

JOHN (FRANKLIN) CANDY. Born 1950, Newmarket, Ontario; died 1994, Durango, Mexico. Actor, writer, director. After working in theater and commercials, John Candy joined Chicago's Second City improvisational theatrical troupe in 1972. Two years later, along with Dan Aykroyd, Gilda Radner, and others, he became a founding member of the Toronto-based sister company. In 1976, with cast members leaving to join NBC's "Saturday Night Live," the Toronto company created "SCTV," adding fellow Canadians Rick Moranis, Dave Thomas, Catherine O'Hara, and Andrea Martin. During each episode Candy's imagination was given free rein. He impersonated Luciano Pavarotti, Orson Welles, Tip O'Neill, and even the late Herve Villechaize! His own characters were no less exotic, including Johnny LaRue, Harry—"the guy with the snake on my face"—and Gil Fisher "The Fishin' Musician." For his work on "SCTV" Candy shared an ACTRA Award for Best Performance in Television in 1978, and won Emmy Awards for Outstanding Writing in 1982 and 1983. By this time, Candy had also appeared in a number of feature films in supporting roles (*Clown Murders; The Silent Partner; Kavik the Wolf Dog*). In 1979 Candy shifted his acting energies to the United States, and emerged as a comic star in *Splash!* (R. Howard, 1984). As his film career took off in the United States, Candy's work in Canada was reduced mainly to television, usually in guest appearances or in unbilled cameos. Due to his large girth and affable exterior, Candy was inevitably cast in comic roles. However, his winsome comic persona enabled him to rise above even the most uninspired material. This persona, an energetic mixture of low cunning and bumbling inefficiency, combined with a streak of sentimentality and vulnerability, created sympathetic and credible characters. Candy returned to Canada to make his two last films: *Canadian Bacon*, the first fiction feature by documentarist Michael Moore, in which Candy plays an American (Bud B. Boomer) intent on invading Canada; and *Hostage for a Day*, a made-for-television film that marked Candy's directorial debut. Sadly, Candy, who showed the same sensitivity and humor in his direction as he had in his acting and writing, died before it was broadcast.

FILMS AS ACTOR: *It Seemed Like a Good Idea at the Time*, 1975; *Clown Murders*, 1976; *Find the Lady*, 1976; *Silent Partner*, 1978; *Kavik the Wolf Dog*, 1978; *Heavy Metal* (voice only), 1981; *The Rocket Boy* (TV), 1986; *Canadian Conspiracy* (TV), 1986; *Reilly Weird Tales*, 1987; *Hostage for a Day* (TV; also dir.), 1994; *Canadian Bacon* (US), 1995.

Sergio Angelini

CARCAJOU ET LE PÉRIL BLANC/KAUAPISHIT MIAM KUAKUATSHEN ETENTAKUESS. Arthur Lamothe (with the collaboration of Rémi Savard), Northeast Quebec, 1973–74, 582 min. (8 films), 16mm. From 1973 to 1983,

Arthur Lamothe directed, with the close collaboration of Quebecois anthropol-
ogist Rémi Savard, the "Chronique des Indiens du Nord-Est du Québec," a series
divided into two parts: *Carcajou et le péril blanc* (eight films) and *La terre de
l'homme* (five films). This series of thirteen films was projected in more than
twenty-five international events. Also, the first part, *Carcajou*, received the Ses-
terce d'or, the first prize of the Nyon (Switzerland) International Festival in
October 1975 as well as the Quebec Association of Film Critics prize in the
same year. The eight episodes of *Carcajou* show us how, on the lower North
Shore of Quebec, the arrival of white people and industrialization had modified
the traditional life of First Nations people, especially that of the Montagnais.
The first episode, entitled *Mistashipu/La Grande Rivière*, constitutes a general
introduction to the world of the Montagnais. (Mistashipu is also the Montagnais
name for the river Moisie.) Mostly, it traces the destiny of this river from the
opening up of the adjacent territories to the exploitation of mining. The second
episode, entitled *Ntesi Nana Shepen/On disait que c'était notre terre (1ère par-
tie)* exposes us to the native people who were expelled from their land and
harassed by the bureaucracy, while *Ntesi Nana Shepen 2* shows us an old man
who teaches his grandson the rudiments of hunting. In . . . *Shepen 3*, it is bear-
hunting which is explained to us, including the rituals linked to it. Then, . . .
Shepen 4 shows the origins of the Sept-Îles region and how the indigenous
inhabitants are dispossessed of its rich natural resources to profit multinational
corporations. Following this, we can learn how one speaks to the stones in order
to communicate with the spirits in *Kuestetsheskamit/L'Autre Monde*, and how
tents are transformed into houses in *Patshiantshiuapa Mak Mistikussiupapa/Le
passage des tentes aux maisons*; and, finally, we follow the installation of a
summer camp along the river Saint-Augustin in *Pakuashipu/La Rivière Sèche*.
Overall, the eight episodes of *Carcajou et le péril blanc* provide us with a global
image of the Montagnais culture, not just a description of their natural habitat.
For the first time in cinema history, we hear the speech of First Nations people
in their own language, transmitting to us with an astonishing sincerity their
material problems, their conception of "man," time, space, and their mythology;
all thanks to the oral tradition, the privileged mode of expression for aboriginal
people. Thus, as people respect nature's cycles and accommodate themselves to
the logic of these cycles without looking to upset the order of things, so filmmaker Arthur Lamothe has respected the duration of Montagnais speech and
has done so without breaking spatiotemporal continuity.

Isabelle Morissette

TANTOO CARDINAL. Born Sara Winnemuca, 1951, Fort McMurray, Alberta.
Actor. Tantoo Cardinal is one of Canada's most critically acclaimed actresses.
She was given her first role in a 1971 docudrama about Albert Lacombe as a
result of her reputation as a political activist and as the president of a youth
group dedicated to getting schools on native reservations. Faced with an overwhelming flood of American entertainment on the market, there was a move-

ment within the Canadian film industry to emphasize the stories of indigenous people, and Cardinal's career quickly developed in this context. By the time she moved to the United States in 1986, Cardinal had already become a familiar face on Canadian screens. She quickly discovered that Native American characters in the U.S. film industry were still often played by actors of other ethnic groups. Cardinal's breakthrough film, director Kevin Costner's *Dances with Wolves*, attempted to break with this tradition. She won the part as wife of Kicking Bird the medicine man by auditioning in her native Cree language. As a member of the Metis Nation, Cardinal acknowledged the controversy generated by inaccuracies in the film but defended the project by saying, "*Dances* was a culmination of our experience in Hollywood films . . . but I think we should move onto stories where native people are in the lead." After a supporting role in Bruce Beresford's *BLACK ROBE*, Cardinal starred with Rip Torn in Jay Craven's *Where the Rivers Flow North* (U.S., 1993), a film that chronicled the relationship between a First Nations woman, Bangor, and her older, log-driver employer. In a recent role Cardinal appeared as a Cree woman married to a white man in the 1994 Hollywood epic *Legends of the Fall*, directed by Ed Zwick. Her many awards include the Eagle & Spirit Award for contribution to the Native American community and the *McLean's Magazine* Honour Roll Actress of the Year (both in 1991) and an honorary doctorate from the University of Rochester in 1993.

FILMS AS ACTOR INCLUDE: *Marie-Anne* (TV), 1979; *Death Hunt*, 1981; *Running Brave*, 1982; *Loyalties*, 1986; *Candy Mountain*, 1987; *Black Robe*, 1991; *Silent Tongue; Mustard Bath; Spirit Rider* (TV), 1993; *Lakota Woman: Siege at Wounded Knee* (TV), 1994; *Tecumseh: The Last Warrior* (TV), 1995; *Grand Avenue* (TV), 1996; *Silence; The Education of Little Tree*, 1997.

BIBLIOGRAPHY: Joel Engel, "Always a Tribeswoman, Never a Lawyer," *New York Times* (April 10, 1994); Cathy Thompson-Georges, "A Dark Horse on a Dark Night," *Entertainment Today* (December 9–15, 1994).

Alice Black

CAREFUL. Guy Maddin, Manitoba, 1992, 100 min., color. *Careful*, GUY MAD-DIN's third feature, solidified his status as Canada's most archaically inventive, and eccentric, visual stylist. *Careful* is an absurdly comic Freudian fairy tale set in Tolzbad, a Swiss Alp town so precariously situated among the mountains that citizens must guard their every word to avert an avalanche. Only in certain places protected by "acoustic shelters" can normal levels of sound be allowed. The town takes anal measures to safeguard its security: domestic animals have their vocal cords severed, children are tied and gagged, and even the voice-over narrator speaks in a hushed voice. The muted lifestyle in Tolzbad is an obvious metaphor for social and sexual repression. The film's ingenuity rests in a visual style that serves the theme of repression well, and also engages in a fascinating, synchronic patchwork of film history. Maddin's unnatural use of color (orange, yellow, green, blue, violet) recalls both silent cinema (in its color tinting and toning) and the German Weimar period "mountain films." There are other German film references: the Nazi-like "Frau Teacher" (JACKIE BURROUGHS); the Werner Krauss/Dr.Caligari look-alike Herr Trotta (Victor Cowie); and the exclusive studio bound, UFA-like sets. The other important film history touchstone in *Careful* is the horror genre. The external nocturnal sets are patterned after the Universal Frankenstein films; the use of shadows in certain early scenes is reminiscent of Carl Dreyer's *Vampyr* (1932); the forlorn brother Franz (Vince Rimmer), locked in the attic and cobwebbed to his chair, recalls the "man by the window" in *Eraserhead* (1977); and there are scenes of exceedingly graphic violence: the coroner drives a large nail through the heart of each dead citizen; as punishment for his Oedipal desires, Johann (Brent Neale) mutilates his mouth with a hot poker and then cuts off four of his fingers with garden shears. Some of these allusions are merely playful citations, but others are used to underscore theme, and help ground Maddin's inimitable visual style in something vaguely familiar.

BIBLIOGRAPHY: Jim Hoberman, "Heights: Careful," *Village Voice* 37 (October 13, 1992): 57; Gabriel Alvarez, "Watch Out!," *Film Threat*, no. 13 (December 1993): 46–49.

Donato Totaro

GILLES CARLE. Born 1929, Maniwaki, Quebec. Director, scriptwriter, and producer. Before joining the Office National du Film in 1960, Gilles Carle studied at the École des Beaux-Arts in Montreal. He was a draftsman for the newspaper *Le Soleil*, and founded the publishing company Éditions de l'Hexagone with friends Gaston Miron and Louis Portugais, as well as working for Radio-Canada. His first works as a documentarist at the NFB did not go unnoticed, since—as he demonstrated in his shorts *Patinoire* (1962) and *Percé on the Rocks* (1964)—he knew how to infuse a large element of fantasy and freshness into a genre previously locked in conventions. Feeling increasingly constrained in the documentary genre, Carle subtly transformed a documentary project about snow-removal into his first feature-length fiction film, *LA VIE HEUREUSE DE LÉOPOLD Z*. Faced with the impossibility of being able to direct other fiction films at the ONF, Carle left and began working on his own. Onyx Films released his next three features, *Le viol d'une jeune fille douce* (1968), *Red*, and *Les mâles*, which enjoyed popular success. In 1971 he and Pierre Lamy founded their own production company, Les Productions Carle-Lamy, which produced some of the most noteworthy Quebecois films of the first half of the 1970s, including his own *LA VRAIE NATURE DE BERNADETTE*, *IL ÉTAIT UNE FOIS DANS L'EST* (André Brassard, 1973), and *Gina* (DENYS ARCAND, 1975). It was with this company that Carle directed some of his most personal films, with his "muse," the actress CAROLE LAURE. *La mort d'un bûcheron, La tête de Normande St-Onge*, and *L'ange et la femme* (1977) are like poems to the wild and sensual beauty of the actress. Introducing more sinuous narrative trajectories, these films carry an undeniable breath of eroticism. The 1980s proved to be Carle's most difficult years. Although *Les Plouffe* was favorably received by critics and audiences alike, both the musical comedy *Fantastica* and *Maria Chapdelaine* (1983) met with mixed responses. *La guêpe* (1986) was a complete failure. It should be noted that during the 1980s Carle resumed the documentary practice at which he had always been a master. *La postière* (1993) marked a strong, though less ambitious, return to the fiction film, as always characterized by a petulant sense of humor.

FILMS AS DIRECTOR INCLUDE: *Patinoire*, 1962; *Percé on the Rocks; Solange dans nos campagnes*, 1964; *La vie heureuse de Léopold Z.*, 1965; *Place à Olivier Guimond*, 1966; *Le viol d'une jeune fille douce*, 1968; *Red*, 1969; *Les mâles*, 1970; *La vraie nature de Bernadette*, 1972; *Les corps célestes; La mort d'un bûcheron*, 1973; *La tête de Normande St-Onge*, 1975; *L'ange et la femme*, 1977; *L'âge de la machine*, 1978; *Fantastica*, 1980; *Les Plouffe*, 1981; *Jouer sa vie* (co-dir., Camille Coudari), 1982; *Maria Chapdelaine*, 1983; *O Picasso* (co-dir., Coudari); *Cinéma, cinéma* (co-dir., Werner Nold), 1985; *La guêpe*, 1986; *Vive Québec!*, 1988; *Le diable d'amérique*, 1990; *La postière*, 1993; *The Other Side of the Law* (Can/Fr), 1994; *Blood of the Hunter* (Can/Fr), 1995; *Pouding chômeur*, 1996.

BIBLIOGRAPHY: Carol Faucher and Michel Houle; Michel Coulombe (1995).

Louis Goyette

CARRY ON, SERGEANT! Bruce Bairnsfather, Ontario, 1928, 100 min, b+w, silent. *Carry On, Sergeant!* has the dubious distinction of being the film that bankrupted Canadian International Films, one of a succession of fledgling production companies established in Trenton, Ontario. Bruce Bairnsfather, an English dramatist and cartoonist who had enjoyed considerable success with his earlier theatrical treatments of World War I, had complete control over the production of the film in spite of his complete inexperience as a film director; his extravagance is in part responsible for the film's (then) enormous budget of $500,000. Conceived as an antidote to American war films, which emphasized the late entry of the United States into the war while ignoring the contributions of the other participants, the film deals with the activities of Canadian soldiers, culminating in the battle at Ypres in 1915. When war breaks out, Jim McKay (Hugh Buckler) leaves his recent bride, Ruth (Nancy Ann Hargreaves), in order to enlist in the Canadian Scottish regiment. A subplot involves an enemy spy who uses his unsuspecting wealthy Canadian and American friends to sabotage the war effort. Critics were scandalized by McKay's willingness to find comfort from the ravages of war in the arms of a French woman in an *estaminet*. Although the film is marred by jingoistic sabre-rattling and some ill-conceived comedic moments featuring burlesque comic Jimmy Savo, *Carry On, Sergeant!* occasionally manages to step away from its patriotic stance in an effort to portray the humanity of soldiers on both sides of the front lines, and is admirable for its convincing battle scenes.

BIBLIOGRAPHY: Peter Morris (1978).

Mitch Parry

LE CHAT DANS LE SAC The Cat in the Bag [The Cat in the Sack]. Gilles Groulx, ONF (Montreal), 1964, 74 min., b+w. Beginning as a short film on winter, *Le chat dans le sac* became a feature film on the problems of Quebecois youth during the Quiet Revolution. The film relates the progressive erosion of the relationship between Claude, a "French-Canadian in search of himself," and Barbara, a young Jewish anglophone who loves the theater. The director, GILLES GROULX, said of the film's subject, "In particular, I have investigated the dullness of the quotidian, which I consider to be like a general state of Quebec francophones, a life with no escape, pitiful, which goes around in circles. For this reason, I created this character, a guy who does nothing more than smoke cigarettes." In truth, Claude's character is worth more than this. He reflects on the condition of the minority in an anglophone Canada, criticizes the Catholic Church, and reproaches Barbara for behaving like a marionette. Groulx filmed *Le chat dans le sac* on a modest budget of $32,000, using nonprofessional actors to interpret all the roles in the film. Although shot on 35mm, his film respects the techniques of *cinéma direct* on several levels: everyday speech (often improvised), shoulder-mounted camera, shooting in continuity on location, the respect for natural light. One can detect the influences of Brecht and Godard in the testimony of a political discourse, the many jump cuts, and actors addressing the camera, as well as the reflexive nature of the film. Directed more than thirty years ago, *Le chat dans le sac* seems not to have aged at all and still seems very immediate. The film won the Grand Prix for best feature film at the Festival du cinéma canadien (1964).

BIBLIOGRAPHY: Robert Daudelin.

Louis Goyette

LE CHÂTEAU DE SABLE/THE SAND CASTLE. Co Hoedeman, ONF, 1977, 13 min., 16mm, color, no dialogue. *Le château de sable/The Sand Castle* is the best known work of Dutch-born animator Co Hoedeman, whose other works include *Oddball* (1969), *The Owl and the Lemming* (1971), *Tchou-Tchou* (1972), *Lumaaq* (1975), and *The Treasure of the Grotoceans* (1980). As with his other works, Hoedeman painstakingly blends characters, sets, and style to create a world where allegory meets playful entertainment. In *Le château* a Gumby-like sand creature appears from under the sand floor and gives creation to a group of oddly shaped fellow sand creatures. Under the leader's (God's?) guidance, the sand creatures, all with their own unique physical skills and attributes, jubilantly construct an elaborate sand castle. A celebration dance ensues, but is disrupted by a windstorm that forces the sand creatures to take refuge inside the castle. The windstorm reduces the landscape to its original state. Hoedeman's open-ended world can be interpreted in many ways: biblically (ashes to ashes, dust to dust), ecologically (humanity and nature working in harmony), or existentially (as a Sisyphean fable). In any case, it remains a bittersweet tale enjoyed by both the young and the old, and has won more prizes (twenty-three), including an Oscar, than any other Canadian film.

BIBLIOGRAPHY: Joan Irving, "Castles in the Sand: Co Hoedeman," *Cinema Canada,* no. 46 (April–May 1978): 28–31; Michael Mills, "The Sand Castle," *Cinema Canada,* no. 46 (April–May 1978): 31.

Donato Totaro

MAURY CHAYKIN. Born 1950, New York. Actor. Called a "true eccentric actor" by Pauline Kael, Maury Chaykin is one of the most vivid presences in Canadian movies. Chaykin studied theater at New York State University in Buffalo, where he rubbed shoulders with the likes of Allen Ginsberg. His first notoriety came as one of the founders of a touring theater troupe called Swamp Fox, who in 1970 crashed Toronto's Festival of Underground Theatre. This act caught the attention of festival director Ken Gass, who in 1974 invited Chaykin to collaborate on a theater piece called *Hurray for Johnny Canuck.* From there, Chaykin drifted into Canadian film and television, with his big breakthrough being the eponymous character in the 1985 TV movie *Canada's Sweetheart: The Saga of Hal C. Banks,* DONALD BRITTAIN's account of the life and work of the notorious thug, strikebreaker, and ukulele-player. Chaykin granted Banks an eerie malevolence that marked most of his portrayals from then on. Chaykin has often been utilized to provide a welcome burst of underground-theater edginess to Hollywood fare as diverse as *Dances with Wolves* (1990), *My Cousin Vinny* (1992), and *Beethoven's 2nd* (1993). His real work, however, has been the series of memorable portraits he has contributed to the current renaissance of Canadian cinema. A large, imposing figure with his 300-pound girth, Chaykin's acting has always gone beyond mere menace. His psychotic kidnapper in COLD COMFORT, his reclusive Brian Wilsonesque rock star in *Whale Music,* and, especially, his deranged husband in *The Adjuster* (1991), are all endowed with a miraculous sense of play. The latter performance is particularly gripping, with Chaykin's key scene being his wandering monologue in the guise of a real-estate buyer—a brilliant index of his character's psychic disintegration. Proof of Chaykin's formidable prowess is the impression he makes with his unbilled cameo in *EXOTICA,* the sad beatific grace with which he gazes at a table dancer, showing up Egoyan's overrated film for the shallow concoction it really is—and hinting at the film it might have been if Chaykin had played the lead.

FILMS AS ACTOR: *Riel* (TV), 1979; *Nothing Personal,* 1979; *Hockey Night,* 1984; *Canada's Sweetheart: The Saga of Hal C. Banks* (TV), 1985; *Meatballs III,* 1987; *Cold Comfort,* 1989; *The Adjuster,* 1991; *The Pianist,* 1992; *Camilla; Whale Music; Exotica,* 1994; *Strip Search* (US/Can); *Northern Lights* (TV, US/Can); *Love and Death on Long Island* (UK/Can); *The Sweet Hereafter,* 1997.

Mark Carpenter

"CHRONIQUE DE LA VIE QUOTIDIENNE" SERIE "Chronicle of Daily Life," series. Jacques Leduc in collaboration with Pierre Bernier, Jean Chabot, Roger Frappier, Gilles Gascon, Claude Grenier, Jean-Guy Noël, (Montreal) ONF, 1977–78, 268 min., color. *Dimanche—granit* [Sunday—Granite], 29 min.; *Lundi—une chaumière, un coeur* [Monday—A Thatched-Roof Cottage, a Heart], 45 min.; *Mardi—un jour anonyme* [Tuesday—An Anonymous Day], 27 min.; *Mercredi—petits souliers, petits pains* [Wednesday—Little Shoes, Little Loaves], 34 min.; *Jeudi—à cheval sur l'argent* [Thursday—On Horseback, on the Money], 17 min.; *Vendredi—les chars* [Friday—The Cars], 24 min.; *Samedi—le ventre de la nuit* [Saturday—The Belly of the Night], 82 min.; *Le plan sentimental* [The Sentimental Shot], 10 min. While stretching the observational concept of Quebecois *cinéma direct* to the limit, "Chronique de la vie quotidienne" is also remarkable for demonstrating how montage alone can create rhetoric. Not necessarily shot in order, and certainly not shot on a single day of the title, each film in the series is structured to represent one day in Montreal and focuses on aspects of quotidian life. Most also employ montage in implicating the power of money over ordinary people. *Lundi* initially intercuts the scene of a building site with a car show, a wedding, and a divorced woman searching for a partner through an agency. A house is viewed in increasingly developed stages of construction while a young bourgeois wife asks the builder for changes. The film, moreover, "constructs" the message that the happiness of a young couple is dependent on the purchase of a car and a house, which, in turn, depends on the labor of the workers. Whereas long takes are employed to objectively view and admire the skilled operations of various craftsmen, a few short scenes are interspersed which show them exchanging their hard-earned money for lunch at a mobile canteen. *Mardi* begins in the morning with milk being sold, intercut with its production in a dairy, and moves to children renting bicycles. *Mardi* develops into the most charming film of the series, viewing old and young on the street with humor and affection, ending with patrons of a bar singing Quebecois songs. *Jeudi*, however, is the most overtly rhetorical film in the series, where (apparently) candid betting transactions at the Blue Bonnets harness racing venue dominate screen time, and where, repeatedly, a tracking shot scanning a futuristic city model is juxtaposed with a reverse lateral track past the slums which the "future city" is intended to replace. The most remarkable work in the "chronicle," though, is the longest, *Samedi—le ventre de la nuit*. Like *Lundi*, it begins on an empty space, which is here filled with a circus tent, the site of one or more of the entertainments—bingo, hypnotism, dance marathon, fairground side-shows, an auction—designed to take the people's money. Comic relief within the montage is provided by a group of young people (possibly university students) viewed on their terrace, resisting the exploitation of the camera for painfully long periods by "performing" only when they choose to. As with all of the films, there is no narration, and the camera views each scene from a distance and mostly from a rigidly fixed position. The sound is as "direct" as the cinematography, but associations are made between events by carrying sound over, and the matching of gestures, lighting, and other visual elements connects events together as being similarly hypnotic. Indeed, as Hélène Samson suggests, JACQUES LEDUC and his collaborators brilliantly connected form and content in *Samedi*, exposing the cinema as being the hypnotic medium that it is and allowing the audience of their film to see through its "effects."

BIBLIOGRAPHY: Hélène Samson, "L'effet hypnotique en *Le ventre de la nuit*," *Copie Zéro*, no. 14 (1982): 36–39.

Peter Rist

CHURCHILL'S ISLAND. Stuart Legg, (Ottawa) NFB, 1941, 22 min., b+w. One of the first productions of Canada's newly formed National Film Board, and the fourth in the series "Canada Carries On," *Churchill's Island* won the very first Oscar for Documentary Film (1941), on February 26, 1942. (The fifth "Canada Carries On," *Warclouds in the Pacific*, was one of the other eight nominated documentary films.) Both films, intended originally for Canadian audiences, were also included in the NFB "World in Action" series, which was distributed internationally by United Artists (hence the Oscar recognition). Both series consisted of compilations of mostly found footage (with some action filmed specifically for the series), music, sound effects, and voice-over narration. LORNE GREENE's voice came to be known as the "voice-of-God" narration because of its authoritative and declamatory nature. Indeed, it is the bombastic soundtrack which dates the work and labels it clearly wartime propaganda. *Churchill's Island* was made in an effort to make Canadian audiences sympathetic to the plight of Britain defending itself against its Nazi foes. Initially, the film shows the island nation getting beaten, but the tide of the Battle of Britain is shown to turn, and some interviews with very calm, low-keyed subjects demonstrate a matter-of-fact defiance. Typically, the editing of the images is the film's strong suit. STUART LEGG, assisted by his stock shot researcher/"student" TOM DALY, often employed Eisensteinian graphic contrasts, for example, juxtaposing a shot of an anti-aircraft gun firing to the upper right of screen with a shot of another gun firing upper-left.

BIBLIOGRAPHY: Gary Evans (1984).

Peter Rist

CITY OF GOLD. Wolf Koenig and Colin Low, NFB, 1957, 22 min., b+w. One of the NFB's most celebrated films, having won over twenty awards, including one at Cannes, *City of Gold* is most notable for having organically integrated the use of the animation camera to documentary film (a technique recently popularized by Ken Burns' "Civil War" series on U.S. television). It also introduced Pierre Berton's evocative voice to worldwide audiences as he recounts the history of Dawson City and the Klondike's gold rush in the Yukon of winter 1897 and summer 1898. Berton, who was born in Dawson, and who was already a well-known journalist, later became one of Canada's most popular writers and television personalities. Directors Wolf Koenig and COLIN LOW cleverly mixed live action footage of Dawson City of the 1950s—rendered as a sleepy, peaceful ghost town—with photographs of the past. Ironically, Douglas Roberts' animation camera, which scans the photographs, gives dynamic, vibrant life to the past while Koenig and Low's "moving pictures" deliberately evoke stillness. The poetic effect throughout *City of Gold* is underscored by Eldon Rathburn's honky-tonk score, and live action shots of old men, who (Berton suggests) stayed behind even though they didn't find their pot of gold, are contrasted with shots of young boys playing baseball. It is also springtime, as pollen in the air doubles up the effect of a renewal of life, elegantly shifting the emotional tone from nostalgia to hope. *City of Gold* is one of the most brilliantly constructed of the NFB's huge output of films, and one that editor (and producer) TOM DALY remains most proud of.

BIBLIOGRAPHY: Tom Daly, "The Still Photo in Cinema," *Pot Pourri* (Summer 1977): 2–4; Peter Harcourt, "The Innocent Eye," *Sight and Sound*, 34, no. 1 (Winter 1964–65) (reprinted in Feldman and Nelson, 70–75).

Peter Rist

BOB CLARK. Born 1947, New Orleans, Louisiana. Director, producer, writer. Bob Clark's feature debut was the enjoyable camp parody of George Romero's *Night of the Living Dead* (1968), *Children Shouldn't Play with Dead Things* (1972). Clark then moved to Canada and made a string of mainly good films. After the mega-success of *PORKY'S*, Clark moved back to the United States, where he has made a string of mainly bad films. Beginning with *Children Shouldn't Play with Dead Things, Deathdream, Black Christmas*, and *Murder by Decree* (1978), it seemed that Canada had a genuine horror auteur in the making. In *Deathdream*, a reworking of W. W. Jacobs' classic short story "The Monkey's Paw" (1902), a mother wishes for her son to return home from Vietnam, unaware that he has already died. The son returns home as a sickly, spectral figure with a progressively decomposing body. In many ways, *Deathdream* packs a stronger anti-Vietnam message than mega-budget Hollywood films *The Deerhunter* (Michael Cimino, 1978) and *Apocalypse Now* (Francis Coppola, 1979). *Black Christmas*, an unacknowledged prototype for *Halloween* (John Carpenter, 1978), is a taut, efficient horror film. Like the latter, it begins with killer point-of-view shots stalking and entering a home; features grisly murders during a holiday, and contains a similar twist ending. *Murder by Decree* is arguably one of the best (and most horrific) Sherlock Holmes films. *A Christmas Story* notwithstanding, Clark has never displayed a great sense of comic timing. With such disastrous U.S. comedies as *Rhinestone* (1984), *Turk 182!* (1985), *From the Hip* (1987), and *Loose Cannons* (1990), one wonders why Clark persists in this genre. Clark failed even with an attempt to recapture the past glory of *A Christmas Story*, with the limp sequel *It Runs in My Family* (United States,

1994). Perhaps Clark should return to the horror genre, one he seems better suited for—or perhaps come back to Canada.

THEATRICAL FEATURE FILMS AS DIRECTOR: *Deathdream (Dead of Night)*, 1972; *Deranged* (prod.), 1974; *Black Christmas (Silent Night, Evil Night)*, 1974; *Breaking Point*, 1976; *Murder by Decree*, 1978; *Tribute*, 1980; *Porky's*, 1981; *Porky's 2: The Next Day*, 1982; *A Christmas Story*, 1983.

BIBLIOGRAPHY: Dennis Fischer; Keith Bearden, "Bob Clark: Horny Teens, Sherlock Holmes & Zombies!," *Psychotronic Video*, no. 16 (1993): 49–55.

Donato Totaro

COLD COMFORT. Vic Sarin, Alberta, 1989, 92 min., color. This adaption of James Garrand's cult theater play provided longtime cinematographer Vic Sarin with a wonderful vehicle to showcase his considerable visual acumen for his directorial debut. A macabre variation on the "traveling salesman" story finds Steve (Paul Gross) rescued from a blizzard on the prairies by Floyd Lucas (MAURY CHAYKIN), an eccentric man who lives an isolated life with only his daughter Delores (Margaret Langrick) as a companion. Steve's growing realization of his entrapment comes amid a series of "family" events in which Delores and, particularly, Floyd demonstrate their aberrant behavior. Steve's attempts to escape only increase the severity of his treatment, until he is eventually manacled to the homestead itself. In the meantime, Floyd's realization of his loss of control of the situation, including his daughter's unwavering affection, propels the film toward its tragic conclusion. Chaykin's portrayal of the deranged Floyd is one of his best performances. His combination of deadpan comedy and near psychotic mania adds a quality of menace to the entire film. Sarin's gifted camerawork envelops the characters in a claustrophobic environment. His exteriors establish the isolation of the Lucas homestead (which is never actually fixed as a place, but rather exists as a zone between other cities and towns on the prairie). For his interiors, Sarin emphasizes blue tones, as if all three characters were contained in a fishbowl.

BIBLIOGRAPHY: Anon, "Power/Knowledge or a New Meaning for Agency," *Take One*, no. 5 (Summer 1994).

Dave Douglas

JANIS COLE. Born 1954, Chatham, Ontario. Director, producer, editor. **HOLLY DALE.** Born 1953, Toronto, Ontario. Director, producer, editor, actor. Janis Cole and Holly Dale are two multitalented filmmakers who co-created a number of compelling feminist documentaries in the 1980s. Dale appeared as an actor in the TV films *Dream on the Run* and *Starship Invasions* (both 1976), but in 1976 she and Cole, whom she had met while studying at Sheridan College under experimental filmmaker RICK HANCOX, teamed up to co-direct, co-produce, and co-edit *Minimum Charge No Cover* and, in 1977, *Thin Line*. It was, however, the disturbing and sensitive documentary *P4W: Prison for Women* (1981), an examination of the difficulties faced (and overcome) by female prison inmates, that solidified their reputations for insightful and challenging documentary. Resolutely insisting that these women be allowed to tell their own stories, *P4W* also establishes the two filmmakers' approach to documentary practice. *Hookers on Davie*, perhaps their most accomplished and best known film, followed in 1984; this controversial film about prostitutes working Vancouver's infamous Davie Street was criticized in some quarters for its perceived fence-sitting in response to the sex trade. Nevertheless, by following the sex workers of the title as they seek out johns and comment on their lives, the film manages to present a fascinating and often moving portrait of individuals often overlooked by the mainstream population. The film was nominated for the Best Documentary Genie Award in 1985. After the somewhat disappointing *Calling the Shots* (1988), about the long history of women filmmakers, Cole and Dale parted company to work on solo projects, including Dale's *Up on the Roof* (1988) and Cole's *Shaggie* (1990), leaving behind an impressive body of work which highlights film's potential for true collaboration. In 1996, Cole wrote the fiction feature *Dangerous Offender*, which was directed by Dale.

FILMS AS CO-DIRECTOR: *Thin Line*, 1977; *P4W: Prison for Women*, 1981; *Hookers on Davie*, 1984; *The Making of Agnes of God* (TV), 1985; *Calling the Shots*, 1988.

BIBLIOGRAPHY: David Clandfield, 35–36.

Mitch Parry

THE COMPANY OF STRANGERS [*Strangers in Good Company*, United States]. Cynthia Scott, (Quebec) NFB, 1990, 101 min., color. *The Company of Strangers* is Cynthia Scott's first feature film following numerous shorts for the NFB, many of which received critical acclaim, including Oscar-winning *Flamenco 5:15* (1983). The feature was the seventh production in the NFB's "Alternative Drama" series, where non-actors were asked to play themselves within a fictitious scenario. In this case, the plot begins with a bus breaking down in the countryside, leaving seven elderly women and their younger bus driver stranded and forced to fend for themselves. In the process of finding shelter and food, the women defy any presumptions about their age group by displaying ingenuity, creativity, and strength. Most important they talk openly to each other, revealing their secrets and fears about loss and death, while sharing their passion for living. Although the framing story within the film is fictitious, it does reflect the experience shared by each cast member in making the film. These women were plucked from their separate walks of life, deposited in an isolated setting, and asked to interact with a group of strangers. The stories they tell are their own, and so they contribute both their presence and their own history to the making of the film, and it is their sincerity and personal charm that make the film a warm personal experience. Often categorized as a semi-documentary, semi-fiction, and/or docudrama, *The Company of Strangers* gently walks the fine line between fiction and reality as a means of documenting the very real existence of a heretofore unrecognized group of people.

Stacey Abbott

LE CONFESSIONAL The Confessional. Robert Lepage, UK/Canada (Quebec), 1995, 100 min., color and b+w. Although *Le confessional* is not the masterpiece everyone was expecting from multimedia *wunderkind* Robert Lepage, it nonetheless stands high in the corpus of contemporary Canadian films. Those already familiar with Lepage's theatrical work will recognize some of his thematic preoccupations in this story of two long-lost brothers briefly reuniting after one of them uncovers the mystery of their parentage: the quest for identity—here, a sexual, cultural, and historical proposition—and its philosophical counterpart, defining the nature of postmodern man and charting his horizons. *Le confessional* is both a deeply personal film, as can be witnessed in the many autobiographical elements of the screenplay, and one which cannot help but resonate more broadly given the archetypal undertones of the drama *and* Lepage's surprising use of Hitchcockian motifs and references. One of the most original aspects of the film is that it situates parts of its intrigue in and around Alfred Hitchcock's shooting of *I Confess* in Quebec City in 1952, the master's film echoing the drama which is splitting apart Lepage's heroes. In an even more daring coup, Lepage complicates his own narrative by constantly shifting back and forth in time and space, and from *I Confess*' diegesis to his own. The result is a mesmerizing and intellectually challenging puzzle in which the emotion is translated not so much through the actors but rather, in pure Lepage fashion, through formalist *trouvailles*.

BIBLIOGRAPHY: Collective, "Dossier Robert Lepage," *Séquences*, no. 180 (September/October 1995): 24–31; Bernard Perron, "À la sortie de l'église," *Ciné-bulles* 14, no. 3 (Autumn 1995): 12–14.

Johanne Larue

CORRAL. Colin Low, (Alberta) NFB, "Canada Carries On" series, 1954, 11 min., b+w. Usually regarded as being the first NFB documentary to break away from too great a reliance on the spoken word, *Corral* is also the film that first distinguished TOM DALY as a producer of actuality films at Unit B (and COLIN LOW as a director of same). It was intended to be part of the "Faces of Canada" series, where Low went back to the ranchland Alberta of his birth to focus on an individual of his choice, a cowboy. Seen today, *Corral* seems to be a very slight (perhaps simplistic) portrait of an Albertan cowboy breaking a horse. But, remarkably for its time, it managed to fulfill the NFB mandate of "educating" without recourse to voice-over narration, while simultaneously providing a lyrical view of its subject. Also, with its low-key guitar accompaniment (variously attributed to Stan Wilson/Al Harris and Rey de la Torre) and Wolf Koenig's hand-held Ariflex 35mm cinematography, *Corral* is distinctly different from a

Hollywoodian, epic representation of the cowboy. And the deserted, rolling hills that cowboy and horse traverse at the film's conclusion suggest a wild, Canadian freedom in contradistinction to the confines of the training arena of the corral and the taming of the wilderness that underlines traditional Hollywood Westerns.

Peter Rist

MICHEL CÔTÉ. Born 1950, Alma, Quebec. Actor, writer. Michel Côté received a diploma from the École Nationale de Théâtre in 1973. Following this, he taught improvisation and introductory acting to students of the Option Théâtre at Ste-Thérèse, until 1977. Two years later, he was also the co-founder of the little theater of Voyagements, where the play *Broue* was supposed to run for a month. But the play became phenomenally successful (in total, by 1997, it had run for more than two thousand performances). Paralleling his theatrical career playing in *Broue* since 1979, Côté's status as a film actor was established with *Au clair de la lune* (MARC ANDRÉ FORCIER), a film which rests essentially on his improvisations with GUY L'ÉCUYER. His intelligent acting did not go unnoticed, nor did his ability to inhabit so many disguises. Above all, his talent is shown in the way he transmits the emotions of these characters to the audience, even when they become contradictory. Such is the case in the short film *Transit* (R. Roy), but especially in *T'es belle, Jeanne* (R. Ménard), where the role of Bert gained him the public's trophy (for Best Actor) in balloting for Grandes Premières Stella Artois. He shifted readily from drama to comedy. He played the part of a marginal character (together with RÉMY GIRARD) in *Dans le ventre du dragon*, directed by Yves Simoneau (1989). During the same year, he put on four new faces in the comedy *Cruising Bar*, the screenplay for which he had devoted a whole year to writing (with Ménard). Each of *Cruising Bar*'s four principal characters, played by Côté came from a different social milieu, but each explored the universal theme of male seduction. The action of the film and the actor's multiple role-playing can be compared to the play *Broue*, which featured only three actors—the same ones for almost twenty years—playing no less than eighteen roles. And, following the play, *Cruising Bar* was a big screen success. In fact, in the fall of 1994, the film still held the all-time Canadian record for the number of admissions to a film. In 1990, Michel Côté quietly returned to drama by playing an old beggar (*La fille du maquignon*) and an ambiguous character in Richard Roy's *Moody Beach*. Then, he obtained a number of roles representing members of the legal profession, that did justice to his disciplined acting. These include the role of Pax Plante in the television series "Montréal, ville ouverte" and the judge Savard in *Liste noire* (J.-M. Vallée, 1995). In rapid succession he played two detectives: in *Erreur sur la personne* (G. Noël) he approached his role from the interior, and then demonstrated a penchant for understatement while playing the central character in the TV series "Omertà."

FILMS AS ACTOR: *Vie d'ange*, 1974–79; *Bleu brume* (short), 1982; *Au clair de la lune*, 1979–83; *La fuite* (short), 1985; *Exit; Transit* (short), 1986; *T'es belle, Jeanne*, 1988;

Dans le ventre du dragon; Cruising Bar, 1989; *La fille du maquignon; Moody Beach*, 1990; *Miss Moscou*, 1991; *Le vent du Wyoming* (Can/Fr), 1994; *Liste noire*, 1995; *Erreur sur la personne*, 1996.

BIBLIOGRAPHY: Edith Madore, "Michel Côté: 'C'est exitant d'être tricheur,' " *Ciné-Bulles* 9, no. 1 (September-October 1989): 22–25.

Isabelle Morissette

CRAC! Frédéric Back, (Montreal) SRC, 1981, 15 min., color. Surely the most quintessentially Canadian (and Quebecois) film ever to win an Oscar (for Best Animated Short in 1982), *Crac!* provides a beautiful and truly "animated" capsule history of Quebec culture in only fifteen minutes. The central character of the film is a rocking chair whose journey is followed from the time it is hand-made and painted with a happy face in the 19th century to its contemporary rescue and placement in art gallery "retirement" by a kindly old security guard. The chair is given by its peasant craftsman maker to a young girl. Rapidly the film traverses her youth, marriage, and motherhood and shows her children using it as a toy and as a vehicle of transportation. The seasons change (the chair is used as a sled in winter), allowing director Frédéric Back to demonstrate a remarkable sense of color and rhythm where the family's leisure activities are accompanied by gorgeous reds and yellows, and where fiddle music, by the group Le rêve du diable, dynamically orchestrates the festivities. Back was born in Germany in 1924. In Europe he studied fine arts and worked as a book illustrator before immigrating to Canada in 1948. Settling in Montreal, he became a teacher and began working at Radio Canada in 1952, where he has stayed most of the time ever since, developing his film animation techniques. His first works as a director, *Abracadabra* (co-dir., Graham Ross, 1971), bringing children of all races together, and *Inon ou la conquête du feu* (1971), based on an Amerindian story, showed an early mastery of color, a delicate touch with fabric backgrounds, and a strong interest in ecology and human rights. All of his stylistic and thematic strands seem to combine in the life affirmative *Crac!*, which moves into a humorous criticism of technological domination and the cold abstraction of modern art in the latter part of the 20th century. When children get tired of looking at abstract paintings they line up to sit in the old rocking chair, and at night the chair returns to its roots, where music, color, and movement oneirically reliven the film. *Crac!*'s great charm eventually garnered twenty-three international prizes. Back's next film, *L'homme qui plantait des arbres* (1987), also won the Animation Oscar as well as the Grand Prix at the Annecy Animation Festival (and twenty other awards), and gained him renown as an important spokesperson for conservation throughout the world.

Peter Rist

CRASH. David Cronenberg, Toronto, 1996, 110 min., color. DAVID CRONEN-BERG's thirteenth feature was based on J. G. Ballard's 1973 novel, *Crash*. It continues key themes present in his earlier films: ideas of human physical and psychic transformation as representative of societal (r)evolution. Indeed, the revolt of mind and body against the status quo and their impending doom within normalcy are quite literalized in *Crash*. The film moves beyond society's increasing isolationism and lack of intimacy to focus on the root cause of enforced loneliness, the cause of our discomfort with others and within ourselves—technology. This is shown in the film's first sequence: after an incredible dolly shot through a hangar the camera stops on Catherine (Deborah Unger), alone as she opens her blouse and pulls her breast out of her bra, rubbing her nipple on the cold, smooth metal of an airplane. A faceless, nameless man enters the frame. When he begins to touch Catherine from behind she deliberately places her breast back into its hidden position, denying him what she is prepared to share with the machine. Clearly, mechanical intimacy has become more compelling and desirable than physical-human touch. The sequence ends with the recounting of her adventure to her husband James (James Spader), who proceeds to take her, again from behind, "rear-ending" (or "bumper to bumper"), the analogy blurring the division between human and machine. *Crash* becomes metaphoric of people's increasing distance being appropriated by an intimacy with new, mechanical skin. Such extension of the human body is realized in the film when James, Catherine, and Vaughn (Elias Koteas), who leads the accident fetishists and has devoted himself to finding the path to a new technological flesh, happen upon a freeway accident. What they, and we, see is a virtual orgy of twisted forms and broken metal, blood, grips, clamps, pierced flesh, jaws of life pulling and tearing at vagina-like holes. As Vaughn states, "the car crash is a fertilizing rather than destructive event." *Crash* created a furor and received a new Special Jury Prize for "daring and audacity" at the 1996 Cannes Film Festival. Cronenberg stated at the festival that it was "appropriate that they had to create a special prize to accommodate the film."

Rob Cotterill

FRANK "BUDGE" CRAWLEY. Born 1911, Ottawa, Ontario; died 1987. Director and producer. **JUDITH CRAWLEY.** Born 1914, Ottawa, Ontario; died 1986. Director and producer. Budge Crawley began work as an amateur filmmaker in the 1930s. His first film of note was *Île d'Orléans* (1938), made in collaboration with his longtime personal and creative partner, Judith. Their first sponsored film was *Canadian Power* (1939). During the early forties, the Crawleys made a number of films for the NFB, including *Canadian Landscape* (1941) and *West Wind* (1942), which were the best of the "Canadian Artists" series initiated by the Crawleys in collaboration with Graham McInnes. Crawley Films was incorporated in 1946, and until 1982 was responsible for a number of classic Canadian documentaries and feature films, frequently dealing with Canadian cultural topics. The most famous of these included the award-winning *THE LOON'S NECKLACE, Newfoundland Scene* (1950), *Beaver Dam*, and *Saskatchewan Jubilee* (1955). The Crawleys were responsible for a number of Canadian "firsts": Budge produced the first animated series for Canadian television, "The Tales of the Wizard of Oz" (1962), and the first Canadian television production shown in both French and English Canada, "Au pays de Neufve-France" (1959–60). THE LUCK OF GINGER COFFEY was a co-production between Crawley Films and a U.S. producer, and won an award for the best feature film at the Canadian Film Awards. Budge Crawley acted as executive producer for *The Rowdyman*, a critical and commercial success noted for its social realism, and for the Canadian Film Awards winning documentary on rock star Janis Joplin, *Janis*. As a director, Judith Crawley's contributions were mainly in the making of films about children, including the "Ages and Stages" television series (1949–57), which featured her own children. After 1961, Judith did not direct films, but continued to write scripts, most memorably for *The Man Who Skied Down Everest*, which won an Academy Award for best feature-length documentary in 1976.

FILMS INCLUDE: *The Loon's Necklace*, 1948; *Newfoundland Scene*, 1950; *Beaver Dam*, 1956; "Au Pays de Neufve-France" (series), 1959–60; *Top of a Continent*, 1961; "The Tales of the Wizard of Oz," 1962; *Return to Oz; The Luck of Ginger Coffey*, 1964; *Saskatchewan Jubilee*, 1965; *The Rowdyman*, 1971; *Janis*, 1974; *The Man Who Skied Down Everest*, 1975.

Helen and Paul Salmon

CRIME WAVE. John Paizs, Manitoba, 1985, 80 min., 16 mm (blown up to 35mm), color. John Paizs is one of the key members of the Winnipeg Film Group, a co-op which began in 1974 and includes directors GUY MADDIN, John Kozak, Greg Hanec, Shereen Jerrett, and Bruce Duggan. Paizs' early films were a series of offbeat comic shorts that featured himself in the role of a mute, alienated anti-hero: *The Obsession of Billy Botski* (1980), *Springtime in Greenland* (1982), and *The International Style* (1983). With a $50,000 budget, *Crime Wave* became Paizs' first (and, thus far, only) feature, and continued his unique contribution to the Winnipeg Film Group aesthetic (which *Cinema Canada* referred to as "Prairie Postmodernism"). *Crime Wave* is about the relationship between Steven Penny (Paizs), an introverted scriptwriter of lurid crime stories, and Kim (Eva Kovacs), a young girl who helps him through his creative blocks. The story is told mainly from Kim's point of view, as if she were reciting a "what-I-did-during-the-summer" term paper. *Crime Wave* is steeped in a junk culture potpourri of film, television, pop music, and comic books. The pop cultural mix is characterized by Paizs' uncanny ability to recreate an ambiguous period style (rural and urban, 1950s–1970s). However, Paizs' style, marked by a static camera, post-sync sound, and voice-over narration, underscores a sense of emotional alienation behind the nostalgic parody. In the monograph *Dislocations* this alienation is explained in terms of the cultural dislocation brought on by the prairie experience. *Crime Wave* premiered at the Toronto Film Festival in 1985. According to Geoff Pevere, criticism concerning the second half of the film led Paizs to reshoot it. Unfortunately, he was not able to procure distribution for this second version, which remains unseen. The original *Crime Wave* is available on video under the title *The Big Crime Wave*.

BIBLIOGRAPHY: Geoff Pevere, "Radical Marginalia: Subversive Signs from the Hinterland," *Cineaction*, no. 6 (Summer/Fall 1986): 50–56; Gilles Hébert.

Donato Totaro

DAVID CRONENBERG. Born 1943, Toronto. Director, writer. David Cronenberg graduated from the University of Toronto in 1967 with a general B.A. in literature. After hedging between a future in science and literature, he did a typically Cronenbergian thing and fused them into one, cinema. A consistency in quality (he has never made a "bad" film), theme (diverse treatments of the nature/culture split), and style (wide-angle, emotionally detached aesthetic) has made Cronenberg a darling among auteurist critics. To Cronenberg's detriment, this has sometimes led to reductive readings that strip his films of their social and philosophical complexity. An increasingly fascinating aspect of his work is the way it continually draws from the horror and science fiction genres, yet resists being exclusively defined by them. A principal reason for this is that Cronenberg uses one of the central horror and science fiction tropes, transformation and metamorphosis, but in a much more probing and metaphorical fashion than is generally used in those genres. Transformation and metamorphosis appear in countless variations in the horror and science fiction genres: living to (un)dead (zombies, vampires, mummies); good/civilized to evil/barbaric (lycanthropy, cannibalism, Dr. Jekyll & Mr. Hyde); inanimate to animate (the Golem, Frankenstein's monster, technology); human to alien (body possession, scientific mutation, nuclear contamination). However, in Cronenberg's film world such polarities are never morally or psychologically unequivocal, but are twisted and confused, metaphorical rather than literal. In *The Dead Zone* (United States, 1983), for example, a mild-mannered schoolteacher (Christopher Walken) comes out of a five-year coma with the power to foretell a person's future. What seems to be a miraculous "touch" soon alienates him from society and makes him a martyr for world salvation. In *The Fly* (United States, 1986) an accident during a teleportation experiment results in a scientist's (Jeff Goldblum) body being genetically fused with that of an insect. As the fateful victim-scientist slowly transforms into a hideous creature, he and his girlfriend Veronica (Geena Davis) attain a deeper, metaphysical understanding of humanity and love. These Cronenbergian transformations produce existential dilemmas rather than the traditional moral dilemmas (good vs. evil) associated with horror and science fiction genres. For example, transformation and metamorphosis lead to alienated relationships in *SHIVERS, Rabid, The Brood*, and the non-horror film *M. Butterfly* (United States, 1993); while characters become alienated from society in *The Dead Zone, NAKED LUNCH, The Fly*, and *CRASH*. Cronenberg continues to live and work in Toronto, where he maintains creative immunity from Hollywood homogenization, and continues to draw from a distinctly Canadian ambivalency toward technology. Regardless of how you label his films, there is little doubt that he is Canada's most consistently innovative and provocative filmmaker.

FILMS AS DIRECTOR: *Stereo*, 1969; *Crimes of the Future*, 1970; *Shivers* (a.k.a. *The Parasite Murders, They Came from Within*), 1975; *Rabid*, 1976; *Fast Company*, 1979; *The Brood*, 1979; *Scanners*, 1980; *Videodrome* (US/Can), 1982; *Dead Ringers*, 1988; *Naked Lunch*, (UK/Can), 1991; *Crash*, 1996.

BIBLIOGRAPHY: Chris Rodley; *Postscript* 15, no.1 (Fall 1995) (Special Cronenberg Issue).

Donato Totaro

LA CUISINE ROUGE [The Red Kitchen]. Paule Baillargeon and Frédérique Collin, Quebec, 1979, 82 min., color. A work of radical feminism and avant-garde drama, *La cuisine rouge* almost never was. It was rejected by the NFB, which was expecting a film on nude dancers, and was finished thanks to the financial contribution of the actors, the crew, and the public when Le Grand Cirque Ordinaire, the theater troupe to which the directors and many of the cast belonged, put on a benefit show. Revolutionary, excessive, and alienating, the film is constructed like a surreal, pessimistic, violent, and biting pamphlet exploring the tensions and irreconcilable differences between women and men. Two groups of actors, physically separated by a kitchen, address different gender-related issues and problems of domestic politics through improvisational confrontations. The action takes place on the day of a wedding. The men occupy a dark and dirty tavern. They are framed from afar, shot in long, rather static takes, and are shown raving and getting drunk. Things get even uglier when the men intrude upon the women's kitchen, where they find their spouses frozen in a catatonic state, a nightmarish still-life of domestic horror. The women are only given their lives back after the men retreat and they, in turn, are given access to the exterior garden in which they can celebrate their rebellion. They bathe and frolic under an idyllic sunlight, their joy and feminine sensuality captured by the hand-held camera and the dynamic montage of short, burst-like, shots: a welcomed allegorical liberation. Profoundly anchored in the ideology of its time, the experience of *La cuisine rouge* was not to be repeated. It remains one of a kind.

BIBLIOGRAPHY: Denise Pérusse.

Johanne Larue

PIERRE CURZI. Born 1946, Montreal. Actor, writer. Pierre Curzi was among a group that left L'École Nationale de Théâtre in 1968, protesting against their traditional approach, and joined his colleagues in Le Grand Cirque Ordinaire. His first film role was in *ON EST LOIN DU SOLEIL* (1970), and André Théberge offered him his first lead in *Les allées de la terre* (1972). In a heavily symbolic piece about an actor couple who separate in order to get to know each other better, Curzi gives a solid performance, yet in the 1970s he only appeared in minor roles. In 1980, GILLES CARLES cast him as Napoléon in *Les Plouffe*, an enormous success which brought Curzi wide attention as the obedient elder son. Curzi believes the cinema to be a collective creative endeavor, and this is perhaps why he excels in supporting roles; witness the timid farmer Eutrope Gagnon in Carles' *Maria Chapdelaine* or as part of an ensemble piece, for example, as Pierre, the photographer in JEAN PIERRE LEFEBVRE'S *LES FLEURS SAUVAGES*. A fine comedian as well as a dramatic actor, Curzi also has the charisma to carry a leading role, turning in a powerful performance as the idealistic activist in the title role of *Lucien Brouillard* (1983). Curzi brought all his talents—his collective instinct, his comic timing, his dramatic force, and his star charisma—to perhaps his finest role, as Pierre in *LE DÉCLIN DE L'EMPIRE AMÉRICAIN*. As the counterpoint to the jolly buffoonery of RÉMY GIRARD, Curzi's ruthless search for pleasure betrays the emotional void at the center of the lives of the group and their risqué stories. His career has continued to flourish. He played a robber involved in a botched heist in *POUVOIR INTIME* alongside real-life companion Marie Tifo. A highly regarded and generous actor on screen, Curzi is also an accomplished scriptwriter, having co-written *Pouvoir intime*, and also the fantasy *Le jour "S . . ."*(Lefebvre), in which he also starred.

FILMS AS ACTOR: *Trouble-fete*, 1964; *On est loin du soleil*, 1971; *Les allées de la terre; Tu brûles . . . tu brûles*, 1973; *Bulldozer*, 1971–74; *L'amour blessé* (voice only), 1975; *Parlez-nous d'amour*, 1976; *Anastasie oh ma chérie* (short); *Avoir 16 ans; Riel; L'homme en colère*, 1979; *La cuisine rouge*, 1979; *Suzanne; Fantastica*, 1980; *Les Plouffe*, 1981; *Les fleurs sauvages; Les yeux rouges ou les vérités accidentelles; On n'est pas sortie du bois* (short); *En plein coeur* (short), 1982; *Lucien Brouillard; Maria Chapdelaine*, 1983; *Le jour "S . . ."*(also scr.); *Amour de quartier; La petite nuit* (short); *Le crime d'Ovide Plouffe*, 1984; *Caffè Italia Montréal; Le million tout-puissant*, 1985; *Pouvoir intime* (also co-scr.); *Le déclin de l'empire américain; Evixion; Les somnambules*, 1986; *T'es belle, Jeanne*, 1988; *Dans le ventre du dragon*, 1989; *Baby Love*, 1990; *April One*, 1993; *C'était le 12 du 12 et Chili avait les blues*, 1994; *Le cri de la nuit*, 1995.

BIBLIOGRAPHY: "Pierre Curzi répond à quelques questions," *Copie Zéro*, no. 22 (October 1984): 18.

Simon Brown

HENRY CZERNY. Born 1959, Toronto. Actor. Henry Czerny studied fine arts at York University and musical theater at the Banff School of Fine Arts, eventually graduating from the National Theatre School in 1982. Czerny worked on stage (Shakespeare, Chekhov) and television before landing a bit role in David Wellington's *I LOVE A MAN IN UNIFORM* (1993). Czerny's next role laid the foundation for many of his subsequent characters. *Cold Sweat*, a Hitchcockian thriller directed by Gail Harvey, presents a wickedly immoral universe peopled with such despicable characters that the most redeeming person is a hired killer (Ben Cross). Czerny puts in a cold, calculating performance as a young, murderous businessman that slithers along with the film's many ludicrous plot twists. Harvey achieves a morose, black humor by casting Dave Thomas (comic persona) and Czerny (boyish good looks) against type—the first of several times that Czerny's handsome features would serve as a counterpoint to a character's dubious morality. The most striking contrast in this regard is Czerny's ground-breaking performance as the pedophiliac priest Peter Lavin in John N. Smith's *The Boys of St. Vincent* (1993). The controversial TV film was unanimously praised, with Czerny's performance singled out for its restrained intensity and ability to render a human, near sympathetic face to evil. Czerny reprises a clergy role in PATRICIA ROZEMA's *When Night Is Falling*, portraying a budding chaplain–theology professor whose career is ruined by the scandals surrounding his fiancée's lesbian relationship. The clergy character is again not likeable, though decidedly less pernicious than Peter Lavin. The critical exposure of *The Boys of St. Vincent* has helped Czerny land "officious bad-guy" roles in the big-budget American productions *Clear and Present Danger* (1994) and *Mission Impossible* (1996). It remains to be seen whether Czerny will escape such typecasting.

FILMS AS ACTOR: *A Town Torn Apart* (TV); *Deadly Matrimony* (TV), 1992; *I Love a Man in Uniform*, 1993; *Cold Sweat; Buried on Sunday* (a.k.a. *Northern Extreme*); *The Boys of St. Vincent* (TV), 1993; *Ultimate Betrayal* (TV); *Anchor Zone*, 1994; *When Night Is Falling; Notes from the Underground; The Michelle Apartment; Jenipapo; Choices of the Heart: The Margaret Sanger Story* (TV) 1995; *For Hope* (TV); *Promise the Moon* (TV), 1996.

BIBLIOGRAPHY: Jim Hoberman, "The Boys of St. Vincent," *Village Voice* (June 7, 1994): 49; David Denby, "The Boys of St. Vincent," *New York* (June 13, 1994): 83.

Donato Totaro

D

HOLLY DALE. *See* Janice Cole/Holly Dale

TOM DALY. Born Thomas Cullen Daly, 1918, Toronto. Producer, executive producer, editor, director. In many people's eyes, Tom Daly was the most influential individual at Canada's National Film Board during its glory years, the 1950s and 1960s. As the head of the creative Unit B from 1951, Daly produced many of the most significant films ever made in Canada, including works of animation (*My Financial Career*, Gerald Potterton), fiction (*Nobody Waved Goodbye*), experimental film (*Very Nice, Very Nice*, Arthur Lipsett), and, especially, documentary (*Lonely Boy*). But according to D. B. Jones' excellent biography, *The Best Butler in the Business*, Daly's greatest contribution to the NFB was as an editor, and as a person whose "central creative contribution lay in helping others create." He was credited as editor and producer on many more key films (e.g., *The Romance of Transportation in Canada*, Colin Low; *Corral; City of Gold; Labyrinthe*, Low and Roman Kroitor), but his influence on films where he was only credited as producer often extended to major structural (i.e., editing) decisions. (See the entry on *Sad Song of Yellow Skin*.) In 1940 Daly received a B.A. from the University of Toronto and was on the verge of going to Harvard to do graduate work in English literature when he was hired by John Grierson as a researcher at the NFB. His first assignment was on the "Canada Carries On" short film, *Battle for Brains* (Stuart Legg, 1941), after which he became responsible for locating stock footage. He began taking notes on every shot and claims to have learnt from Legg that "the line of a film follows the line of attention in a frame." Jones cites *Road to the Reich* (1944–45) as Daly's first assignment as director (and producer). A year after the unit system began in 1950, Daly was made an executive producer, heading up a staff of forty people at Unit B, mandated to make animation and films on art, classroom, science, experimental, and sponsored films. He encouraged the development of some of the best directing talents at the NFB in the 1950s, including Low, Kroitor, and Wolf Koenig, through their combination of creative expression and recording reality. And in 1958–59 he executive produced thirteen "Candid Eye" films for television, adding the direct cinema documentarian Terence Macartney-Filgate and the eloquent, compelling, yet quotidian voice of Stanley Jackson to his talent pool. This series remains the standard for slice-of-life, objective, documentary reportage, and as a whole constituted Daly's greatest achievement. After the unit system was abandoned in 1964, Daly continued to produce films and to influence and encourage new, young filmmakers, including Michael Rubbo, DEREK MAY, Mort Ransen, and Robin Spry. Although generally considered to be an apolitical (perhaps conservative) man, Tom Daly, as D. B. Jones notes, "championed an appreciation for Native Canadian cultures throughout his career," and "more than most English-speaking Canadians can claim, he empathized with the political and cultural aspirations of French-speaking Canadians." He retired in May 1984.

FILMS INCLUDE (AS PRODUCER, EXCEPT WHERE STATED): *Atlantic Crossroads* (dir., ed.); *Guilty Men* (also, dir., scr., ed.), 1945; *Out of the Ruins*, 1946; *The People Between*, 1947; *Hungry Minds* (also dir., scr., ed., research), 1948; *Royal Journey* (color), 1951; *Lismer* (color), 1952; *The Romance of Transportation in Canada* (color), 1953; *Paul Tomkowicz: Street-Railway Switchman; Corral* (also ed.), 1954; *Gold*, 1955; *City of Gold*, 1957; *The Days Before Christmas; Blood and Fire; Police* (all exec. prod., for "Candid Eye" series), 1958; *The Back-Breaking Leaf; Glenn Gould: On the Record; Glenn Gould: Off the Record* (all, exec. prod., for "Candid Eye" series), 1959; *Universe* (also ed.), 1960; *New York Lightboard; Very Nice, Very Nice; Lonely Boy* (exec. prod.), 1962; *My Financial Career* (color); *Runner*, 1962; *21–87*, 1963; *I Know an Old Lady Who Swallowed a Fly* (color, exec. prod.); *Nobody Waved Goodbye* (feature, exec. prod.), 1964; *Stravinsky* (exec. prod.), 1965; *Labyrinthe* (color, ed.), 1967; *Christopher's Movie Matinee* (color feature), 1968; *Prologue* (feature), 1969; *Sad Song of Yellow Skin* (color); *A Film for Max* (color feature); *Un pays sans bon sens* (feature), 1970; *Cold Journey* (color feature, ed.), 1972; *Coming Home* (color feature); *Action: The October Crisis of 1970* (color feature); *Reaction: A Portrait of a Society in Crisis* (color), 1973; *Waiting for Fidel* (color); *Running Time* (color feature), 1974; *One Man* (color feature), 1977; *North China Commune* (color feature), 1979; *Musical Magic: Gilbert and Sullivan in Stratford* (color), 1984.

BIBLIOGRAPHY: D. B. Jones (1996).

Peter Rist

DANCING IN THE DARK. Leon Marr, Toronto, 1986, 98 min., color. Prior to 1985, Leon Marr's credits as a filmmaker were television commercials and two half-hour dramas, in addition to work as assistant director for CLAUDE JUTRA, ALLAN KING, and several other notable Canadian directors. He chose Joan Barfoot's *Dancing in the Dark* (1982), which examines the blighted life of a "perfect housewife," as the basis of his first feature, despite the ruminative novel's "uncinematic" interior-placed conflict and lack of incident. Exclusively subjective in its austere, antiseptic visuals and in its grinding pace, the film immerses the viewer in Mrs. Edna Cormick's abject subordination. The flashback structure, with catatonic Edna narrating and interpreting her past in voice-over, blends images of a psychiatric ward and the fanatically maintained Cormick home. Vic Sarin's cinematography makes the home hazily and darkly cloister-like, and the ward an overlit series of harsh visual fragments; the viewer feels entombed in both places. MARTHA HENRY's remarkable depth of characterization empowers the film. Her unrelenting physical stasis and her deliberate diction make the largely static film unsettling and suspenseful. In the climactic scenes, Henry rivets the viewer in stoic close-up as the fury Edna can't comprehend takes control of her. Marr's very focused and direct portrayal of repression outweighs by far the film's weaknesses, which include the caricaturish portrait of the career-absorbed husband and the unlikely furtive phone call that apprises Edna of his infidelity. *Dancing in the Dark*, chosen for the Directors' Fortnight in Cannes, divided critics there. Few praised it, and some, responding to the long sequences occupied with scrubbing, vacuuming, and dusting, found it risible (one reportedly thought it was a comedy). In Canadian festival showings and theatrical release, it was unfairly overshadowed by LE DÉCLIN DE L'EMPIRE AMÉRICAIN.

BIBLIOGRAPHY: Martin Knelman, "*Dancing in the Dark*'s Leon Marr Plunges into Cannes Whirlwind," *Cinema Canada*, no. 131 (June 1986): 4; Knelman (1987), 171–72.

Ian Elliot

DE LA TOURBE ET DU RESTANT. Fernand Bélanger*, (Montreal) ONF, 1980, 89 min., color. The evolution of the documentary form in Quebec cinema was significantly altered in the late 1970s. *Cinéma direct*'s concern with capturing reality gave way to a much more reflexive style of filmmaking. This shift is well represented by Fernand Bélanger's *De la tourbe et du restant*. A difficult film to describe due to its thematic and stylistic complexity, it is, ostensibly, a study of the peat moss industry in rural Quebec. Bélanger, however, used the film as a poetic statement on exploitation, the environment, and filmmaking itself. The influence of the *direct* movement is clear in the opening sequence of a dust-ridden factory in which workers package peat moss. This impression changes slightly as the handwritten titles appear, and return throughout the film commenting on the images and the soundtrack. By cutting from the immediacy of "work" sequences to relaxed interviews (in which the crew's presence is usually called attention to), a critique of industrialism is combined with a heartfelt humanism. This is especially apparent in the interview scenes in which the camera isolates details on individual faces of those in this community. A new approach to *direct* techniques is also apparent in the use of the soundtrack

*In some places, Bélanger is credited as co-director with Yves Angrignon and Louise Dugal, but they seem mostly to have been involved in the post-production, editing phase, and are thus not listed here.

wherein language (French and English) is an essential part of the film's lyricism. Pauses and repetitions reflect on identity, and when combined with the recurring sounds of machinery and coughing (a result of lungs destroyed by working conditions), create a poetic motif. Bélanger also relies upon the influence of Edmond Plourde, a local painter/filmmaker/projectionist. By making the presence of the artist and the act of viewing explicit, *De la tourbe* marks another step in the evolution of the documentary form in Quebec—one that is concerned with the individual's relationship to the world, and the ways in which it is depicted.

Judes Dickey

DEAD RINGERS. David Cronenberg, Toronto, 1988, 113 min., color. *Dead Ringers* is the culmination of DAVID CRONENBERG's long-standing interest in the theme of the "new flesh," and the film that marked his departure from the genres of science fiction and horror. Cronenberg enlisted the talents of Jeremy Irons to play twin brothers, Beverly and Elliot Mantle, who develop their childhood fascination with the body into a highly specialized gynecological clinic which deals only with cases of female infertility. In the course of their work the twins encounter Claire Niveau (GENEVIÈVE BUJOLD), an actress who wishes to have children. Claire's particular case fascinates the twins, and both masquerade as Beverly to pursue an affair with her. Her discovery of the twins' secret and her rejection of their desires sets in motion a chain of events that sees both twins descend into drug dependency and increasingly irrational behavior in pursuit of their "research." After Beverly develops and attempts to use "primitive" surgical tools on a patient, the twins' world falls apart. Isolating themselves to "try and get in sync," they descend further into obsession over their interconnected psyches, until Beverly attempts to sever their relationship, killing Elliot in the process. The next morning, realizing his action, Beverly dies in the arms of Elliot. Though controversial at the time of its release, critics acknowledged that the film was a visual tour de force. Sets and decor matched the contrast between the two main characters: antique/Renaissance with the urban and modern. The strong use of blue tones echoed the antiseptic illustration of the future that Cronenberg first explored in *Crimes of the Future* (1970). This primitive/modern dichotomy was furthered through costume design. The twins' magnificent red operating garb gives one simultaneously the impression of a cleric as well as a doctor. Selected to open the 1988 Festival of Festivals in Toronto, the film went on to considerable international acclaim, and garnered Cronenberg his second Genie for Best Director.

BIBLIOGRAPHY: Peter Morris (1994).

Dave Douglas

LE DÉCLIN DE L'EMPIRE AMÉRICAIN *The Decline of the American Empire*. Denys Arcand, Quebec, 1986, 102 min., color. The recipient of nine Genies, *Le* *déclin de l'empire américain* also earned the Critics' Prize at the Cannes Festival, as well as a nomination for the Foreign Language Film Oscar. In this corrosive study of morals, DENYS ARCAND approaches the theme of contemporary "amorous disorder" by analyzing the behavior of a group of intellectuals who have become disillusioned with love. Privileging a comparative approach, Arcand resorts, in the first part of his film, to parallel editing which interweaves the discussions of four women with those of four men, all of whom talk of sex with a malign pleasure. Even though a certain harmony appears to reign in the heart of each group, it soon becomes otherwise when, in the second part of the film, Arcand brings together the men and women, who are husbands, wives, lovers, and single people to varying degrees. During a memorable meal the numerous tensions develop and unravel in a tragic and unexpected conclusion. The success of *Le déclin* in itself constitutes a veritable tour de force. Essentially based on provocative characters and propelled by their dialogue, the film nevertheless possesses an amazing dynamism. Certainly, the quality of the dialogue is important, as Arcand doles out humor and cynicism with brio. However, it should also be remembered that the "metronomic" precision and choreography of the mise-en-scène impart an impeccable rhythm to *Le déclin*. The intensity of the performances by Dorothée Berryman and RÉMI GIRARD stand out in particular among a fairly equal cast, even if one finds it difficult to believe in the performance of Dominique Michel, who seems to be miscast in the role of an intellectual. While one cannot adhere to the constant pessimism Denys Arcand presents, it must be acknowledged that he never bores us.

BIBLIOGRAPHY: "Dossier Denys Arcand," *24 Images*, nos. 44–45 (Autumn 1989): 38–68.

Louis Goyette

ROCK DEMERS. Born 1933, Ste-Cécile de Lévard, Quebec. Producer. As president of Les Productions La Fête, Rock Demers has become one of the most prolific and successful producers in Quebec. This fact, however, should not eclipse the other achievements that have insured Demers' place in the province's history, filmic and otherwise. Not surprisingly, Demers, renowned for his films aimed at younger audiences, began his career in education. After obtaining a teaching diploma in 1957, followed by studies at the Audiovisual Centre of St. Cloud in Paris, Demers' interest in the educational potential of film earned him a grant to research the field. This training was combined with the founding of several Ciné-clubs, *Images*—the first Canadian film journal—and a trip around the world. Industry work, first at Art Films as head of marketing (1960–62), then as director of the Montreal International Film Festival (1962–67), led to the founding of Faroun Films, a distribution company specializing in educational and recreational films. These professional ventures were once again balanced with a devotion to social causes. Demers was at the forefront of the implementation of the Cuisenaire-Gattegno method for math education, co-founder of the

Cinémathèque canadienne, and president of L'institut québécois du cinéma, an organization established to support the private sector. Not one to rest on his laurels, after receiving the Governor General's Award for his work in film (1978), Demers founded Les Productions La Fête. His first film, *La guerre des tuques* (1984), worked its way into a whole generation's memory and paved the way to over a dozen films, as well as continued commercial success, over the next ten years. This success has led to places on festival juries around the world, as well as prestigious honors, including the Prix François Truffaut-Giffoni, Officer of the Order of Canada, Chevalier des Arts et des Lettres (France), and the Prix Albert-Tessier (Quebec). It seems, however, that education has maintained its importance in Demers' career, as he continues to teach at the University of Quebec and has recently co-founded L'Institut National de l'Image et du Son (INIS).

FILMS AS PRODUCER INCLUDE: *La guerre des tuques*, 1984; *The Peanut Butter Solution*, 1985; *Bach et Bottine*, 1986; *Le jeune magicien; C'est pas parce qu'on est petit qu'on peut pas être grand; Tommy Tricker and the Stamp Traveller*, 1987; *La grenouille et la baleine*, 1988; *Fierro . . . l'été des secrets; Bye bye chaperon rouge*, 1989; *Pas de répit pour Mélanie; Vincent and Me; Why Havel?*, 1990; *Tirelire, Combines et cie*, 1992; *The Flying Sneaker; The Return of Tommy Tricker*, 1993; *V'là l'cinéma; La vie d'un héros*, 1994; *Reflets du patrimonie*, 1995; *Le silence des fusils*, 1996; *Viens danser . . . sur la lune*, 1997.

Judes Dickey

LES DERNIÈRES FIANÇAILLES The Last Betrothal. Jean Pierre Lefebvre, Quebec, 1973, 91 min., 16mm, color. One of the most profoundly humanistic films ever made in Canada, *Les dernières fiançailles* is also a highly personal work for its director, JEAN PIERRE LEFEBVRE, in exhibiting great stylistic rigor. *Fiançailles* focuses on the last three peaceful days in the lives of Armand Tremblay (J. Léo Gagnon) and his wife Rose (Marthe Nadeau). Only one other character enters the narrative, their family doctor (MARCEL SABOURIN), who tries to persuade Armand to go to a hospital for treatment of his heart trouble, while all the action takes place in a single house and garden. The film begins on a static long shot view of the house as the sun rises above it. The camera follows Rose into the kitchen to observe her making tea and then picks up Armand as he adjusts one of his clocks to match the other. The pace is slow and deliberate, but perfectly matches the pure and simple, yet arduous lifestyle that the seventy-five-year-olds have developed. At once reminiscent of Japan's Yasujiro Ozu in its emphasis on the simple details of quotidian life, and of France's Jean Renoir in its moving camera expressing a harmonious connection between people and the world outside, *Fiançailles* is also very much reflective of traditional Quebec life in the Cantons de l'Est where it was shot, and of Lefebvre's own interests. The latter is particularly evident in the director's decisions to structure the film around the cycle of daily life, to present the characters warmly but unsentimentally, and to combine realism with "magic." *Les dernières fiançailles* matter-offactly presents the appearance of two young girls as angels to escort the couple's ghosts, and the image fades to white at the end of the last shot of the foursome. It is as if Lefebvre represents them in death as the characters would wish it to be—Rose had apparently chosen to die immediately following her husband's passing.

BIBLIOGRAPHY: Susan Barrowclough; Peter Harcourt (1981), 66–70, 136–37.

Peter Rist

DEUX FEMMES EN OR *Two Women in Gold.* Claude Fournier, Montreal, 1970, 107 min., color. Following in the footsteps of Denis Héroux, who had been very successful with *Valérie* (1969) and *L'initiation* (1970), two soft-core productions that marked the beginnings of the sexploitation wave that won over Quebec cinema in the 1970s, Claude Fournier made his fiction debut with *Deux femmes en or*. This film, a low-budget suburban sex farce, would remain the most profitable made in Quebec until 1986 and *LE DÉCLIN DE L'EMPIRE AMÉRICAIN*. The sitcom-like, simple story line focuses on two bored Brossard housewives, who lure numerous workers from different public services into their homes to have sex with them. Ultimately, this activity brings the women before a tribunal, which exonerates them, and they find fortune and fame through a Broadway producer who shows interest in their story. The repetitive nature of the narrative limits the mise-en-scène to the bare essentials, but with sufficient rhythm and humor to sustain the viewer's attention. Some criticism of men is provided through ironic dialogue and the use of voice-over, where we hear the characters' thoughts, which contradict their actions. The feminist undertone is quickly neutralized, though, by the sheer exploitation of gratuitous scenes of nudity, primarily involving women. Despite all this, *Deux femmes en or* stands as a peak in the sex film trend of the 1970s, if only because of its conquering anarchy, its celebratory presentation of pleasure, and its absence of moralizing pretensions. Most important, Fournier's film suggested the possibility of a national cinema that was popular and appealing to mass audiences, who willingly responded, temporarily giving Quebec cinema a public that it is still struggling to galvanize and recaptivate.

Alain Dubeau

BERNARD DEVLIN. Born 1923, Quebec City; died 1983, Montreal. Director, scriptwriter, producer. After completing his military service, Bernard Devlin entered the National Film Board in 1946, at a time when very few French Canadians were working there. In 1950, while working for the NFB series "Vigie," Devlin directed *Contrat de travail*, a staged documentary short film supporting trade unions. Strongly attracted to the fiction mode, Devlin made two shorts in 1952, *L'abatis/The Settler* (co-dir., Raymond Garceau), which retraced the settling of Abitibi, and *L'homme aux oiseaux/The Bird Fancier* (co-dir., Jean Palardy), a comedy written by the novelist Roger Lemelin (*Les plouffe*). With the arrival of television, production expanded at the ONF, and the work of French Canadian researchers, technicians, and directors became more important. Several TV series saw the light of day. Devlin collaborated as a director of the documentary report series "On the Spot," and then its francophone equivalent, "Sur le vif." Devlin also played the key role on the series "Passe-partout" and "Panoramique," which he produced and directed. It was for "Panoramique" that Devlin directed one of his best fiction films, *Les brûlés/The Promised Land*. This feature-length work (originally four episodes of thirty minutes each) relates anew the saga of Abitibi colonization. Recognizing that the characters are some-what unidimensional, the film nevertheless possesses a number of good qualities. In addition to the details of historical reconstruction, *Les brûlés* is notable for its rigorous description of the settlers' customs and the beauty of George Du-faux's photography of the landscape. From 1964 to 1974, Devlin worked chiefly in English on behalf of the NFB. He retired in 1977. It has been said that Devlin was a convinced anti-nationalist, and yet his dynamism as a producer/director has undeniably contributed to the development of francophone production at the Film Board during the 1950s.

FILMS AS DIRECTOR INCLUDE: *Contrat de travail*, 1950; *L'abatis/The Settler* (co-dir., Raymond Garceau); *L'homme aux oiseaux/The Bird Fancier* (co-dir., Jean Palardy), 1952; *Alfred J.*, 1956; *Les brûlés/The Promised Land*, 1958; *L'héritage*, 1960; *Dubois et fils*, 1961; *A Question of Identity—War of 1812; Once upon a Prime Time*, 1966; *The End of the Nancy J.*, 1970; *A Case of Eggs*, 1974.

BIBLIOGRAPHY: Carol Faucher.

Louis Goyette

COLLEEN DEWHURST. Born 1926, Montreal; died 1991, South Salem, New York. Actor. Colleen Dewhurst was one of the grand dames of the American theater, receiving the Drama Desk Award for *Mourning Becomes Electra* (1974), the OBIE for *Desire Under the Elms* (1974), and a Tony for *All the Way Home* (1961). Although born in Canada, the daughter of a hockey player, she moved to the United States at the age of seven. In 1946, after dropping out of college, she held various jobs before enrolling in New York's American Academy of Dramatic Arts. This move began a highly respected career on the American stage. Although her training and early experiences were gained in the United States, she returned to Canada regularly to appear in numerous CBC television productions, from "A Cheap Bunch of Flowers" to the internationally successful "Anne of Green Gables" (1985) and its sequel, "Anne of Avonlea" (1987). In fact, it was as Marilla Cuthbert, Anne Shirley's (MEGAN FOLLOWS) sensible but kind guardian, that Dewhurst gained her largest single audience. The role seemed to capture what was most appealing about Dewhurst as an actress and as a personality, which was her ability to convey warmth and charm beneath her harsh and cantankerous exterior. In a career that included far too few per-formances on the big screen, it is to Canada's credit that a large percentage of

her film work took place here. Her roles have predominantly been as independent women in intensely dramatic situations, such as the mother of twins separated at birth in *The Third Walker*, or a Russian scientist who leaks a story
about steroid experiments on Russian athletes to a Canadian journalist in *Final
Assignment*. One of her last films saw her reunited with "Anne" co-star Megan
Follows in *Termini Station* (1990). This time their mother/daughter relationship
took a darker side, as Dewhurst plays an alcoholic who, mourning the loss of
a lover, takes her pain out on the illegitimate child of that relationship. Colleen
Dewhurst was a truly gifted actress who often outshone the material she performed. She was rarely given the opportunity to display on film the full range
of her skills, such as her exemplary comic talent, demonstrated in her television
work.

FILMS AS ACTOR: *Mary and Joseph: A Story of Faith* (Can/Ger/Is), 1979; *The Third
Walker* (Can/US), 1977–80; *Final Assignment; Tribute*, 1980; *The Glitter Dome* (Can/
US), 1984; *Anne of Green Gables* (TV), 1985; *Anne of Green Gables: The Sequel* (TV),
1987; *Termini Station*, 1990.

BIBLIOGRAPHY: Otile E. McManus, "Colleen Dewhurst and the Wolf at the Door,"
After Dark (June 1976): 67–71.

Stacey Abbott

DOUBLE HAPPINESS. Mina Shum, British Columbia, 1994, 87 min., color.
Double Happiness is director Mina Shum's extraordinary debut feature film, and
has deservedly won several major awards, including a special jury citation for
Best Canadian Feature at the 1994 Toronto Film Festival, and the Wolfgang
Staudte Award for Best First Feature Film at the Berlin International Film Festival. Sandra Oh, who stars as the young Asian Canadian woman at the center
of the film, won a Genie for Best Actress, and the film also won a Genie for
Best Editing. In the film Jade Li (Oh) is a twenty-two-year-old struggling to
balance her own acting aspirations with the traditional values and expectations
of her family. Yielding to her family's matchmaking attempts, Jade agrees to
date Andrew (Johnny Mah), a handsome Chinese Canadian lawyer, only to
discover that he is gay. Amid mounting pressure from her family to marry within
the Chinese community, Jade develops a reluctant relationship with Mark (Callum Rennie), a white university student. The conflict that Jade feels between
her family loyalties and the Westernized society that lies outside of the family
circle is brought to a closure of sorts (but not fully resolved) when she leaves
home in a bittersweet ending to the film. Like Shum's formally innovative documentary, *Me, Mom and Mona* (1993), *Double Happiness* draws directly upon
the director's experiences as a young woman and explores the complex dynamics of traditional family values which encounter and conflict with modern Western societal values. Both films make use of comedy, visual vignettes, and
carefully scripted dialogue, although *Double Happiness* provides a far more
extended and sophisticated treatment of these strategies. Although billed by crit-

ics as the first Chinese Canadian woman to direct a feature film in Canada, Shum defiantly rejects acting as a spokesperson for her cultural community, preferring to practice the art of filmmaking by drawing upon but not being limited by the specificities of her own experience.

BIBLIOGRAPHY: Kass Banning, "You Taste Canasian: Negotiating *Double Happiness,*" *Border/Lines Magazine,* no. 36 (1995): 24–27; Elizabeth Renzetti, "A Year of Living Famously," *Globe and Mail* (September 9, 1995): C1, C10.

Helen and Paul Salmon

GARTH (HOWARD) DRABINSKY. Born 1948, Toronto. Producer, lawyer, entrepreneur. Perhaps the most important figure of the new breed of Canadian film producers to emerge in the late 1970s, Garth Drabinsky rose from the ranks of an independent commercial film producer (Tiberius Productions) and film distributor (Pan-Canadian, formed with Nat Taylor in 1978) to become the head of the largest film chain in North America during the 1980s. Drabinsky's career in cinema began during the Capital Cost Allowance era—when federal tax laws provided a boom period for the Canadian film industry, at least in financial terms—when he produced such films as *THE SILENT PARTNER, The Changeling,* and *Tribute.* These films, which featured international stars and disguised their Canadian locales, achieved critical and commercial success (*The Changeling* won eight Genies in 1980). In April 1979 Drabinsky moved into the dangerous terrain of film exhibition with his first multiplex theater in Toronto. Unable to secure first-run release Hollywood films, Drabinksy was forced to build his new empire on European and second-run films. When the costs of expansion threatened to bankrupt Drabinsky's Cineplex chain, he answered by challenging the industry's entente cordiale between Paramount's Famous Players Canada and Odeon Theatres, who controlled first-run films. In 1983, when his suit was progressing well in the courts, Hollywood blinked, offering a relaxation of the manner in which film distribution was controlled. But by May 1984, Cineplex had bought up the Odeon Theatre chain, making Drabinsky a player in the industry. From this footing he proceeded to buy American theater chains. Realizing that the Reagan administration would do little to enforce antitrust laws that had kept the industry fractured since the Paramount Decree of 1948, Drabinsky had moved to build a new, vertically integrated film empire. The fall for Drabinsky came at the hands of his American partner, MCA, who used the company's debt load as a rationale to force Drabinsky out in December 1989. In response, Drabinsky left film altogether, to work in theater. Using his Toronto Pantages Theatre as a base to build a new company, Livent Productions, Drabinsky has mounted various high profile musicals since then. By the mid-1990s Drabinsky had built Livent into a major presence on the international theater scene with productions of *Phantom of the Opera, Show Boat,* and *Ragtime.*

FILMS AS PRODUCER: *The Disappearance,* 1977; *The Silent Partner,* 1978; *The Changeling,* 1979; *Tribute,* 1980; *The Amateur,* 1981; *Losin' It,* 1982.

BIBLIOGRAPHY: Ted Magder.

Dave Douglas

DRYLANDERS. Don Haldane, (Saskatchewan) NFB, 1961 (rel. 1963), 69 min., b+w. The story of settlers in Saskatchewan, from 1907 through the Dust Bowl of the 1930s, *Drylanders* was the NFB's first attempt at feature film production. Centered on the Greer family, Don Haldane's film depicts the struggle to cultivate the land, and the land's hostility to its inhabitants. Relocating from Montreal in 1907, Dan (James B. Douglas) and Liza (Frances Hyland) Greer seek a new life for their family. After early failures they prosper, until drought threatens to ruin all they have built. The family struggles with the question of leaving, and one son does leave for the east—only to drift as one of the army of the jobless during the depression. His dream seemingly shattered, Dan dies a broken man. Despite this, Liza insists the family remain on the land, and soon the rains return. In contrast to Hollywood frontier stories, *Drylanders* bears the explicit mark of the NFB, entertaining with dramatic content while remaining faithful to a historical record. The narrative echoes J. Scott Booth's *Heritage* (1939), a Canadian Government Motion Picture Bureau film on the Dust Bowl that was released by the NFB. Shot in 1961, *Drylanders* encountered numerous delays in its production, and the released print was cut considerably from Haldane's original ninety-minute version.

Dave Douglas

JEAN DUCEPPE. Born 1923, Montreal; died 1990. Actor. It is nearly impossible to discuss the arts in Quebec without mentioning Jean Duceppe. He was without a doubt one of the most talented and appreciated actors to grace the stage and screen (big and small), as well as the airwaves. His death in 1990 marked the passing not only of the artist, but also of the man who was loved by his people, *his* Quebec. Born to a merchant family, the young Duceppe's first contact with theater, his passion, came as he worked as an ice delivery boy in Montreal. Trained by Sita Riddez, Duceppe was a part of the venerable Henri Deyglun troupe at eighteen years old. Working with some of the province's most acclaimed actors and directors allowed his sensitive, down to earth style to develop quickly and efficiently. Duceppe's initiation to film came via *TIT-COQ* (1953), an adaptation of a successful play which exposed the actor to a larger audience. This was followed immediately by television stardom in the form of Stan Labrie on "La famille Plouffe" (1953–59), a wildly successful series that did not dissuade Duceppe from constantly accepting theater engagements. In 1957, as president of the Artists' Union, Duceppe was at the forefront of the SRC's directors' strike, a period of upheaval in the province's artistic history. The 1960s represent Duceppe's work ethic quite well. He acted in several films (notably, *YUL 871*, JACQUES GODBOUT), continued working in television ("Ti-Jean Caribou," 1963–65), hosted three radio shows on Montreal's

CKAC, founded a weekly newspaper, and continued his theater work. It was during this period that his reputation as a man of the people was solidified, not only because of his screen persona, but also due to his social engagement. The year 1971 marks Duceppe's crowning achievements in film and television. CLAUDE JUTRA's *MON ONCLE ANTOINE* gave him his strongest film performance, and an SRC adaptation of Steinbeck's *Of Mice and Men* went down in history as one of the best performances on the province's small screen. In 1973, La Compagnie Jean Duceppe was founded, quickly becoming one of the most successful theater companies, presenting classics and introducing Quebecois playwrights to a larger public. Duceppe's devotion to theater became his main focus in the 1980s, and it is on the stage that he gave his final performance in a translation of Neil Simon's *Broadway Bound* (1989).

FILMS AS ACTOR: *Tit-coq*, 1953; *Trouble-fête*, 1964; *La corde au cou*, 1965; *YUL 871*, 1966; *The Act of the Heart*, 1970; *L'apparition*, 1971; *Les colombes; Mon oncle Antoine*, 1971; *Quelques arpents de neige*, 1972; *Alien Thunder; Je t'aime*, 1973; *Bingo*, 1974; *Les vautours*, 1975; *Cordélia*, 1979; *Lucien Brouillard*, 1983; *Le vieillard et l'enfant*, 1985.

Judes Dickey

E

L'EAU CHAUDE L'EAU FRETTE A Pace-Maker and a Side-Car. Marc-André Forcier, Montreal, 1976, 92 min., color. MARC-ANDRÉ FORCIER creates, with *L'eau chaude l'eau frette*, a "hymn to love" in praise of the loveless and of a whole world peopled with marginal beings. An impressive fresco where the little bums of the neighborhood and the emotional misfits come together, Forcier's film harks back in many respects to Italian comedy, notably Ettore Scola's *Brutti, sporchi, e cattivi* (*Down and Dirty*, 1976), in its humorous treatment of a social milieu where the tragedy of life is omnipresent. It has often been said, with reason, that the reality of Forcier's films has been contaminated by Surrealism. The recurrence of the theme of *l'amour fou* (which often leads to murder) in a good number of his films attests to this connection. Even though the narration of *L'eau chaude l'eau frette* remains linear, one finds some scenes which operate like many ruptures made to the traditional chain of cause and effect of the classical narrative. By taking an interest in the social rejects of society, Forcier registers his film right from the start in a cruel and uncompromising realism. But the absurd invention of numerous gags constantly reminds us of the Compte de Lautréamont (a 19th century forefather of Surrealism) who spoke of "the reunion of a sewing machine and an umbrella on a dissection table." Thus, the scene in which little Francine must boost a car battery with her pacemaker is completely indebted to a Surrealist ideology. *L'eau chaude l'eau frette* is certainly a funny and profoundly original film, but it is one in which laughter permits the audience to swallow more easily the bitter pill of despair.

BIBLIOGRAPHY: Line Bouteiller, "Harel, Forcier et Noël: Une étrange contamination du réel," *Copie Zéro*, no. 37 (October 1988).

Louis Goyette

ATOM EGOYAN. Born 1960, Cairo, Egypt. Director, writer. With *THE SWEET HEREAFTER* winning major awards at Cannes in 1997 and receiving Oscar nominations in 1998, Atom Egoyan became the most honored Canadian-based feature filmmaker in history. He is not only the recognized leader of his generation of Canadian film directors, known for their self-conscious artistry, but is now better known throughout the world than almost any other living Canadian filmmaker. (Perhaps DAVID CRONENBERG and James Cameron are the only exceptions.) Born in Egypt of Armenian parents, Egoyan immigrated to Canada when he was only three years old. Surprisingly, his parents elected to live far from other Armenians in the "very British" Victoria, British Columbia. They wanted Atom to grow up as a "real Canadian," and this separation from his own cultural roots has evolved into a major multicultural theme in his films, especially his first feature, *Next of Kin* (1984), about a lonely young Anglo-Canadian man who pretends he is the long-lost son of an immigrant Armenian couple, and *CALENDAR*, which was partially filmed in former Soviet Armenia. Other films have strong autobiographical elements: for example, *The Adjuster*'s central character was based on an insurance adjuster who comforted Egoyan's family after their home was destroyed by fire. Indeed, the family is often used by Egoyan in his films as a microcosm of society, and a dysfunctional one at that. He studied English literature at the University of Toronto, and it was there that he began to make films. His writing has always been an important ingredient leading to the success of his films, and one of the most striking aspects of his scripts is their narrative complexity. The audience is regularly challenged to understand frequent jumps in time and space and to follow the actions of multiple characters. Egoyan's acting style is also distinctive, being restrained, somewhat like Robert Bresson's emotionless style. But the Canadian has been unfairly criticized for a coldness of characterization, whereas invariably his characters are deliberately withholding their emotions in what would otherwise be "operatic" situations. His films are notable for their thematic preoccupation with both voyeurism—most obviously *EXOTICA, FAMILY VIEWING*, and *Speaking Parts* (1989), where a hotel worker obsessively views videos featuring her male colleague, but also *The Adjuster*, where the title character's wife works as censor—and the destructive incursion of media technology into human relations (which can be found in almost all of his films). Importantly, such questions raised by Atom Egoyan's films lead viewers to question their own experience of film viewing, and, not surprisingly, his work is increasingly being written about in scholarly journals.

FILMS AS DIRECTOR: *Howard in Particular* (16mm short), 1979; *After Grad with Dad* (16mm short), 1980; *Peep Show* (16mm short), 1981; *Open House* (16mm short), 1982; *Next of Kin* (16mm), 1984; *Men: A Passion Playground* (16mm short); *In This Corner* (TV), 1985; *Family Viewing*, 1987; *Speaking Parts*, 1989; *The Adjuster*, 1991; *Montréal vu par . . .* (co-dir. with Patricia Rozema, Jacques Leduc, Michel Brault, Léa Pool, and

Denys Arcand); *Gross Misconduct* (TV), 1992; *Calendar*, 1993; *Exotica*, 1994; *Bach Cello Suite #4: Sarrabande* (TV); *The Sweet Hereafter*, 1997.

BIBLIOGRAPHY: Carole Desbarats et al.; Atom Egoyan.

Peter Rist

R. BRUCE ELDER. Born 1947, Hawksbury, Ontario. Filmmaker, theorist, author. Elder is a central figure of the Canadian avant-garde, both for his considerable body of films and for his critical discussion of the entire project of experimental cinema in Canada. As a filmmaker, Elder has inherited the historical legacy of avant-garde cinema in North America and married that bounty of knowledge and practice with his own particular interests, producing in the process a series of increasingly lengthy and visually complex films that he has bound together in the grand project of an epic cycle, *The Book of All the Dead*. This extremely long opus, which began in 1974, consists of three sections: "The System of Dante's Hell," "Consolations (Love Is an Art of Time)," and "Exultations (In Light of the Great Giving)." Elder completed the cycle, temporarily abandoned in 1992, in 1994. At that time it included some twenty-one (film) parts, such as *1857 (Fool's Gold)*, *Lamentations*, and *The Art of Worldly Wisdom*. The cycle maps the transitions from Elder's early cinema, with films such as *Breath/Light/Birth* (1975) and *Barbara Is a Vision of Loveliness* constructing a world largely without points of reference to orient the viewer, to his later films, which center intensively on the body. Some critics have suggested that Elder's development of an interest in the body, disease, and death stems from a serious illness he suffered in 1977, although Elder tends to regard such readings as too literal. An offshoot of his filmmaking struggles was one of the rare manifestos of Canadian cinema, "The Cinema We Need," which he wrote while making *Lamentations*. It appeared in *Canadian Forum* in February 1985. This polemical essay asserted Elder's conviction that the essential importance of a Canadian avant-garde lay not in the current development of "new narrative," which Elder regarded as simply derivative of American cinema, only able to deal with the past. In contrast, he advocated a cinema capable of dealing with what he termed "the here and now," a cinema of "perceptions." The article produced considerable commentary in Canadian avant-garde and academic circles. Elder went on to establish a theoretical foundation for his project of a Canadian avant-garde in his book, *Image and Identity: Reflections on Canadian Film and Culture* (1989). With its equally polemical argument and its avowedly nationalist orientation, the book has met similar responses in some quarters. Having completed *The Book of All the Dead* in 1994, Elder began working on another cycle, entitled *The Book of Praise*.

FILMS INCLUDE: *She Is Away; Breath/Light/Birth*, 1975; *Barbara Is a Vision of Loveliness; Permutations and Combinations*, 1976; *The Art of Worldly Wisdom*, 1979; *Trace*, 1980; *1857 (Fool's Gold)*, 1981; *Illuminated Texts*, 1982; *Lamentations: A Monument for the Dead World*, 1984; "Consolations (Love Is an Art of Time)," includes *The Fu-*

gitive Gods; The Lighted Clearing; The Body and the World, 1988; "Exultations (In Light of the Great Giving)," includes *Flesh Angels,* 1990; *Newton & Me,* 1991; *Exultations (In Light of the Great Giving),* 1992; *Et Resurrectus Est,* 1994; *The Book of Praise: A Man Whose Life Was Full of Woe Has Been Surprised by Joy,* 1997.

BIBLIOGRAPHY: Lianne McLarty, "The Films of R. Bruce Elder: The Evolving Vision," in Feldman, 287–97; R. Bruce Elder, "The Cinema We Need," in Fetherling, 260–71.

Dave Douglas

ELVIS GRATTON: LE KING DES KINGS Elvis Gratton: The King of Kings. Pierre Falardeau, Quebec, 1981–85, 90 min., 16mm. *Elvis Gratton: Le King des Kings* is a Quebecois cult classic that began as a short film made in response to the 1980 Quebec referendum on sovereignty (*Elvis Gratton,* 1981). The short's success (winning a Genie for Best Theatrical Short in 1983) led to two more shorts, *Les vacances d'Elvis Gratton* (1983) and *Pas encore Gratton?!* (1985), which were put together as the feature *Elvis Gratton: The King of Kings.* In the first episode we follow garage-depanneur owner Robert Gratton as he prepares for an Elvis Presley look-alike contest. This is by far the best of the three episodes because it stays truest to its sociopolitical course, and in doing so the slapstick (Gratton's uncouth mannerisms, his lack of physical grace) helps define the satirical style. In the second episode he and his wife, courtesy of the contest, vacation at a Third World resort town, ruled by a pint-sized Hitlerian dictator, Santana Banana. In the weak third episode Gratton hosts a gaudy Hawaiian-style pool party, dies of a heart attack while trying to get into his Elvis costume, and then magically returns to life during his funeral, proclaiming himself as the new messiah (how can a myth die?). Although *Elvis Gratton* works at the specific level of Quebec's sociopolitical scene, it also satirizes the broader question of American cultural colonialism and the general 1980s Anglo-wide swing to the right (Thatcher, Reagan, Mulroney). Regardless of the broader target, members of Quebec society were still offended by the portrayal of Gratton as a petit-bourgeois, ultra–right wing, sexist, xenophobic federalist. This reaction is partly explained by the strong emotions surrounding Quebec separatism. But *Elvis Gratton* remains special in being able to comically reflect these emotions, as both a cynical, bitter response to the failed referendum, and as a hilarious send-up of the worst elements of cultural intolerance and ignorance. Robert Gratton is an overloaded stereotype, but, as PIERRE FALARDEAU and co-writer/lead actor Julien Poulin imply in the scene where each shopper in a depanneur is wearing an Elvis Gratton rubber mask, perhaps there is a bit of Robert Gratton in us all.

BIBLIOGRAPHY: David Edelstein, "Film: Almost There," *Village Voice* 30 (May 14, 1985): 62; Richard Martineau, "Elvis Gratton: Le film," *Séquences,* no. 123 (January 1986): 43–44.

Donato Totaro

EN PAYS NEUFS. L'Abbé Maurice Proulx, Quebec, 1934–37, 66 min., b+w. The first sound documentary feature film to be made in Canada, *En pays neufs* is one of the best-known films of the Catholic priest MAURICE PROULX. He collaborated with Quebec's Société de Colonisation in filming the settlers of Abitibi over a series of several visits to the region. *En pays neufs* offers a more or less idealized image of colonization by exploiting the beauty of the natural landscape in exaltation of the virtues of the Catholic Church and its members. Further, Proulx seemed more interested in making a kind of family album of settlers posing in front of the camera, instead of showing them at work. The highly subjective character of the spoken commentary and the choice of classical music contribute to reinforce the "pastoral" vision of the cineaste-priest. A propagandistic documentary, *En pays neufs* demonstrates a nice mastery of cinematic language on Proulx's part, while privileging a chronological exposition of events. His sense of lyricism is well displayed in the panoramic shots of the countryside, and the montage is fluid and sometimes surprising in its rhythmical structure. Several touches of humor complement these elements, although the view presented of First Nations people seems today to be somewhat contemptible.

BIBLIOGRAPHY: Pierre Demers, "Un pionnier du documentaire québécois: L'Abbé Maurice Proulx," *Cinéma Québec* 4, no. 6 (1975): 17–34.

Louis Goyette

EVANGELINE. E. P. Sullivan and William H. Cavanaugh, Nova Scotia, 1913, 75 min., b+w (tinted and toned), silent. *Evangeline* was the first Canadian-produced feature-length film. It is also the most tragically lost Canadian film— only a few production stills survive. The story of Evangeline is quintessentially Acadian. Acadia (*L'Acadie* in French) is the region of Canada, now spanning parts of the provinces of New Brunswick and Nova Scotia, settled by the French in the 17th century and claimed by the British in 1701. Many Acadians were later expelled to Louisiana, where they formed "Cajun" communities. Henry Wadsworth Longfellow's poem "Evangeline" idyllically represents the village of Grand-Pré, where Gabriel, the blacksmith's son, and Evangeline fall in love. They are torn apart in exile, and, after searching for each other throughout their travels in the central and eastern United States, finally come together in old age with Gabriel on his deathbed. The poem was first adapted into a film by the Kalem Company in 1908. Selig then based another short film on it in 1911, and after the Canadian version, Hollywood made two silent features on the subject, directed by Raoul Walsh (Fox) in 1919 and Edwin Carew (United Artists) in 1929. The Canadian Bioscope film was shot mostly on Canadian and American locations (from Longfellow) and employed Americans, including some actors and the two directors. The production's cost was quite high ($30,000), but this was more than recovered at the box office, being a popular success with audiences in Canada and the United States.

BIBLIOGRAPHY: Peter Morris (1978), 49–51.

Peter Rist

EXOTICA. Atom Egoyan, Toronto, 1994, 104 min., color. ATOM EGOYAN's sixth feature, *Exotica* was, prior to THE SWEET HEREAFTER, his most easily accessible and biggest international box office success. Running for twenty-five straight weeks in Toronto, including one week at the IMAX theater, it grossed $1.75 million at the Canadian box office. Mia Kirschner plays Christina, a dancer who performs a striptease dressed as a schoolgirl each night at the club Exotica. She is watched by Francis (Bruce Greenwood) and by the enigmatic club emcee Eric (Elias Koteas) who, by agreement, has made the proprietress of the club, Zoe (Arsinée Khanjian), pregnant. Meanwhile, Francis is undertaking a tax audit of pet shop owner Tomas (DON McKELLAR). To summarize the plot is to do it an injustice, as it unfolds like striptease, each character initially wrapped in an enigma that slowly peels away to reveal a kind of truth. Dealing with his usual subjects of sex, relationships, and voyeurism, Egoyan here eschews his traditional use of video, except for one key image, creating a more direct fusion between fantasy and reality through the use of the striptease. First we see Francis watching a stripper dressed as a schoolgirl, then we see him driving a young girl home and giving her money. Yet, as Egoyan reveals through a consistent use of one-way mirrors, he conceals what is actually there. The first line of the film, "You have to ask yourself what brought the person to this point," is both advice and a challenge. Egoyan delights in a "journey" through complex crosscutting, subtle lighting, and sound. Focusing ultimately on the melodramatic situation, some viewers find the denouement disappointing. Yet Egoyan's aim is never to explain what has gone before but to offer a key to allow one to return and reassess. *Exotica* won eight Genie Awards including Best Film, Best Director, Best Screenplay, and Best Supporting Actor for Don McKellar.

BIBLIOGRAPHY: "Dossier: Atom Egoyan," *Positif*, no. 406 (December 1994), 74–94; Tony Rayns, "Everybody Knows," *Sight and Sound* 5, no. 5 (May 1995), 3.

Simon Brown

F

PIERRE FALARDEAU. Born 1946, Montreal. Director, videaste, screenwriter. Few critics or journalists will disagree: Pierre Falardeau is the political loud-mouth of Quebec's cinema—a label the director and onetime videaste wears proudly. A student of anthropology at the Université de Montreal, he joined the ranks of the Vidéographe group after graduating to shoot his first documentary, a short video denouncing the mythical construct of professional wrestling (*Continuons le combat*, 1971). His next short works further exposed the rigor and uncompromising nature of his political discourse: *La Magra* (1975) argues that fascism is at the core of contemporary police training; *À force de courage* (1976) celebrates the socialist spirit found in an agricultural coop set up by Algerian farmers; and *Speak White*, shot on 35mm, condemns American imperialism. These three documentaries were co-signed by Julien Poulin, an actor who would star in Falardeau's first foray into fiction film, the *ELVIS GRATTON* series. Though rather crudely directed—in keeping with the subject matter—they proved so popular that they were re-released as a feature film in 1985. But for true critical acclaim, Falardeau would have to await *Octobre* (1994), Quebec cinema's first revisitation of the traumatic October Events of 1970 since MICHEL BRAULT's *LES ORDRES* (1974). For all the dramatic impact of Falardeau's claus-trophobic and intense mise-en-scène of the events leading up to the infamous F.L.Q. tragedy, what remains most striking about this award-winning film is the Marxist slant of its discourse, which repudiates the usual "franco versus anglo" historical reading of the October Events in favor of an "exploited versus ex-ploiter" dialectic. Falardeau doesn't necessarily have it in for English Canada but does for capitalists, regardless of their cultural identity. That much is again made evident upon viewing Falardeau's political tract, the short documentary *Le temps des bouffons* (1993). In this scathing and darkly funny indictment of the Montreal Beaver Club, whose influential members make fools of themselves during a reception they think is being filmed by a "friendly" camera, Falardeau criticizes rich francophones and anglophones alike in a rhyming and rhythmical voice-over narration that propaganda poets would not disavow. It could very well be his best work.

FILMS AS DIRECTOR: *Speak White* (short), 1980; *Elvis Gratton* (short), 1981; *Les vacances d'Elvis Gratton* (short), 1983; *Pas encore Elvis Gratton?!* (short); *Elvis Gratton: Le King des Kings* (anthology of all three shorts), 1985; *Le Party*, 1991; *Le Steak*, 1992; *Le temps des bouffons* (short), 1993; *Octobre*, 1994.

BIBLIOGRAPHY: Maurie Alioff, "The Outsider," *Take One*, no. 6 (Fall 1994): 8–13; Falardeau.

Johanne Larue

THE FALLS: A CAUTIONARY TALE. Kevin McMahon, Ontario, 1992, 89 min., 16mm (blown up to 35mm), color. *The Falls* is a documentary that uses Niagara Falls as a reflection of a universal disharmony between nature and culture in the Western world. With style and intelligence, it relates humanity's changing view of Niagara Falls, from something ugly (17th century), to something of terrible beauty (late 18th century), to something boring, conquered, and to be exploited (early 20th century). By the 20th century, the sideshow (gift shops, amusement parks, honeymoon hotels, restaurants, electrical towers, etc.) has become the main attraction, and the once glorious Falls a necessary appendage. *The Falls* is a powerful plea for heightened environmental consciousness. While never cynical, it is soaked in irony. Irony #1: We witness a museum exhibit entitled "Freaks of Nature" (two-headed animals, etc.); later in the film we learn about the toxic pollutants surrounding the Falls and see one of its victims: a bird with a horribly twisted beak. Irony #2: The area surrounding the Falls is converted into a quaint, family-friendly "model city"; through an interview witness we slowly learn of the science-fictionish health nightmares endured by families living near the chemically contaminated "model city," Love Canal. Irony #3: As a Niagara Falls employee tells us about environmental studies being conducted by the chemical companies, the camera tracks away to reveal a score of ugly toxic waste sites. Irony #4: In one of the film's final shots, the camera takes in the glitzy neon lights, amusement park games, and other frivolous expenditures of electricity. Irony #5: The film's complex visual style (aerial shots, vertical crane shots) renders a certain beauty to the industrial and technological machinery surrounding the Niagara area. Irony #6 (perhaps the crowning irony): *The Falls* was funded by the same federal government largely responsible for the commodification of Niagara Falls. *The Falls* is an engaging and provocative documentary that will forever change the way we perceive Niagara Falls.

BIBLIOGRAPHY: Geoff Pevere, "On the Brink," *CineACTION!*, no. 28 (Spring 1992): 34–37; Barry Keith Grant, "Nature, Culture, Documentary: The Films of Kevin McMahon," *Postscript* 15 no. 1 (Fall 1995): 57–67.

Donato Totaro

FAMILY VIEWING. Atom Egoyan, Toronto, 1987, 86 min., color. *Family View-ing* is a clever recasting of the Oedipal complex as a modernist story about technology's effects on the human condition. A teenager, Van (Aidan Tierney), lives with his father (David Hemblen) and stepmother/lover (Gabrielle Rose) in a high-rise condominium. Van's vacuous existence consists of daytime trips to the old age home to visit his catatonic maternal grandmother and nights spent passively watching television. Things change as Van finds videotapes containing home footage which begin to reconnect him to his (repressed) past. Van dis-covers that his father has been "erasing" their family history by using these tapes to record his sex sessions. This triggers a symbolic battle between Van and his father over the rightful heir of the video apparatus (the power/technol-ogy). Through Van, the apparatus symbolizes positive qualities, such as the past, precious memories, and lived time. Through Stan, it symbolizes alienation, in the form of a perpetual present. Egoyan has referred to Stan as a person suffering from a "20th century disease." And, in fact, many of the film's formal qualities, from the emotionally detached, minimalist, and flatly affected speech patterns, to the monotonous editing rhythms, reflect a schizophrenic's speech behavior. There is also a "schizophrenia" to the visual style (which reflects the temporal theme of past/history versus present): scenes shot on film versus scenes shot on video; video zooms versus film camera movements; "cold" locations versus "warm" locations. In the context of a Canadian technological discourse, Egoyan seems to assume a position equivalent to that of Harold Innis, the leery realist, rather than that of George Grant, the pessimist, or Marshall McLuhan, the uto-pianist.

BIBLIOGRAPHY: Cameron Bailey, "Scanning Egoyan," *CineACTION!*, no. 16 (May 1989): 45–51; Ron Burnett, "Atom Egoyan: An Interview," *CineACTION!*, no. 16 (May 1989): 40–44.

Donato Totaro

THE FAR SHORE. Joyce Wieland, Ontario, 1976, 105 min., color. Set in 1919, *The Far Shore* centers on the unhappy marriage of Eulalie (Céline Lomez), a young French Canadian, to a Toronto businessman, Ross Turner (Lawrence Benedict). He has little time for her, and no appreciation of her love of music. She finds companionship with an obscure painter, Tom McLeod (Frank Moore), and tries to convince her husband to support his painting. Ross sees only the potential for money in becoming a patron, and suggests that Tom paint "more commercial" pictures. When Tom leaves for the north to paint, Eulalie is isolated in Toronto. A chance meeting at a friend's cottage in Northern Ontario offers Eulalie the opportunity to see Tom once again. Mindful of the jealous Ross, Tom remains encamped on the shore opposite the cottage. In desperation Eulalie jumps into the lake, swimming across to Tom. In return, he rescues her by canoe, and the two enjoy a brief moment of joy. Spurred on by a friend, Ross chases the two lovers and murders Tom. *The Far Shore* marks JOYCE WIELAND's transition from the world of experimental film to narrative, a transition that was not an easy one. The film was frequently delayed due to lack of funding, and its release was marked by scathing reviews from critics, most of whom lambasted Wieland for the wooden characters and overt symbolism. In retrospect the film has attained stature as a culmination of Wieland's various artistic interests. Richard Leiterman's cinematography was key to Wieland's desire to construct Eulalie's world in a formally structured manner. Echoing her sculpture, Wieland focused on the texture of objects in Eulalie's home. As with her painting, Wieland's *Far Shore* actively courts associations with a wide body of Canadian art, most notably the landscape paintings of Tom Thompson (the model for the McLeod character). In retelling Thompson's story from the perspective of Eulalie, Wieland fuses her interests in Canadian nationalism and feminism.

BIBLIOGRAPHY: Lauren Rabinovitz, "After the Avant-Garde: Joyce Wieland and New Avant-Gardes in the 1970's," 184–215.

Dave Douglas

LA FEMME DE L'HÔTEL A Woman in Transit. Léa Pool, Quebec, 1984, 89 min., color. Following her experimental art film *Strass Café*, LÉA POOL directed her first feature, to which both the general public and the critics responded more than favorably. While Quebec cinema endured a difficult period on the heels of a precarious economy and public disinterest in Quebec's national cinema, *La femme de l'hôtel* revived all the hopes of renewing the themes of a cinema driven, in the past, by a great nationalist inspiration. Pool's film takes as its starting point the story of two women: Andréa, a filmmaker, and Estelle, a troubled woman caught up in perpetual wandering. Strongly reflexive, the film is interested in the problem of artistic creation, as Andréa takes her inspiration from the enigmatic Estelle in order to create the character of the film she is preparing to shoot. This mirror construction (the film within the film) allows Pool to establish that the line dividing reality from fiction can often be quite fine. Rather than participating in an engaged and revolutionary feminist consciousness, *La femme de l'hôtel*, with its slow and meditative rhythm, maintains instead the "feminine mystique" through the intermediary of a character with a troubled past, all to demonstrate how complicity and solidarity between women can prove rich in fruitful moments. This first feature film prepares the way for the intimate feminine universe of Pool's next film, *ANNE TRISTER*.

BIBLIOGRAPHY: Mary Jean Green, "Léa Pool's *La femme de l'hôtel* and Women's Films in Quebec," *Quebec Studies*, no. 9 (Fall-Winter 1990): 48–62.

Louis Goyette

LES FLEURS SAUVAGES Wild Flower. Jean Pierre Lefebvre, Quebec, 1982, 152 min., 16mm (blown up to 35mm), color/b+w. With *LES DERNIÈRES FIANÇAILLES*, this is the most moving film directed by JEAN PIERRE LEFEBVRE. Opting for a linear narrative structure and restraint in the dramatic action, Lefebvre explores mother/daughter relationships with such realism that one practically forgets that the film is a work of fiction. To achieve this effect requires brilliant direction of the actors. All are excellent, but one most remembers the subtle and interior performances of Marthe Nadeau and Michelle Magny, the mother and daughter who, although displaying an undeniable tenderness toward each other, arrive at closeness with difficulty. The luminous photography of Guy Dufaux constitutes a celebration of the countryside and captures the true essence of the serene pleasures of the return to the land. Lefebvre's only concession to experimentation was to film some scenes in black and white in order to offer a different perspective on scenes first presented in color. Faithful to his usual collaborators, Lefebvre shot his film in the country with a relatively modest budget. *Les fleurs sauvages* was awarded the Prix de la Presse Internationale at the Cannes Film Festival.

BIBLIOGRAPHY: Claude Chabot et al.

Louis Goyette

MEGAN FOLLOWS. Born 1968, Toronto, Ontario. Actor. Megan Follows was born into an acting family. Both her parents, Ted Follows and Dawn Greenhalgh, were screen actors, and their four children each expressed an interest in acting. Megan, however, showed great promise from the beginning and has achieved the most fruitful results. Appearing on both television and film from an early age, her precociousness and tomboy demeanor gained her many roles as intelligent young girls struggling against their traditional place in society. At the age of fourteen Follows gave a touching performance in Rebecca Yates' film *Jen's Place* as a young girl who, in the face of her parents' impending divorce, fights for her right to decide with whom she will live. This was followed by her lead role in the adaptation of Margaret Lawrence's classic short story *Boys and Girls*. Here Follows played a farm girl facing the realization that her approaching adolescence will mark a significant change in her life, as she is expected to abandon her tomboy ways and take on her expected place as her mother's helper in the home. Her natural rebelliousness and sincerity in these early roles were ideal qualities for the role that would bring Follows international attention, as Anne Shirley in the television series adaptation of Lucy Maud Montgomery's *Anne of Green Gables* (1985). Follows was first tested for the role at the age of fourteen and was then forced to wait a year while 3,000 other girls were tested. When CBC finally returned to her, Follows proved to be the definitive Anne with the skill of a seasoned professional. Since the success of "Anne of Green Gables" and its sequel "Anne of Avonlea," Follows faced the most difficult challenge of all child actors: growing up.* Her most recent choice of roles marks a movement away from charismatic young teenagers and toward darker performances as troubled young women. Although films such as *Termini Station*

*Both series were shown on U.S. television as two-part TV movies. "Anne of Avonlea" was called *Anne of Green Gables: The Sequel*, or *The Continuing Story of Anne of Green Gables*.

(where Follows is reunited with "Anne" co-star COLLEEN DEWHURST) and *Deep Sleep* were less successful with audiences, Follows imbues each film with emotional depth and has received consistently positive reactions. She has had a great deal of success in the United States and continues to move back and forth between there and Canada.

FILMS AS ACTOR: *Jen's Place*, 1982; *Boys and Girls* (short), 1983; *Hockey Night* (TV), 1984; "Anne of Green Gables" (TV series), 1985; "Anne of Avonlea" (TV series), 1987; *Termini Station*, 1989; *Deep Sleep; Nutcracker Prince* (voice only), 1990; *Romeo and Juliet* (TV), 1993; *Under the Piano* (TV), 1995; *Major Crime* (TV), 1997.

Stacey Abbott

FORBIDDEN LOVE: THE UNASHAMED STORIES OF LESBIAN LIVES.
Aerlyn Weissman and Lynne Fernie, NFB, 1992, 85 min., color/b+w. Following in the grand tradition of the Women's Studio D of the National Film Board, *Forbidden Love* presents the direct and frank testimony of women, who reveal *The Unashamed Stories of Lesbian Lives*. Nine Canadian women, and one American (the writer of lesbian fiction, Ann Bannon), whose ages range from forty to seventy, share their reminiscences on same sex experiences of the 1950s and 1960s in carefully staged but very relaxed interviews. Amanda White is a Haida Native Canadian, while Nairobi, an Afro-West Indian singer, is the lone Montreal representative. Keelly Moll, complete with cowboy hat, is introduced on her ranch, and talks of her experiences out west, particularly in Vancouver, as do White, Stephanie Ozed, Ruth Christine, a "femme," and Reva Hutkin, who claims to be neither "butch" nor "femme." Three other women discuss the Toronto-area scene. Their stories are often amusing and sometimes sad, and the potential for violence in a prejudicial era is recounted often. The charm of *Forbidden Love* is in its construction: a documentary framed by an invented narrative depicting a young woman, Laura (Stephanie Morgenstern), who travels to the big city and is willingly seduced by Mitch (Lynne Adams). These episodes are presented in washed-out color sequences which dissolve into lurid color covers for the imagined novel *Forbidden Love*. Throughout the film, actual "pulp fiction" lesbian novel covers (e.g., *The Constant Urge, Odd Girl Out*), some by Bannon, are intercut with stock footage of city life, still photographs of lesbian hangouts, and personal snapshots. While the choice of only ten interview subjects may have led to some stereotyping (e.g., of "butch" and "femme" role playing), it allowed for each woman's character to be revealed in great detail. And directors Aerlyn Weissman and Lynn Fernie cleverly withheld some key information on them until the end. We learn that Nairobi has been living with a transplanted heart since 1988, that Ozed has raised a teenage daughter by herself, and that the feisty Lois M. Stuart (Toronto) has become a marching activist.

BIBLIOGRAPHY: Kass Banning, "Sexing the Nation," *Take One*, no. 2 (Winter 1993): 11–15.

Peter Rist

MARC-ANDRÉ FORCIER. Born 1947, Greenfield Park, Quebec. Director, scriptwriter. Justly called the *enfant terrible* of Quebec cinema, Marc-André Forcier has been one of the most original filmmakers of his generation, from the very start of his career. While he was a student at a Franciscan college, Forcier found himself "compelled" to take a course in cinema. It was under the rubric of a course in rhetoric that he made a little film in 8mm, entitled *La mort vue par. . . .* Selected for the television program, "Images en tête," the film was awarded a prize by a jury led by none other than GILLES CARLE. With such encouragement and the support of Onyx Films, Forcier made his first two "real" films: *Chroniques labradoriennes* (1967) and then *Le retour de l'Immaculée Conception*, a work in which classical narration finds itself undermined by a succession of unusual tableaux representing an anarchist youth. Forcier's next films, although more rigorously constructed, present a singular imaginary world where poetry and "the marvelous" rub shoulders with a very concrete social realism found in the poor quarters of Montreal, its bars and cheap motels. *BAR SALON* inaugurates a suite of remarkable films, wherein the cineaste's style is already perfectly recognizable: equal doses of the comic and the tragic; narratives unfolding around a number of impressive, marginalized characters; all served by an aesthetic that refuses to idealize "reality." Such is the style that characterizes *Night Cap* (1974) and *L'EAU CHAUDE L'EAU FRETTE* (1976), the two summits in Forcier's oeuvre. The stylistic unity of this work is equally attributable to the director's insistence on employing regular collaborators. Of the actors, GUY L'ÉCUYER, Jean Lapointe, and several others (often nonprofessional) have appeared in more than one Forcier film. Jacques Marcotte is the perennial accomplice on his screenplays, and François Gill has been the cinematographer on no less than six of the ten films directed by Forcier. The 1980s were marked by a slowing down in the filmmaker's output. If the surrealist *Au clair de la lune* agreeably surprised the critics, the reception accorded to *Kalamazoo* (1988) was relatively lukewarm. Although Forcier remained faithful to his preferred themes in *Kalamazoo*, one does not find the same exuberance that characterized his earlier efforts. But he returned to form with *UNE HISTOIRE INVENTÉE* and *Le vent de Wyoming* (1995), instantaneously regaining his prominence.

FILMS AS DIRECTOR INCLUDE: *Chroniques labradoriennes*, 1967; *Le retour de l'Immaculée Conception*, 1971; *Bar salon*, 1973; *Night Cap*, 1974; *L'eau chaude l'eau frette*, 1976; *Au clair de la lune*, 1982; *Kalamazoo*, 1988; *Une histoire inventée*, 1992; *Le vent du Wyoming*, 1995; *La comtesse de Bâton-Rouge*, 1997.

BIBLIOGRAPHY: Pierre Jutras, ed., "André Forcier: Entretien, témoinages et points de vue," *Copie Zéro*, no. 19 (January 1984).

                                                                                Louis Goyette

LA FORTERESSE. Fedor Ozep, Quebec, 1947, 99 min, b+w. *WHISPERING CITY [Crime City].* Fedor Ozep, Quebec, 1947, 91 min, b+w. With *Whispering*

City and *La forteresse*, Quebec Productions Corporation boldly addressed the global market with the most commercially ambitious pre-television Quebec film enterprise. Paul L'Anglais and René Germain formed the company in 1946 to produce features, each to be shot in French and English versions, for worldwide exhibition. Commanding a $600,000 budget (later exceeded by at least $150,000), they commissioned a screenplay to move the setting of an existing Hollywood-patterned mystery storyline to Quebec City. Recruited Hollywood veterans included the producer, crew members, technicians, and the three lead English-language actors. Fedor Ozep, hired to direct both versions, entered Russian films as a scenarist in 1916. His standout directorial credit, a Soviet/German co-production, *The Living Corpse* (1928), drew notice with its weighty expressionistic style and Vsevolod Pudovkin's presence in the lead. Ozep thereafter made films in Germany, France, Hollywood, and Canada (the well-received *Le Père Chopin*, 1944). Quebec Productions secured distribution through Eagle Lion, a division of the Rank Organization, ensuring exposure in the United States and overseas. Reportedly, the French-language release, retaining the project's working title, "The Stronghold," matches its counterpart closely but has a longer prologue. *La forteresse* had long runs in Montreal and other major Quebec centers, but reviewers objected to the film's Hollywood style and flavor. Understandably, the English version also received poor notices and very disappointing returns. Despite the expense and Ozep's vast experience, *Whispering City*, a leaden, unsurprising "mystery," is stiffly acted, superficial, and static, a weak entry in the *noir* cycle then at its zenith with the work of Robert Siodmak, Jacques Tourneur, and Henri-Georges Clouzot, among many others. Polished, mildly amusing, yet excessive dialogue and somber cinematography make it watchable. Quebec Productions survived to produce (on much smaller budgets) French-language features marketed domestically only, including the successful *Un homme et son péché* (1948). *Whispering City* bore the more urgent title *Crime City* for a 1952 American re-release.

Ian Elliot

DON FRANCKS. Born 1932, Vancouver, British Columbia. Actor, musician. A veteran of Canadian screen and television, Don Francks first came to prominence in the role of Russell, the youngest son of the Greer family in Don Haldane's *DRYLANDERS* (1961–63). During the 1960s Francks enjoyed some success in character roles, both in international productions (Robert Altman's *McCabe & Mrs. Miller*, United States, 1972) as well as on television (Constable Bill Mitchell in the Canadian television series "RCMP"), but breakthrough roles proved elusive. After a period away from the screen in the early 1970s Francks returned as Pete Brennan, a crusading ex-junkie, in Robin Spry's underrated film, *Drying Up the Streets* (1978). Since that time Francks has found steady work in character roles on Canadian screens (*My Bloody Valentine, Prisoner of the Future, The Diviners, Johnny Mnemonic*), as well as numerous voice-character roles on animated television, such as ABC's "Ewoks-Droids Adventure Hour" (1986).

In addition to his acting, Francks has also been a musician, a jazz vocalist, and a member of a barbershop quartet.

THEATRICAL FILMS, AS ACTOR: *Ivy League Killers*, 1959; *Drylanders*, 1961–63; *Drying Up the Streets*, 1978; *Riel; Fast Company; Summer's Children*, 1979; *Fish Hawk*, 1980; *My Bloody Valentine; Heavy Metal* (voice), 1981; *The Tomorrow Man*, 1978–82; *Ring of Power* (voice), 1982; *Rock & Rule* (voice), 1983; *Prisoner of the Future*, 1984; *Terminal Choice*, 1985; *The Big Town*, 1987; *Christmas Wife*, 1988; *Married to It; The Diviners*, 1993; *Paint Cans*, 1994; *Johnny Mnemonic; First Degree*, 1995.

Dave Douglas

JAMES SIMMONS FREER. Born 1855, Woodstock, England; died 1923, Winnipeg, Manitoba. Filmmaker and exhibitor. James S. Freer was the first Canadian filmmaker. He immigrated to Canada in 1888, settling on a farm in Manitoba. He had formerly been a newspaper publisher, which may have helped him make films with a camera he bought from the Edison Company. In the fall of 1897 he shot scenes of harvesting and the Canadian Pacific Railroad (CPR), only a year later than the first filmmaking at Niagara Falls by the Lumière (France), Biograph and Edison (both U.S.) companies. Freer traveled to England in April 1898, where he showed his films on an Edison projector. This, the first "Freer's Tour," was sponsored by the CPR, and his show, called "Ten Years in Manitoba," also included lectures. While in England he shot a couple of London "scenes" which he added to the program. He returned to Canada in the spring of 1899. He apparently filmed his return voyage but was unable to make any more films before being invited back to England for his second tour in 1902. His pioneering work in the area of sponsored film helped to begin the large influx of emigration from the United Kingdom; the CPR upgraded its filmmaking, hiring the British-based Charles Urban Company, and other organizations like the Massey-Harris Company of Toronto followed suit.

FILMS INCLUDE: *Arrival of CPR Express at Winnipeg; Pacific and Atlantic Mail Trains; Premier Greenway Stooking Grain; Six Binders at Work in 100 Acre Wheat Field; Typical Stacking Scene; Harvesting Scene with Trains Passing; Cyclone Thresher at Work; Coming thru' the Rye* [Children Play in the Hay]; *Winnipeg Fire Boys on the Warpath; Canadian Militia Charging Fortified Wall; Harnessing the Virgin Prairie*, all 1897–1898.

BIBLIOGRAPHY: Peter Morris (1978), 30–33.

Peter Rist

FROM NINE TO NINE [The Man with the Umbrella]. Montreal, 1936, Edgar G. Ulmer, 75 min. (62 min. for surviving prints), b+w. *From Nine to Nine* was the first dramatic feature to be shot in a fully equipped sound studio in Canada, and the only one to be filmed at Associated Screen News (ASN) in Montreal (immediately following the fifty-five minute sponsored docudrama *House in Order*, directed by GORDON SPARLING). It is most interesting as an example of a sub-"B" movie, utilizing tiny sets, and shot in only nine days. *From Nine* was directed by the master of such projects, Edgar G. Ulmer. According to archivist D. J. Turner, an earlier version of the script (working title "Death Strikes Again") was slated to be made in Germany by F. W. Murnau before both he and Ulmer left for Hollywood. As it is, *From Nine* is a fairly straightforward murder-mystery thriller, where Ruth Roland, a former "queen of silent serials," plays the exotic Cornelia Du Play (or Prée?), a police detective posing as a jewel thief. Other minor actors were hired for the film, including some from Britain, where the film was targeted for release as a "quota quickie." (It is not known if it was ever released in the UK, or Canada, or the United States). Prior to becoming a director, Ulmer designed sets, and the art deco look of *From Nine* is reminiscent of his *The Black Cat* (Universal, 1934). So small was the sound stage at ASN, though, that a single set seems to have been employed with variations for apartment and hotel rooms alike, and with all the windows painted plain white. Ulmer keeps it somewhat credible, though, with fluid panning and tilting camera movements, close-up cutaways, and some wipes for scene transitions. A few (silent) shots were taken in the hallways of the old Sheraton Mount Royal Hotel, conveniently employing the front of Sachs jewelers, while the limited number of exterior shots betray the snowbound wintry conditions of the February shooting schedule. Remarkably, as Turner has discovered, *From Nine* was not even Ulmer's first Canadian film. *Damaged Lives* (1933), his very first solo directorial effort, and a much more accomplished work, is technically Canadian. Although this propaganda drama, warning against venereal disease, was made in Hollywood, it was sponsored by the Canadian Social Health Council and received its premiere in Toronto. The only print of *From Nine to Nine* in North America, held by Canada's national archives, is missing sound on one reel, but in a European film archive there is a complete print (albeit 16mm, but possibly full length) which had been acquired from the late, great film collector William K. Everson.

Peter Rist

WILLIAM FRUET. Born 1933, Lethbridge, Alberta. Director, screenwriter. Before directing, William Fruet had a varied career that included acting (DRYLAN-DERS), still photography, directing medical films, and editing at the CBC. The critical success of Fruet's first scripts, the DON SHEBIB films GOIN' DOWN THE ROAD and *Rip-Off* (1971), facilitated his entry into directing. Fruet's directorial debut, *Wedding in White*, continued the success by garnering the Canadian Best Feature Award for 1972. Set in Western Canada during World War II, *Wedding in White* is a bleak, claustrophobic drama of lower class, small-town patriarchal oppression. A timid young woman (Carol Kane) is raped and impregnated by her brother's war buddy. To save family honor, a family friend (played by Donald Pleasence) arranges a marriage to a man old enough to be Kane's grandfather. Fruet talked about the emotional drain of such a project, and expressed interest in making more commercial films. Intentionally or not, Fruet's career veered in that direction, to the detriment of his artistic development. The majority of Fruet's subsequent films have been in the thriller and horror genres. His most notorious film, *Death Weekend*, was universally panned by Canadian critics, though it won prizes for Direction and Best Picture at Spain's Sitges International Horror Film Festival. *Death Weekend*, with its crude style and misanthropic vision, remains one of the few genuine Canadian exploitation films. Fruet's later work seems to answer the oppressive patriarchy of *Wedding in White* with strong female characters. In the survivalist thriller *Death Weekend*, a woman is forced to turn on her aggressors; in the *Alien* (United States, 1979) clone *Blue Monkey* (1987), a female doctor becomes a Sigourney Weaveresque heroine; and the otherwise limp thriller *Bedroom Eyes* features a resourceful female psychiatrist in a central role. *Blue Monkey* and *Spasms* are routine "monster-on-the-loose" (respectively, a huge insectoid and a snake) horror films that borrow liberally from *Them!* (United States, 1954), *Alien*, and DAVID CRONENBERG's *SHIVERS* and *Brood*. The better of the two, *Blue Monkey*, oddly enough recalls *Wedding in White* with its primarily single-set location (a hospital) and claustrophobic atmosphere. Fruet has continued working in the horror genre, directing mainly for U.S. television ("Ray Bradbury Theatre," "Friday the 13th: The Series").

FEATURE FILMS AS DIRECTOR: *Wedding in White*, 1972; *Italy* (TV); *Bring Whiskey and a Smile*, 1974; *Death Weekend (House by the Lake)*, 1976; *One of Our Own* (TV); *Search and Destroy (Striking Back)*, 1979; *Cries in the Night (Funeral Home)*, 1980; *Baker County, USA (Trapped)*; *Chatwill's Verdict*, 1981 (TV); *Spasms (Death Bite)*, 1982; *Killer Instinct*, 1985; *Bedroom Eyes; Killer Party*, 1986; *Blue Monkey (Insect, Green Monkey, Invasion of the Bodysuckers)*, 1987.

BIBLIOGRAPHY: George Csaba Koller, "Bill Fruet's *Wedding in White*," *Cinema Canada* (August 1972): 42–47, 57; Piers Handling, "Bill Fruet: 2 or 3 things . . ." *Cinema Canada* (September 1977): 43–46.

                                                                          Donato Totaro

G

CHIEF DAN GEORGE. Born 1899, North Vancouver, B.C.; died 1981. Actor. Born on the reservation of the Tse-Lat Watt band, a branch of the Coatslish First Nations people, with the tribal name of Geswanouth Slaholt, Dan George went to missionary school and became a logger at the age of sixteen. In 1921 he got a job as a stevedore and worked on the docks for twenty-six years until an accident forced him to return to logging and construction. Married at nineteen, he had six children, one of whom, Robert, became an actor, appearing in the TV show "Caribou Country." It was on this series, at the age of sixty-one, that Chief Dan George first appeared as an actor when the white man playing the Indian chief fell ill and a quick replacement was required. Robert suggested his father, who took up acting not just for his son, but also because he saw it as an opportunity to forward the cause of aboriginal people in Canada and the United States, both in life and in their media representation. George, actual Chief of the Coatslish for twelve years, as well as honorary Chief of the Squamish and Sushwap tribes in the early seventies, brought an overwhelming sense of dignity to the parts he played, sometimes against all odds. Working in Canada on such films as *Cold Journey, Alien Thunder*, and *Shadow of the Hawk*, he usually played either a tribal medicine man or storyteller. Offscreen he made speeches on behalf of First Nations Canadians at banquets and presented one-man shows at playhouses and hotels. In 1967 he presented a soliloquy at Canada's centenary celebrations, representing the Native people's contribution to that event. He will perhaps be best remembered for his work in two Hollywood films, Clint Eastwood's *The Outlaw Josey Wales* (1976) and Arthur Penn's *Little Big Man* (1970). He received an Oscar nomination for his majestic supporting performance as Old Lodge Skins in the latter. Although not necessarily a versatile actor, he honed his portrayals of aboriginal people, finding the truth in even the most hackneyed dialogue and the most absurd and even stereotypical situations. Chief Dan George died in 1981, having made a considerable contribution to his dream of seeing his people "raised by my words and example in films and on television . . . to the norms of society."

FILMS AS ACTOR: *Education of Phyllistine*, 1965; *Alien Thunder* (a.k.a. *Dan Candy's Law)*, 1974; *Cold Journey*, 1971–76; *Shadow of the Hawk*, 1976; *Spirit of the Wind*, 1979; *Nothing Personal* (Can/US), 1980.

BIBLIOGRAPHY: Wayne Varga, "His Son Just Happened to Have One at Home," *International Herald Tribune* (March 1, 1971); Ahmed Lat, "Dan George Preaches Equality to Whites, Fellow Indians," *Movieland* (May 14, 1971).

Simon Brown

RÉMY GIRARD. Born 1950, Jonquière, Quebec. Actor. Rémy Girard began a theatrical career in the 1970s, first in Quebec City and subsequently in Montreal. Successful performances at the Theatre du Vieux Québec did not initially lead him into film. He appeared in only a few small roles until 1981, when he received his first major role as the psychiatrist/king in Helen Doyle and Nicole Guigiere's *This Isn't Wonderland*, a modern reworking of the *Alice in Wonderland* story. In 1986 Girard achieved stardom with his explosively comic portrayal of the compulsive womanizer Rémy, in LE DÉCLIN DE L'EMPIRE AMÉRICAIN. In the film's most flamboyant role, Girard dominates the first half, making a potentially loathsome character both appealing and funny. Two years later, Girard appeared with MARIE TIFO in *Kalamazoo*, a film about a bachelor who dreams that the woman he loves is a mermaid. His performance was singled out for praise. His talents were better served by Yves Simoneau in *Dans le ventre du dragon*, in which Girard plays part of a Laurel and Hardy–like double act of leaflet distributors trying to save their friend from the clutches of a mad scientist. A witty script and a fine rapport with co-star MICHEL CÔTÉ enabled Girard to give one of his funniest and most technically accomplished performances. With an eye for a good role, Girard chose a supporting part in JÉSUS DE MONTRÉAL. Again, Girard provides the comic highlights of the film, this time teamed with director Robert Lepage (clearly having enormous fun). In *L'homme idéal* (1996), Girard offers a male rendition of the orgasm scene from Hollywood's *When Harry Met Sally*. Very popular in Quebec, Girard is an undiscovered comic talent, internationally.

FILMS AS ACTOR: *La conquête*, 1973; *Les beaux souvenirs; C'est pas le pays des merveilles/This Isn't Wonderland* (short), 1981; *Les yeux rouges ou les vérités accidentelles*, 1982; *Le crime d'Ovide Plouffe*, 1984; *Trouble* (short), 1985; *Le lys cassé*, (short); *Le déclin de l'empire américain*, 1986; *Kalamazoo; Le chemin de Damas*, 1988; *Dans le ventre du dragon; Jésus de Montréal; Les portes tournantes*, 1989; *Montréal vu par . . . ; Amoureux fou; La pagaille*, 1991; *La Florida*, 1993; *Le secret de Jérôme*, 1994; *Lilies; Fish Tale Soup; L'homme idéal*, 1996; *Les Boys; Le siège de l'âme*, 1997.

Simon Brown

JACQUES GODBOUT. Born 1933, Montreal. Director, novelist, poet. Jacques Godbout is part of the 1960s generation of Quebec filmmakers that collectively revolutionized French-language filmmaking at the NFB/ONF. After completing his master's thesis on the poet Arthur Rimbaud, Godbout moved to Ethiopia, where he taught philosophy and French for three years. Upon returning to Montreal in 1958 he began a long, fruitful career at the NFB. Alongside his films, Godbout has published two collections of poems, written several celebrated novels, founded the magazine *Liberté* (1959), and been the recipient of several arts and letters prizes. The breadth of subject matter and intellectual rigor of his extensive documentary work reflect this cultural richness. His documentaries include biographies on the Quebec modernist painter Borduas (*Paul-Emile Borduas*); Ernest Dufault, who withheld his true Quebecois identity to become a legendary "American" cowboy (*Alias Will James*); the Quebec writer and filmmaker Hubert Aquin (*Deux episodes dans la vie d'Hubert Aquin*); and Hans Selye, the Viennese psychologist who pioneered stress analysis (*Pour l'amour du stress*). Other documentaries include a trilogy of films deconstructing various aspects of media (*Derrière l'image, Feu l'objectivité, Distortions*), and studies on international politics (*Un monologue nord-sud*) and Quebec-Canada politics (*Le mouton noir, Le sort de l'Amerique*). Godbout's formal choices consistently enrich his thematics. For example, in *Alias Will James*, he includes footage of Hollywood Westerns based on Will James' writings. Likewise, to mirror Aquin's complex life, Godbout intercuts between footage from a spy film featuring Aquin, *Faux Bond*, and interviews with people who knew him. Though primarily a documentarist, Godbout has excelled in his few fictional forays. These include *Kid Sentiment* (1967), a Richard Lester/Jean Rouch–inspired film in which go-go meets *cinéma direct; IXE-13* (1971), the classic musical comedy; and *La gammick* (1974), a thriller about a small-time Quebec gangster. After nearly forty years, Godbout decided to leave the ONF. *Le sort de l'Amerique* represents his last Film Board work.

FILMS AS DIRECTOR INCLUDE: *Les administrateurs* (short, co-dir., Fernand Danserau), 1960; *Paul-Emile Borduas* (short), 1963; *Rose et Landry* (co-dir., Jean Rouch), 1963; *Huit témoins*, 1965; *YUL 871*, 1966; *Kid Sentiment*, 1967; *L'homme multiplié* (short), 1969; *Les vrais cousins*, 1970; *IXE-13*, 1971; *La gammick*, 1974; *Aimez-vous les chiens?*, 1975; *Arsenal*, 1976; *Derrière l'image*, 1978; *Deux episodes dans la vie d'Hubert Aquin*, 1979; *Feu l'objectivité* (short), 1979; *Distortions*, 1981; *Un monologue nord-sud*, 1982; *Québec Soft* (short), 1985; *Alias Will James; En dernier recours*, 1988; *Pour l'amour du stress*, 1991; *Le mouton noir*, 1992; *L'affaire Norman William*, 1994; *Le sort de l'Amerique*, 1996.

BIBLIOGRAPHY: Claude Racine, "Entretien avec Jacques Godbout," *24 Images*, no. 62–63 (Summer 1992): 66–70; Martine Rainville, "Jacques Godbout: A Happy Phoenix" (trans. Erica Pomerance), *Point of View*, no. 30 (Fall 1996): 13–17.

Donato Totaro

GOIN' DOWN THE ROAD. Donald Shebib, Toronto, 1970, 87 min., color, 16mm (blown up to 35mm). Released in 1970 at the height of the artistic and academic debate concerning a Canadian national identity, *Goin' Down the Road* was quickly and warmly embraced as the quintessential Canadian film—a designation which has long since haunted both the film itself and the character of Canadian cinema. The film has, certainly, established itself as a watershed in English-language Canadian cinema, and clearly set up what were to become characteristics of Canadian film in the 1970s. The story follows two Cape Breton Islanders, Pete (Doug McGrath) and Joey (Paul Bradley), as they drive west to Toronto in the hope of escaping the poverty and ennui of maritime living, only to discover that the city is not as hospitable as they had imagined. Undiscouraged, the pair search for jobs, eventually working together loading trucks at a pop factory. Joey meets Betty (the brilliant Jayne Eastwood), a waitress, and the two quickly establish a relationship; when Betty becomes pregnant, Pete urges Joey to travel further west with him, but Joey refuses and marries Betty. The duo—now a trio, with a fourth on the way—are eventually forced to move into a squalid Cabbagetown rooming house and become increasingly disheartened. Following a bungled attempt to rob a grocery store of some food, Betty leaves, and the two men are evicted. The film ends with an ironic recapitulation of the energetic opening sequence as the two drive west, into the sunset. *Goin' Down the Road* was shot on 16mm, most often with a hand-held camera, which gives the film a *cinéma direct*, documentary quality; director DON SHEBIB enhances this effect through careful and subtle direction. In its portrayal of downtrodden, alienated Canadians, its use of documentary techniques, and its relentless pessimism, *Goin' Down the Road* established (at least in the eyes of audiences) many of the characteristics of Canadian cinema in the 1970s.

BIBLIOGRAPHY: Marshall Delaney, "Nothing but Heartaches," in Feldman, 13–15.

Mitch Parry

GOLDEN GLOVES. Gilles Groulx, (Montreal) ONF, 1961, 28 min., b+w, 16mm. An essential work of the *cinéma direct québécois, Golden Gloves*, while providing a portrait of young aspiring boxers and also describing their social milieu, is a documentary sporting a dazzling technical virtuosity. The "participating camera" (in Gilles Marsolais' words) is here exploited to its maximum potential: the proximity of the mobile camera glimpsing the boxers in their training sessions; frequent variations in camera angle. To this dynamism of the image is added a utilization of montage which allowed Groulx not only to elaborate on an audacious rhythm, but also to provide an ironic commentary. Thus, when a man crashes to the canvas after suffering a knockout punch from Ronald Jones, Groulx superimposes in voice-off the commentary of the same defeated boxer exclaiming that "Jones isn't a hard puncher." The credit sequence, during which one sees the boxers in training, also demonstrates the director's editing talents. Over one of Les Jérolas' songs, Groulx multiplies short shots of boxers skipping, wherein the rhythm of the images is apparently in perfect time with the song (through montage). Spoken by CLAUDE JUTRA, the narration of *Golden Gloves* is, above all, informative, revealing the social world of boxers and, further, the pressures to which they are exposed through the competition for the Golden Gloves. Faithful to the spirit of *direct*, Groulx equally leaves a lot of space for the boxers to express themselves freely and with spontaneity in front of the camera. That is especially the case for Ronald Jones, a charismatic young black boxer living on unemployment insurance, whom Groulx doesn't cease to foreground throughout the film, allowing us to discover the director's love for the underprivileged.

BIBLIOGRAPHY: Robert Daudelin.

Louis Goyette

GRAHAM GREENE. Born 1952, Brantford, Ontario. Actor. One of a group of male First Nations actors* to have recently come to prominence in Canadian film and television, Graham Greene was in the forefront of this movement when he was nominated for an Oscar for Best Supporting Actor in Kevin Costner's *Dances with Wolves* (United States, 1990). Born on the Six Nation reserve, the second of six children, he dropped out of school at age sixteen and left for the United States, only to return to Canada to study welding in Toronto. After working in a Hamilton factory, he got involved in the music business, working in a sound studio and as a roadie, and got his first acting job in 1974, as a Native American. Before getting his big Hollywood break, Greene had really paid his dues, interspersing acting with a variety of trades, including welding, landscape gardening, carpentry, bartending, and high-steel work. He was often cast in First Nation roles, including the stereotypic "drunken Indian," and unfortunately was forced to battle alcoholism off-stage as well. His first film role came in 1982 with *Running Brave*, where he played a friend of the Olympic champion and Native American long distance runner Billy Mills (Robbie Benson). After a difficult period in the 1980s, he returned to the screen in Jonathan Wacks' *Powwow Highway* (United States, 1989), a kind of First Nations "road movie," and found success on the Toronto stage in Cree author Tomson Highway's *Dry Lips Oughta Move to Kapuskasing*. Following *Wolves*, he was offered numerous Hollywood film roles, and smartly chose John Fusco's fictionalized script of the Oglala, South Dakota, incident, playing the part of the Sioux reserve's wily police officer, Walter Crow Horse, in *Thunderheart* (Michael Apted, 1992). Although he is best known for his U.S. films, Greene has been able to expand his acting range in his Canadian work, stretching his tough, proud persona into the crazed defender of aboriginal rights in *Clear-Cut* (1991), the powerful but misguided first Canadian feature for Polish refugee Richard Bu-

*Others include Tom Jackson (Canadian TV series, "North of 60"), Gary Farmer (*Powwow Highway*; Jim Jarmush's *Dead Man*, 1996, United States), and Russell Means (*Last of the Mohicans*, Michael Mann, 1992, United States).

gajski. He has also played the gullible Will, a successful photographer who is tricked into reintegrating himself to his Alberta native home, in *Medicine River* (perhaps the first film to consistently and successfully represent First Nations humor), and was memorable, appearing for only a few minutes, as a scene-stealing Georgia con man who poses as an aristocratic record producer in Asian Canadian Deepa Mehta's *Camilla* (UK/Canada, 1994).

FILMS AS ACTOR: *Running Brave*, 1983; *Where the Spirit Lives* (TV), 1989; *Clear-Cut; Lost in the Barrens*, 1991; *Medicine River* (TV); *Spirit Rider*, 1993; *Camilla* (UK/Can); *Rugged Gold* (TV, NZ/Can), 1994; *Dead Innocent; Sabotage*, 1996; *Heart of the Sun* (NZ/Can); *Wounded; The Education of Little Tree*, 1997.

BIBLIOGRAPHY: Brian D. Johnson, "Dances with Oscar: Canadian Actor Graham Greene Tastes Stardom," *Maclean's* (March 25, 1991): 60–61.

Peter Rist

LORNE GREENE. Born 1915, Ottawa, Ontario; died 1987, Santa Monica, California. Actor, narrator. Lorne Greene will be best remembered as the ultimate patriarch, Ben Cartwright, in the long-running and oft-repeated U.S. TV series "Bonanza." He should be equally remembered, however, as the authoritative voice of Canada, whose strong and confident narration set the patriotic tone for the National Film Board's wartime documentaries. His career as an actor began at Queen's University when he joined the university's drama guild. By the time he graduated with a degree in engineering, he had performed in and directed numerous productions and won a fellowship to New York's Neighborhood Playhouse, where he stayed for approximately two years. When he returned to Canada, he began to work in radio and was eventually named chief announcer for the CBC. It was his powerful voice that brought him to the attention of the newly formed NFB, who enlisted Greene as narrator for their new wartime documentary series, "Canada Carries On." The films, many of which were directed by STUART LEGG, were designed to boost the national morale and confidence in the Canadian contribution to the war effort. Greene narrated over twenty-two of them between 1940 and 1945. In 1942, when the NFB launched its second documentary series, "World in Action," Greene was once again taken on board. As a narrator, he had become familiar to audiences around the world. His booming voice, which commanded the audience's attention, left no room for doubt or hesitancy. Following the war, Greene returned to radio and co-founded the Jupiter Theatre in Toronto. In the 1950s, he moved to New York and relaunched his own acting career by taking on the role of Big Brother in Studio One's version of George Orwell's *1984*. He continued to appear on stage, at the Stratford Shakespeare Festival in Canada and on Broadway, while simultaneously making numerous TV appearances. His TV roles would eventually lead to his being cast in "Bonanza" (1959–71), when Lorne Greene himself would become as famous as his voice.

FILM AS ACTOR: *Klondike Fever*, 1979.

FILMS AS NARRATOR INCLUDE: "Canada Carries On"—*Atlantic Patrol; Wings of Youth*, 1940; *Guards of the North; Churchill's Island; Battle for Oil; Warclouds in the Pacific*, 1941; *Geopolitik—Hitler's Plan for Empire; Women Are Warriors*, 1942; *Fighting Norway; Up from the Ranks*, 1943; *UNNRA—In the Wake of the Armies; Homefront*, 1944; *Back to Jobs; Gateway to Asia*, 1945; *River Watch; Tomorrow's Citizens; What's on Your Mind?*, 1947; *Arctic Jungle; Maps We Live By* (revised), 1948; *A Capital Plan; White Fortress*, 1949; *Hunters of the North Pole; Horizons of Quebec*, 1950. "World in Action"—*Inside Fighting Russia; Inside Fighting China; The Mask of Nippon*, 1942; *Battle Is Their Birthright; The War for Men's Minds*, 1943; *Our Northern Neighbour; Battle of Europe*, 1944; *Balkan Powderkeg; Food—Secret of the Peace*, 1945. Features: *A Matter of Fat*, 1969; *Wings in the Wilderness*, 1974; *That's Country*, 1976.

Stacey Abbott

THE GREY FOX. Phillip Borsos, British Columbia, 1982, 91 min., color. *The Grey Fox* is both a loving paean to the Western and a revisionist critique of its codes and conventions. Based on the life of Arizona's "Gentleman Bandit" Bill Miner, the film begins in 1901 with Miner released from prison after a thirty-three-year sentence. Miner (Richard Farnsworth), not your typical gunslinger, is a calm, reflective outsider trying to adjust to a changed society; he is a social alter ego rather than a "civilizing agent." For example, he quickly sees through the exploitative mining industry, and sympathizes with the plight of immigrants ("They're a world away from home," also a cultural reflection on his own societal alienation). Unlike the traditional Westerner, Miner falls in love, and not with a schoolmarm but with a feisty, independent, and politically progressive Eastern blue-blood, Kathlyn Flynn (JACKIE BURROUGHS in a performance modeled on Katharine Hepburn). PHILLIP BORSOS gives us other atypical Western characters, such as a corporal torn between duty and his admiration for Miner, and—typically—a polite RCMP officer. Borsos uses reflexive touches to recall the West, such as shooting in an early film style (black and white, undercranked shots) and intercutting footage from *The Great Train Robbery* (1903). However, the film's authenticity owes much to Frank Tidy's remarkable period cinematography. Tidy uses low-key lighting, reflecting surfaces, and on-location nighttime photography to recreate a turn of the century kerosene lamp atmosphere. While *The Grey Fox* won seven Genie Awards, including Best Feature Film and Best Direction, Tidy lost out to MICHEL BRAULT (*Threshold*, 1983) for Best Cinematography.

BIBLIOGRAPHY: Pauline Kael, "The Grey Fox," *New Yorker* (August 8, 1983): 87; Vernon Young, "Of Mice and Wolves and Hounded Men," *Hudson Review*, no. 37 (1984): 289–94.

Donato Totaro

GREY OWL'S LITTLE BROTHER. Gordon Sparling, Montreal and Alberta, 1932, 11 min., b+w. *Grey Owl's Little Brother* was compiled from two earlier silent films (*Beaver People*, 1928, and *Beaver Family*, 1929) made by Englishman William J. Oliver, who had settled in Calgary in 1910 and become a free-lance photographer. According to film historian Peter Morris, Oliver's films, which he wrote, designed, shot, and edited for the National Parks Bureau, stood out from other documentaries of their period, having "a superior photographic quality" as well as "unity, warmth and human interest." Some of these films, which featured "Grey Owl," a naturalist whom we now know to have been English posing as an "Indian," were re-edited with sound added by Canada's most successful filmmaker of the 1930s, GORDON SPARLING. Whereas Sparling's work with music and voice-over narration now seems considerably dated, it is clear that the effect of anthropomorphizing animals, in this case the "little brother" beaver, was ahead of its time. Ever since *Gertie the Dinosaur* in 1911, film audiences had become familiar with the personification of cartoon animals, but Sparling pioneered the nature film exploited later by Disney, while simul-taneously creating a Canadian documentary genre through the combination of light comedy, self-deprecation, and a treatment of nature as wild and unspoiled, yet harmonious. As we see the beaver cleaning himself, Corey Thomson's voice tells of "table manners." One can well imagine the hard work ethic of an emerg-ing nation rubbing off on the beaver when we see him rapidly gnawing a twig, and hear that he only has a limited time to build his "house."

BIBLIOGRAPHY: Peter Morris (1978), 169–72, 230–31.

Peter Rist

JOHN GRIERSON. Born 1898, Deanston, Scotland; died 1972, Bath, England. Although he never directed, or even produced, a single film in Canada, John Grierson is arguably the single most important figure in the development of Canadian film. Both of his parents were teachers, and his father was headmaster of a Calvinist village school, a heritage that no doubt influenced his didacticism. His studies at Glasgow University were interrupted by World War I, in which he served on a minesweeper, but he returned and earned an M.A. in philosophy with distinction in 1923. He lectured at Durham University, then at the Univer-sity of Chicago on a Rockefeller Fellowship (between 1924 and 1927). After his return to England he was appointed films officer of the Empire Marketing Board in 1929, beginning his almost evangelical mission to create documentary films (a term he invented). There he directed his only film, *Drifters*, which was clearly inspired by Soviet films of the 1920s. In 1930 he established the "film unit" at the Board, which trained filmmakers and produced over 100 films before it was disbanded in September 1933. Grierson moved to the GPO, where his efforts enabled some of history's greatest documentaries to be made. In May 1938 he arrived in Canada, and showed great bureaucratic skill, encouraging the drafting of the National Film Act to establish the National Film Board of Can-ada, which passed on March 6, 1939. In October, he reluctantly accepted the position of NFB Film Commissioner in which he was to function as an adviser. But he immediately began hiring people from Britain, including STUART LEGG, and gradually eliminated the rival Motion Picture Bureau of Canada (under Captain Frank C. Badgeley). In February 1940, the first wartime "informational" series of films was launched, "Canada Carries On." By December 1942, the NFB was employing 293 people, and by April 1945, it was the largest producer of documentaries in the world (with a staff of 739). Grierson preferred to hire young Canadians with a good degree in political science or economics, saying that "if they really wanted to make movies they weren't hired." Though he championed creativity and hired filmmakers such as NORMAN MCLAREN, Grierson's emphasis on the content of social documentaries characterized the NFB for years to come. He resigned his position as commissioner in 1945, and, after being hounded out of the United States for alleged communism, he spent many years in Europe before returning to Canada to teach at McGill University in 1969, stimulating a new following for Grierson and his own particular brand of filmmaking. In recent years, though, his status has been called into question, with him being regarded variously as authoritarian, patriarchal, and colonialist (see Joyce Nelson, for example).

BIBLIOGRAPHY: James Beveridge; the John Grierson Project: McGill University; Joyce Nelson.

Peter Rist

GILLES GROULX. Born 1931, Montreal; died 1994. Film director, editor, screenwriter. Before becoming Quebec cinema's premier modernist and Marxist filmmaker from the mid-1960s onwards, Gilles Groulx was a painter and a poet, one inspired by Paul-Émile Borduas' famous *Refus global* manifesto. Groulx's rebellious nature and keen intellect were surely instrumental in his teaming up with cinematographer/director MICHEL BRAULT, with whom he paved the way for *cinéma direct*. The first short they shot together, *LES RAQUETTEURS* (1958), simultaneously marks the birth of the movement, the true beginnings of the NFB's French Office National du Film, and a truly remarkable film career for Gilles Groulx, one spent almost exclusively in the ranks of the ONF, an institution which, ironically, he very often had to fight and trick to fulfill his creative vision. Whereas he got to shoot *GOLDEN GLOVES* (1961) with minimal interference, that wasn't the case with most of his films. *Les raquetteurs* was almost shelved when it didn't comply with the "4 minute objective reportage" rule. Groulx took his name off *Normétal* (1959) when the NFB asked him to depoliticize his documentary about a small mining town. In 1965, he softened the discourse of his award-winning *Un jeu si simple*, a poetic and political documentary on hockey, so it could be released. A year before, he secretly turned a short documentary commission about winter into his first feature-length fiction film, *LE CHAT DANS LE SAC*, to great critical acclaim. Groulx pulled the same trick again with *Où êtes-vous donc?* (1968), morphing an expected documentary study of *Québécois* pop music into a Brechtian fiction analyzing the state of Quebec's culture and society, a kaleidoscopic collage on a par with Jean-Luc

Godard's best work. But nothing equals the five-year battle which surrounded *24 HEURES OU PLUS* . . . (1971–77), his best and most ambitious documentary but also his most political. Perhaps Groulx's radical creativity would not have blossomed in a more hospitable environment. Yet, in quieter times, he continued to grow as an artist and an activist. In 1969, he directed *Entre tu et vous*, a modernist autopsy of one couple's alienation in a media and publicity driven world. In 1977, a co-production deal between the NFB and Mexico made it possible for him to shoot a documentary on the militant efforts of Mexican farmers demanding agricultural reforms (*Primera pregunta sobre la felicidad/ Première question sur le bonheur*). And he surprised everyone with his final opus, *Au pays de Zom* (1982), Quebec's only filmed Marxist opera/fable! If only a violent car accident hadn't seriously impaired Gilles Groulx in the early eighties, he would surely have continued to rock the boat, surprise us, and enrich Quebec and Canadian cinema for many years to come.

FILMS AS DIRECTOR: *Les raquetteurs* (co-dir., M. Brault) (short), 1958; *Normétal* (short), 1959; *La France sur un caillou* (co-dir., C. Fournier) (short), 1960; *Golden Gloves* (short), 1961; *Voir Miami* . . . (short), 1963, *Le chat dans le sac*, 1964; *Un jeu si simple* (short), 1964–65; *Quebec* . . . (co-dir., G. Godin) (short), 1966; *Où êtes-vous donc?*, 1968; *Entre tu et vous*, 1969; *Place de l'équation* (short), 1973; *24 heures ou plus* . . . , 1971–77; *Primera pregunta sobre la felicidad/Première question sur le bonheur*, 1977; *Au pays de Zom*, 1982.

BIBLIOGRAPHY: Jean-Pierre Bastien (1978); Roger Bourdeau, "L'utilisation du montage dans l'oeuvre de Gilles Groulx," *24 Images*, no. 5 (May 1980): 54–62.

Johanne Larue

LUCE GUILBEAULT. Born 1935, Montreal; died 1991. Actor, director. Luce Guilbeault's first filmmaking experience came in 1956 when she and her then husband Guy Borremans borrowed a camera from CLAUDE JUTRA and shot an experimental film in a cabin by a lake. She acted and later wrote the narration. Entitled *La femme, l'oiseleur et la maison*, it has since been lost. Although a successful stage actress, Guilbeault had to wait fifteen years before working in film again. It was the up and coming DENYS ARCAND who brought her back to the medium by casting her as the lead in his first feature, *La maudite galette* (1971), and confirmed her star status by giving her the title role in *RÉJEANNE PADOVANI*. Guilbeault was captivated by the medium and the talented young filmmakers emerging in Quebec in the 1970s, and as a result she began working continuously in film, appearing in three more films in 1971 alone. She quickly became critical of the stereotypical roles offered to her, mostly waitresses and housewives, but fortunately found her way into a successful collaboration with ANNE-CLAIRE POIRIER which enabled her to stretch her talents. In *Le temps de l'avant* Guilbeault brings warmth and understanding to her role as a mother contemplating abortion, while in the ensemble piece *La quarantaine*, about life after the age of forty, she provides a sincere performance as an actress facing middle age. In 1972, while appearing in JACQUES LEDUC's collaborative production *Tendresse ordinaire*, she assisted in its production as well as performing in it. This sparked her own desire to make films, which would later come to fruition in 1975 with the release of her documentary *Denyse Benoît, comédienne*. The film follows the work of the title actress, who used drama and theater as a form of therapy for the residents of a retirement home. Guilbeault's two subsequent films as director, *Some American Feminists* and *D'abord ménagère*, each address distinct aspects of womanhood and give equal voice to women, whether housewives or renowned feminists, speaking about their life and work. In the 1980s, Guilbeault's presence on screen began to decrease and she turned more to teaching and production. In 1991 she was made president of Rendezvous du Cinéma Québécois. One of Quebec's leading actresses, she was awarded the NFB's Iris Award for her career achievements.

FILMS AS ACTOR INCLUDE: *La femme, l'oiseleur et la maison* (short), 1957; *Percé on the Rock* (short; voice only), 1964; *La maudite galette; IXE-13; Le temps d'une chasse; Françoise Durocher, Waitress* (short), 1971; *Le grand sabordage* (Can/Fr); *Tendresse ordinaire; OK . . . la liberté; Réjeanne Padovani*, 1972; *Souris, tu m'inquietes*, 1973; *Les beaux dimanches; Par une belle nuit d'hiver* (short), 1974; *Mustang; Le temps de l'avant*, 1975; *J. A. Martin, photographe*, 1976; *Angela* (Can/US), 1978; *Mourir à tue-tête*, 1979; *La quarantaine; Albédo*, 1982; *Qui a tiré sur nos histoires d'amour* (short), 1986; *Petit drame dans la vie d'une femme* (short), 1990.

FILMS AS DIRECTOR: *Denyse Benoît, comédienne* (short), 1975; *Some American Feminists*, 1977; *D'abord ménagères*, 1978.

BIBLIOGRAPHY: Jacques Leduc, "Luce Guilbeault: Paralle-mene," *Cinéma Québec* 1, no. 6 (December 1971).

Stacey Abbott

H

RICK HANCOX. Born 1946, Toronto, Ontario. Director, writer, editor, camera operator. Rick Hancox has influenced a generation of young avant-garde film-makers, both through the examples offered by his films and through his work as a teacher. Hancox was born in Toronto, but spent much of his childhood traveling across the country. He studied English literature at the University of Prince Edward Island, and considered poetry as his first artistic medium. However, at university he became interested in film, and in avant-garde film in particular, and began making his own films. After completing his undergraduate degree, he continued his film studies at the graduate level at New York University, and received his M.F.A from Ohio University in 1973. He was part of the Toronto Filmmakers' Co-op in the early 1970s, but his real period of involvement with other filmmakers followed his decision to teach film at Sheridan College in Oakville, Ontario, where he resided from 1973 to 1985. He left Sheridan to teach in the Communications Studies Department at Montreal's Concordia University. As a teacher, he has influenced (and been influenced by) students as diverse as MIKE HOOLBOOM, JANIS COLE, and HOLLY DALE. Hancox's oeuvre is quite varied, ranging from experimental collage (*Rose*) to dramatic narratives (*Tall Dark Stranger*); above all, Hancox is concerned with the role landscape plays in the creation of Canadian experimental film, which he has treated in what he calls his "poetry films"—*Waterworx*, which won first prize at the Eighth San Francisco Poetry Film Festival, *LANDFALL*, and *Beach Events*, which took first prize at the Third Experimental Film Coalition Festival in Chicago (1986). Perhaps as a result of his early work as a poet, Hancox is interested in issues of time and memory, and he attempts to deconstruct the privileging of the present over the past. Although his works explore formal aspects of filmmaking, they also deal with broader philosophical and existential issues.

FILMS AS DIRECTOR INCLUDE: *Rose*, 1968; *Cab 16*, 1969; *Tall Dark Stranger*, 1970; *Next to Me*, 1971; *House Movie*, 1972; *Wild Sync*, 1973; *Home for Christmas*, 1977; *Zum Ditter*, 1979; *Reunion in Dunnville*, 1981; *Waterworx (A Clear Day & No Memories)*, 1982; *LANDFALL*, 1983; *Beach Events*, 1986; *Moose Jaw (There's a Future in Our Past)*, 1992.

BIBLIOGRAPHY: Rick Hancox and Catherine Jonasson.

Mitch Parry

HARD CORE LOGO. Bruce McDonald, British Columbia, 1996, color. BRUCE MCDONALD's fourth film, and the conclusion to an "unofficial trilogy" of road movies—which began with ROADKILL (1989) and *Highway 61* (1991)—*Hard Core Logo* focuses directly on a fictional punk band from Vancouver as it tries to make one last tour of the Canadian midwest, and, metaphorically on the passage of youth. McDonald employs the familiar techniques of the *cinéma vérité* documentarist to present this fictional band. While comparisons to Rob Reiner's satirical *This Is Spinal Tap* (United States, 1984) are inevitable, McDonald's film infuses its comedic moments with a far darker perspective. The leader of the band, Joe Dick (Hugh Dillon), fabricates the story of a tragic injury to a former punk icon and friend of the group, Bucky Haight (Julian Richings), to cajole his former mates into one last tour. The other principal member of the group, Billy Tallent (Callum Keith Rennie), has aspirations of making it big in Seattle (aspirations he conceals from Dick). Mid-tour the band makes a rendezvous with Haight, and the members realize that Dick has lied to get them together. Amid expressions of despair, paranoia, and betrayal the tour ends, culminating in an onstage altercation between Joe and Billy. With the realization that he cannot maintain his life as it is or go back to where he was, Joe Dick decides to commit suicide on-camera at the film's conclusion. Many who read Michael Turner's collection of poems, songs, and ramblings would consider the question of filming *Hard Core Logo* an impossibility, and it is a credit to McDonald's vision and his considerable skills as a director that he was able to pull off filming such a source. McDonald plays with the numerous clichés of the "rockumentary" throughout, deriving both comedic and critical value from their repetition. The use of nonprofessional actor Dillon, lead singer of the group The Headstones, provides the film with a powerful onscreen stage performance, one that makes us believe the viability of the fictional group. After opening at the Vancouver Film Festival the film enjoyed both popular and critical success, garnering Genie nominations for Best Picture, Directing, and Screenplay, ultimately losing that year to CRASH and LILIES.

BIBLIOGRAPHY: Michael Turner.

Dave Douglas

HARVEY HART. Born 1928, Toronto; died 1989. Director. The most prolific English Canadian film director of his generation, Harvey Hart was once thought to be a filmmaker to watch after the promise of *Bus Riley's Back in Town* (United States, 1965). Hart was educated at the University of Toronto and began working at CBC television in one of its first production units during the 1950s with Robert Allen, PAUL ALMOND, Arthur Hiller, Norman Jewison, and Sydney Newman. After apprenticing in New York he began directing live drama and films in the "Festival" series, including "The Crucible," "The Luck of Ginger Coffey" (both 1959), "The Dybbuk," and "Enemy of the People" (both 1960). From 1963 to 1971 he worked mostly in the United States directing episodes of TV series such as "Alfred Hitchcock Presents," and theatrical features, including *Bus Riley* and *The Sweet Ride* (1968). His first Canadian theatrical feature is also his best known, *Fortune and Men's Eyes* (1971). Filmed on location in Quebec Prison and adapted from John Herbert's controversial play depicting the brutalities of prison life, *Fortune* maintains the tendency of Canadian film and television to be more realist than its U.S. counterparts. It is also graced with some fine acting by mostly unknowns and deliberately drab color cinematography by Georges Dufaux which brilliantly evokes entrapment by insistently viewing the male prisoners through bars, doorways, shelving, and so on. But it teeters on hysterical melodrama, and, in its relentlessly depressing homophobic action, does little to encourage prison reform. Over the next sixteen years, based mainly in Canada, Hart directed no less than thirty-one feature films, many of which were made for television. His last film, *Bloodsport*, was shot in Toronto and British Columbia for U.S. television and released in 1989, the year that he died of a heart attack.

CANADIAN THEATRICAL FEATURE FILMS, AS DIRECTOR: *Fortune and Men's Eyes*, 1971; *The Pyx*, 1973; *Mahoney's Last Stand*, 1971–76; *Shoot; Goldenrod*, 1976; *The High Country*, 1979–81; *Utilities* (also called *Getting Even*), 1980–83.

BIBLIOGRAPHY: Eleanor Beattie.

Peter Rist

THE HART OF LONDON. Jack Chambers, Ontario, 1968–70, 79 min., 16mm, color and b+w. Jack Chambers, who is best known as a painter, was a leading light in the prominent London, Ontario, art scene of the 1960s and 1970s and one of the founders of the London Film Co-Operative (with fellow experimentalists Greg Curnoe and Kee Dewdney). His first film, *Mosaic*, made in 1966, presents strong images of birth and death, which are also at the center of *The Hart of London*. But by the time he made this, his most celebrated and last finished film, he knew that he was dying of leukemia, so that the continual juxtaposition of what he called "the life-death-life cycle" here became a more profound thematic gesture. The first section of *The Hart of London* comprises old photographs, newsreels, and "home movies," rephotographed so that, initially, it is difficult to discern exactly what is being viewed. The effect is somewhat impressionist, especially through the addition of waves on the soundtrack which smooth out the often jagged visual collage contrasts. Chambers' paintings, as well as his films, are delicately textural, and although the director personally oversaw the striking of each print of *Hart*, it is impossible to view the film in its original state, so subtle is the play of image on surface. Gradually, one can begin to recognize various sights of London and environs, and a scene of a deer (the "hart" of the film's title) being captured comes to dominate. Toward the end of the film, the "hart" reappears in the form of a young deer at London's Springbank Park zoo, being approached and fed gingerly by Chambers' two young sons, Diego and John. On the soundtrack we repeatedly hear a voice (presumably that of the boys' mother) say "you must be very careful." At the very end of the film, the camera repeatedly tilts and pans to unite air (the sky) with the earth (Griffith Park) through water (the River Thames) and back again. Thus the film ends very optimistically. But the effect of this can never eliminate the shock of the mid-section, where the film first turns to color on a scene of fire, which is linked to the difficult birth of a child by the bright color, red. In turn, *Hart* cuts to a shocking long take scene of a lamb being slaughtered and left to bleed, which Chambers filmed in Chinchon, Spain, in 1969. Whereas the film's first section brilliantly achieves Chambers' goal of representing "perceptual realism," perhaps the prolonged scene of slaughter overextends his ideal "white light . . . moment of perception," but the anguish translated to the spectator helps him/her better understand Chambers' struggle to survive.

BIBLIOGRAPHY: R. Bruce Elder, "Forms of Cinema, Models of Self: Jack Chambers' *The Hart of London*," in Feldman, 264–74; Tom Graff.

Peter Rist

HEAVY METAL. Gerald Potterton, United States/Canada (Toronto), 1981, 90 min., color. *Heavy Metal* was a massive animated feature undertaking based on the adult science fiction/fantasy comic of the same name. The overall production, supervised by director Gerald Potterton, involved seventeen countries and over 1,000 people (which explains the nearly six-minute-long end credits). The respective directors of the sequences are: "Soft Landing" (credit sequence): Jimmy T. Murikami; "Grimaldi" (framing story): Harold Whitaker; "Harry Canyon": Pino Van Lamsweerde; "Den": Jack Stokes; "Captain Sternn": Paul Sabella, Julian Szuchopa; "B-17": Barrie Nelson, Lee Mishkin; "So Beautiful & So Dangerous": John Halas; "Taarna": John Bruno. The film begins with a space-age Pandora's Box, a "lochnar," unleashing primal evil onto the universe. The subsequent episodes are nebulously held together by the lochnar's trail of violence, aggression, and destruction across varying time frames and settings. The episodes range from science fiction noir ("Harry Canyon"), to horror ("B-17"), to swords and sorcery ("Taarna"), with the strongest being "Harry Canyon," "Captain Sternn," and "Taarna." *Heavy Metal* was aimed largely at a male adolescent audience, which accounts for the sophomoric humor, generic heavy rock music, and soft porn content. The film lacks the unifying vision that would raise it above this level (as in Bakshi's *Heavy Traffic* [United States, 1973], for example). For this reason *Heavy Metal*, which achieved a formidable cult status stature in its time, appears somewhat dated today. If, however, taken as "brain candy," you can enjoy the film's diverse animation styles and take pleasure in recognizing the voices of JOHN CANDY, Eugene Levy, Harold Ramis, Joe Flaherty, and JOHN VERNON. *Heavy Metal* won 1982 Genie Awards for sound editing and overall sound. It was re-released in 1996, perhaps to cash in on the popularity of recent rude and crude television animation series such as "Beavis and Butt-head" and "Ren & Stimpy."

BIBLIOGRAPHY: Carl Macek; "Heavy Metal," *Film Review Annual, 1982*, 543–48.

Donato Totaro

MARTHA HENRY. Born Martha Buhs, 1938, Greenville, Michigan. Actor. Martha Henry's late-coming film credits are a worthy supplement to her long, consistently triumphant theater career. Residing in Canada from 1959, Henry attended the National Theatre School in Montreal and then performed at several major Canadian theater centers. Her reputation ascended rapidly when she joined Ontario's Stratford Festival in 1961. She won accolades for her forceful, high-precision diction and for her command of a wide range of classical roles, including Desdemona in *Othello* (1974). In 1985, she began to direct. From 1988 to 1995, she served as artistic director at the Grand Theatre in London, Ontario. Inducted into the Order of Canada in 1981, Henry has received, among many other honors, the 1970 Theatre World Award, the 1979 Guthrie Award, an LL.D. from the University of Toronto, and the 1996 Canadian Governor General's Performing Arts Award. She reached her largest audience playing a principal role in the six-part CBC television series "Empire, Inc." (1983). She has won Genie Awards for every one of her five film appearances. *DANCING IN THE DARK* hinges on her authoritative central performance, her best work on film. In a supporting role as a psychologically scarred eccentric recluse she transcends the aimless oppressiveness of Darrell Wasyk's dejected character study, *Mustard Bath*. A successful 1994 Stratford Festival production of *A Long Day's Journey into Night* was smoothly adapted to film, preserving Henry's vivid Mary Tyrone.

FILMS AS ACTOR: *The Newcomers 1978* (short), 1980; *The Wars*, 1983; *Dancing in the Dark*, 1986; *Glory Enough for All: The Discovery of Insulin* (TV, Can/UK), 1988; *Mustard Bath*, 1992; *A Long Day's Journey into Night*, 1996.

BIBLIOGRAPHY: Martin Knelman (1982); Rota Herzberg Lister, "Martha Henry," in Benson and Conolly, 264.

Ian Elliot

UNE HISTOIRE INVENTÉE An Imaginary Tale. Marc-André Forcier, Montreal, 1990, 91 min., color. Following the relative setback of *Kalamazoo*, MARC-ANDRÉ FORCIER triumphantly returned to the proven formula of the fresco (where many characters appear) which created the success of *L'EAU CHAUDE L'EAU FRETTE*. Faithful to his habitual obsessions, the director once again takes marginal characters who are in search of love and moves one step further by considering the theme of *l'amour fou*. Thus, Gaston Turcotte, the Don Juan of the trumpet, falls in love with Soledad, the daughter of Florence Desruisseaux, who is in love with Gaston. Tibo, performing opposite Soledad in the play *Othello*, is madly in love with his partner, even though he continually cheats on her, while the prolific Florence drags behind her fallen lovers who have been literally paralyzed by passion. These manifestations of excessive lovers lead inevitably to that other emotion that *l'amour fou* can engender: jealousy, that which blinds, which pushes one to murder and suicide. A nonstop comedy run through with tragic outbursts, *Une histoire inventée* happily integrates that other great drama of jealousy, Shakespeare's *Othello*, while adding a reflexive dimension important to the heart of Forcier's film. Indeed, jealousy clearly presents itself in Shakespeare's play, but is equally divided among a good number of the characters in *Une histoire inventée*. Forcier and Jacques Marcotte have concocted a scenario that is true to their reputations as *enfants terribles*, although they have softened the anarchic character encountered with great pleasure in their previous films—doubtless with the goal of appealing to a much larger public. *Une histoire inventée* was awarded the prize for Best Canadian Film as well as the Air Canada Prize, awarded to the most popular film, at the Festival des Films du Monde in 1990.

BIBLIOGRAPHY: Marie-Claude Loiselle, "Le théâtre de la vie," *24 Images*, nos. 50–51 (Autumn 1990): 12–17; André Roy, "L'amour réinvente," *24 Images*, nos. 50–51 (Autumn 1990): 8–11.

Louis Goyette

MIKE HOOLBOOM. Born 1958, Toronto, Ontario. Director, writer, editor, camera operator. Mike Hoolboom has become well known as one of the most innovative and prolific experimental filmmakers currently working in Canada, producing a large body of highly personal and disturbing works. Hoolboom's parents immigrated to Toronto from Holland in order to avoid the military draft. After finishing high school, he traveled across Canada, hitching rides and hopping trains. At the age of twenty-one he founded a Toronto performance group, White Noise Labs, which fueled an interest in experimental filmmaking. He then attended film school at Sheridan College (studying under RICK HANCOX), and began making films. His first, *Song for Mixed Choir* (1980), established his stylistic objectives for the next several years: the film uses music to provide its structure, and features heavy manipulation of the images. Around this time, Hoolboom became associated with the Toronto experimental film group the Funnel, and began experimenting with optical printing. His work from this period emphasizes the physical attributes of film while at the same time addressing theoretical and political concerns. For example, *White Museum*—the final film in a trilogy dealing with the idea of the movie theater—calls into question the power of the image by presenting thirty minutes of voice over white leader, followed by two minutes of silent black and white picture. A trip to Holland for the AVE Film Festival resulted in *Bomen* (1989), an expressionistic, anxiety-ridden self-exploration using footage of trees (Hoolboom's own name contains the Dutch word for "tree"). Upon returning to Canada, Hoolboom tested HIV positive; his immediate response was the angry pairing of *Was* and *Eat* (both 1989), two collage films which used earlier footage of him with his first lover. Hoolboom began working at the Canadian Filmmakers' Distribution Centre (an artist-run experimental film co-op) and edited their journal, *The Independent Eye*. In 1990 he and Ann Marie Fleming collaborated on *Man*, which was followed the next year by *The New Man*. Since then he has completed several films, most notably *Frank's Cock*, his contribution to the omnibus film *Breaking Up in Three Minutes*, and the futuristic satire *Kanada*.

FILMS INCLUDE: *Song for Mixed Choir*, 1980; *Self Portrait with Pipe and Bandaged Ear*, 1981; *White Museum*, 1986; *Fat Film*, 1987; *Scaling; At Home*, 1988; *Bomen; Was; Eat; Brand*, 1989; *two* (with Kika Thorne); *Towards; Man* (with Ann Marie Fleming), 1990; *Red Shift; The New Man* (with Ann Marie Fleming), 1991; *Mexico*, 1992; *Frank's Cock; Kanada*, 1993; *Valentine's Day*, 1995.

BIBLIOGRAPHY: Mike Hoolboom, "Watching Death at Work: My Life in Film," *Cantrill's Filmnotes*, 69/70 (March 1993): 34–49.

Mitch Parry

GERMAIN HOUDE. Born 1952, Petit Saguenay, Quebec. Actor. Germain Houde began to work in the theater with a troupe at the Jonquière Cégep. Finishing his studies at the Dramatic Art Conservatory of Quebec in 1976, he followed the generation of actors which was exploring the cinema as much as the theater. In the same year that he made his debut on the stage with *La Complainte des hivers rouges* (1979), he made his remarkable entrance into the "seventh art scene" by playing the merciless rapist in *MOURIR À TUE-TÊTE* (ANNE-CLAIRE POIRIER) and the simpleton "Ti-Guy" in *LES BONS DÉBARRAS* (FRANCIS MANKIEWICZ, rel. 1980). These two first roles in the cinema surely demanded a great deal of courage on his part, and he was very convincing in them. Justly, he won the Genie for Best Actor in a Supporting Role for *Les bons débarras*. Later he won the same award for his role as Charlie, an unsympathetic and brutal character in *UN ZOO LA NUIT*. In between these performances, during the 1980s, he continued to appear on stage (e.g., *Macho Man, Vu du pont*) and in several short films. He also appeared in a couple of English-language TV films and in some popular *téléromans* including "L'or du temps" and "Le parc des braves." But his playing of the patriarch Caleb Bordeleau in the prime-time TV series "Les filles de Caleb" (1990–91) allowed him once again to carry off the title of Best Supporting Actor; this time a Prix Gémeaux. Finally, it was in this period when Houde was given the chance to play two leading roles in film, allowing him to explore characters connected to his own profession in great depth. He played Charles, a filmmaker who puts together a collective creation in *Love-moi* (M. Simard), and then an out-of-work actor who occupies the post of night watchman at a film studio in the children's film *L'assassin jouait du trombone* (R. Cantin). In 1992, the journal *Séquences* rewarded him with the prize of Best Actor in the Cinema for these two roles.

FILMS AS ACTOR INCLUDE: *Mourir à tue-tête*, 1979; *Les bons débarras*, 1980; *Lucien Brouillard*, 1983; *Shellgame* (TV); *Prettykill*, 1986; *Un zoo la nuit*, 1987; *The Rainbow Warrior Conspiracy; La nuit avec Hortense; Lonely Child—Le monde imaginaire de Claude Vivier*, 1988; *Terminal City Ricochet*, 1989; *Love-moi*, 1990; *L'assassin jouait du trombone*, 1991; *Léolo; Montréal ville ouverte* (TV), 1992; *Le secret de Jérôme; Craque la vie!* (TV), 1994; *La vengeance de la femme en noir; Matusalem II: Le dernier des Beauchesne*, 1997.

BIBLIOGRAPHY: André Lavoie, "Entretien avec Germain Houde," *Ciné-Bulles* 10, no. 4 (July-August, 1991): 4–7.

Isabelle Morissette

WILLIAM HUTT. Born 1920, Toronto. Spanning several decades, William Hutt's acting and directing career is as widespread as it is diverse. He began acting professionally in 1947 with a summer stock company in Bracebridge, Ontario, after serving in the Canadian army in World War II (and winning the Military Medal). He joined the Stratford (Ontario) Shakespearean Festival Company in its first year (1953), playing in *Richard III* and *All's Well that Ends Well.* Hutt displayed his skill and talent in the years that followed, creating an expansive list of roles that varied from Shakespeare to O'Neill, and Molière to Albee. In 1954 he was the first recipient of the Tyrone Guthrie Award for his portrayal of the Leader of the Chorus in *Oedipus Rex*, and two years later he appeared in the film version of this production (his first film performance). In the 1960s Hutt firmly established his international appeal when he starred at the Bristol (England) Old Vic and in several TV films for the BBC. He then toured the United States in Noel Coward's *Waiting in the Wings*, and toured with the Canadian Players, principally as Shakespeare's King Lear. (Years later he led the Stratford National Theatre's European tour in this role.) He began directing plays at Stratford, Ontario, in 1968 and over the next two decades became established as Canada's preeminent man of the theater, winning numerous awards and citations, including the Companion of the Order of Canada (1969), the Key to the City of Ottawa, and official recognition by the Speaker of the House of Commons (1984), culminating with the Governor General's Lifetime Achievement Award in Performing Arts in 1992. Surprisingly, his performances in Canadian films have been rare, possibly because he is better known as an actor in British and U.S. plays, rather than Canadian ones. But his aura has contributed to his winning the Canadian Film Award for Best Leading Actor virtually every time he has put in an appearance (three) since 1975: an Etrog for Best Performance in a Dramatic Short Film, *The National Dream*; a Genie for starring in Robin Phillips' version of *The Wars* (based on Timothy Findlay's novel), made following Hutt's stint as artistic director at Theatre London (Ontario); and a Genie for refashioning the role of Eugene O'Neill's James Tyrone, Sr., in David Wellington's film version of the Stratford (Ontario) Company's *Long Day's Journey into Night* (which he had reincarnated at least twice before in major stage productions since playing the part for the Bristol Old Vic).

FILMS AS ACTOR: *Oedipus Rex*, 1956; *There Was a Crooked Man* (UK), 1960; *Henry V* (TV), 1996; *The Fixer* (US), 1967; *The National Dream: The Last Spike* (short, TV), 1975; *The Shape of Things to Come* (voice only), 1979; *The Wars; Covergirl*, 1981; *The Kid Who Couldn't Miss* (voice only), 1983; *Much Ado About Nothing* (TV), 1987; *Long Day's Journey into Night*, 1996.

BIBLIOGRAPHY: Keith Garebian.

Sandra Sabathy/Peter Rist

I

I LOVE A MAN IN UNIFORM [*Man in Uniform*, United States]. David Wellington, Ontario, 1993, 97 min., color. Although *I Love a Man in Uniform* is not David Wellington's first feature, it is remarkable in that it is perfectly poised between authorial exploration and commercial appeal. Like DAVID CRONENBERG before him, David Wellington uses a well-known and popular genre—in this case, the psychological thriller—to reflect upon issues both Canadian and universal in nature: the angst of contemporary life and the search for a (distinct) identity. The film follows the downward journey of Henry Adler (Genie Award winner Tom McCamus), an actor who loses himself so completely in the role he must play—that of a policeman—that he finds himself performing it in the real world to disastrous effect. Though the plot isn't new and overtly borrows from other similarly themed films (William Friedkin's *Cruising*, United States, 1980; Martin Scorsese's *Taxi Driver*, United States, 1976), Wellington's work remains fresh and potent because of the finesse and probing aspects of his character study. On the one hand, Adler can be seen as a cynical caricature of the Canadian WASP, a national identity-challenged individual. On the other hand, his lack of personality and his compulsive need to perform, which hide the void of his existence, can also be read as metaphors for the postmodern artist and the creative dead-end which excessive referential work can lead to. Moreover, by choosing the figure of the policeman for McCamus' "character in character," Wellington is able to discuss power, authority, and the importance of role-playing, or theatricality, in our everyday life. The only difference between the officer Adler impersonates and those he meets on the street isn't that *he* is an actor whereas *they* aren't, but that *he* forgets he's playing a part while *they* never do.

BIBLIOGRAPHY: Johanne Larue, "I Love a Man in Uniform," *Séquences*, no. 172 (May–June 1994): 39; Stephen Farber, "Northern Exposure," *Movieline* 5, no. 10 (July 1994): 30–31.

Johanne Larue

IF YOU LOVE THIS PLANET. Terre Nash, NFB, 1982, 26 min., color. *If You Love This Planet* is a surprisingly powerful documentary—surprising because its success is in part a result of the relative simplicity of its form. The film is, essentially, a lecture delivered by Dr. Helen Caldicott, an outspoken critic of nuclear proliferation and president of Physicians for Social Responsibility in the United States. Caldicott provides convincing arguments against the nuclear arms buildup and urges her audience—both in the auditorium and in the theater—to participate in the fight against nuclear madness. Footage of Caldicott delivering the lecture (and of her audience's reactions to the material) is intercut with footage of nuclear tests and the survivors of Hiroshima, and with scenes from U.S. War Department and Information Agency films. Particularly chilling, given the context of the documentary, is the inclusion of clips taken from one such film: *Jap Zero* (1943), starring a pre–White House Ronald Reagan. The urgency behind Caldicott's argument ("If you love this planet," she declares at the film's conclusion, "you will realize that you are going to have to change the priorities of your life") is quite real: she cites testimony by the Joint Chiefs of Staff in 1975, which claimed that there was "a fifty-fifty chance of nuclear war by 1985"; she also discloses the inefficiency of the U.S. military and recounts an episode that placed the world on nuclear stand-by for six minutes—fourteen minutes away from total war. The simplicity of its style further emphasizes the urgency of the film's position; the viewer is offered nothing that might distract from the gravity of the nuclear arms buildup of the 1980s. In fact, this singleness of purpose encouraged many to view the film as outright (and primarily anti-American) propaganda. Even so (and, perhaps, as a result), the film won the Best Documentary Oscar for 1983.

BIBLIOGRAPHY: David Clandfield.

Mitch Parry

IL ÉTAIT UNE FOIS DANS L'EST Once Upon a Time in the East. André Brassard, Montreal, 1973, 100 min., color. A man of the theater above all else, André Brassard gave to Quebecois cinema three important films directed in close collaboration with the playwright Michel Tremblay: *François Durocher, waitress* (1972), *Il était une fois dans l'est* (1973), and *Le soleil se lève en retard* (1976). An exception in the landscape of Quebec cinema, *Il était une fois dans l'est* presents itself as a digest of Tremblay's theatrical universe, bringing together characters and situations from the plays *Les belles-soeurs, La duchesse de Langeais, Hosanna*, and *À toi pour toujours ta Marie-Lou*. "A raw gay film having as its theme the crises of the queens, lesbians, waitresses and housewives" (Thomas Waugh), *Il était une fois* is constructed on the model of the fresco (an impressive number of characters, numerous narrative threads) and, essentially, relies on a theatrical aesthetic influenced by the world of nightclubs. Apart from the uniformity of the performances (all the actors are remarkable, the unforgettable Denise Filiatrault in particular), the film features an elaborate use of parallel editing and multiple narrative lines which meet in a dramatic momentum of profound hopelessness. *Il était une fois* contains numerous anthology scenes in which biting humor (the monologue of the duchess in the plane) borders on the tragically cruel (the downfall of Hosanna during the drag show). Clearly, the film marks an important moment in the representation of gays and lesbians in Quebec cinema.

BIBLIOGRAPHY: Thomas Waugh, "Nègres blancs, tapettes et 'butch': Les lesbiennes et les gais dans le cinéma québécois," *Copie Zéro*, no. 11, Cinémathèque Québécoise, (1981): 12–29.

Louis Goyette

ILSA, TIGRESS OF SIBERIA [*The Tigress*, United States]. Jean Lafleur, Montreal, 1977, 91 min., color. The *Ilsa* trilogy is Canada's "great" contribution to exploitation cinema. The other films in the series are *Ilsa, She Wolf of the SS* (Canada/United States, 1974) and *Ilsa, Harem Keeper of the Oil Sheiks* (1976), both directed by Don Edmonds. A fourth unofficial entry is the unrelated *Wanda the Wicked Warden* (Switzerland/Federal Republic of Germany, 1977, Jesus Franco), which was retitled *Ilsa, the Wicked Warden* in 1983 to capitalize on the *Ilsa* notoriety (it does star the original Ilsa, Dyanne Thorne). The *Ilsa* series is part of a surprisingly extensive subgenre, the wartime torture-experiment film, which ranges from arthouse (*The Night Porter*, Italy/United States, 1973, Lilliana Cavani) to exploitation (*Men Behind the Sun*, Hong Kong/China, T. F. Mous, 1987). A key to the *Ilsa* series' success is the imposing, statuesque presence of former Las Vegas cabaret entertainer Dyanne Thorne in the title role. Along with Thorne, *Tigress* contains the two other series constants: a series of brutal (and creative) tortures, along with experiments supervised by commander Ilsa Koch; and a male prisoner or government agent who either "tames" the sexually omnivorous Ilsa with his sexual prowess, or overpowers her "will" by resisting her body. *Tigress*, shot in Montreal, begins in Siberia, 1953, with Ilsa as commander of a Russian concentration camp for political dissidents, Gulag 14. (Just how a German woman achieved such a position in the Russian army is never explained!) Forty minutes into the film Ilsa receives news of Stalin's death. With the prisoners trapped within, she sets the camp on fire and leaves. The film flashforwards to Montreal, 1977, where Ilsa and her henchmen run a brothel/torture house. Throwing logic to the wind, Ilsa and a sole camp survivor have not aged a day! The film ends weakly with a three-way confrontation among Ilsa, local Mafia kingpin Pasolini (a homage to *Salo*?), and KGB agents. *Tigress*' poor box-office showing spelled the end of the *Ilsa* series (though a strong cult following still exists today).

BIBLIOGRAPHY: Norman Taylor, "Mistress of Mayhem," *The Dark Side* (July/August 1993): 5–9; John Martin, "It's a Nazi Business," *The Dark Side* (February/March 1995): 56–60.

Donato Totaro

MICHAEL IRONSIDE. Born 1950, Toronto. Actor. Ironside's career began at the age of fifteen when a play he had written was performed by the Toronto Workshop Theatre. He subsequently studied at the Ontario College of Art, where he wrote, directed, and starred in his first film, *Down Where the Lights Are* (1975). He began by taking acting courses run by the NFB, and made his feature debut playing a drunk in OUTRAGEOUS! (1977). Since his breakthrough role, as the psychotic Darryl Revok in DAVID CRONENBERG's *Scanners* (1981), Ironside has been prolific, appearing in over fifty features. His heavy-set build and steely-eyed features have made him a target for typecasting, either as the villain or as the cop tracking down the lead villain. He has said of himself, "I've got a reputation for giving two dimensional parts a sense of reality no matter how poorly written they are" (*Starburst*, no. 145, September 1990), and he seems to be content with the path his career has taken. After *Scanners*, he again played a villain, this time without psychic powers, in *Visiting Hours* (J.-C. Lord), in which he was one of the few involved to be praised by the critics. Often Ironside's films have been badly written and poorly directed, but he never gives less than his best performance. In 1983 he moved to Los Angeles, feeling that his career was not progressing in Canada, and finally achieved fame playing the lead role in the TV series "V" (1985). Now best known for American movies such as *Total Recall* (P. Verhoeven, 1990), Ironside returns frequently to Canada to work. In the midst of many mainstream appearances, Ironside co-wrote, executive produced, and starred in *Chaindance* (A. Goldstein). Clearly a labor of love on Ironside's part, he played a hard-boiled prisoner who, as part of a radical reform program, is handcuffed to the wheelchair of a cerebral palsy sufferer (superbly played by Brad Dourif). The film charts the relationship that develops between the two men. Ironside clearly relished the opportunity to play beyond the limits of his usual roles and develop a well-rounded character from the inside out, instead of making the best of someone else's stereotypes. It is a heart-warming, beautifully acted piece and quite a revelation for Ironside fans.

FILMS AS ACTOR: *Down Where the Lights Are* (short; also dir., scr.), 1975; *Outrageous!*, 1977; *High-Ballin'*, 1978; *Summer's Children; Stone Cold Dead*, 1979; *I, Maureen*, 1977–80; *Suzanne*, 1980; *Surfacing; Scanners*, 1981; *Off Your Rocker; Double Negative*, 1979–82; *Visiting Hours; Community Standards*, 1982; *American Nightmare; Cross Country; Spacehunter*, 1983; *Best Revenge*, 1980–84; *The Surrogate*, 1984; *Nowhere to Hide*, 1987; *Office Party*, 1988; *Hello Mary Lou: Prom Night 2; Destiny to Order*, 1989; *Mind Field; Chaindance* (also scr, co-prod.), 1990; *Cafe Romeo; Killer Image*, 1992; *Sweet Killing*, 1993; *Tokyo Cowboy; Bolt; Killing Machine*, 1994; *Kids of the Round Table*, 1995; *Portrait of a Killer*, 1996; *The Arrow* (TV), 1997.

Simon Brown

ISABEL. Paul Almond, Quebec, 1968, 108 min., color. The first theatrical feature film for PAUL ALMOND and the first film of a trilogy starring GENEVIÈVE BUJOLD marked Almond as a director distinct among his contemporaries. *Isabel* presents the story of a woman (Bujold) who returns home to the Gaspé region following the death of her mother, only to rekindle the dark secrets of her family's tragic past, which is rife with incest and death. In contrast to the dominant Canadian style of documentary realism applied to the fictional text, Almond's film features a complex narrative structure, which defies linearity. The past returns to Isabel in a series of dreams, flashbacks, and possibly flashforwards. The effect constructs a world of psychological terror, where the question of reality itself must be considered. As Peter Morris has noted, Almond's manipulation of time and space emulates that seen in Alain Resnais' *L'année dernière à Marienbad* (France, 1961) and the visualization of madness echoes the work of Sweden's Ingmar Bergman. Upon its release the film was accorded some critical acclaim, winning four Etrogs (Canadian Film Awards) in 1968, as well as a nomination for Almond as Best Director by the Directors Guild of America, but public recognition of Almond's work was slow. Almond became a marginalized figure in the predominantly francophone Montreal film community.

BIBLIOGRAPHY: Janet Edsforth.

Dave Douglas

I'VE HEARD THE MERMAIDS SINGING. Patricia Rozema, Toronto, 1987, 81 min., color. Made on a modest budget, and in only a little over a month, this film was the unexpected hit of the 1987 Cannes Film Festival (winning the Prix de la Jeunesse), garnering rave critical reviews and achieving considerable financial success. As PATRICIA ROZEMA's second film (her first feature film), *I've Heard the Mermaids Singing* was notable for the performance of Sheila McCarthy as Polly Vandersma, described by Rozema as "a quirky and vulnerable Innocent whose inept exterior belies a vast and vivid internal universe." Through the eyes of Polly, a whimsical and naive temporary secretary, we observe the pretensions of the contemporary Canadian art scene. In her new job at an art gallery, Polly develops a voyeuristic adoration for her beautiful and arrogant boss, the Curator (PAULE BAILLARGEON), and her lover, Mary (Ann-Marie MacDonald). Rozema charts Polly's course from infatuation to disillusionment to ultimate renewal with considerable visual wit and charm. Particularly noteworthy is the film's evocation of the rich inner life that underlies Polly's awkward and unsophisticated exterior. *I've Heard the Mermaids Singing* was anticipated by Rozema's first film, *Passion: A Letter in 16mm* (1985), which employed a number of innovative stylistic devices to capture the complexity and nuances of the female lead's personality and unique point of view.

BIBLIOGRAPHY: Michael Posner, "The Little Movie that Did: *I've Heard the Mermaids Singing*," in Posner, 213–34.

Helen and Paul Salmon

IXE-13. Jacques Godbout, ONF, 1971, 114 min., color. *IXE-13* is a unique Quebecois musical-comedy spoof that caricatures both the social world (Maoists, Nazis, French Canadians, anglophones, the clergy) and pop culture (musicals, spy films, pulp serials). Though primarily a parody, there are also satirical touches that speak directly to Quebec's political and cultural history (the caricature of the Church, the archetypically English boss). The film is based on a popular 1950s serial by Pierre Saurel featuring the "French Canadian" spy-hero IXE-13. JACQUES GODBOUT adapts the novel's serial pulp form into a live-action comic book world of bold colors and artificial sets that could be best described as "Pop Art Meets Expressionism." The story, set in 1949, pits a Canadian spy-wrestling organization (replete with lesbian and midget wrestlers) against a Maoist/Nazi espionage ring. When Canadian wrestler-spy Bob West is murdered, the chaste, clean-cut hero IXE-13 is brought in to solve the case. The film flows in a series of sketches featuring the four-member Quebec comedy troupe, The Cynics (who play all the male characters). In today's heightened social and political climate some elements of *IXE-13* may not play well. For example, much of the film's humor comes at the expense of race and culture (white actors in outrageous oriental makeup speaking with equally outrageous Chinese accents; a Chinese man eating Rice Krispies with chopsticks, buffoonish Nazis). However, the outlandish, cartoon style and lighthearted sensibility keep it from becoming mean-spirited.

BIBLIOGRAPHY: George Csaba Koller, "Jacques Godbout: *IXE-13*," *Cinema Canada*, no. 7 (April–May 1973): 36–39; Yves Lever, 1995.

Donato Totaro

J

J. A. MARTIN, PHOTOGRAPHE *J. A. Martin, Photographer.* Jean Beaudin, ONF, 1977, 101 min., color. One of the first key Quebecois feature films to be set in the past, *J. A. Martin, photographe* is also significant for presenting a portrait of a married woman struggling to assert her individuality. Periodically, Rose-Aimée Martin (MONIQUE MERCURE) has to stay at home for six weeks, looking after her children, while her husband goes on a road trip to Maine visiting various clients and making them photographs. She decides that this year she is going with him, and after unsuccessfully asking neighbors to mind her children, she persuades her maiden aunt Aline (Marthe Nadeau) to do so. Their journey is interspersed with conflicts, but it ends with the rekindling of their love and J. A.'s appreciation of his wife's talents and free spirit. MARCEL SABOURIN, who collaborated on the script, very generously underplays J. A.'s character, allowing Mercure to shine. Beautifully shot in 1975 in a variety of rural Quebec locations (and Montreal), Pierre Mignot's cinematography gracefully pans across natural exteriors and Vianney Gautier's interiors alike, linking the characters with the world they live and work in. Indeed, one of the most remarkable aspects of *J. A. Martin* is the degree to which *work* is emphasized. The film begins on a flame lighting an oil lamp to introduce the details of J. A. preparing a photographic plate and continually cross-cuts to Rose-Aimée, doing her household chores. As historian Peter Morris has noted, it is hard to imagine this film, which often moves at a deliberately slow pace to match the place and time it is representing, made anywhere in North America other than the NFB/ONF. The audience also has to work hard to fully understand the actions and psychological states of the principal characters, so subtle is the exposition. The repeated fading in and out of scenes (and occasionally single shots) adds to the impression that so much is being elided, while a nostalgic, yet verisimilar account of 19th century Quebec life is being presented. *J. A. Martin, photographe* won seven Etrogs (Canadian Film Awards) in November 1977, for Best Feature

Film, Performance by a Lead Actress, Art Direction, Cinematography, and Sound Re-recording (Jean-Pierre Joutel), as well as two for JEAN BEAUDIN, for Best Direction and Editing (shared).

BIBLIOGRAPHY: Peter Morris (1984), 26–27, 155.

Peter Rist

JÉSUS DE MONTRÉAL *Jesus of Montreal.* Denys Arcand, Montreal, 1989, 118 min., color. One of the most exciting and important films to emerge from Quebec in the 1980s, *Jésus de Montréal* is an intense investigation of both the spiritual hollowness of modern society and the enduring human impulse for artistic expression and spirituality. The film's central character, Daniel Coulombe (LOTHAIRE BLUTEAU), and a fellow group of actors are asked by a priest to update the Passion play for modern audiences. Their version of the play, with Daniel as Christ, proves to be a popular success with the public but outrages the Catholic hierarchy, who threaten its termination. Arrested by the police in mid-performance, Daniel is seriously injured, dies despite the efforts of his friends, and undergoes a modern version of resurrection as his eyes and heart are used for organ transplants. The main structuring principle of the film involves an interplay between contemporary and biblical events, and the parallel between Daniel and Christ is particularly well drawn and powerfully performed. The film has a fine satirical edge, .which is expressed through dark humor, self-conscious theatricality, and a skillful use of religious allegory and debased symbolism. *Jésus* continues the critique of Western culture so powerfully handled in DENYS ARCAND's previous film, *LE DÉCLIN DE L'EMPIRE AMERICAIN* (1986), and shares that film's trademarks of brilliant ensemble acting and a powerful screenplay. In both films, music is carefully integrated into the film's thematic core in a way that is effective and at times greatly moving. Although some of Arcand's fellow Quebecois filmmakers have decried in his films what they term an abandonment of direct political engagement, *Jésus de Montréal* illustrates Arcand's ability to speak meaningfully to the human condition in its broadest and most universal sense.

BIBLIOGRAPHY: Michael Posner, "The Big Chill with a PhD," in Posner, 213–39; André Loiselle and Brian McIlroy.

Helen and Paul Salmon

JOUR APRÈS JOUR *Day After Day.* Clément Perron, ONF, 1962, 29 min., b+w. A gem of *cinéma direct, Jour après jour* was supposed to be a straight-forward documentary on paper making, but its director conceived his film as an indictment of the industry, showing the harsh labor conditions and the resulting existential dead-end the workers found themselves in. Not surprisingly, the film was issued its release visa only after Clément Perron agreed to cut out or obscure any direct reference to the company's name. Ironically, the absence of a clearly identified corporate nemesis only broadened the film's critical impact. This award-winning film not only boasts a powerful philosophical and ideological discourse, but also possesses formal qualities that still amaze contemporary audiences. A combination of modernist and poetic aesthetics, the film impresses the senses before addressing itself to the mind, combining striking images with an almost surreal voice-over narration in a contrapuntal and associational montage driven onwards by stream-of-consciousness: ominous machines—the dark sheen of metal, expressionistically lit—are juxtaposed to workers trapped by telephoto lenses, their oppression suggested by composition and the deadly glance they sometimes throw at the lens; series of repetitious movements, both mechanical and human, create a hypnotic rhythm which interfaces with the disjunctive heartbeat of industrial sounds orchestrated by Maurice Blackburn, and so on. True, the construction and discourse of *Jour après jour* betray the elitist background of its makers, but the film does not condescend to its subjects or the public. The honesty of its youthful bravado is still palpable and exciting after all these years.

BIBLIOGRAPHY: Léo Bonneville.

Johanne Larue

CLAUDE JUTRA. Born 1930, Montreal; died 1986. Director, screenwriter, editor, actor. Solid studies in medicine could not prevent Claude Jutra from devoting himself to the profession of filmmaker. Equally passionate about the dramatic arts, it was at the age of eighteen that Jutra created his first cinematic efforts, which already demonstrated the emergence of a strong personality. *Le dément du Lac Jean-Jeunes* (1948) established one of the recurrent themes of his work: the exploration of childhood. His next film, the astonishing *MOUVE-MENT PERPÉTUEL*, is a formal and narrative experiment in the same line as the U.S. trance films of Maya Deren and Kenneth Anger. Jutra joined the ONF in 1954. In France, he directed *Anna la bonne* (1959), produced by François Truffaut, and collaborated with Jean Rouch on the documentary *Le Niger, jeune république* (1961). While *cinéma direct* was at its peak at the ONF, he co-directed *LA LUTTE* with MICHEL BRAULT, Marcel Carrière, and Claude Fournier. The year 1963 was an important one in the history of Quebecois cinema, since it was in that year that Jutra directed *À TOUT PRENDRE*, an independent film that is admirable in many respects. *MON ONCLE ANTOINE*, though much more classical, remains nevertheless the director's most celebrated film. In 1973, Jutra directed the Canadian/French co-production *Kamouraska*, a luxurious adaptation of the novel by Anne Hébert. After the failure of *Pour le meilleur et pour le pire*, Jutra felt unable to film as he wanted to in Quebec. He accepted an offer from the CBC and left for Toronto. He made some television films there, including *Ada* (1977), a touching adaptation of a Margaret Gibson Gilboord novel about the lives of patients in a psychiatric institute, and *Dreamspeaker*, which recounts the friendship between a wise old Amerindian and a young pyromaniac. It was also in Toronto that Jutra directed two films with substantial budgets:

Surfacing, a problematic adaptation of the Margaret Atwood novel, and *By Design*, a charming comedy about a lesbian couple who want to have a child. Jutra's career, at first interrupted by illness, ended tragically in 1986 when he took his own life. Two years earlier he had directed his final film, *La dame en couleurs*.

FILMS AS DIRECTOR INCLUDE: *Le dément du Lac Jean-Jeunes*, 1948; *Mouvement perpétuel*, 1949; *Pierrot des Bois*, 1956; *A Chairy Tale* (co-dir., N. McLaren), 1957; *Les mains nettes*, 1958; *Anna la bonne; Félix Leclerc troubadour*, 1959; *Le Niger, jeune république; La lutte*, 1961; *Québec—USA ou l'invasion pacifique*, 1962; *À tout prendre; Les enfants du silence* (co-dir., M. Brault), 1963; *Comment savoir; Rouli-roulant*, 1966; *Wow*, 1969; *Mon oncle Antoine*, 1971; *Kamouraska*, 1973; *Pour le meilleur et pour le pire*, 1975; *Ada; Dreamspeaker*, 1977; *Seer Was Here*, 1978; *The Wordsmith*, 1979; *Surfacing*, 1980; *By Design*, 1981; *La dame en couleurs*, 1984.

BIBLIOGRAPHY: Pierre Jutras, ed., "Claude Jutra: Filmographie et témoignages," *Copie Zéro*, no. 33 (September 1987); Jean Chabot.

Louis Goyette

K

KANEHSATAKE: 270 YEARS OF RESISTANCE. Alanis Obomsawin, (Quebec) NFB, 1993, 119 min., color. Alanis Obomsawin, an Abénaquise Indian, took on the difficult task of relating the salient events known as the Oka Crisis, without a doubt the most important political crisis to have taken place since the events of October 1970. With *Kanehsatake*, she directed a militant and denunciatory documentary in which the rigorous description of the events is equal to the unbearable tension associated with this crisis—a tension pushed to its culmination thanks mainly to extraordinary montage. In the beginning, there is the decision to expand a golf course by encroaching on land belonging to Mohawk Indians. This constitutes the initial affront, that raised the thorny issue of territorial rights once again. For 270 years the Mohawks have resisted, for better or worse, successive governments who have tried every means available to monopolize a territory that doesn't belong to them. In 1990, this sad history was repeated anew. Alanis Obomsawin investigates the present by creating a return to the past, and reveals to us the gray areas of our history—those areas marked by profound injustices committed against First Nations people. Like those presented in the film, the governments clearly did not have a winning hand in this crisis, like the Sûreté du Québec and the Canadian army, who are painted in an unflattering light. The real "heroes" were the Mohawks and the Warriors, defending their ancestral lands, willing to be buried six feet under for the sake of their children's future. One may well argue that the film has been made from a highly subjective viewpoint, but it is important to recognize that the historical detour effected by Obomsawin lends her militant discourse an undeniable credibility. Certainly, it has been a long time since one has seen a documentary that moves with such an immediate force, reflecting the intensity and seriousness of a political crisis.

BIBLIOGRAPHY: Michel Saint-Germain, "Entretien avec Roger Rochat," *Terres en vues* 1, no. 2 (Spring 1993): 3–4, 18.

Louis Goyette

LARRY KENT. Born 1937, Johannesburg, South Africa. Director, writer. One of the pioneering filmmakers of the 1960s, Larry Kent emerged not from the NFB or CBC, but from the ranks of interested amateurs. Beginning in theater at the University of British Columbia in 1963, Kent self-distributed his first feature, THE BITTER ASH, across the country using other university film societies and "midnight" movie houses. With two follow-up films he quickly established himself as both a director and an independent producer before leaving Vancouver for Montreal. In contrast to the documentary influence seen in NOBODY WAVED GOODBYE (1964), Kent's early work demonstrated a quality of visual experimentation similar to the films of the New American Cinema. Influenced by the literature of the Beat generation, Kent's early films evinced a free-form energy. His subject matter typically focused on the conditions of the working class or down-and-out individuals in their struggle to cope with the pressures of society. Controversy followed Kent's early career, due principally to his use of graphic language, sexual imagery, and adult situations. *The Bitter Ash* was censored at many venues, and *High* was prevented from being shown at the Montreal Film Festival in 1967. In addition to battles over censorship, Kent was often vilified by Canadian film critics for the same visual excess that drew audiences to his work. His last Vancouver film, *When Tomorrow Dies* (1965), was attacked for its depiction of the banality of middle-class values. His subsequent relocation to Montreal brought renewed critical acclaim with *High*, but Kent's willingness to further his experimentations with film form drew further criticism of his daring project *Façade*. After the failure of this film Kent attempted to ingratiate himself with the burgeoning commercial sector. Following *High*, Kent ceased to produce his own films. With the exception of *The Apprentice/Fleur bleue* (1970), this move proved to have increasingly negative results for Kent's career. Like many of his generation, Kent found the quest for commercial success in the 1970s elusive. Returning to his strength, he ended the decade with some critical success with his family melodrama *This Time Forever (Yesterday)*. Despite this, Kent's work trailed off in the 1980s, when he worked primarily in TV. In 1992 he returned to independent producing with *Mothers and Daughters*.

FILMS AS DIRECTOR: *The Bitter Ash*, 1963; *Sweet Substitute*, 1964; *When Tomorrow Dies*, 1965; *High*, 1967; *Façade*, 1968; *The Apprentice/Fleur Bleue*, 1970; *Saskatchewan* −45° *below* (short), 1971; *Cold Pizza* (short), 1972; *Keep It in the Family*, 1973; *The Slavers*, 1977; *This Time Forever (Yesterday)*, 1979; *High Stakes; Mama's Boy*, 1986; *Dragon Slayer*, 1987; *Mothers and Daughters*, 1992.

BIBLIOGRAPHY: Piers Handling, "Larry Kent Lost and Found: A Critical Rehabilitation," *Cinema Canada*, no. 127 (February 1986): 10–16.

                                                                                                          Dave Douglas

RICHARD KERR. Born 1952, St. Catharines, Ontario. Director. One of the central figures of the Canadian avant-garde to emerge in the late 1970s, Richard

Kerr has produced a large body of work in multiple media, working in film and video and as a visual artist. As a student at Sheridan College in the mid-to-late 1970s, Kerr was influenced by avant-garde filmmaker RICK HANCOX and began making a series of films that bridged the gap between documentary and avant-garde cinema. Some works, such as *Vesta Lunch*, evinced a style echoing *cinéma vérité*, while others, such as *Hawkesville to Wallenstein* and *Canal*, maintained a documentarist eye, albeit one infused with a poetic quality. Kerr's later work focused on the Canadian landscape, seeking to explore the metaphysical nature of a Canadian identity with films such as *Plein Air* and *Plein air Etude* (both 1991), which document a trip driving through the Canadian Shield. In the late 1980s Kerr turned his interests to the American landscape with works such as *Last Days of Contrition*. In 1984, Kerr signaled his further interest in combining the personal-diaristic forms of expression with which he had been working with the question of narrative cinema. The result was one of his early great works, *On Land over Water (Six Stories)*. In the 1990s he extended this interest in the fusion of the avant-garde with narrative to a feature-length film, *The Willing Voyeur*.

FILMS AS DIRECTOR: *Hawkesville to Wallenstein*, 1976; *Vesta Lunch*, 1979; *Dogs Have Tales*, 1980; *Luck Is the Residue of Desire*, 1981; *Canal*, 1982; *On Land Over Water (Six Stories)*, 1984; *The Last Days of Contrition*, 1988; *The Machine in the Garden; Plein Air Etude; Plein Air*, 1991; *Cruel Rhythm*, 1992; *McLuhan*, 1993; *Out of Control—Behind the Scenes of Willing Voyeur*, 1994; *The Willing Voyeur*, 1996.

BIBLIOGRAPHY: Bart Testa, "Richard Kerr: Overlapping Entries," in Cindy Richmond, 8–48.

Dave Douglas

MARGOT KIDDER. Born 1948, Yellowknife, Northwest Territories. Actor. Margot Kidder spent most of her youth relocating from one mining town to the next following her father's career as a mining engineer. At the age of sixteen, she settled in Vancouver where she studied at the University of British Columbia. It was not long, however, before she relocated once again, but in this case it was to benefit her own career, as she moved to Toronto to begin work as an actress. One of her earliest breaks was to be cast in Norman Jewison's film *Gaily, Gaily* (aka *Chicago, Chicago*, 1969), playing a prostitute who becomes the object of the young hero's affections. Although the film was not a success, it did bring Kidder attention and the offer of further Hollywood roles. An independent, strong-willed woman, Kidder returned to Toronto and explored alternative career options. She worked briefly for CBC as well as assisting with the editing of Robert Altman's *Brewster McCloud* (1970). Kidder has continued to oscillate between her work as an actress and her ambitions toward filmmaking. In 1975 she was awarded a place on the AFI's Directing Workshop and later resumed making short films in Canada. Although it was her Hollywood films from the mid-1970s that brought Kidder international attention and stardom, her talent had been recognized in Canada much earlier. In 1969 she received a special Canadian Film Award as an "outstanding new talent" for her work in *Does Anybody Here Know Denny?* In 1975, she received the Canadian Film Award for her performances in both *Black Christmas* and *A Quiet Day in Belfast*. In fact, Kidder has continued to return to Canada in search of interesting roles to complement her more mainstream Hollywood output. In 1981 she chose to star in the small-scale women's road movie *Heartaches*, and her sensitive portrayal of Rita, the eccentric lovelorn traveler, won her a Genie in 1982. Often described as a women's version of GOIN' DOWN THE ROAD (also directed by DON SHEBIB), *Heartaches*, the story of two women who are drawn together out of a mutual need for freedom and friendship, finds much of its emotional strength in Kidder. She shows no restraint, allowing Rita to come across as vulnerable and gaudy without masking her strength of will and passion. Kidder clearly illustrated that she has range beyond the feisty female leads for which she is famous. Her path to stardom has not, however, been a straightforward one. Due to her regular career shifts toward filmmaking and her personal obligations, Kidder frequently disappears from the screen. This has also been exacerbated in the last few years by a series of health problems. As a result, she is repeatedly forced to fight her way back to remind audiences of her skill and determination.

FILMS AS ACTOR: *The Best Damn Fiddler from Calabogie to Kaladar* (short), 1968; *A Quiet Day in Belfast; Black Christmas*, 1974; *Heartaches*, 1981; *Louisiana* (Can/Fr); *The Glitterdome* (Can/US), 1984; *Keeping Track; Mob Story*, 1987; *White Room*, 1989; *To Catch a Killer*, 1992; *La Florida*, 1993; *Henry and Verlin*, 1994; *Young Ivanhoe* (Can/Fr/UK), 1995; *Silent Cradle; The Planet of Junior Brown* (TV), 1997.

BIBLIOGRAPHY: "She's Not Proud of Her Revolting Brat Days," *TV Guide*, no. 46 November 17, 1984).

Stacey Abbott

ALLAN (WINTON) KING. Born 1930, Vancouver, British Columbia. Director, producer. One of the most successful and durable filmmakers to emerge in Canada during the 1960s, Allan King built a career upon challenges to the conventional wisdom of what Canadian filmmaking ought to be. Unlike many of his contemporaries, King gained his entry into cinema not through the NFB in Montreal, but through the CBC's Vancouver Film Unit. The unit, which was formed in 1954 under the direction and influence of Stan Fox and Jack Long, offered King his first opportunity to direct a documentary film. After a scant two years working at the unit, King, with Long and editor Arla Saare, seized the opportunity to direct *Skid Row*, a portrait of the unemployed and indigent of Vancouver's Gastown district. Although the documentary conscience of the Griersonian model was evident, *Skid Row* also evinced the lyrical and less didactic quality of the new *cinéma vérité* style. King followed the success of his first film with equally successful portraits of other West Coast communities, most notably in *Pemberton Valley*. King then turned his eye on international subjects, directing such films as *Saigon* and *Rickshaw*. In 1961 he relocated to London, while still making contributions to the CBC's "Document" series. It was during this period that King began working with cinematographer Richard Leiterman (a collaborative relationship that has extended to most of his later films) and began to evolve his own style of documentary, beyond the free-form codes of *cinéma vérité*. King's new direction took an increasingly dramatic form, which Peter Harcourt termed the "actuality drama"—structurally orchestrated films employing non-actors in unscripted situations. King introduced this new style with the film *Running Away Backwards* (1964), but his later works, the controversial WARRENDALE and A MARRIED COUPLE, remain the best known films of this period. The latter garnered a sizeable box office upon its theatrical release, an extreme rarity for Canadian cinema of the late 1960s. A further project along these lines, *Come On Children*—a project that saw King take a group of disaffected youth out of the city and onto a farm, allowing them largely to decide their own daily activities—forced King to reconsider ethical issues connected to his methodology. In 1977 he first attempted fiction with his adaption of W. O. Mitchell's WHO HAS SEEN THE WIND. Since then King has continued to work in the dramatic mode for both cinema and television from his base in Toronto. While he has directed episodes of mainstream TV series "Danger Bay" and "Road to Avonlea," King has maintained his longtime interest in figures who exist at the margins of society. His feature *Termini Station* took the actress MEGAN FOLLOWS (then playing Anne of Green Gables) and transformed her into a woman in a small northern community, trapped in a life of prostitution and dreaming of escape. King's social conscience on display here harkens back to his first film and remains his truest and most lasting contribution to Canadian cinema and society.

FILMS AS DIRECTOR INCLUDE: *Skid Row; The Yukoners*, 1956; *Portrait of a Harbour; The Pemberton Valley*, 1957; *Morocco*, 1958; *Bull Fight; Saigon* (also cin.), 1959; *Rickshaw; India—14 Years After*, 1960; *A Matter of Pride; Three Yugoslavian Portraits*, 1961; *Joshua, a Nigerian Portrait*, 1962; *The Peacemakers; The Field Day*, 1963; *Christopher Plummer; Running Away Backwards*, 1964; *The Most Unlikely Millionaire*, 1965; *Warrendale* (also co-prod.), 1966; "Children in Conflict" series; *Who Is . . . James Jones* (also prod.), 1967; *I Was Born Greek* (co-dir., with W. Brayne, also prod.), 1968; *A Married Couple* (also prod.), 1969; *Mortimer Griffen, Shalinsky and How They Settled the Jewish Question*, 1971; *Come On Children*, 1972; *A Bird in the House*, 1973; *Pity the Poor Piper*, 1974; *Six Years War*, 1975; *Red Emma*, 1976; *Who Has Seen the Wind*, 1977; *Silence of the North*, 1981; "Home Fires" series; *Who's in Charge?*, 1983; *Tucker & the Horsethief*, 1984; *The Last Season*, 1986; *Termini Station* (also prod.), 1989; *All the King's Men*, 1990.

BIBLIOGRAPHY: Peter Harcourt, "Allan King: Filmmaker," in Feldman, 69–79.

Dave Douglas

KISSED. Lynne Stopkewich, British Columbia, 1996, 80 min., color, 35 mm (blow-up). *Kissed* concerns a young woman's (Molly Parker) obsession with death. In a brief flashback we see a pubescent Sandra performing bizarre, part-Christian, part-pagan animal burial rites. During one of the rites Sandra is seen holding a dead mouse tightly in her hand. The scene cuts to a close-up of blood trickling down her leg. This symbolic link between death and sexual development (menstruation) is the only psychological insight we get into Sandra's future necrophilia. Sandra attempts a relationship with a young man, Matt (Peter Outerbridge), but sex with the living can not duplicate the wonderful "cross-over" sensation she experiences during necrophilic sex. Distraught and confused, Matt commits suicide so that he can gain Sandra's eternal love. The media has tended, wrongly I feel, to play up the film's "controversial" subject matter. If *Kissed* is about necrophilia, then one could take offense at Stopkewich's romanticization of it (eroticized, no graphic scenes, sympathetic character). But *Kissed* uses necrophilia as a pretext to explore one woman's quest for spiritual transcendence. Cues also suggest that the film can be read as Sandra's subjective fantasy, which would temper the "reality" of necrophilia, for example, the otherworldly white light seen in otherwise realist spaces (Sandra refers to the life emanating from each corpse as "the light"). Even at its slim eighty minutes, *Kissed* feels padded. Once Matt's love goes unrequited, the ending becomes predictable and the film less engaging. Perhaps developing the film's subjective-fantasy angle or the psychological dimension of Sandra's necrophilic-spiritual journey could have effectively fleshed out the length. Minor criticism aside, *Kissed* scored big at the 1997 Genie Awards, winning prizes for Best Actress (Parker), Best Cinematography, Best Direction, and Best Picture.

BIBLIOGRAPHY: Maurie Alioff, "Sweet Necrophilia," *Take One* 5, no. 15 (Spring 1997): 12–16.

Donato Totaro

L

JEAN-CLAUDE LABRECQUE. Born 1938, Quebec City, Quebec. Director, scriptwriter, cinematographer. At the Office National du Film, Jean-Claude Labrecque acquired a solid reputation as a camera operator. He was the d.o.p. on several significant Quebec films of the 1960s, notably *LE CHAT DANS LE SAC* (GILLES GROULX) and *LA VIE HEUREUSE DE LÉOPOLD Z.* (GILLES CARLE). His debut as a film director came in 1965 with the documentary short *60 Cycles*, about the cycling tour of Saint-Laurent. The film astonished with its audacious images and dynamic montage. Furthermore, it received a Special Mention at the Festival du Film Canadien, and the First Prize for Short Films at Moscow. Following this success, Labrecque made several documentaries, where he set himself the task of "fixing on film some significant moments in Quebec's sporting, cultural and political history" (Francine Laurendeau). With JEAN BEAUDIN, Marcel Carrière, and Georges Dufaux, he directed the "official" film of the 1976 Olympic Games in Montreal, *Games of the XXI Olympiad*. Labrecque showed himself to be particularly adept at capturing Quebec's greatest cultural events on film. *La nuit de la poésie 28 mars 1980* is a remarkable visual anthology of the contemporary Quebecois poetry scene, in which it is a pleasure to see some of Quebec's best poets reunited in one place. Conventionally constructed, the film is nevertheless a faithful reflection of a sparkling era when there seemed to be no limits on creativity. Further, Labrecque always knew how to recreate an intimate relationship between the camera and his filmed subjects. His portraits of artists are the quintessence of "testimonial" documentaries. *Marie Uguay* is a touching portrait of a young poet, stricken by illness, who reveals her reflections on art, life, and death only a few months before her own death. *André Mathieu, musicien*, another big success for Labrecque, relates the rise, then fall of the prodigious pianist Mathieu through a clever arrangement of archival footage and testimonies that produce a troubling response in the spectator. With *Les smattes* (1972), Labrecque made his first attempt at fiction. *Les vautours* remains his best film in this register. Another fiction film, *Le Frère André*, once again attests to Labrecque's fascination with Quebec's history and its celebrities. In 1992, Jean-Claude Labrecque was awarded the Prix Albert-Tessier.

FILMS AS DIRECTOR INCLUDE: *60 cycles*, 1965; *La visite du Général de Gaulle au Québec*, 1967; *Les canots de glace*, 1969; *La nuit de la poésie 27 mars 1970; Essai à la mille*, 1970; *Les smattes*, 1972; *Claude Gauvreau, poète; Les vautours*, 1975; *Games of the XXI Olympiad*, 1977; *L'affaire Coffin*, 1979; *La nuit de la poésie 28 mars 1980*, 1980; *Marie Uguay*, 1982; *Les années de rêve*, 1984; *Le Frère André*, 1987; *Bonjour Monsieur Gauguin*, 1988; *La nuit de la poésie 1991*, 1991; *André Mathieu, musicien*, 1994.

BIBLIOGRAPHY: Réal Larochelle (1971).

Louis Goyette

EVE(LYN) LAMBART. Born 1914, Ottawa, Ontario. Animator, director. It is possible that Eve Lambart, modest about her diligent, supportive role at the NFB, like Alma Reville on her work with husband Alfred Hitchcock, has yet to receive full recognition for her career in film, overshadowed as she was by the "master" animator, NORMAN MCLAREN. After studying at the Ontario College of Art, Lambart was hired by the NFB in 1942. Initially she drew maps and graphic designs for films in the wartime propaganda series "The World in Action," which were collected into a single film, her first as a director, *Maps in Action* (1945). McLaren claims to have helped her on the "technical side" of map animation. Her best known map project is *O Canada*, where Canada's national anthem is accompanied by an apparently single traveling shot from coast to coast, achieved through dissolving between shots where the camera moves vertically downwards on an animation stand. To this day, Lambart's idea continues to be evoked every night on CBC television at sign-off with a similar "map" film. She next worked with McLaren on perhaps his most experimental film, *BEGONE DULL CARE*, as co-director, no less. She continued to work with him on at least nine more films, and in a major interview conducted by Maynard Collins, McLaren argued that she functioned as more of a collaborator than an assistant, although "not usually on the basic idea of the film." She worked mainly on educational films, and after 1965 she began to develop her own paper cut-out technique on animal characters in (fable) films for children. She never fully retired, and in 1978 Margaret Wescott directed a documentary on her life for the NFB, *Eve Lambart*.

FILMS AS DIRECTOR AND ANIMATOR INCLUDE: *Maps in Action*, 1945; *The Impossible Map*, 1947; *Family Tree; Begone Dull Care* (co-dir.), 1949; *O Canada*, 1952; *Rhythmetic* (co-dir., co-anim.), 1956; *Lines Vertical* (co-dir., co-anim.), 1960; *Lines Horizontal* (co-dir., co-anim.), 1962; *Mosaic* (co-dir.) 1965; *Fine Feathers*, 1968; *Paradise Lost*, 1970; *The Story of Christmas*, 1973; *The Lion and the Mouse*, 1976; *The Town Mouse and the Country Mouse*, 1980.

OTHER FILMS WITH NORMAN MCLAREN (WITH ROLE IN PARENTHESES): *La poulette grise* (anim. assistant), 1947; *Around Is Around; Now Is the Time* (production asst.), 1951; *Neighbours* (production asst.), 1952; *A Chairy Tale* (production asst., chair anim.), 1957; *Le Merle* (co-anim.); *Short and Suite* (co-anim.), 1958.

BIBLIOGRAPHY: Maynard Collins; Marjah Tajibnapis, "Foregrounding Women: An Annotated Index of 52 Canadian Women Filmmakers." *Resources for Feminist Research*, 8, no. 4 (1979): 25–26.

Peter Rist

ARTHUR LAMOTHE. Born 1928, Saint-Mont, France. Director, editor, producer, writer. Born into a Gascogne peasant family, Arthur Lamothe immigrated to Canada in 1953, where he performed a number of different jobs, including working as a lumberjack. After studying political economy at Université de Montréal, he worked as a researcher and writer for the Radio-Canada news bureau while teaching the cinema. He was also one of the founders of the magazine *Images* (1955–56) and collaborated on SRC's Ciné-club. It was in 1961 that he really began his career in cinema by joining the ONF, researching and writing three short films, *Manger* (L. Portugais), *Dimanche d'amérique* (GILLES CARLE), and *Pour quelques arpents de neige* (G. Dufaux and JACQUES GODBOUT, 1962). In 1962 he directed his first film, *BÛCHERONS DE LA MA-NOUANE*, a documentary on the problems encountered in a lumberjack camp. Then he directed four other films, including his first fictional work (*La neige a fondu sur la Manicouagan*) and *La moisson*, before leaving the ONF in 1966, desiring to become an independent producer/director. In the same vein, he became one of the founding members of the Professional Association of Quebec Filmmakers (1964) as well as president of ARRFQ and of APFQ (1966). Further, in 1965, he founded the Société générale cinématographique, which became the Ateliers audio-visuels du Québec in 1979, and which produced his own work and about fifty other documentaries. In 1980, Lamothe became the first recipient of the Prix Albert-Tessier. Between 1967 and 1973, he directed some commissioned and educational films. It was in 1967 that he directed his first short film dealing with the reality of Montagnais life, *Le train du Labrador*, bearing witness to his social engagement with these First Nations people, who became the focus of the majority of his later films. In fact, from 1973 to 1983 Lamothe devoted himself to the making of an important documentary series of thirteen films, "Chronique des Indiens du Nord-Est du Québec," comprising two parts (*CARCAJOU ET LE PÉRIL BLANC* and *La terre de l'homme*). Shot in Montagnais, each "Chronicle" allowed the people themselves to recount their culture, their problems of dispossession, and their vision of the future, all in their own language. Moreover, all of the work completed by Lamothe from 1974 to 1983 was recorded in Montagnais: the last of these films, *Mémoire battante*, presented the spiritual Montagnais world. In the same year he inaugurated an archive consisting of his audiovisual documents (in all, eighty videotapes), which he donated entirely to an Attikamek-Montagnais cultural organization. Reflections on the tragic condition of people to whom he always listened—whether they were First Nations people, lumberjacks, or workers—or testaments affirming the conservation of their culture and way of life, the films of Arthur Lamothe are driven by a conscientious humanity and have made him one of the most respected filmmakers in the world.

FILMS AS DIRECTOR INCLUDE: *Bûcherons de la Manouane* (short; also ed.), 1962; *De Montréal à Manicouagan* (short), 1963; *La neige a fondu sur la Manicouagan*, 1965; *La moisson* (short), 1966; *Poussière sur la ville*, 1965–68; *Le train du Labrador* (short), 1967; *Ce soir-là, Gilles Vignault . . .* , 1968; *Pour une éducation de qualité* (6 TV shorts), 1969; *Le mépris n'aura qu'un temps*, 1970; *Le technicien en arpentage minier* (short), 1971; *Le système de la langue française* (7 shorts), 1972; *À propos de méthodes* (5 shorts), 1973; *Carcajou et le péril blanc* (8 films: 3 features, 5 shorts), 1973–74; *La chasse aux Montagnais* (short), 1974; *La terre de l'homme* (5 films, including 4 features), 1974–78; *Montage de la tente; Géographie Montagnaise* (shorts), 1978; *Mémoire battante* (3 TV films; also scr., narr., prod.), 1982–83; *Équinoxe*, 1986; "Cultures amérindiennes" (80 videos), 1984–88; *Ernest Livernois, photographe* (TV), 1988; *La conquête de l'Amérique II*, 1990; *La conquête de l'Amérique I*, 1992; *L'écho des songes*, 1993; *Le silence des fusils*, 1996.

BIBLIOGRAPHY: Gérald Baril; Rémi Savard, "Hommage à Arthur Lamothe, cinéaste," *Terres en vues* 2, no. 3 (1994): 25.

Isabelle Morissette

MICHELINE LANCTÔT. Born 1947, Montreal. Director, actor. Micheline Lanctôt is the rare filmmaker for whom the term "Renaissance Woman" seems only justified. Lanctôt started her film career as an animator at the NFB; from there she moved to Potterton Productions, where she worked on the Oscar-nominated short *The Selfish Giant*. Her career took an unexpected turn when GILLES CARLE developed a script with a central character inspired by what he saw as a contrast between the urban sophistication of her manner and her healthy countrified look. The result was the role of Bernadette in *LA VRAIE NATURE DE BERNADETTE*, a frustrated Montreal housewife who breaks out of stifling city life by returning to nature. Lanctôt won the 1972 Canadian Film Award for Best Actress and went on to become a leading star of the burgeoning Quebec cinema of the time. Her roles throughout the seventies tended to derive in greater and lesser degrees from the husky-voiced high-spiritedness of her signature role, particularly her guileless, good-hearted Yvette in *THE APPRENTICESHIP OF DUDDY KRAVITZ*— unfortunately, a thanklessly ill-conceived caricature of a Quebecoise Peasant Woman as Nurturer. In 1980, having already directed an NFB animated short in 1975 (*A Token Gesture*), she began a new stage of her filmmaking career with the release of her first feature as writer and director, *L'homme à tout faire*. This Chaplinesque comic fable of a handyman unlucky in love did little to prepare audiences for her next film, *SONATINE*, a story about two adolescent girls bonded by their disaffection within a mechanized urban dystopia (represented by a gray, pitiless Montreal). Lanctôt allies the melancholy humanism of her previous work as actor and director with a steely, modernist sense of space—

a formalist abstraction that renders the movement of ships, buses, and the subway with both a near-balletic grace and a profound sense of loss and foreboding.
This bleak *Modern Times* for the eighties has been followed by sporadic directing assignments, including 1993's *Deux actrices*.

FILMS AS DIRECTOR: *A Token Gesture* (short, also anim.), 1975; *L'homme à tout faire*, 1980; *Sonatine*, 1984; *Onzieme speciale*, 1989; *Deux actrices*, 1993; *La vie d'un heros*, 1994.

Mark Carpenter

CAROLE LAURE. Born 1948, Shawinigan, Quebec. Actor. At age eighteen, Carole Laure went to the theater for the first time and was bitten by the acting bug, auditioning for and joining the New World Theatre in Montreal shortly thereafter. She was discovered for the cinema by Jean Chabot, who cast her in the short film *Un bicycle pour Pit* (1968) and *Mon enfance à Montréal*. Her big break came when she auditioned for GILLES CARLE for *LA VRAIE NATURE DE BERNADETTE*. She didn't get the part, but Carle was inspired to write *La mort d'un bûcheron* (1972) with Laure in mind. He offered her the part of bar singer Maria Chapdelaine, a name usually recognized as that of Louis Hémon's famous folkloric heroine, a character she would eventually get to play in the 1983 Carle production, *Maria Chapdelaine*. *La mort* went to Cannes, and brought Laure considerable attention and offers, including the lead in *Emmanuelle*, which she turned down. She returned to Canada to make part of *Sweet Movie* (1974), a disastrous enterprise that ended in a legal battle with director Dusan Makavejev, but which nonetheless brought Laure more exposure. She continued to work with her mentor Gilles Carle, in *La tête de Normande Saint-Onge* and *L'ange et la femme*, before returning to France to make *La menace* with Yves Montand (1977). There, disillusioned with the lack of opportunities in the Quebec film industry, she settled in Paris with her partner, Canadian musician and composer Lewis Furey, whom she had met while making *Normande Saint-Onge*. In Paris, she returned to singing and dancing (skills she acquired during her time with the New World Theatre), and appeared at the Palace Theatre in a show written by Furey, and shortly after, on film, in Bertrand Blier's massive international hit *Préparez vos mouchoirs* (1977). Dividing her time since then between France and Canada, she has worked with directors such as Joyce Bunuel in France (*La jument vapeur*, 1977) and old friends in Canada such as Gilles Carle (*Fantastica*) and Lewis Furey (*Night Magic*), coming full circle in 1987 by being reunited with Jean Chabot for *La nuit avec Hortense*.

FILMS AS ACTOR INCLUDE: *Un bicycle pour Pit* (short), 1968; *Mon enfance à Montréal; Fleur Bleue*, 1971; *IXE-13*, 1972; *La mort d'un bûcheron; Les corps célestes* (Can/Fr), 1973; *Sweet Movie* (Can/Fr/Ger), 1974; *La tête de Normande Saint-Onge; Born for Hell* (Can/Fr/Ger/It), 1975; *Spécial Magnum*, 1976; *L'eau chaude l'eau frette; L'ange et la femme; Exit; La menace* (Can/Fr), 1977; *Inside Out*, 1970–79; *Au revoir . . . à lundi* (Can/Fr), 1979; *Fantastica*, 1980; *Maria Chapdelaine* (Can/Fr), 1983; *The Surrogate*;

Stress, 1984; *Night Magic* (Can/Fr), 1985; *Sauve-toi, Lola,* 1986; *La nuit avec Hortense,* 1988; *Thank You, Satan,* 1989; *Flight from Justice/Justice à Eden River* (Can/US/Fr), 1993.

BIBLIOGRAPHY: "Interview," *Take One* 7, no. 4 (March 1979).

Simon Brown

JEAN-CLAUDE LAUZON. Born 1953, Montreal; died 1997. Director, screenwriter. Jean-Claude Lauzon was Quebec cinema's *enfant terrible,* a controversial and equally vocal filmmaker with whom the media had a field day whenever they provoked his passionate ire. Even with only two feature films to his credit and two shorts, the uniqueness and raw emotional power of Lauzon's vision was such that one could not help but see in him a true author, whatever one may have thought of the artistic value of his productions. The director, who also specialized in advertising art, was a diamond in the rough, as his uneven and self-indulgent yet brazenly imaginative works of fiction can testify to. While a student at the Université de Québec à Montréal (UQAM), he shot his first short, *Super Maire l'homme de 3 milliards* (1979), a wickedly funny if unnuanced satirical criticism of Jean Drapeau, Montreal's famous *über*-mayor. Fame came to Lauzon with the release of his first feature, *UN ZOO LA NUIT,* a dramatic hybrid of genres and tones. Half New Wave noirish gangster film and half masculine melodrama, this violent *and* tender film keeps the viewer in a constant state of unrest and intellectual perplexity, while introducing into Quebec's naturalistic cinema the cool, slick imagery of commercials, a dubious aesthetic contribution. Lauzon's greatest qualities and flaws are again apparent, and exacerbated, in *LÉOLO.* This largely autobiographical yet fantastical account of his very troubled childhood strikes one as a cry from the heart and a plea for artistic and spiritual freedom—Lauzon's very own *refus global.* It haunts us with painful and nightmarish images, postcards from a feverish mind which, intentionally or not, have opened up Quebec cinema's worn-out landscapes to encompass horrific urban views, surreal mental scapes, and exotic lands. Alas, the film is also pretentious and heavy-handed, overburdened with an insistent voice-over narration and more flash than mise-en-scène. Which didn't stop it from making *Time* magazine's top ten film list the year it came out, a rare achievement for a foreign film, let alone a Quebec production. Lauzon's last feature before his tragic death (his plane crashed in the Quebec wilderness), *Léolo* is now looked upon as his living will and testament.

FILMS AS DIRECTOR: *Super Maire L'homme de 3 milliards* (short), 1979; *Piwi* (short), 1981; *Un zoo la nuit,* 1987; *Léolo,* 1992.

BIBLIOGRAPHY: Robin Wood, "Toward a Canadian (Inter)national Cinema (part 1 of a 2-part article)," *CineACTION!,* no. 16 (Spring 1989): 59, 63; Richard Corliss, "The Art of Childhood," *Time* (Toronto) 141, no. 16 (April 19, 1993): 63–64.

Johanne Larue

GUY L'ÉCUYER. Born 1931, Montreal; died 1985. Actor. In theater and television, Guy L'Écuyer was one of the most engaging Quebec actors of his generation. Equally, he has lent his thickset frame to several striking characters of the Quebecois cinema. In GILLES CARLE's *LA VIE HEUREUSE DE LÉOPOLD Z.*, L'Écuyer first revealed his talent for film acting in 1965. Here, he incarnated a sympathetic snow remover who has to deal with the whims of both his boss and his wife while maintaining a good attitude on life. Throughout his career, L'Écuyer excelled in interpreting naive and charming characters who lacked malice and with whom audiences related with much pleasure and emotion. MARC-ANDRÉ FORCIER is the Quebecois filmmaker who sought his services most often, writing no less than four roles specifically for the actor: in *BAR SALON*, L'Écuyer played a bar owner faced with financial problems; in *Night Cap* (1974), his character dies unexpectedly in a tavern toilet after winning a frozen turkey; in *L'EAU CHAUDE L'EAU FRETTE*, he is Panama, a gay head cook; then, in *Au clair de la lune* (1982), he plays Bert, a former bowling champion reduced by rheumatism to being a sandwich-man. Guy L'Écuyer has also leant his services to a good number of first works by young filmmakers, evidence of his willingness and pleasure in rising to challenges. It is worth mentioning here, among others, *Le temps d'une chasse* by FRANCIS MANKIEWICZ, *Tu brûles . . . tu brûles* by Jean-Guy Noël, and *L'heure bleue* by Hubert-Yves Rose. Each year, the "Rendez-vous du cinéma québécois" awards the Prix Guy-L'Écuyer for the best performance by a male or female Quebecois actor over the previous year.

FILMS AS ACTOR: *Les mains nettes*, 1958; *La vie heureuse de Léopold Z.*, 1965; *Le martién de Noël*, 1970; *Élisa 5 ou les inquiétudes d'Élisa*; *Les indrogables*; *Le temps d'une chasse*, 1972; *Trois fois passera . . . ; Tu brûles . . . tu brûles*; *Bar salon*, 1973; *Night Cap*; *Une nuit en Amérique*, 1974; *Lies My Father Told Me*; *Les vautours*; *La fleur aux dents*, 1975; *Ti-mine, Bernie pis la gang . . . ; Ti-Cul Tougas*; *J. A. Martin, photographe*; *L'eau chaude l'eau frette*; *Parlez-nous d'amour*; *L'heure bleue*, 1976; *Jacob Two Two Meets the Hooded Fang*, 1978; *The Lucky Star*, 1980; *Au clair de la lune*, 1982; *Maria Chapdelaine*, 1983.

Louis Goyette

JACQUES LEDUC. Born 1941, Montreal. Director, cinematographer, camera operator. Along with MICHEL BRAULT, Jacques Leduc probably has the most diversified filmography in the history of Quebec cinema. He also worked as a director of photography and wrote film criticism for the reputable *Objectif* magazine from 1960 to 1967. In 1962, he joined the ranks of the ONF, first as assistant cameraman, then assistant director, until finally he got to try his hand at directing in 1967 (*Chantal en vrac*). One of his early shorts, *Là où ailleurs*, co-directed with editor Pierre Bernier, belongs as much to the avant-garde as to the documentary tradition. In a sweeping and cunningly sarcastic montage of seemingly disparate images and sounds, the film looks at one region's struggle with *passéist* Catholic traditions, American and English-Canadian imperialism, and the rise of consumerism in the face of rampant unemployment. The more recent docudramas *Albédo* and *Le dernier glacier*, again co-created with colleagues, still show Leduc's fondness for hybrid forms, but he also shot documentaries in the less flamboyant direct style ("CHRONIQUE DE LA VIE QUOTIDIENNE"; *Charade chinoise*). When turning to fiction, Leduc directed three remarkable films: *ON EST LOIN DU SOLEIL*, *Tendresse ordinaire* (1973), and *Trois pommes à côté du sommeil* (1988). The first two challenge the viewer with slow-paced elliptical narrative structures in which long takes predominate; zen-like modernist films, really, where, amid alienation techniques, emotion slips in unawares. The third sports a more abrupt montage style suiting the sarcastic tone of Leduc's criticism of his hero, a man possibly not unlike himself, a disillusioned intellectual looking for meaning in the morose aftermath of Quebec's failed referendum on independence. Jacques Leduc is still shooting and creating; his segment of *Montréal vu par . . .* ("La Toile du temps") is a tribute to his undying interest in original filmic experimentation as he tells us of Montreal's history through the spatiotemporal journey of a painted portrait caught up in a postmodern dance of blue screen projections, collages, and humorous wit.

FILMS AS DIRECTOR INCLUDE: *Chantal en vrac* (short); *Nominigue depuis qu'il existe*, 1967; *Là où ailleurs* (short; co-dir., P. Bernier), 1969; *On est loin du soleil*, 1970; *Je chante à cheval avec Willie Lamothe* (short; co-dir., L. Ménard), 1971; *Tendresse ordinaire*, 1973; "Chronique de la vie quotidienne" (series of 8 different films on which many directors collaborated), 1977–78; *Albédo* (short; co-dir., R. Roy), 1982; *Le dernier glacier* (co-dir., R. Frappier), 1984; *Charade chinoise; Trois pommes à côté du sommeil*, 1988; *L'enfant sur le lac*; "La toile du temps" (short) in *Montréal vu par . . .* , 1991; *La vie fantôme*, 1992; *L'âge de braise*, 1997.

BIBLIOGRAPHY: Jean-Pierre Bastien and Pierre Véronneau.

Johanne Larue

JEAN PIERRE LEFEBVRE. Born 1941, Montreal. Director, scriptwriter, producer, actor. Undoubtedly one of the most prolific Quebecois directors, Jean Pierre Lefebvre directed no less than twenty-two feature films between 1965 and 1991—an average of one feature per year. This productivity, fairly unique in Quebec, is explained by the fact that Lefebvre primarily shoots on a modest budget and that on the whole he practices the art of cutting corners: his films have an artisanal quality; they are shot in 16mm, favoring the long take; he films on location in exteriors or in natural settings. Contrary to the vast majority of cineastes of his generation, who began their careers on the documentary path with the ONF, Lefebvre was drawn to independent cinema, and, by founding his own production company—Cinak—with his wife Marguerite Duparc in 1969, he ensured total control over the direction of his films. His passage through the ONF was of fairly brief duration, allowing him time to direct two films, *Mon amie Pierrette* (1967) and *Jusqu'au coeur*. Frequenting cine-clubs led Lefebvre to film criticism (most notably for the magazine *Objectif*) as well as to the directing of his own films. With his first short film, *L'homoman* (1964), the tone was established: a sort of poem-essay in which the filmmaker puts into play his delirious imagination, this surrealist film is a good indicator of the formal and narratival experiments that run through many of his films. Behind an occasionally unbridled humor hangs a biting critique of Quebecois society, of its political and cultural mores. Thus in *Jusqu'au coeur* (1968), Lefebvre denounces the passivity and inertia of the Quebecois by demonstrating how they can be susceptible to brainwashing by the mass media and advertising. In *Q-Bec my love ou un succés commercial*, the spectator is confronted with a scathing indictment denouncing the wave of sexploitation films initiated by Denis Héroux's *Valérie* (1968). Following the example of Brecht and Godard, Lefebvre's "experimental" films abound in fragmented narratives, alternating between black and white and color, long take and montage, and manipulating the soundtrack in an unconventional manner. This experimentation clearly reveals the rich style of the filmmaker, but in the most extreme cases Lefebvre is not exempt from eliciting from the spectator a certain exasperation, as in the baffling *Ultimatum* (1973). One also finds in Lefebvre's oeuvre some classically constructed films: *Il ne faut pas mourir pour ça* (1967), LES DERNIÈRES FIANÇAILLES, and LES FLEURS SAUVAGES are perhaps the most beautiful and moving of Lefebvre's films, in which the director observes his characters with much tenderness. Following Duparc's death in 1982, Lefebvre began a new stage in his career, filming *Au rythme de mon coeur*, an introspective film essay based on a private journal. His subsequent films and videos are often directed in highly artisanal conditions and, even if they occasionally lack cohesion, maintain an indisputable creative integrity.

FILMS AS DIRECTOR INCLUDE: *L'homoman*, 1964; *Le révolutionnaire*, 1965; *Patricia et Jean-Baptiste*, 1966; *Il ne faut pas mourir pour ça; Mon amie Pierrette*, 1967; *Jusqu'au coeur*, 1968; *La chambre blanche, Q-Bec my love ou un succés commercial*, 1969; *Mon oeil*, 1970; *Les maudits sauvages*, 1971; *Les dernières fiançailles; On n'engraisse pas les cochons à l'eau claire; Ultimatum*, 1973; *L'amour blessé*, 1975; *Les gars des vues*, 1976; *Le vieux pays où Rimbaud est mort*, 1977; *Avoir 16 ans*, 1979; *Les fleurs sauvages*, 1982; *Au rythme de mon coeur*, 1983; *Le jour "S . . ."*, 1984; *Laliberté Alfred Laliberté sculpteur 1878–1953*, 1987; *La boîte à soleil*, 1988; *Le fabuleux voyage de l'ange*, 1991; *La passion de l'innocence*, 1995.

Louis Goyette

STUART LEGG. Born 1910, London, England; died 1988, Wiltshire, England. Director, editor, producer. Stuart Legg, one of Canada's best-known war documentarists, began his career in Britain as part of the socially conscious group of 1930s filmmakers that included JOHN GRIERSON, Basil Wright, Humphrey Jennings, Harry Watt, and Arthur Elton. While Legg was employed at the Empire Marketing Board, he collaborated in the making of such well-known classics of British documentary as *Coalface* and *Nightmail* (both 1936). In 1939, Legg joined John Grierson in immigrating to Canada. He initially worked at the

Canadian government's Motion Picture Bureau, directing two famous documentaries as part of the Dominion Youth Training Plan, *The Case of Charlie Gordon* and *Youth Is Tomorrow*. Legg soon moved to the newly formed National Film Board and began producing a series of influential and groundbreaking films in the "Canada Carries On" and "World in Action" series. A number of these films, such as CHURCHILL'S ISLAND (1941), *The War for Men's Minds* (1943), and *Atlantic Patrol* (1940), were widely distributed at the time. *Churchill's Island* won for the NFB its first Oscar, and *Warclouds in the Pacific* (1941) greatly helped to draw attention to Canada's film board. Legg's particular strengths in all of these productions were his skillful, economical editing style and his use of powerful and evocative voice-over commentaries. After the war, Legg joined Grierson in New York to work on other documentary series, returning to Britain in 1957 to become chairman of the government's Film Centre International.

FILMS AS DIRECTOR INCLUDE: *The Case of Charlie Gordon; Youth Is Tomorrow*, 1939; *Atlantic Patrol; Letter from Aldershot; Home Front*, 1940; *Churchill's Island; Warclouds in the Pacific*, 1941; *Labour Front; The War for Men's Minds*, 1943; *Global Air Routes; Our Northern Neighbour; Fortress Japan*, 1944; *Balkan Powder Keg*, 1945.

BIBLIOGRAPHY: Forsyth Hardy, 1979; Gary Evans, 1984.

Helen and Paul Salmon

LÉOLO. Jean-Claude Lauzon, Canada (Quebec)/France, 1992, 107 min., color. JEAN-CLAUDE LAUZON's second feature film, *Léolo*, is narrated from the point of view and voice-over of a coming-of-age boy, Léo Lozeau (Maxime Collin). Léo fantasizes that he is of Italian parentage (in contrast to his other siblings) and insists that he be called Léolo Lozone. Fearing that he will follow the rest of his family, excepting his mother (Ginette Reno), as a patient in the psychiatric ward, Léolo escapes through his writing and dreams, allowing him to refute his family reality with the mantra "because I dream, that is not what I am." Lauzon contrasts Léolo's idealistic dreams of Sicily, inspired by his crush on a neighborhood girl, Bianca, with the dark, grungy Montreal alleyways of Léolo's neighborhood and his family's starkly lit apartment. Lauzon also uses contrast to show us the sordidness of Léolo's real sexual experiences compared to his dreams of Bianca. These sexual experiences are impaired for Léolo, either visually (glimpsed through keyholes or through dirty or fogged glass, or under the influence of alcohol) or physically (the uncomfortable locations of a bathroom or a construction site). The veracity of Léolo's mantra is demonstrated at the end, when he finds himself unable to dream anymore, and joins his family in the psychiatric ward (in a catatonic state). The film oscillates between reality and fantasy, both with the inclusion of dream sequences and by using a character called the Word-Tamer (Pierre Bourgault), who functions as an omniscient godlike observer, privy to Léolo's thoughts and actions through the boy's discarded writings. The dreamlike environment resonates through Lauzon's choice of choral music on the soundtrack, suggesting the possibility of spiritual transcendence.

BIBLIOGRAPHY: Maurice Alioff, "Jean-Claude Lauzon's Léolo," *Take 1* 1, no. 1 (1992): 15–19, 33–35; Michel M. Buruiana, "Jean-Claude Lauzon: Interview," *Séquences*, no. 158 (June 1992): 33–34.

Sandra Gallant

LA LIBERTÉ D'UNE STATUE A Statue's Liberty. Olivier Asselin, Quebec, 1990, 90 min., b+w. *La liberté d'une statue* is to Quebec cinema what GUY MADDIN's *Archangel* (1990) is to English Canadian cinema, an independent avant-garde feature-length fiction film, a very rare offering in our day and age. The two films share further traits—a postmodern sensitivity toward the visual aesthetics of early cinema and a rather esoteric philosophical discourse—yet both remain ferociously original in their particulars. Olivier Asselin's poetic filmic essay concerns itself with the ontological nature of cinema, a serious subject which it nonetheless explores with a delicious and sometimes absurd sense of humor. The film opens with the voice of a young Belgian scientist explaining, over black leader, that he is presently sitting in our projection booth, with his assistant, Mademoiselle Scott, to oversee the post-synchronization of the footage we are about to see. He apologizes for the inconvenience and further explains that this near-century-old film was excavated somewhere in Egypt, the contents of its dialogue reconstituted by an expert team of deaf-mute lip readers! The satirical slant of the film is further established when the attentive viewer soon realizes that Mademoiselle Scott is able to dub actors who either have their backs to the camera or have temporarily left the frame. The understated humor extends to the visual pastiches Asselin creates. His images are at once reminiscent of Edison's early films, Carl Dreyer's austere and minimalist compositions, and Georges Mélies' almost surreal visions. As is the case when Anne, the thaumaturge heroine of the fictional fiction, is persuaded by capitalist extraordinaire P. T. Robertson to step inside a makeshift rocket (which doubles as camera obscura) to reach the stars, where her destiny lies. In the end, though, it is the narrator and Mademoiselle Scott who best embody the mysterious, magical, and subversive power of cinema: our unseen hosts have fallen in love during the course of the projection and decide to elope, leaving us alone with an unfinished film.

BIBLIOGRAPHY: Gilles Marsolais and Marcel Jean, "Dossier: La liberté d'une statue," *24 Images*, no. 49 (Summer 1990): 4–11; Johanne Larue, "Archangel et La liberté d'une statue: Fictions expérimentales de jeunes cinéastes," *Séquences*, no. 150 (January 1991): 45–46.

Johanne Larue

LIES MY FATHER TOLD ME. Jan Kadar, Montreal, 1975, 103 min., color and b+w. Anglo Québécois films are sadly rare. Not that there are no English-speaking films shot in the province of Quebec, but most of them are American productions (often looking for locations with a European feel), and of the truly Canadian projects filmed there, very few have taken upon themselves to illustrate the human and social specifics of the anglophone experience in the land of Québécois. And almost none have shown members of the two "Canadian solitudes" interrelate in their drama, a strange but telling phenomenon. *Lies My Father Told Me* is an endearing exception. Not that the film solely preoccupies itself with the Canadian/Québécois dynamic. It does not. In fact, it is but one of the multiple facets to be found in the social fresco imagined by the film's creators. First and foremost, this 1920s drama concerns itself with the chronicle of one Montreal-based Jewish family, living modestly on St-Urbain Street, where the Hassidic Mile-End section of Montreal meets Outremont, two neighborhoods where Jews of various economic levels live in close proximity with other ethnic groups, including the French-speaking blue-collar Catholics or their more bourgeois counterparts. It is a heterogenous and lively tapestry that Czech director Jan Kadar lovingly illustrates, with humor and nostalgia, from a screenplay by Ted Allan. Their production was privileged in that it was picked up by Columbia Pictures and widely distributed across North America, winning the Golden Globe for Best Foreign Film and receiving an Academy Award nomination for Best Original Screenplay. Had producers learned the lesson taught by this film, we might find more English Canadian/Quebec ventures today.

BIBLIOGRAPHY: S. Adilman, Review of *Lies My Father Told Me, Variety* (September 17, 1975): 18.

Johanne Larue

LIFE CLASSES. William D. MacGillivray, Nova Scotia, 1987, 116 min., color. *Life Classes* is without a doubt one of the great films Canadian cinema has given us in the last fifteen years. The film recounts, with moving simplicity, the transitory passage of Mary Cameron from a small Cape Breton village to the city of Halifax. This journey is for her the occasion to bring into the world and raise alone her daughter Marie; above all, it provides the opportunity to realize herself fully, both as a woman and as a visual artist. Touching on a number of social themes as well as the question of individual identity, BILL MACGILLIVRAY is never didactic or moralizing, even while allowing here and there some caustic comments on the pretentious character of modern art. The slow, meditative rhythm of the film, which breathes a marine air from beginning to end, is an image of the peaceful life of the insular world of Nova Scotia. The film also contains numerous admirable long takes—true moments of grace!—like the circular traveling shot which reveals the students at a fine arts school drawing the nude body of Mary, who is posing before them. The impression of sobriety that one finds in *Life Classes* recalls the most beautiful films of JEAN PIERRE LEFEBVRE (who, incidentally, was an adviser during the writing of the film). The sensitive and restrained performance of Jacinta Cormier in the role of Mary adds to the gentle character of the film, as does the music of Alexander Tilley, inspired by Welsh folklore.

BIBLIOGRAPHY: Pierre Véronneau (1991), 66–87.

Louis Goyette

LILIES. John Greyson, Quebec, 1996, 95 min., color. Indefatigable and pushed forward by the international triumph of his musical about AIDS, *Zero Patience* (1995), the prolific John Greyson went on to shoot for the big screen one of the most critically acclaimed Quebec plays of recent history: *Les feluettes* by Michel Marc Bouchard. The playwright transposed his drama himself, in a first effort for cinema, and remained fairly true to his original text. In fact, a lot of *Lilies'* dialogue is taken directly from the play. This tale of love, jealousy, betrayal, and vengeance, set within a religiously oppressive school in 1912, is told through the fake confession of a prisoner to an old friend, now a bishop. More precisely, some forty years after the fact, Simon Doucet (the criminal) has invited Monsignor Bilodeau in the hope of shedding light on the past, with the help of his fellow prisoners, who reenact the fatal events that caused him to be incarcerated. With such material to film, it is evident that the interplay between past and present would inevitably result as the key to a successful mise-en-scène. Although Greyson's style was probably influenced by Robert Lepage's LE CONFESSIONAL, from the previous year, it is nonetheless original in its lyrically evanescent conception of time and space. The bathtub sequence toward the end, where, against all odds, two young boys meet again to lose themselves in a taboo embrace, is certainly a good example of that feeling. Greyson blends the stage in the church (inside the detention center) with spaces from the past, where the action effectively occurred, while falling leaves from another time progressively fill the present space of the prison: a truly poignant moment. Also, while some criticism has been levelled at the sometimes hesitant performances from the actors, mainly young emerging talents, this unusual trait actually testifies to Greyson's intelligent direction, as it reflects the fact that what is being shown is delivered by convicts, and not professionals. This detail is revelatory of the filmmaker's path to maturity, already well embodied by *Lilies* as a whole. It is no surprise, then, that the film was awarded the 1996 Genie for Best Picture.

Alain Dubeau

ARTHUR LIPSETT. Born 1936, Montreal; died 1986. Director, editor. Arthur Lipsett, who tragically committed suicide after spending much of his adult life in a state of depression, was one of Canada's finest filmmakers and a pioneer experimentalist whose influence extended far beyond the country's borders. After studying art and design at l'École des Beaux-Arts de Montréal he joined the NFB's animation unit in 1957. While with Unit F he co-directed and co-animated his first film, *Hors d'oeuvres* (1960). At Unit B he made his first solo film as a director, *Very Nice, Very Nice* (1961), which was a collage of (mostly) still photographs accompanied by sound clips from other film board documentaries. It provides a scathing critique of contemporary society's dependency on technology in an era of atom bomb paranoia, where editing links world political figures with destruction and creates outrageous associations—for example, Einstein with death. Although made after Bruce Conner's similarly apocalyptic *A Movie* (1958), it's doubtful that Lipsett would have seen the Californian's work, and, in any event it is the Canadian film which was widely seen and had the greater influence, both stylistically and thematically: it was even nominated for the 1961 Oscar in the Live Action Short Subject category! Lipsett's next film, *21–87*, carried the collage principle further with slightly longer duration, (mostly) moving shots (rather than photographic stills), many of which appear to have been filmed by the director. Here, we can sense a very personal vision of the world emerging, where Lipsett sympathizes with old and marginalized people, apparently alienated and outcast by an encroaching technological nightmare, while including many shots of these people looking up to the sky. The thin ray of hope in his dark world seems to be through an unidentified spiritual or mystical force. The strength of these films and his next, *Free Fall*, released in 1964, is that they provide both an intense visual play of graphics, light, movement, and texture, and interpretive associations within and between shots and sound elements. Like the best Canadian experimental films, they work on a number of levels. One cannot be certain of one's understanding of Lipsett's intentions, but he himself said of *Free Fall* that its construction was deliberately neither "logical" nor "rational." He completed only four more films, leaving two unfinished works. Arthur Lipsett's important oeuvre is only now beginning to receive the recognition it deserves in Canada. In 1993, Richard Magnan defended his master's thesis at the Université de Montréal on "Les collages cinématographique d'Arthur Lipsett comme 'métaphore épistémologique.' "

FILMS AS DIRECTOR AND EDITOR: *Hors d'oeuvres* (co-dir. with five others), 1960; *Very Nice, Very Nice*, 1961; *21–87* (also cin.), 1963; *Free Fall* (also cin.), 1964; *A Trip down Memory Lane* (also co-prod.), 1965; *Fluxes*, 1967; *N-Zone* (also co-scr., co-cin.), 1970; *Strange Codes*, 1972; *Blue and Orange* (co-dir. with Tanya Tree), 1975—unfinished; *Traffic Flow*, 1978—unfinished.

BIBLIOGRAPHY: Lois Siegel, "Montreal Cowboy," *Cinema Canada*, no. 44 (February 1978): 16–17; Lois Siegel, "A Clown Outside the Circus," *Cinema Canada*, no. 134 (October 1986); 10–14.

Peter Rist

LISTEN TO THE PRAIRIES. Gudrun Bjerring Parker, (Manitoba) NFB, 1945, 21 min., b+w. Along with Jane Marsh Beveridge, Gudrun Parker was one of the first Canadian crop of documentarists hired by the NFB during the war. During this period STUART LEGG's influence determined the structure and tone of the board's documentary voice; films produced under the banner of the "Canada Carries On" series were hard-hitting and authoritative wartime propaganda. Following Legg's departure after the war a new style began to emerge, a looser style, with greater interest in observation over prescription. Parker's *Listen to the Prairies* is an early example of this style. The film, which documents the

Manitoba Annual Music Festival, eschews the formality of the previous board style for a more lyrical approach. The prologue and epilogue of the film situate the importance of the festival by locating it in the context of the cultural life of the city. A montage of images presents the city when introducing the festival, and the film concludes by segueing from the festival to the plains at sunset. The film features topics familiar to Parker's longtime interests, namely, music, the expression of Canadian culture, and the lives of young people. An eleven-minute abridged version of the film was released under the title *A City Sings*. In the 1950s Parker further pushed the traditional codes of documentary in two key films, *Opera School* (1952) and *A Musician in the Family* (1953). Both films wrapped a dramatic story around the real events in question. Again the films centered on music, culture, and Canada's youth.

Dave Douglas

LONELY BOY. Wolf Koenig and Roman Kroitor, NFB, 1962, 26 min., b+w, 16mm. The last film in the "Candid Eye" series produced by Unit B, *Lonely Boy*'s stated intention is to provide "a candid look at Paul Anka, from both sides of the footlights," and to document "the astonishing transformation of an entertainer into an idol worshipped by millions of fans around the world." Shot on 16mm with a hand-held camera and portable Nagra sound recording system, the film follows Anka on a tour of various performances, each preceded by his trademark "Anchors Aweigh" intro. As perhaps might be expected, *Lonely Boy* is characterized by what Bruce Elder refers to as "detached, ironic humour." For example, at one point Anka's monologue about his song-writing skills provides the voice-over for a series of shots of the entertainer silently singing, gesturing, and mugging for the audience. After the performance, Anka presents a gift to Yule Podell, owner of the Copacabana Club in New York; Anka's gift, an enormous framed picture of himself, leaves Podell embarrassed and speechless. Later, during a performance at the New York amusement park Freedomland, Anka's singing is drowned out by the screaming of his fans; the film then cuts to footage of the fans themselves, their screams drowned out by the pop idol's singing. At the time of its release, *Lonely Boy* was a groundbreaking (and award-winning) documentary; its loose, episodic structure and disjointed editing were considered highly innovative. Today the film retains much of that appeal, especially in light of Anka's subsequent decline into Las Vegas club land.

BIBLIOGRAPHY: Peter Harcourt, "The Innocent Eye: An Aspect of the Work of the National Film Board of Canada," in Feldman and Nelson, 67–77.

Mitch Parry

THE LOON'S NECKLACE. Frank Radford "Budge" Crawley, Ottawa, Ontario, 1948, 11 min., 16mm, color. Crawley Films (*see* JUDITH & FRANK "BUDGE" CRAWLEY) produced this adaptation of a West Coast Tsimshian myth in the minimal spare time allowed by their prolific schedule of promotional and instructional films. Shot intermittently over several years with the creative input of all the Crawley staff, *The Loon's Necklace* displays startling inventiveness. While a stentorian voice-over tells completely the simple, linear story, the film's inspiration is visual. Befitting the tale of a withdrawn blind medicine man regenerating his spirit and finally his sight, an expressionistic mise-en-scène gives way to realism in the end. Native masks from the National Museum of Canada occupy most of the film, embodying the characters, rendering the climate, and evoking the mood. Their severity dramatizes the hardships of famine, wolves, and winter while imposing an elemental feel that authenticates the myth. Judiciously lit and framed close-ups, combined with skillful montage amid Graham Crabtree's accomplished painted and sculpted landscape, propel the narrative lucidly. Already cited among the eleven most outstanding noncommercial films of the world at an Edinburgh festival, it won Film of the Year at the first Canadian Film Awards in 1949. Imperial Oil then took on sponsorship, giving it an unusually wide and hugely successful distribution. The film became an enduringly popular, warmly revered staple of library, school, and community screenings, bringing to the Crawleys their lasting reputation for resourceful and inspired filmmaking.

Ian Elliot

COLIN LOW. Born 1926, Cardston, Alberta. Director, producer, cinematographer, animator. One of the NFB's pioneering documentary and animation filmmakers, Colin Low combined interests in creativity and technology, culminating in his most recent work with spectacular large screen Omnimax and IMAX projects. He joined the NFB in 1945, working initially as an animator, and in 1952 directed the groundbreaking, Oscar-nominated *Romance of Transportation in Canada*, which gently ridiculed Canada's historical dependence on the growth of transportation systems. It also introduced the world to a comic, narrative-driven style of NFB animation, very different from the experimental work of NORMAN MCLAREN's studio. Low's first documentary film was also an NFB landmark, the tone poem on a cowboy, CORRAL (1954). He continued to thrive as a director of documentaries, under TOM DALY's guidance, and for over three years he worked on the spectacular multi-screen/chamber presentation for Expo '67, *Labyrinthe*, which historian Peter Morris calls "the last and most complete, statement of the collective humanist ethos of the NFB's Unit B." Low then pioneered the NFB's "Challenge for Change" program with a series of films made with the direct participation of the people themselves on Fogo Island, Newfoundland. He later produced some of the most successful films in this community development series, including *Cree Hunters of Mistassini* (dir. Tony Ianzelo and Boyce Richardson, 1974). While still employed by the NFB he became increasingly interested in spectacle, especially working on 3-D experiments, which resulted in the IMAX film at the Vancouver Expo in 1986, *Transitions*, and eventually in the very high definition, 3-D IMAX work, *Momentum*, filmed and projected at 48 f.p.s. (double the normal rate) and made as the cen-terpiece of the Canada pavilion at Expo '92 in Seville, Spain.

FILMS AS DIRECTOR INCLUDE: *Cadet Rousselle*, 1947; *The Romance of Transpor-tation in Canada*, 1952; *Corral*, 1954; *Gold*, 1955; *City of Gold* (co-dir., Wolf Koenig), 1957; *City out of Time*, 1959; *Universe* (co-dir., Koenig); *Circle of the Sun*, 1960; *The Days of Whiskey Gap*, 1961; *Labyrinthe* (co-dir., Roman Kroitor), 1967; "Fogo Island" series (28 films), *Atmos* (Omnimax), 1980; *Pete Standing Alone*, 1982; *Transitions* (IMAX; co-dir., Tony Ianzelo), 1986; *Emergency* (IMAX; co-dir., Ianzelo), 1988; *Mo-mentum* (IMAX, 3-D; co-dir., Ianzelo), 1992.

BIBLIOGRAPHY: Peter Morris (1984), 170–71, 184–85; René Villeneuve, "Interview with Colin Low, Tony Ianzelo, Ernie McNabb," *Perforations* 11, no. 2 (April 1992): 34–36.

Peter Rist

THE LUCK OF GINGER COFFEY. Irvin Kershner, United States/Canada (Mon-treal), 1964, 100 min., b+w. Filmed in Montreal, by an American director, *The Luck of Ginger Coffey* is, in many respects, the direct precursor of DON SHEBIB's *GOIN' DOWN THE ROAD*. The film follows James Francis "Ginger" Coffey (Rob-ert Shaw), an Irish immigrant who has come to Montreal with his wife Vera (Mary Ure) and teenaged daughter Polly. Although he is unable to find mean-ingful employment, Ginger tells his friend Joey, a sportswriter for the (fictional) *Montreal Tribune*, "I'm willing to bet on Canada." Joey urges Ginger to apply for a position as an editor with the *Tribune*. However, Ginger is offered a position as a proofreader instead, and his unwillingness to admit this to Vera causes her to leave him and begin what appears to be an unconsummated affair with Joey. Polly leaves her mother in order to live with Ginger, who is now forced to take on another job with a diaper delivery service. He begins to ac-tively assert himself in both workplaces, coming up with an idea for crib rentals at the diaper service, which leads his employer to offer him a job as his assistant. However, Ginger turns down the job and resigns from his delivery job, still holding out for a reporter's position at the *Tribune*. When the film seems to be threatening to turn into a Horatio Alger story, Ginger loses both his hopes of becoming a reporter and his position as a proofreader, and he finds himself, once again, impoverished and without prospects. Ginger is arrested for urinating in an alleyway; at the trial the judge mildly ridicules him as Vera looks on. Ginger appears to have learned humility, and the film ends with an ambiguous shot of Ginger opening the door to Vera's apartment. *The Luck of Ginger Coffey* exemplifies many "quintessentially Canadian" qualities—the irresponsible male character; the downbeat tone; the ambiguous ending. The film is highlighted by the strong performances of the principal actors and by highly convincing art direction which successfully captures the atmosphere of English Montreal in the 1960s.

Mitch Parry

LA LUTTE *Wrestling*. Michel Brault, Marcel Carrière, Claude Fournier, and Claude Jutra, (Montreal) ONF, 1961, 28 min., b+w. *La lutte* is one of the seminal French Unit (ONF) *cinéma vérité* films, and one that exemplifies the differences between the French and English schools of "direct" filmmaking. While the English "Candid Eye" films stressed nonintervention of the pro-filmic event, their French counterparts shared a closer rapport with their subjects. The filmmaker's voice, held back in the "Candid Eye" films, is felt everywhere in *La lutte*. The film is full of humor, reflexivity (the interjection of silent film–style intertitles), and irony. Borrowing from Roland Barthes' study on myths, *La lutte* is an engaged study of a lower-class, urban entertainment form steeped in emotional catharsis and ritualistic violence. In a series of remarkable close-ups we witness audience members vicariously involved in the Manichean battle of hero versus villain, their emotions swayed by the rhythm of the wrestling match. Stylized music (organ, harpsichord) marks the wrestling arena as a shrine. *La lutte* demonstrates how sport, with its ritualistic aspects (the fan participation, the Reichian pregame preparations), has come to signify the new secular religion of a modern, urban Quebec. The greater empathy felt by the French filmmakers toward their subjects no doubt grew out of the cultural positioning of these young filmmakers within the broader Quiet Revolution of the late 1950s and early 1960s. For the *cinéma vérité* revolution, sports became an ideal locus for this shift from the folkloric and rural to the modern and urban.

BIBLIOGRAPHY: David Clandfield, "Films of the French Unit at the NFB," in Feldman, 112–124.

Donato Totaro

M

WILLIAM D. MACGILLIVRAY. Born 1946, St. John's, Newfoundland. Director. While he received his film training at the London School of Film Technique (now the London International Film School), where he produced the film *7:30 A.M.* for his diploma, Bill MacGillivray has maintained a close connection to the Maritimes and to his native Newfoundland throughout his career. In 1973, he was a founding member and the first president of the Atlantic Filmmakers' Co-op (AFCOOP) in Halifax, Nova Scotia. It was here that MacGillivray made one of his most moving documentary films, *Linda Joy*, on the life of Linda Joy, the coordinator of AFCOOP, who contracted and died of breast cancer. The basis of the film is an interview with Joy done in a series of single takes (shortly before she died). To this MacGillivray added other material from Joy's life, all interspersed with fades to black. At the film's conclusion the director discusses his last visit with her in the hospital prior to her death. After a series of sponsored films including *The Author of These Words* (1980), MacGillivray began to make the transition to narrative filmmaking. Early efforts such as *Aerial View* (1979) and *Stations* (1981) mark this transition, but both retain a sense of MacGillivray's interest in the avant-garde, as both rework their narrative lines in a manner that refuses linearity. The culmination of the transition is to be found in *LIFE CLASSES*. Nominated for five Genies, the film proved to be a breakthrough for MacGillivray. Since that time he has maintained an interest both in fictional work—*Understanding Bliss, The Vacant Lot*—and in documentary—*I Will Not Make Any More Boring Art* (1988), a film recounting the influence of the avant-garde on the Nova Scotia College of Art and Design (NASCAD) during the late 1960s and early 1970s. His most recent work has been on television, creating "Gullages," a comedy series about a cab company in St. John's, Newfoundland, in 1996.

FILMS AS DIRECTOR: (shorts) *Talkautobanden*, 1970; *7:30 A.M.*, 1971; *Lil and Mr. Bill*, 1973; *Breakdown*, 1977; *Aerial View*, 1979; *The Author of These Words*, 1980;

Stations, 1981; *Alistair MacLeod*, 1984; *Abraham Gesner; Linda Joy*, 1985; (features) *Life Classes*, 1986; *I Will Not Make Any More Boring Art; My Brother Larry*, 1988; *The Vacant Lot*, 1989; *Understanding Bliss*, 1990.

BIBLIOGRAPHY: Peter Harcourt, "Planting Pictures: An Appreciation of the Films of William D. MacGillivray," *Cinema Canada*, no. 146 (November 1987): pp. 14–21.

Dave Douglas

GUY MADDIN. Born 1956, Winnipeg, Manitoba. Director, screenwriter. Guy Maddin, sprung from the nurturing confines of the Winnipeg Film Group, is one of cinema's most idiosyncratic and remarkably original stylists. Maddin met his future producer Greg Klymkiw at the University of Manitoba, where they both took a film class taught by George Toles, Maddin's eventual screenwriting collaborator. Together they formed a repertoire that includes actors Kyle McCulloch, Michael Gottli, Victor Cowie, and Sarah Neville. Maddin's inimitable style, alienating to some, surreally engaging to others, is marked by a self-conscious use of historical anachronism. With all of film technology at his disposal, Maddin prefers to employ low-tech, in-camera effects (greased lenses, soft focus, iris effects, superimpositions), high contrast lighting (usually black and white), and manipulated soundtracks that recreate the look and sound of silent and early sound film history. Most of Maddin's film references are pre-1940 (German expressionism, *kammerspiel*, Universal horror). This appropriation of film history rarely exists in a pure, unadulterated state (why some critics have referred to his style as "postmodern expressionism"). In *Archangel* (1990), for example, the characters and setting are pre-revolutionary Russia, but the aesthetic sensibility is far more Germanic. Pinpointing a single source for his films would be impossible. *Archangel* owes much to Joseph von Sternberg's *Scarlet Empress* (United States, 1932) for its histrionic performances and anachronistic art direction. But its catalogue of film references also includes Soviet films of the twenties/thirties, Carl Dreyer, German expressionism, and Maddin's own earlier works. His films may look and feel ancient, but they are laced with comical anachronisms (for example, during a battle scene in *Archangel* we see two men carrying a huge, modern bomb). Thematically and narratively his films are marked by foregrounded Freudianism (Oedipal complexes, social/sexual repression, bisexuality), eruptions of graphic violence, twisted humor, and an underlying streak of sexual perversion (the homoeroticism between Lt. Boles and the young boy in *Archangel*). *Gimli*'s concluding ass-grappling showdown between the two male leads is a textbook example of all the above elements. Unfortunately, given the market-driven nature of the film industry, Maddin continues to have difficulty getting projects off the ground. Perhaps he can take solace in the worldwide cult recognition he has received (Canada's only genuine cult director?) and the fact that, at the age of thirty-nine in 1995, he became the youngest recipient of the Telluride Lifetime Achievement Award.

FILMS AS DIRECTOR: *The Dead Father* (short), 1985; *Tales from the Gimli Hospital*, 1988; *Archangel*, 1990; *Careful*, 1992; *Odilon Redon* (short), 1995; *Twilight of the Ice Nymphs*, 1997.

BIBLIOGRAPHY: Geoff Pevere, "Guy Maddin: True to Form," *Take One*, 1, no. 1 (1992): 4–11; Gilles Hébert.

Donato Totaro

MADELEINE IS . . . . Sylvia Spring, British Columbia, 1971, 90 min., color. Sylvia Spring's first feature, the first feature film directed by a woman in Canada (in 1970), explores the coming of age of the title character, Madeleine, amid the controlling desires of the men in her life. As a French Canadian woman in Vancouver, Madeleine is initially an outsider and dependent upon, first, her chauvinist boyfriend Toro, and then, subsequently, an ineffectual friend, David, whom Madeleine imagines to be a clown in her dreams. Her reactions to both men's desires to control her are manifested in this dreamscape, in the form of a clown who encourages her to follow him. When both relationships prove unfulfilling Madeleine makes changes in her life. She leaves Toro, begins her painting career, and asserts control over her own sexuality. At the film's conclusion she finds herself free from the desires of those around her. Spring combines fiction with a strong social sense by mixing Doug McKay's documentary-influenced camera style with more formally styled sequences. In addition, Spring experiments with sound, often using *musique concrete* to create an alienating image of the commercial world. A photo collage reinforces this distinction by presenting the image of the dispossessed in Vancouver, in a manner that recalls ALLAN KING's *Skid Row* (1956). The film's message of empowerment and self-awareness reflects the growing influence of feminism on Canadian filmmakers.

Dave Douglas

NICK MANCUSO. Born 1949, Mammola, Calabria, Italy. Actor. Born in Italy and raised in Toronto, Nick Mancuso began acting in high school, but majored in psychology while at the University of Toronto. It was only upon graduating that he decided to pursue an acting career. He spent the early 1970s traveling across Canada, performing in theaters from Vancouver to Halifax. He also spent a year at the Stratford (Ontario) Festival in productions of *A Midsummer Night's Dream* and *Antony and Cleopatra*, among others. Mancuso's big screen debut came in 1974 by providing the narration for BOB CLARK's sorority house horror film *Black Christmas*. His first on-screen appearance, however, was a small role in Allan Eastman's *A Sweeter Song*, which was followed by a supporting role in the horror film *Death Ship*. It was as the brainwashed member of a religious cult in *TICKET TO HEAVEN* that Mancuso was finally given an opportunity to demonstrate the acting skills he had successfully shown on stage. Mancuso reveals the vulnerability and terror involved in the gradual submission of one's own identity and makes a startling physical transformation, from a healthy young man to an expressionless cult member with hollow eyes and a ghostly pallor. It is a sensitive performance for which he won the Best Actor honors at the 1980 Genie Awards. This was followed by the romantic lead in the classic French Canadian story *Maria Chapdelaine*, directed by GILLES CARLE. Here Mancuso demonstrates power and magnetism as the woodsman lover of the title character. Sadly, he has not yet achieved the stardom expected after these notable performances and his earlier stage work. Mancuso has since worked predominantly in television, giving topnotch performances such as his role as a world-weary gangster in the U.S. TV movie *Double Identity* (1991).

FILMS AS ACTOR: *A Sweeter Song*, 1976; *A Thousand Moons*, 1975; *Death Ship* (Can/UK), 1980; *Ticket to Heaven*, 1981; *Maria Chapdelaine* (Can/Fr); *Tell Me that You Love Me* (Can/Is), 1983; *Paroles et musique* (Can/Fr), 1984; *Night Magic* (Can/Fr), 1985; *Toronto Trilogy*, 1984; *Crowd*, 1985; *Tom Alone* (TV), 1987; *Double Hope/Haute tension* (Can/Fr); *Last Train Home* (TV), 1990; *Milena*, 1991; *Komanche Street*, 1994; *Young Ivanhoe* (TV, Can/Fr/UK), 1995; *Twists of Terror* (TV), 1996: *The Ex* (Can/US), 1997.

Stacey Abbott

FRANCIS MANKIEWICZ. Born 1944, Shanghai, China; died 1993, Montreal. Director, screenwriter. Francis Mankiewicz began his career in England, shooting six documentaries before returning to Quebec in 1969 and pursuing his career as a film technician and director. Unlike some of the more distinguished Quebec filmmakers of his generation, Mankiewicz did not embrace the modernist tradition or have an overt political agenda. If truth be told, his filmography counts more mainstream commissioned films than personal projects, and many of the former he directed for English Canada. Nonetheless, Mankiewicz is now remembered for the latter, which include *Le temps d'une chasse*, LES BONS DÉBARRAS, *Les beaux souvenirs* (1981), and *Les portes tournantes* (1988). Although the last three are adaptations of literary works, their thematic unity makes them Mankiewicz's own, as does the warmth with which he infuses his direction, the naturalistic acting he demands of his actors, and the undercurrent of romanticism which threatens, at any given moment, to topple the classical order structuring the narratives. In all four films, a child, whether young or grown up, struggles for the affection of one of his parents. The violent impulse of that need and the inadequacy of the respondent leads always to tragedy or sorrow. In *Le temps*, the father dies after having ignored his son during a weekend-long hunting party. In *Débarras*, the daughter alienates her mother's lover and precipitates her uncle's death to secure her mother's attention. In *Les beaux souvenirs*, a father's incapacity to love his daughter leads her to suicide. And finally, *Les portes tournantes* shows an already cast-aside son trying to piece together an image of his mother through artefacts he finds in a trunk. That his own son succeeds where he has failed (the young boy rejoins his grandmother at the end of the film) shows that, maybe, Mankiewicz was ready to turn over a new leaf and introduce some hope in his tormented personal films, when cancer claimed him.

FILMS AS DIRECTOR INCLUDE: *Le temps d'une chasse*, 1972; *Un procès criminel* (short), 1973; *L'orientation* (short), 1974; *Expropriation* (short), 1975; *What We Have Here Is a People Problem* (short), 1976; *I Was Dying Anyway* (short), 1977; *Une amie d'enfance*, 1978; *Les bons débarras*, 1980; *Les beaux souvenirs*, 1981; *And Then You Die*, 1987; *Les portes tournantes*, 1988; *Love and Hate* (TV), 1989; *Conspiracy of Silence*, 1990.

BIBLIOGRAPHY: J. Beaulieu, "Un réalisateur: Francis Mankiewicz," *Séquences*, no. 100 (April 1980): 11–29.

Johanne Larue

RON MANN. Born 1959, Toronto, Ontario. Director, writer, editor. Toronto-based Ron Mann has made a handful of provocative documentaries about subjects unusual to the tradition of Canadian documentary cinema. Mann attended Bennington College and the University of Toronto. Upon graduation he made his first film, *Imagine the Sound* (1981), an examination of American avant-garde jazz in the 1960s. This was followed in 1982 by *Poetry in Motion*, which dealt with luminaries of contemporary poetry, concentrating on poets of the Beat generation and their Canadian and American descendants. Some of the poets examined in the film, including bp Nichol and David McFadden, had cameo appearances in Mann's first (and only, to date) feature-length fiction film, *Listen to the City*, a political allegory dealing with unemployment, municipal politics, and the machinations of the corporate world. *Poetry* was also instrumental in establishing the subject matter of *Echoes Without Saying*, a documentary about the collective behind the well-known Canadian publishers, Coach House Press. Mann's greatest success, both critically and popularly, was *Comic Book Confidential* (1989), an attempted history of comic strips. Although the film has been accused of an overly brief treatment of comics before the 1960s, it contains interviews with some of the major figures of "underground" comics in the 1970s and 1980s (e.g., Lynda Barry). In 1992 Mann released *The Twist*. Ostensibly a documentary about the dance craze of the early 1960s, the film examines the complex relationship between black and white popular culture in the United States. Mann's interests are, clearly, diverse; perhaps more important, his films reflect his own conviction that being Canadian also means being part of a larger, North American culture. An outspoken advocate of a genuinely independent cinema, Mann is an important figure in Toronto's film community.

FILMS AS DIRECTOR: *Imagine the Sound*, 1981; *Poetry in Motion*, 1982; *Echoes Without Saying*, 1983; *Listen to the City*, 1984; *Comic Book Confidential*, 1989; *The Twist*, 1992.

BIBLIOGRAPHY: David Segal, "An Interview with Ron Mann," *Cineaste*, 17, no. 2 (1989): 45.

Mitch Parry

MANUFACTURING CONSENT: NOAM CHOMSKY AND THE MEDIA. Mark Achbar and Peter Wintonick, NFB, 1985–92, 167 min., color. *Manufacturing*

Consent is a biography of Noam Chomsky, arguably the most important intellectual alive. The film operates principally as a vehicle for Chomsky's political philosophy on the "manufacture of consent" (a phrase taken from the American journalist/philosopher Walter Lippmann). Chomsky posits that the mainstream media operate as a tool for propaganda and ideological control by deliberately deceiving the majority of society for corporate and government profit. This manipulation and thought control are underscored when Chomsky points to the media's flagrant neglect of Indonesia's orchestrated genocide in East Timor, where the West had profitable interests. This is held up against the equally horrible but much smaller-scale atrocities perpetrated by Pol Pot in Cambodia, which met with a considerable amount of outcry in the media. (East Timor was invaded by Indonesia in 1975, and Pol Pot's regime lasted from 1975–79.) Chomsky's point is that the dominant elites defend humanitarian issues only when profit is involved. The film is structured as a reflexive tool on media-constructed reality, and forces the viewer into a heightened sense of critical engagement. There are many ironic visual metaphors that use found footage to highlight the danger of mediated consent. The obvious propaganda films of old have now become more subtle and dangerous. Chomsky is filmed in absurd locales, like Montreal's Olympic Stadium, projected on an immense screen, booming into an empty complex, echoing his and our marginalization through disinformation. In substitute locations for the media world, the sports arena and advertisements reveal the elimination or diversion of thought. *Manufacturing Consent* is a fascinating look at the dominant forces that control many societal actions and reactions. The film, which Achbar began in 1985, was constructed over the course of seven years, employing the ideology it promotes; the filmmakers used a democratic approach with extensive consultative screenings that eventually allowed over 600 people to be involved in the development of the final product. The film works as an emotional vanguard, thankfully manufacturing dissent.

Rob Cotterill

MARGARET'S MUSEUM. Mort Ransen, UK/Canada (Nova Scotia), 1995, 118 min., color. The fourth feature film by veteran NFB docudrama director Mort Ransen, *Margaret's Museum* took five years to secure its funding, and only became a reality when international star Helena Bonham Carter (Margaret MacNeil) joined the cast. The story focuses on the life of Margaret, a woman who lives in the shadow of the harsh conditions for coal miners on Nova Scotia's Cape Breton Island in the 1940s. A woman of fierce independence, Margaret swears she will not become like her embittered mother (KATE NELLIGAN) and all others in the community: widows to the "pit." The arrival of Gaelic poet and bagpipe playing drifter Neil Currie (Clive Russell) alters Margaret's life, and the two enjoy a brief period of happiness before economics forces Neil to work in the mines with Margaret's brother Jimmie (Craig Olejnik). The death of the two men precipitates the creation of Margaret's "Museum": a tragic monument to lives bitterly wasted. The moving portrayals of the principal characters by Bonham Carter, Nelligan, Russell, and Kenneth Welsh ensured the success of the film, winning Best Acting Genies for Bonham Carter and Nelligan (Supporting). The film's success marked Ransen's final acceptance as a feature film director after his extended period as a documentarian and house director at the NFB (which he had joined in 1961).

BIBLIOGRAPHY: Ingrid Randoja, "Ransen Rising," *Take One*, no. 9 (Fall 1995): 28–31.

Dave Douglas

A MARRIED COUPLE. Allan King, Toronto, 1969, 96 min. (originally 112 min.), color, 16mm. Like *POUR LA SUITE DU MONDE* (1963) and *NOBODY WAVED GOODBYE* (1964) before it, *A Married Couple* is one of the key films to test the boundaries of documentary and fiction—a specialty of Canadian cinema. Shot over a period of ten weeks in 1968 as a documentary about a couple experiencing problems in the seventh year of their marriage, it was released in Canada in 1969 as a fiction feature. In focusing on moments of conflict (out of the seventy hours of footage obtained), director ALLAN KING fashioned a very "dramatic" film out of real life. The small crew of King, cinematographer Richard Leiterman, and Christian Wangler, on sound, spent two weeks with Billy and Antoinette Edwards in their house, slowly setting up, in order to acclimatize everyone with the situation of making a "direct cinema" documentary before actually shooting film. King thought that the Edwardses, who were friends of his, would make good subjects because they were very charismatic and would probably rise to the occasion, even in a situation of crisis. Even though it is hard to believe in the veracity of private moments where the filmmakers clearly intrude—for example, when Leiterman actually gets on the bed to get closer to the couple, who are contemplating making love—there are times where the couple seem genuinely to forget that King and company are there—for example, where an argument over the use of the family car turns physical. King and editor Arla Saare structured the material to include moments of calm and relative harmony between the conflicts, but like *WARRENDALE*, his previous film, *A Married Couple* seems to work best as therapy to alleviate anger, for the filmmaker and film subjects alike. The bad language used extensively by the Edwardses was unprecedented in a Canadian film, but only the Ontario government (and nowhere else in Canada, or the United States and UK, where it was also released) demanded cuts. The film stands today as a wonderful time capsule of marriage in the 1960s, with Billy and Antoinette self-destructively testing the limits of their relationship.

BIBLIOGRAPHY: Alison Reid; Alan Rosenthal, "*A Married Couple*, An Interview with Allan King," in Feldman and Nelson, 179–93.

Peter Rist

MASALA. Srinivas Krishna, Toronto, 1991, 105 min., color. A remarkable, edgy, somewhat rude first feature film for writer/director/actor Srinivas Krishna, *Masala* is also the first feature to be directed by a South Asian–Canadian man. Daringly opening on a representation of the infamous, unsolved Air India flight 182 bombing, on June 23, 1985, Krishna, playing his namesake, whose immediate family has perished in the disaster, immediately risks alienating many in his potential Indian audience. From here, *Masala* (which means "sauce") mixes drama and comedy and adds the "spices" of fantasy/dream sequences and bizarre musical numbers that parody traditional, Bombay-made Hindi musicals. Celebrated British-Asian actor Saeed Jaffrey is captivating in three roles: the popular Indian god of love, Krishna, who appears blue-faced as a TV character; a prosperous sari dealer, Lallu Bhai, young Krishna's uncle; and Mr. Tikkoo, a postal worker. Krishna is good friends with Rita, Tikkoo's daughter (played by Jaffrey's daughter, Sakina), but is in conflict with virtually everyone else. His punkish character stands in youthful rebellion against Indian tradition, which is shown to support hypocrisy and greed. Tikkoo, who seeks social standing rather than money, finds a very rare and valuable 3d (three penny) 1867 stamp, which could easily be the family salvation: "Grandma" (Zohra Segal), who worships Krishna at her TV shrine, shockingly tells her son to take the "fucking" money. He wants Rita to be a doctor, but she would rather be an airplane pilot. Indeed, the image of aircraft—repeatedly shown overhead in low angle shots—is a key motif in *Masala*, which cleverly juxtaposes various Canadian and Indian cultural icons, especially in its fantasy sequences. The god Krishna, in a Toronto Maple Leafs uniform, shoots a hockey puck at a postal van, enabling Tikkoo to capture the $5 million stamp; male and female red-jacketed "Mounties" raid Lallu Bhai's sari store, searching for terrorists, only to find Sikhs in the basement innocuously planning to market toilet rolls marked with Sikh history—"everyone has time to read on the 'loo' "—in India. Perhaps not every element works in *Masala*, yet the film clearly lives up to its title, and the colorful conjunction of Paul Sarossy's cinematography, Tamara Deverell's production design, and Alexa Anthony's art direction help to augment Srinivas Krishna's bold attempt at organic unity through dialectical conflict: ancient and modern, old and young, Indian and Canadian, "good" and "bad" taste. Krishna has since completed another dramatic feature, *Lulu* (1995), starring Kim Lieu as a Vietnamese mail-order bride whose character seems to metaphorically represent all Third World victims.

BIBLIOGRAPHY: Cameron Bailey, "Srinivas Krishna: *Masala* Filmmaker's Heady Hybrid Redesigns Standards of Style," *Now*, February 6, 1992; Hussain Amarshi, "Power/ Knowledge, or a New Meaning for Agency" (interview with Srinivas Krishna and Vic Sarin), *Take One*, no. 5 (Summer 1994): 12–15.

Peter Rist

THE MASK Eyes of Hell [*Face of Fire/The Spooky Movie Show*]. Julian Roffman, Ontario, 1961, 83 min., b+w. *The Mask* is Canada's first and as yet only

3-D feature film. Although its Montreal-born director and producer, Julian Roffman, came primarily from a documentary tradition (the U.S. "March of Time" series, NFB World War II shorts), he has also produced features: *Explosion* (1969); *The Pyx* (1973). Budgeted at $300,000, the film was given wide distribution by Warner Brothers during a mini 3-D revival in the early 1960s. Shot in Toronto (mainly at the Toronto International Studios), the film lacks any Canadian specificity and was treated by Warner Brothers as an indigenous American product. The film tells the story of a psychiatrist, Dr. Barnes (Paul Stevens), who comes across an ancient Aztec mask which causes the wearer to experience hallucinogenic visions (enter the 3-D sequences) and succumb to the base desires of the subconscious. The film falls within the horror tradition of the overreacher plot where the search for scientific knowledge comes at the expense of the scientist's humanity. Hence, the mask functions narratively like the potion in *The Invisible Man* (United States, 1933) or *Dr. Jekyll and Mr. Hyde* (United States, 1932). The film rises above its stock plot and characters (doctor caught between science and the supernatural; unscientific, doting girlfriend; understanding secretary) with the 3-D sequences (three, totalling approximately fifteen minutes) designed by SlavkoVorkapich (his final film), which owe much to the French surrealism of Jean Cocteau (*Orphée*, 1950) and Georges Franju (*Les yeux sans visage*, 1959).

BIBLIOGRAPHY: R. M. Hayes; Sylvain Garel and André Pâquet.

Donato Totaro

BILL MASON. Born 1929, Ottawa, Ontario; died 1988. Filmmaker, environmentalist, author, artist. As perhaps Canada's best-known nature documentarist, Bill Mason made eighteen films (many of which won awards) during his career. After graduating from the University of Manitoba School of Art, Mason worked as a quite successful commercial artist, escaping annually to spend each summer canoeing in the wilderness. He gradually began photographing and later filming his canoe trips and began working with Crawley Films (*see* FRANK "BUDGE" CRAWLEY and JUDITH CRAWLEY) as an animator and photographer, assisting his friend Chris Chapman with the making of the award-winning film *Quetico Park* (1958). Mason later went on to make films for the National Film Board from 1962 to 1984. An ardent environmentalist and canoeist, Mason's films spoke to his deep love of the wilderness and his Christian faith. Notable for their stunning photography, his films were intended to educate viewers about the preciousness of Canada's wilderness resources, and to share with the audience Mason's own passion for the wilds. Indeed, Mason frequently incorporated elements of his own life (himself, family, friends) into his films and writings, as in *Blake*, which portrays Mason's close friend and fellow wilderness lover, Blake James. Similarly, *Song of the Paddle* centers around a Mason family summer trip by canoe, and *Path of the Paddle* (both 1978) narrates the way in which Mason passes on his knowledge of wilderness canoeing to his young son

Paul. Mason's deep fascination with wolves (which he raised) was captured in his trilogy of films, *Death of a Legend*; his most commercially successful film, *Cry of the Wild*; and *Wolf Pack*. After making *Waterwalker* in 1984 (with a soundtrack by the popular Canadian musician Bruce Cockburn), Mason retired from filmmaking to concentrate on painting—a pursuit cut short by his death in 1988 of cancer.

FILMS INCLUDE: *Wilderness Treasure*, 1962; *Paddle to the Sea*, 1966; *The Rise and Fall of the Great Lakes; Death of a Legend*, 1968; *Blake*, 1969; *Cry of the Wild*, 1971; *In Search of the Bowhead Whale; Wolf Pack*, 1974; *Face of the Earth*, 1975; *Song of the Paddle; Path of the Paddle*, 1978; *Coming Back Alive*, 1980; *Breadalbane*, 1983; *Waterwalker*, 1984.

BIBLIOGRAPHY: Wilber Sutherland, "In Tribute: Bill Mason (1929–1988)," *Quill & Quire* 55, no. 2 (February 1989): 8; Gene Walz, "A Motion and a Spirit: Bill Mason's Nature Films," *Border Crossings* (Spring 1989): 37–40.

Helen and Paul Salmon

DEREK MAY. Born 1932, London, England; died 1992. Director, editor, art director, painter. Though not as prolific a filmmaker as many NFB directors, Derek May produced a body of work that garnered wide respect. A British import to the board in 1965, May began as an art director—working on DON OWEN's *The Ernie Game* (1967)—prior to directing his own films. His early films balanced experimental and documentary tendencies. His first short film, *Angel* (1966), featured a dreamlike encounter of a woman and a man as they attempt to fly with butterfly wings. *Niagara Falls* and *McBus* offered daring travelogue "anti-documentary" encounters with contemporary society. In both films May offers dissonant and obscure visions of contemporary values. *Niagara Falls* is notable both for the presence of actor Michael J. Pollard—fresh from his role in *Bonnie & Clyde* (United States, 1967)—as guide, and for May's initial interest in the legacy of First Nations Canadians. His investigation of Native culture would be followed later with *Sananguagat*, a documentary on Inuit artworks that coincided with a national exhibition of the Canadian Eskimo Arts Council in 1974. *Pandora* (1971) remains one of May's last experimental films, employing color, light, and sound to symbolically reconstruct the ancient myth. Through the late 1970s and into the 1980s he became increasingly interested in topics of identity, language, and the role of art in society, preoccupations that mirrored his own personal life, that of an anglophone filmmaker living in a bilingual city. This challenge was elaborated on film in the autobiographical *Mother Tongue*, which featured May and his wife, actress Patricia Nolan, negotiating their bilingual marriage. May's interest in art and artists produced a series of films that examined the relationship between the works themselves and society, in *The Boulevard of Broken Dreams*, and the lifestyle of the artists in relationship to their work and society, in *Off the Wall* and *Krzysztof Wodiczko: Projections*.

FILMS AS DIRECTOR: *Angel* (also scr.), 1966; *Niagara Falls* (also scr.), 1967; *McBus*, 1969; *A Film for Max*; 1970; *Pandora*, 1971; *Sananguagat Inuit Masterworks of 1,000 Years* (also ed.), 1974; *Pictures from the 1930's* (also scr. & prod.), 1977; *Mother Tongue* (also co-ed.), 1979; *Off the Wall*, 1981; *Other Tongues*, 1984; *Do the Crawl*, 1985; *The Boulevard of Broken Dreams*, 1987; *Krzysztof Wodiczko: Projections*, 1991.

BIBLIOGRAPHY: Piers Handling, "The Films of Derek May," in Feldman, 217–28.

Dave Douglas

BRUCE MCDONALD. Born 1954, Toronto. Director, editor, producer. Bruce McDonald, one of the more popular directors to emerge from Toronto in the late 1980s, has built a career on typifying the figure of the "outlaw" within Canadian cinema. Emerging from Ryerson Polytechnical Institute in the early 1980s, McDonald was among a number of new Canadian filmmakers who were influenced by the New Wave and punk movements of the late 1970s and channelled this experience to produce an edgy style of filmmaking. At the time, McDonald was a figure of importance both on and behind the scenes, helping to found the Liaison of Independent Filmmakers of Toronto (LIFT). Although he has worked with numerous well-established figures in Canadian film, editing productions by RON MANN (*Comic Book Confidential*), ATOM EGOYAN (*FAMILY VIEWING* and *Speaking Parts*), and PETER METTLER (*The Top of His Head*), in addition to working with Norman Jewison, McDonald's persona is that of a filmmaker on the outside of the mainstream. From his early short mock documentaries to his string of road movies to his recent work on television, McDonald has continually focused on characters who identify themselves as outsiders. His characters are those people who are searching the depths of their own identity, questioning their role in society—in short, his figures are those engaged in the quest. McDonald's first feature, *ROADKILL*, proved to be the vehicle to launch him from the margins into the limelight: at the Toronto Festival of Festivals, after *Roadkill* was awarded the $25,000 prize of the Toronto-City Award for Best Canadian Feature, the director, in an offhand remark, suggested that the money could buy a big chunk of hash. McDonald teamed up with actor/ writer DON MCKELLAR for a second road feature, *Highway 61*, in 1991. The period in between this film and his next afforded McDonald the time to "park" long enough to attend the Canadian Film Centre. McDonald's return to filmmaking, *Dance Me Outside*, was seen by many as a valiant effort, but one too cautious in its approach to issues surrounding teens on a First Nations Reserve. The director who had made his living on the outskirts had reached unfamiliar territory. Once again McDonald got on the (tour) bus with his next feature *HARD CORE LOGO*, which forsook earlier themes of identity in favor of the darker terrain of nostalgia and remembrance of promises unfulfilled; the scenery is more stark, more unforgiving. A parting gesture to marginality, McDonald repaid the B.C. backers of the film with the premiere at the Vancouver Film Festival. Although the film appeared to suggest that McDonald himself was moving beyond the world of youth, music, and fringe, McDonald has not forsaken his roots, and his next production, the CBC television movie *Platinum*, finds the director on familiar roads once again.

FILMS AS DIRECTOR: *Let Me See* (. . .) (short), 1982; *Knock! Knock!* (short), 1985; *Roadkill*, 1989; *Highway 61*, 1991; *Dance Me Outside*, 1994; *Hard Core Logo*, 1996; *Platinum* (TV), 1997.

BIBLIOGRAPHY: Marc Glassman, "Rockin' on the Road: The Films of Bruce McDonald," *Take One*, no. 8 (Summer 1995); Ken Anderlini, "Bruce McDonald's *Hard Core Logo,*" *Take One*, no. 13 (Fall 1996).

Dave Douglas

DON MCKELLAR. Born 1963, Toronto. Writer, actor, director. Recognized as an eclectic character actor, Don McKellar is also an award-winning screenwriter and director. He began his dramatic career by entertaining audiences with magic shows while in high school and also touring with his own children's theater company. Now an established playwright, he is the co-founder of the experimental theater group, the Agusta Company, who have staged *Indulgence, Drinking, Red Tape, The Book of Rejection*, and *86*. McKellar is internationally known for his work as the author and star of two of director BRUCE MCDONALD's films: *ROADKILL* (nominated for a Genie Award, Best Original Screenplay) and *Highway 61* (1991). He also co-wrote the acclaimed film *THIRTY-TWO SHORT FILMS ABOUT GLENN GOULD* (nominated for a Genie Award, Best Original Screenplay) and a third McDonald film, *Dance Me Outside* (1994). As an actor McKellar has collaborated with two of Canada's leading filmmakers: ATOM EGOYAN, on *The Adjuster*, and *EXOTICA*, which won him a Genie Award for Best Supporting Actor; and PATRICIA ROZEMA, on *When Night Is Falling*. After attending the Canadian Film Institute McKellar completed his directorial debut, a short film titled *Blue* (1992), starring DAVID CRONENBERG, which won McKellar the Gold Plaque at the Chicago Film Festival.

FILMS AS ACTOR INCLUDE: *Roadkill*, 1989; *Highway 61; The Adjuster*, 1991; *Thirty-Two Short Films About Glenn Gould*, 1993; *Exotica; Camilla; Arrowhead*, 1994; *When Night Is Falling*, 1995; *Never Met Picasso; Joe's So Mean to Josephine; In the Presence of Mine Enemies* (TV), 1996; *Vinyl*, 1997.

FILMS AS WRITER INCLUDE: *Roadkill*, 1989; *Highway 61*, 1991; *Blue* (short; also dir.), 1992; *Thirty-Two Short Films About Glenn Gould*, 1993; *Dance Me Outside*, 1994.

FILM AS DIRECTOR: *Blue*, 1992.

Alice Black

NORMAN MCLAREN. Born 1914, Stirling, Scotland; died 1987, Hudson, Quebec. Animator, director. Until the recent surge of interest in DAVID CRONENBERG and ATOM EGOYAN, Norman McLaren was almost certainly the best known

Canadian filmmaker both inside and outside his adopted country. He is also Canada's most honored filmmaker, having won over two hundred prizes at film festivals and award ceremonies all over the world. Considering that McLaren made predominantly short, animated films throughout his career, and that most of these films could be termed "experimental," these are remarkable achievements. At the age of eighteen, he became an interior design student at the Glasgow School of Art and also joined the Glasgow Film Society, where he began to make films. In 1935 he entered his third complete film in the Glasgow Amateur Film Festival, where it won a prize, after which the one-man jury, JOHN GRIERSON, offered him a job at his newly formed GPO film unit. *Love on the Wing* (1938), a color commercial for air mail, with metamorphosing figures hand painted over rolling multiplane backgrounds, was the first animated film Grierson produced at the GPO. Inspired by Emile Cohl's early metamorphoses, Oscar Fischinger's stick figures, and the work of his colleague, Len Lye, directly on film stock, *Love on the Wing* began McLaren's forte: formal experimentation in the cause of education. In 1941, Grierson brought McLaren to Canada from New York, where he had become a landed immigrant in 1939. Initially working on wartime propaganda, McLaren continued to animate in an abstract mode and in 1944 began to draw on black card, first with gouache (*C'est l'aviron*) and later with pastels (e.g., *LA POULETTE GRISE*), where delicate changes were created through a combination of erasing and in-camera dissolves. He set up the NFB's animation studio and trained the first generation of film animators there. As the prizes accumulated, McLaren became increasingly independent, eventually becoming the envy of all would-be experimental filmmakers, a kind of "civil servant as artist" who could work at his own pace on his motion studies. From the brilliant scratching and painting on film abstractions of *BEGONE DULL CARE* and the anthropomorphizing of paper cut-out numbers in *Rythmetic* to the pixillation of CLAUDE JUTRA's chair in *A Chairy Tale* (1957) and the multiple exposures of dancers' movements in *PAS DE DEUX*, McLaren expanded his repertoire of animation techniques while continuing to entertain and educate. He was as interested in film sound as image, even to the extent of drawing and scratching on (optical) soundtracks, and he worked closely with innovative composers and musicians like Maurice Blackburn and Ravi Shankar. His film experiments weren't always successful, especially when he was working with purely geometrical figures, and he dwelt rather too extensively late in his career on distending human movement (from *Pas de deux* through *Ballet Adagio*, to *Narcissus*, 1981). But, ultimately, he is best remembered as a humanist artist and teacher, concerned equally with the potential beauty of the film medium and the potential for people to come together as one. In this view, the experimental nature of his work is far less significant than its social effect, and *NEIGHBOURS* is, perhaps, his most definitive film, arguing against war and national boundaries, and having been made in between two educational stints with UNESCO in China (1949) and India (1953).

FILMS AS DIRECTOR AND ANIMATOR: *Mail Early; V for Victory*, 1941; *Five for Four; Hen Hop*, 1942; *Dollar Dance*, 1943; *Alouette* (co-anim., co-dir., René Jodoin); *Keep Your Mouth Shut; C'est l'aviron*, 1944; *Là-haut sur ces montagnes*, 1945; *A Little Phantasy on a 19th-Century Painting; Hoppity Pop*, 1946; *Fiddle-de-dee; La poulette grise*, 1947; *Begone Dull Care* (co-dir., Eve Lambart), 1949; *Now Is the Time; Around Is Around*, 1950–51; *Neighbours; Two Bagatelles*, 1952; *A Phantasy*, 1948–53; *Blinkity Blank*, 1955; *Rythmetic* (co-dir., Lambart), 1956; *A Chairy Tale*, (co-dir., Claude Jutra); *La Merle* (co-anim., Lambart), 1958; *Short and Suite* (co-anim., Lambart); *Serenal; Mail Early for Christmas*, 1959; *Lines Vertical* (co-anim., co-dir., Lambart); *Opening Speech*, 1960; *New York Lightboard; New York Lightboard Record*, 1961; *Lines Horizontal* (co-anim., co-dir., Lambart), 1962; *Canon*, 1964; *Mosaic* (co-dir., Lambart), 1965; *Pas de deux*, 1967; *Spheres*, 1969; *Synchromy*, 1971; *Ballet Adagio*, 1972; *Pinscreen*, 1973; *Animated Motion*, Parts 1–5, 1976–78; *Narcissus*, 1981.

BIBLIOGRAPHY: Maynard Collins; Guy Glover; Donald McWilliams.

Peter Rist

MEATBALLS. Ivan Reitman, Ontario, 1979, 94 min., color. IVAN REITMAN built on his success with *Animal House* by teaming with Bill Murray of "Saturday Night Live" for *Meatballs*. Early in his career, Murray delivered a stellar performance as Tripper, the semi-responsible prankster head counselor of Camp White Pine. Leading a cadre of counselors, Tripper engages in a series of pranks, many perpetrated on camp owner Mortie (Harvey Atkin). Along the way Tripper befriends a loner (Chris Makepeace) and helps the teenager come out of his shell by developing his skills as a distance runner. At the same time Tripper himself learns he must grow up somewhat to maintain his relationship with his counterpart, Roxanne (Kate Lynch). The episodic nature of the narrative allows Murray to excel in his comic shtick, with Atkin as his principal foil. A deal to release the film through Paramount Pictures helped make it the highest box office grosser in Canadian cinema until the success of *PORKY'S.* At the 1980 Genies the film won awards for Best Original Screenplay and Best Actress (Lynch).

Dave Douglas

MONIQUE MERCURE. Born Monique Hémond, 1930, Montreal. Actor. As a child, encouraged by her aunt, Monique Hémond followed a music career. While studying at the Vincent-D'Indy School she met and married composer Pierre Mercure, following him to Europe. Returning to Montreal following the breakup of their marriage, she began taking method acting classes in the late fifties. She won notice in 1963 in *L'Opera de Quat'Sous* at the Théâtre du Rideau-Vert, having taken over from the lead, who broke her leg. A month later, Mercure herself broke a leg, and, unable to gain paid work, appeared in CLAUDE JUTRA's *À TOUT PRENDRE* unpaid. Returning to the theater, a chance encounter with Claude Fournier in 1969 led her to star in his sex comedy *DEUX FEMMES EN OR.* It was the hit of the year in Quebec and made her a household name. She followed this with a small but key role in MON ONCLE ANTOINE, but her big break came in 1975 when she was cast as Rose-Aimée Martin in *J. A. MARTIN, PHOTOGRAPHE*, which won her Canada and Quebec's first Best Actress prize at Cannes. Mercure's portrayal is so sensitive that she becomes a sort of Everywoman, reaching out in a modest way for the chance to revel in her own marriage. The international success that was predicted for her after *Martin* proved elusive. Since then, the focus of Mercure's career has been playing small but key roles, such as the Mother Superior in *La dame en couleurs* or the maid Fadela in DAVID CRONENBERG's *NAKED LUNCH*. Mercure is one of Quebec's strongest actresses, capable of turning what is essentially a cameo into a highlight of a film, whether in comedy, such as Yves Simoneau's *Dans le ventre du dragon*, or in a serious drama such as "A Canvas in Time," JACQUES LEDUC's vignette from *Montréal vu par.* . . . Mercure works predominantly in Quebec, preferring not to move from her home. In 1987 and 1989, she served as president of les Rendez-vous du cinéma québécois.

FILMS AS ACTOR INCLUDE: *Tit-Coq*, 1952; *Félix Leclerc, troubadour*, 1959; *À tout prendre*, 1963; *Ce n'est pas le temps des romans* (short), 1964; *Le festin des morts*, 1966; *Waiting for Caroline*, 1967; *Don't Let the Angels Fall*, 1969; *Love Is a Four Letter Word; Deux femmes en or*, 1970; *Mon oncle Antoine; Finalement*, 1971; *Françoise Durocher, Waitress; Le temps d'une chasse*, 1972; *Il était un fois dans l'est*, 1974; *Pour le meilleur et pour le pire; Les vautours; L'amour blessé* (voice only), 1975; *J. A. Martin, photographe; L'absence; Parlez-nous d'amour*, 1976; *La chanson de Roland*, 1978; *Stone Cold Dead*, 1979; *The Third Walker* (Can/US), 1977–80; *La cuisine rouge*, 1980; *Odyssey of the Pacific* (Can/Fr); *Une journée en taxi; La quarantaine*, 1982; *Contrecoeur*, 1979–83; *Les années de rêves; Blood of Others* (Can/Fr), 1984; *La dame en couleurs; Tramp at the Door*, 1985; *Les bottes; Qui à tiré sur nos histoires d'amour?*, 1986; *Dans le ventre du dragon*, 1989; *Histoire de chasse* (TV), 1990; *Montréal vu par . . . ; Naked Lunch*, 1991; *La fête des rois*, 1994; *Whiskers* (TV), 1997.

BIBLIOGRAPHY: André Guy Arsenault, "Monique Mercure Balancing Act," *Cinema Canada*, no. 144 (September 1987).

Simon Brown

PETER METTLER. Born 1958, Toronto. Director, cinematographer. Peter Mettler is part of a vanguard of English Canadian filmmakers, known as the Ontario "New Wave," whose careers blossomed in the early 1980s (ATOM EGOYAN, BRUCE McDONALD, PATRICIA ROZEMA, RON MANN, JANIS COLE). Mettler graduated from Toronto's Ryerson Polytechnical Institute and quickly became one of Canada's most gifted cinematographers. In his early career, Mettler alternated between directing his own films and photographing those of fellow New Wavers Egoyan (*Next of Kin; FAMILY VIEWING*), McDonald (*Knock! Knock!*), and Rozema (*Passion*). With his last three films, Mettler has established himself as a visionary filmmaker with a thirst for philosophical and spiritual exploration. Mettler's films are reflexive paradoxes that search for knowledge and truth, while acknowledging the limitations of cinema as a means for recording, understanding, and unveiling reality. As Mettler's voice-over from *Picture of Light* (1995) implies, this is largely because it is impossible to separate the reality cinema makes from that which it records. *Tectonic Plates* (1992), based on Robert Lepage's stage production, is Mettler's most impressive cinematic achievement thus far. Mettler takes the scientific theory of shifting earth plates as a central metaphor for parallel "shifts" in art, humanity, and culture. Foreground/background and time/space constantly shift by means of rear projection, lighting, set effects, and moving camera, like the earth's crust and the human events depicted. *Picture of Light*, shot in Churchhill, Manitoba, is a poetic documentary in which Mettler sets out to film the Northern Lights (aurora borealis). When the calculatingly built-up moment arrives, it is not a disappointment. We are treated to a spectacular light show of tornado-like swirls of green, yellow, and orange. *Picture of Light* is Mettler's attempt to refute Werner Herzog's apocalyptic claim that "there are no more new images." In a sense Mettler succeeds, but with a self-serving paradox. We have not witnessed the real Northern Lights, but an artist's rendition captured with a special computerized camera shooting at the rate of three frames per minute. As an earlier cinematic visitor to the Canadian North, Robert Flaherty, once said, sometimes you have to lie to tell the truth.

FILMS AS CINEMATOGRAPHER INCLUDE: *I.I.I.*, 1983; *Knock! Knock!; Next of Kin*, 1984; *Divine Solitude*, 1984–86; *Passion: A Letter in 16mm*, 1985; *Artist on Fire; Family Viewing*, 1987.

FEATURE FILMS AS DIRECTOR: *Scissere* (also cin., ed., scr., prod.), 1982; *Eastern Avenue* (also cin., ed., prod.), 1985; *Lolita* (also cin.), 1987; *The Top of His Head* (also cin., scr., co-ed.), 1989; *Tectonic Plates* (UK/Can), 1992; *Picture of Light*, 1995.

BIBLIOGRAPHY: Salome Pitschen and Annette Schönholzer; Jason McBride, "Peter Mettler: Making the Invisible Visible," *Point of View*, no. 30 (Fall 1996): 33–34.

Donato Totaro

GEORGE MIHALKA. Born 1952, Budapest, Hungary. Director. George Mihalka moved to Canada from his native Hungary in 1961. Since studying film production at Montreal's Concordia University Cinema Department, Mihalka has worked steadily in film and television to become one of Canada's most prolific and versatile directors. Mihalka is a throwback to the Hollywood studio contract director, a true *metteur-en-scène* adapting himself to each new project, regardless of its relative merit: comedy (*Pinball Summer; La Florida*); horror (*My Bloody Valentine; The Blue Man; Relative Fear; The Psychic*); thriller (*The Office Party; The Final Heist; Bullet to Beijing*). Without a distinct style, Mihalka is only as good as his material. When given a decent budget and cast, as in *Bullet to Beijing*, with Michael Caine and Michael Sarrazin, or in *La Florida* (a smash hit in Quebec), with RÉMY GIRARD, he produces serviceable entertainment. Mihalka's best film may be *The Blue Man*, an effective horror film about a guru named Janus (Karen Black) who uses astral projection to commit murders in search of host bodies ("spiritual vampirism"). The astral projection sequences contain some remarkable steadicam and aerial camera work by Christian Du-guay. *The Blue Man* won the Prix du Public at the Avoriaz Fantastic Film Festival, France, 1987. When budget and aspirations are low, as in *Scandale*, Mihalka hits rock bottom. *Scandale* is a farcical exposé of a real-life scandal involving disgruntled Quebec civil servants who used government resources to make pornographic films (the incident was labeled "Pornobec"). However, the satirical premise slowly becomes a pretext for hard-core pornographic scenes. To his credit, Mihalka is one of the few independent Quebec filmmakers who moves freely between English and French productions.

CANADIAN THEATRICAL FILMS AS DIRECTOR: *The Private Agony of Jimmy Quin-lan*, 1978; *Pinball Summer*, 1979; *My Bloody Valentine*, 1980; *Old Hippies*, 1981; *Scan-dale*, 1982; *Humbug*, 1982; *The Blue Man* (a.k.a. *Eternal Evil*), 1985; *The Office Party* (a.k.a. *Hostile Take Over*), 1988; *Psychic*, 1991; *La Florida*, 1993; *Relative Fear* (a.k.a. *The Child*), 1994; *Bullet to Beijing*, (UK/Can/Russia) 1995; *L'homme idéal*, 1996.

CANADIAN TELEVISION FILMS AS DIRECTOR: *Midnight Magic*, 1987; *Straight Line*, 1988; *Le chemin de Damas*, 1988; *The Final Heist*, 1992; *Le flic et la séductrice; Windsor Protocol* (Can/NZ); *Thunder Point* (Can/NZ), 1996.

BIBLIOGRAPHY: Denyse Therrien, "Voyages en comédie avec Georges Mihalka," *Ciné-Bulles* 15, no. 4 (Winter 1997): 28–31.

Donato Totaro

THE MILLS OF THE GODS: VIET NAM. Beryl Fox, CBC, 1965, 56 min, b+w. Assembled with extensive life-risking hardship, this thorough, uncompro-misingly graphic documentary overwhelmed television audiences, then generally unfamiliar with the ground-level character of the Vietnam conflict. Showing a distinct egalitarian vision, the film has a fluid, supple, and urgent style rooted in the noneditorializing "direct cinema" approach developed by the NFB's Unit B filmmakers and at the CBC. Beryl Fox here involves the viewer intimately with her subjects by the most direct of means: faces continually occupy the screen, distinguishing each of the morale-deficient Americans, the resilient farm-ers and villagers, the captured and brutalized Viet Cong, and South Vietnam's own highly capable military force. Fox achieves a profoundly, persuasively hu-manist record of dangers, privations, and carnage while showing with clarity the war's ideological and tactical muddle. The final segment demonstrates the film's adroit focus, taking the viewer on the mission of a personable, chatty bomber pilot swept away with his own professionalism, delighting in the technology—precisely governing napalm discharges through the treelines—that enables him to rout and kill "Charlie." The film stays airborne in patient close company with the pilot for several minutes, distanced from the contorted corpses and intrac-tably burned survivors depicted in a lengthy early sequence. Showing uninter-ruptedly and sympathetically the man's protected moral myopia as well as his daunting resources for slaughter, Fox ends the film wrenchingly. Never sur-passed in its reputation as a chronicle of the war, it won two Canadian Film

Awards in 1966: a Certificate of Merit for television journalism, and Film of the Year.

BIBLIOGRAPHY: Alan Rosenthal (1980), 227–31.

Ian Elliot

MON ONCLE ANTOINE *My Uncle Antoine* [*Silent Night*]. Claude Jutra, Quebec, 1971, 104 min., color. At the time of a vote held by Canadian film professionals and critics in 1984, *Mon oncle Antoine* was named "Best Canadian Film of All Time." The action of the film takes place in the mining village of Black Lake, where Benoît, an adolescent, simultaneously discovers sexual desire, death, and the hypocrisy of the adult world. The scenario by Clément Perron develops according to a structure that is quite original: in the first part of the film, two initially independent narrative threads join together to form a single thread which propels the drama and leads, finally, to a sad and equivocal conclusion. In addition to the originality of the scenario, one can also admire the psychology of the characters who populate the film. Happy and seemingly enjoying a peaceful life without history, the characters remain nevertheless subject to all sorts of weaknesses and reveal, in the second half of the film, the dark sides of their personalities. Antoine, an embalmer by profession, gets drunk and cries because he is afraid of the dead; meanwhile, his wife Cécile cheats on him with Fernand, the sales clerk at the general store Antoine manages. These revelations are achieved through the increasingly disenchanted gaze of Benoît. Interestingly, the time period of the film is quite ambiguous. The historical reconstruction of the Duplessis era is accompanied by a nationalist sentiment and by a level of language connected to the 1970s, which situate the film in a sort of "no time's land." All the actors are remarkable, and the participation of the inhabitants of Black Lake as extras contributes to the authenticity of the film. Highly esteemed in Canada, *Mon oncle Antoine* also won eight Canadian Film Awards, including Best Film and Best Director for CLAUDE JUTRA.

BIBLIOGRAPHY: Jean Chabot.

Louis Goyette

MONTREAL MAIN. Frank Vitale, Montreal, 1972–74, 88 min., 16mm, color. The first in a series of three semi-autobiographical, apparently improvised films, shot on location in downtown and east Montreal, and featuring many characters playing themselves, *Montreal Main* set the pattern for a number of loosely structured and somewhat eccentric, group-made anglophone features to be filmed in the city over the next two decades. American-born Frank Vitale (Jacksonville, Florida, 1945), who came to Montreal to study at McGill University in the 1960s, co-directed his first film, *Country Music*, with Allan Moyle in 1971. The following year, Vitale shot his first feature, *Montreal Main*, on video, and then remade it in 16mm (a clue to its questionable spontaneity). He starred himself as Frank, a gay, misunderstood, 1960s-ish artist living on Boulevard St. Laurent (affectionately dubbed "The Main" by Montreal residents) who wants to adopt a teenager (John Sutherland) from the suburbs. Sutherland's parents (also playing themselves) and his best friends (Stephen Lack and "Bozo" Moyle) struggle to come to terms with the relationship. Even more loosely scripted than *NOBODY WAVED GOODBYE*—attributed in the credits to "the cast" of the film—*Montreal Main* was notable for dealing with (real) members of the city's marginalized gay and artistic communities and introducing the "social problem" of age differential in homosexual relationships in a very personalized way. *Main* wasn't released in Canada until 1974, finally appearing in Montreal with a subtitled version in October. During its local release, Vitale, Moyle, Lack, and other *Main* participants, including Peter Brawley and Pam Marchant, began shooting the sequel, *THE RUBBER GUN*. In 1975, Vitale directed, co-produced, and co-wrote (with Moyle) the least successful of the three features, *East End Hustle*. This film, which was released in 1976 (before *Rubber Gun*), mixed francophone actors with anglophones and focused on the life of a prostitute who tries to help her fellow sex workers. Vitale, who had worked on a number of short documentaries over the feature-making period, left Canada to live and work in New York State at the end of the 1970s.

BIBLIOGRAPHY: John Hofsess, 103–14; Michel Coulombe and Marcel Jean, 474–75.

Peter Rist

MOURIR À TUE-TÊTE A Scream from Silence/[Primal Fear]. Anne-Claire Poirier, ONF, 1979, 96 min., color. *Mourir à tue-tête* was the first of ANNE-CLAIRE POIRIER's films to have been seen extensively outside Canada, primarily through screenings at the Cannes and New York film festivals of 1979. Its notoriety stems from the controversy it stirred up not only because of its subject matter—rape—but also because of its style: rhetorical in parts, but detachedly objective in others, oscillating between documentary and fiction in a way similar to that of Jean-Luc Godard's "essay" films. *Mourir* presents a series of "texts" which the audience must "read." In the film's first sequence, "rape" is universalized by having the same actor, GERMAIN HOUDE, identified in a number of guises—grocer, doctor, husband, film director—by the off-screen voice of his victim. Then, in a shocking sequence, filmed in almost real time, we witness the rape of a young woman, Suzanne (Julie Vincent). But in a remarkably original and appropriate stylistic choice, the incident is seen directly through her eyes: during the rape we view the rapist, not the victim. Occasionally, her facial reactions are shown in reverse-angle shots, but mostly the camera views Houde's face, rendered uglier through its jerky movements across the frame and through the low-angle position. In filming the scene this way, never showing genitalia and never showing the man and woman as a couple, Poirier tried to de-eroticize rape. The powerful emotional impact of the rape scene is then abruptly broken by a scene of the apparent film director (Monique Miller) and editor MICHELINE LANCTÔT) discussing the universality and erotic effect of what has transpired.

The film begins to analyze itself. Questions are raised, but no definite answers are given, and Suzanne's continuing, depressing story is repeatedly interrupted by other discursive passages. After the director states that the real Suzanne did, in fact, commit suicide, and a reconstruction of her denouement is shown, a female voice-over announces that at least mothers should teach their daughters to wear a whistle so that they can send out a distress signal. Brilliantly, *Mourir* ends with a series of nighttime shots of empty, potentially dangerous spaces: indoor and outdoor parking lots, parks, and alleyways. The sound of whistles builds on the soundtrack in consort with a police siren: a "scream from silence" indeed. At the New York Film Festival, the ending of *Mourir à tue-tête* was accompanied by a cacophony of whistles blown by women in the audience, responding to the film with a determined, defiant, collective optimism. By raising an unmentionable issue in a, by turns, emotionally wrenching and intellectually stimulating way, Poirier fashioned an important and unusual film essay on rape.

BIBLIOGRAPHY: Carole Zucker, "Les oeuvres récentes d'Anne Claire Poirier et Paule Baillargeon." *Copie Zéro*, no. 11 (1981): 52–55; Peter Rist, *"Primal Fear,"* in Magill (1985), 2461–66.

Peter Rist

MOUVEMENT PERPÉTUEL Perpetual Movement. Claude Jutra, Quebec, 1949, 15 min., b+w, 16 mm, no dialogue. The greatest thing about this 1949 short experimental film by CLAUDE JUTRA (and cinematographer MICHEL BRAULT) is that, by its very existence, it challenges our perception of a uniformly conservative and aesthetically retrograde cinema in Quebec prior to the advent of *cinéma direct* in the late fifties. Indeed, for those lucky enough to have seen this rare and unsung film, *Mouvement perpétuel* shines like a beacon through the artistically depressing years of *la grande noirceur*—the Duplessis era. It is the cinematic answer to Paul-Émile Borduas' manifesto, *Le refus global* (1948). Shot while the director was a medical student at the Université de Montréal, *Mouvement perpétuel* was clearly influenced by the early surreal works of Luis Buñuel and Jean Cocteau and has much in common with the avant-garde cinema of Maya Deren and Kenneth Anger, North American contemporaries of whose work Jutra was apparently aware. Filmed in slow motion, and paced to the hypnotic cyclical rhythms of a slowed-down musical piece by Novacek, the film presents us with a disjunctive and oneiric tale of desire and alienation between two men and a woman. In so doing, Jutra violently sets himself apart from other Quebec directors of the time, not only because he chooses to explore modern modes of filmmaking but because he dares to go against the dominant sexual ideology found in film and society—first, by clearly representing female desire on screen (the heroine caresses the naked and sweaty torso of her unconscious boyfriend), and second, by implying, through subtle use of montage and acting, homosexual desire between the two men (shots of a man and woman kissing are juxtaposed to shots of the men's faces slowly converging as if to repeat the kiss; elsewhere the men's hands lock in embrace when the two are supposed to be fighting, etc.). The film's twofold beauty, its impressionistic sensuousness and intellectual complexity, is matched only by the raw emotional angst it still imparts.

BIBLIOGRAPHY: M. Guilet.

Johanne Larue

MY AMERICAN COUSIN. Sandy Wilson, British Columbia, 1985, 92 min., color. *My American Cousin* was the first English Canadian fictional feature film directed by a woman in nearly ten years, since JOYCE WIELAND'S *THE FAR SHORE*. It was made on a low budget (of $1.2 million) and in Penticton, British Columbia, well removed from the mainstream of Ontario and Quebec. Yet it garnered six Genies in March 1986, including Best Film, Director, Screenplay, Editing, Actress, and Actor. In the process, *My American Cousin* upset the aspirations of those connected with *Joshua Then and Now*—the most expensive Canadian film made at that time, with a budget of more than $11 million—and ushered in a fresh new wave of quality Canadian production. Sandy Wilson, the writer/director, had made a number of short films after 1974, and she conceived the idea for *American* in 1982, after receiving a scriptwriting grant for another project. While listening to Johnny Horton's hit song "The Battle of New Orleans" on a Vancouver radio station, she was reminded of the summer of 1959, when her own American cousin visited the family ranch. The resulting film is largely autobiographical and was shot on the Penticton ranch in summer 1984. Apart from the two leads and three other actors, all the cast members were from Wilson's hometown, including her mother, sister, brother, and their children. Sandy Wilcox (i.e., Wilson) is twelve, and she and her siblings and friends are bored picking cherries for her father (Richard Donat), a very English ex-major, when cousin Butch (John Wildman) arrives in his mother's red Cadillac. In the short time that he is around before his parents come to retrieve him (he has run away), everyone, it seems, falls for him, including, of course, Sandy. The portrait of Sandy, as a modest and self-effacing young Canadian, mildly rebelling against authority and longing to be somewhere else, is beautifully realized by Margaret Langrick, and the interrelationships with her girlfriends and younger sisters are equally well conveyed. But the adults are caricatured to varying degrees, lending an unevenness to the film's acting. A good feeling for the late 1950s is evoked through the young performances. Further, the music and costumes accurately represent teenage tastes of the times. Richard Leiterman's cinematography presents a somewhat garish, picture postcard view of the place and period while also displaying the world in pop art poster color as though it were seen through a young person's eyes. Hugely enjoyable for Canadian audiences, *My American Cousin* was far less successful in the United States, where it was the flagship release for dynamic young Linda Beath's new pan–North American distribution company, International Spectrafilm. Unfortunately, Wilson failed to match her first feature's success with the sequel, *American Boyfriends*, Langrick's star image gradually faded, and Beath's daring venture also missed its mark.

BIBLIOGRAPHY: Peter Rist, *"My American Cousin,"* in Magill (1987), 318–22; Joanne Yamaguchi, "Who Is the American Cousin? Canadian Cinema, Cultural Freedom, and Sandy Wilson's *American Cousin*," *CineACTION!*, no. 16 (May 1989): 70–72.

Peter Rist

N

NAKED LUNCH. David Cronenberg, Toronto, 1991, 115 min., color. Outside of DEAD RINGERS (thirteen Genies), *Naked Lunch* is DAVID CRONENBERG's most celebrated Genie Award–winning film (eleven). *Naked Lunch* is not so much an adaptation of the William S. Burroughs novel but a "making of" told from the point of view of a drug addicted, sexually confused, guilt-ridden writer, Bill Lee (Peter Weller). Cronenberg mixes scenes from the novel with biographical events (Burroughs' accidental shooting of his wife, his visit to Tangiers, his job as an exterminator). The result is an ambitious but ultimately dissatisfying mélange of pop culture and high art references (*Orphée, Vertigo*, film noir, the Beat Generation, Paul and Jane Bowles, Kafka). At best *Naked Lunch* adds to that minor subgenre of writing-process-as-hell films which include *The Shining* (United States, 1980) and *Barton Fink* (United States, 1991). Where it fails is in its decision to undercut the novel's horror or feeling of dread. Lee, the Burroughs surrogate, slips into a hallucinogenic writer's block that sees his typewriter turn into a bug with a talking sphincter, and people into bug-eyed monsters. But Lee is not frightened or remotely surprised by these intrusions into reality because he realizes, at some level, that they are part of his creative thought process. This complacency to his surreal surroundings nullifies any dread an audience may feel toward the imagery. Lee's imaginary state of mind, his "Interzone," is a fantasy land rather than a nightmare. The only scene that echoes the novel's nightmarish imagery is the sex-murder scene between Kiki (Joseph Scorsiani) and Cloquet (Julian Sands). Searching for something genuinely surreal, I was struck by an odd coincidence: Bill Lee, a Burroughs pseudonym, is the namesake of eccentric, nonconformist Boston Red Sox and Montreal Expos pitcher "Spaceman" Bill Lee!

BIBLIOGRAPHY: Chris Rodley, 157–69; Amy Taubin, "The Wrong Body," and Mark Kermode, "Interview with David Cronenberg," *Sight & Sound* 1, no. 11 (March 1992): 8–11, 11–13.

Donato Totaro

NANOOK OF THE NORTH. Robert Flaherty, United States/France, 1922, 65 min., b+w. Made by an American, independently funded by a French company, and shot in Canada (Western Ungava of the Hudson Bay area), *Nanook of the North*, like THE SILENT ENEMY and THE VIKING, is a Canadian film by proxy. Quintessentially Canadian in many respects (documentary form, reverential depiction of nature, survivalist theme), *Nanook* is justifiably canonized as the first modern documentary film. *Nanook* immediately raised issues which have remained seminal to the documentary discourse: objectivity, realism, authenticity, and the effect of the filmmaker's intervention on the pro-filmic reality. Though contemporary critics lauded the film for its naturalness and ready-made Inuit life drama, *Nanook* dramatized the survivalist saga by employing narrative storytelling devices. For example, the final scene crosscuts between Nanook's "family" (constructed, not real) inside the igloo to his sled dogs outside the igloo. The spaces are narratively contiguous but were filmed separately in different locations: an example of "creative geography" before Lev Kuleshov. This scene also contains the film's most famous example of ingenious staging. The regular igloos were far too small and dark for interior filming, so through a trial-and-error process Robert Flaherty and his Inuit crew constructed a half-igloo which allowed for interior filming (though unnatural shadows hamper the illusion). Flaherty realized, as subsequent documentarists have, that when reality is in conflict with art, "the aggie [film] must come first." Contemporary audiences may disparage the film's Rousseauian vision of the noble savage or its restricted view of Inuit culture, but *Nanook of the North* maintains an authentic visual poeticism that has rarely been surpassed in the documentary form.

BIBLIOGRAPHY: Peter Morris (1978), 196–200; Jay Ruby, "A Reexamination of the Early Career of Robert J. Flaherty," *Quarterly Review of Film Studies* 5 (1980):434–57.

Donato Totaro

NEIGHBOURS/VOISINS. Norman McLaren, NFB, "Documentary Showcase" series, 1952, 8 min., color, no dialogue. Having won numerous prizes, including an Oscar, NORMAN MCLAREN's *Neighbours* was for years Canada's best known film, internationally and at home, being shown regularly on television and in schools and libraries. It is also the most notable example of McLaren's combining artistic creativity with a social conscience. *Neighbours* constructs an allegory of nations fighting over land, clearly in criticism of the Korean War. Two men, Grant Munro and Jean-Paul Ladouceur, reclining in lawn chairs, read their newspapers, proclaiming "Peace Certain If No War" and "War Certain If No Peace." Through pixilation, a flower pops up in the middle of a lawn and each man, as magician, successively moves a fence row of white pickets to contain his property, including the flower. Simple music, scratched onto the soundtrack by the director, percussively accompanies the stop-motion of the fence pieces. Eventually, the men use these to beat each other. Until 1969, the next scene in the film was censored, where Munro and Laduceur batter each other's wife and child, represented by puppets, behind painted flats of houses. At the end of the film a new flower grows out of each man's grave. Typically, for McLaren's dialogue-free films, a title is inserted at the end in a number of languages, "Love Thy Neighbour."

BIBLIOGRAPHY: Donald McWilliams, 29–30, 67–73.

Peter Rist

KATE NELLIGAN. Born 1951, London, Ontario. Actor. A classically trained actress, Kate Nelligan left Canada at the age of eighteen to study at the Central School of Speech and Drama in London, England. Following graduation, she spent a year at the Old Vic theater in Bristol performing over thirteen leading roles and later made her London debut in David Hare's play *Knuckle*. On her way to establishing an enviable career on the stage, she surprised both critics and audiences alike by moving to Los Angeles in 1981 to become a film actress. Up to this point in her career, her film work had consisted of a handful of small roles in mostly Canadian and British films. Her most notable work in Canada had been to star opposite DONALD SUTHERLAND in the CBC drama *Bethune* (1977) as the wife of the famous Canadian doctor, for which she received a great deal of praise and was viewed as a budding new talent in Canada. It was only in the late 1980s, however, that Nelligan began to work in her native Canada on a regular basis, appearing in television productions like *Love and Hate: The Story of Colin and Joann Thatcher*, playing a battered wife of a Canadian politician. In 1990, she teamed up with MARGOT KIDDER and Sheila McCarthy to star in PATRICIA ROZEMA's *White Room*, playing a woman of mystery struggling to conceal a dark secret. In this role, she convincingly conveys her character's vulnerability without sacrificing her strength. Nelligan is best suited for this type of dramatic role, playing deeply emotional characters whose passions lurk beneath a cool exterior. In *MARGARET'S MUSEUM*, for which Nelligan won both critical acclaim and a Genie for Best Supporting Actress, she gives a moving performance as a Maritime miner's wife who stoically accepts the hardships of her life and the dangers of the mine.

FILMS AS ACTOR: *Bethune* (TV), 1977; *Mr. Patman*, 1981; *White Room*, 1990; *Love and Hate: The Story of Colin and Joann Thatcher* (TV), 1989; *Great Diamond Robbery*, 1992; *Margaret's Museum*, 1995.

Stacey Abbott

NOBODY WAVED GOODBYE. Don Owen, (Toronto) NFB, 1964, 80 min., b+w, 16mm. Knowing full well that they were trying to make a feature film, director DON OWEN, producer TOM DALY, and cinematographer John Spotton were able to clandestinely exploit the generous resources of the NFB, between August and December 1963, under the pretense of making a dramatized documentary short about juvenile delinquency. The completed film, *Nobody Waved Goodbye*, became the second English-language fiction feature made by the film board and is now understood to be a groundbreaking work of Canadian film.

Episodic in narrative structure, shot on location in the Toronto suburbs with a predominantly nonprofessional cast, using lightweight 16mm equipment with direct sound and a minimal script, *Nobody* is the prototype for de-dramatized, realist fiction, as different from Hollywood as the European art film. It features relatively unsympathetic characters viewed objectively, often from a distance, and, in a most original strategy, Owen gave each of the principal actors little information about the others in the scene, forcing them to improvise. An angry young man, Peter (Kastner), is flunking out of high school while trying to maintain a relationship with Julie (Biggs). (Having the young actors play the central characters with their own given names adds to the realism.) The film then documents Peter's conflictual relationships with his parents (Claude Rae and Charmion King), the police, unemployment and parole officers, and a crooked car park operator, as his boss (JOHN VERNON). At the end of the film, with Julie pregnant, Peter is left to cry, sitting in a stolen car on the side of a highway. Peter's overwhelmingly negative plight and his inability to overcome his problems leaves many viewers cold, but these elements ultimately distinguish *Nobody Waved Goodbye* as quintessentially Canadian, and look forward to profound changes in Hollywood narratives of the early 1970s, for example, *Five Easy Pieces* (1971), *Badlands* (1973), and *Payday* (1973), which was directed by Canadian Daryl Duke. Also setting a pattern for Canadian film, *Nobody* needed to receive acclaim elsewhere before being recognized in its own country. It bombed on its December 1964 release in Toronto, and "eminent exhibitor and distributor" N. A. Taylor called it "garbage" and "amateur night in Hicksville." But after winning an award in Mannheim, Germany, as well as the British Film Academy Flaherty Award (for Best Documentary!), and after a successful run at Cinema V in New York (and great reviews), it returned triumphantly to the Nortown in Toronto.

BIBLIOGRAPHY: Natalie Edwards, "Who's Don Owen? What's He Done, and What's He Doing Now?," *Cinema Canada*, no. 8 (June/July 1973), reprinted in Feldman and Nelson, 160–78.

Peter Rist

NOT A LOVE STORY (A FILM ABOUT PORNOGRAPHY). Bonnie Sherr Klein, NFB, 1981, 69 min., color, 16mm. *Not a Love Story*, which is revealed in the end credits to be "a film about pornography," is one of the most controversial films ever made in Canada (and one of the two most popular all-time rentals from the NFB). Banned for a long time in the province of Ontario, where much of it was shot, *Not a Love Story* ironically presents an argument for censorship of hard-core pornography. Like most documentaries produced by the Women's Unit, Unit D, it consists mainly of interviews, allowing a number of different points of view on erotica and pornography to be presented. On the one hand, we hear from erotic artist Kate Millett, *Penthouse* photographer Suze Randall, a particularly fascinating subject, and pornographic film producer Ron

Martin; on the other, reformed porn star Marc Stevens laments the degradation of women and poet Robin Morgan compares violent pornography to Nazism. But the crew also visited sex parlors in U.S. cities, including New York and San Francisco, without backing away from their graphic, sleazy events (even intercutting hard-core pornographic film clips and photographs). Here, the viewer's guide is former stripper Linda Lee Tracy, spurred on by on-screen director Bonnie Sherr Klein to become aware of the humiliations women are subjected to in the sex industry. Whereas the first half of the film presents a balanced account of what may or may not constitute erotica and pornography (through interviews), its second half is decidedly didactic, with an anti-pornography rhetoric. Strangely, the film has offended everyone: for its being against pornography, and its emphasis on misogyny in the form, but, conversely, for its alleged titillation by including sexually explicit material. Perhaps the filmmakers tried to cover too much ground in this one film, but *Not a Love Story* stands as a landmark documentary in attempting to bring to light the problem of violent and degrading misogyny within the sex industry.

BIBLIOGRAPHY: Susan Barrowclough, "Not a Love Story," *Screen* 23, no. 5 (November/December 1982): 26–36.

Peter Rist

O

?O, ZOO! (THE MAKING OF A FICTION FILM). Phil Hoffman, Ontario, 1986, 23 min., color, 16mm. Invited by Peter Greenaway to the Netherlands to observe the filming of *A Zed and Two Noughts*, Phil Hoffman used the occasion to make a document of the experience that both employed and confounded the traditions of the Griersonian model of documentary filmmaking. Hoffman employs a narrator to recast events, culminating in the death of an elephant at the zoo, but at the same time subverts that authority by creating a character to go with the role of narrator. Personalizing the role of the narrator allows Hoffman to bring memory and family into the body of the film. Shots of his film log and places he visited overseas further a sense of connection, and render the film in a diary format. Finally, Hoffman explicitly undercuts the truth value of documentary by brazenly lying to us, offering images that do not correspond to the voice-over explanation of them. The ethical dilemma of whether or not to supply the footage of the elephant dying to the viewer (the scene originally plays over black leader) is resolved at the film's conclusion, with Hoffman supplying the footage after the credits, and then, in addition, more footage to show that the elephant did not in fact die and that the dilemma itself was a fabrication. Upon the film's release it was an immediate success, winning awards at the Athens International Film Festival, Ohio (United States), and was nominated for a Genie, ironically in the "Documentary" category.

Dave Douglas

ALANIS OBOMSAWIN. Born 1932, Odanak Reservation, Quebec. Director, producer. A respected member of the Abenaki nation, Alanis Obomsawin spent most of her early professional years traveling around Canada, the United States, and abroad to sing and stage concerts showcasing the culture of her people. She began her film career in 1967 as a consultant for the NFB, where documentaries about aboriginals were frequently produced but rarely so by First Nations people. Obomsawin tipped the balance when she stepped forward to shoot her first short, a documentary entitled *Christmas at Moose Factory* (1971). By the mid-seventies, her productions become more clearly political (*Amisk*) and study the role of women in aboriginal society (*Mother of Many Children*). In the 1980s the filmmaker still paid attention to Native domestic life and strife (*Richard Cardinal: Cry from a Diary of a Metis Child; Poundmaker's Lodge—A Healing Place*, and *No Address*), but it is for her more radical political documentaries— namely, *Incident at Restigouche* (1984) and *KANEHSATAKE: 270 YEARS OF RE-SISTANCE*—that Obomsawin is acclaimed. In these, Obomsawin uses very effective montage techniques to counterpoint the diverging philosophies of whites and aboriginals and, more provokingly, the mechanisms of racism and the injustices of the "double standard." In *Incident at Restigouche*, she uses her investigation of a "fishing rights" confrontation between Mic Macs and Sûreté du Québec police officers to show the parallels between the Natives' demands for more respect and autonomy and the Quebecois' dream of independence, the irony being that the Mic Macs' requests are being denied by a government suffering the same affront at the hands of a bigger "fish." Although the inside view she offers of the Oka Crisis would suffice to validate the film, given how the media brainwashed the public with its own biased coverage at the time, her work is at its most effective when she again uses contrapuntal montage to catch white officials in a lie or show the ludicrous and ineffectual yet dangerously fascist involvement of the Canadian army in the confrontation with the Mohawks. At her most courageous, Alanis Obomsawin questions the reality of a democracy we all take for granted and have always associated with a moderate and peace-loving Canada.

FILMS AS DIRECTOR: *Christmas at Moose Factory* (short), 1971; *Mother of Many Children; Amisk* (short), 1977; *Sounds from Our People* (in six short parts), 1979; *Incident at Restigouche* (short), 1984; *Richard Cardinal: Cry from a Diary of a Metis Child* (short), 1986; *Poundmaker's Lodge—A Healing Place* (short), 1987; *No Address* (short), 1988; *Le Patro* (short), 1991; *Kanehsatake: 270 Years of Resistance*, 1993; *My Name Is Kahentiiosta* (short), 1995; *Spudwrench*, 1997.

BIBLIOGRAPHY: Sandy Greer, "Mohawks and the Media: Alanis Obomsawin's *Kanehsatake: 270 Years of Resistance*," *Take One*, no. 4 (Winter 1994): 18–21.

Johanne Larue

ON EST AU COTON "We're in Cotton."* Denys Arcand, ONF, 1968–1970 (rel. 1976), 159 min., b + w. It took six years for the ONF to allow the distribution of DENYS ARCAND's first feature-length film, a bleak and angry documentary about the textile industry. Though not as overtly revolutionary-minded as GILLES GROULX's *24 HEURES OU PLUS . . .*, *On est au coton* builds an impressive case for radical change. Early in the film, we see a shot of a dust-covered crucifix hanging in a textile factory, which Arcand inserts in the midst of an unbearable

---

*A Quebecois expression meaning "We're at the end of our rope."

interview with a very sick and exploited worker. Not surprisingly, the film was accused of propaganda. But as Arcand has always tried to explain, he *did* want to show the owners' side of the problem but had to cut out the scenes in which they appeared, at the specific request of Edward F. King, the president of Dominion Textile. It goes without saying that the whole incident greatly disgusted the filmmaker. The film was produced, and shelved, during politically turbulent times (the October Crisis, the rise of the labor movement and its clashes with law enforcement), but then finally released the same year the nationalist and (then) left-wing Parti Québécois was elected for the first time in the province. Sadly, by then, the film had lost its raison d'être. It felt *dépassé*. To more contemporary eyes, of course, *On est au coton* shines as a brilliant example of rhetorical filmic argumentation; the film's rigorous analytical structure and contrapuntal editing are a showcase for Arcand's scholarly training as a historian.

BIBLIOGRAPHY: Raynald Poirier; Collective (1973).

Johanne Larue

ON EST LOIN DU SOLEIL We're Far from the Sun. Jacques Leduc, (Montreal) ONF, 1970, 70 min., b+w (last shot in color). Avant-garde fictions like *On est loin du soleil*, shot without care for commercial appeal, were made possible by the patronage of the NFB/ONF who, in the 1960s and 1970s, did not have to perform at the box office and could therefore give the green light to feature-length formal and discursive experimentations. Commissioned to film a portrait of Brother André, a modest priest and thaumaturge responsible for the erection of St-Joseph's Oratory in Montreal, a globally known shrine of the Catholic Church, Leduc chose only to allude to his subject. His film opens with a voice-over giving out biographical information over black leader, followed by a silent shot of the subject's picture. Then, abruptly, the film cuts to the lives of ordinary and down-on-their-luck citizens, their fictional drama unfolding without any more references to Brother André. Or so we think. On closer inspection, we notice fragments of the priest's biography creeping up in the characters' profiles, and we begin to understand that they *all* stand for the missing subject. This extraordinary case of transfiguration—dare we say filmic transsubstantiation?— not only enlightens our understanding of the subject's bond with French Canadian Catholics but proposes an eye-opening definition of the Quebecois as an orphaned, self-effacing, and sickly . . . loser. It is a very harsh portrait for sure— predating Quebec's political coming of age—but one that finds itself alleviated by the tranquil inner beauty of the central character, Isabelle, who faces death with a disconcerting yet very moving serenity. Leduc also endows the style of his film with its subject's personality. Brother André's asceticism is mirrored in the austere quality of the long take mise-en-scène, sometimes reminiscent of Dreyer's later films, while the puzzling contradictions of his life are reflected in the maddening narrative structure, which keeps all the characters apart only to reveal, in the last ten minutes of the drama, during Isabelle's funeral, that they were all related.

BIBLIOGRAPHY: V. Lacroix, "Un parti pris d'écriture," *Copie Zéro*, no. 14 (December 1982): 40–51.

Johanne Larue

LES ORDRES Orders. Michel Brault, Quebec, 1974, 107 min., color and b+w. During October 1970 the F.L.Q. (Front de Libération du Québec) kidnapped government ministers Richard Cross (UK) and Pierre Laporte (Quebec). At 4:00 A.M. on the night of October 16, the Canadian government invoked the War Measures Act, which gave police officers unlimited powers to arrest any citizen suspected of illegal activity, "real or apprehended," and keep them incarcerated for up to twenty-one days without charge. *Les ordres* is a dramatic reenactment of these events. In preparation for the film, Michel Brault interviewed over 40 of the 465 people who were arrested under this act. These collective experiences were synthesized into five characters, who recount their individual ordeals in a flashback interview style. Brault "universalizes" the event by avoiding any references to the October Crisis. While this decision accentuates the Kafkaesque nature of the experience, it also depoliticizes the event. Outside of the brief interview scenes, there is very little here to remind the viewer that Brault was one of the founding figures of the *cinéma direct* movement. The film adopts a somber yet exacting and highly controlled style which serves to underscore the collective loss of control felt by the victims. The soundtrack consists only of sounds and diegetic music. Color is intercut with black and white for thematic and ironic effect: black and white for scenes outside the prison, and color to depict the "modern, clean, cold" prison atmosphere. Most of the camera movements are smooth, precise dolly and tracking shots that reflect a sense of control and order. One of the few times Brault uses a hand-held documentary-like movement is when Marie Boudreau (Hélène Loiselle) is freed and the camera follows her jubilant run down a prison corridor. The film concludes with a dramatic crane shot that moves from Clermont Boudreau (Jean Lapointe) on his balcony (the specific) to the roof of the apartment building looking out over the city (the general). *Les ordres* succeeds as a nightmarish depiction of an individual's helplessness against totalitarian state authority. Knowing that this scenario took place in Montreal, *Les ordres* leaves us with the discomforting feeling that any political system, democracy included, has a point at which order and self-preservation take precedence over individual rights and civil liberty. *Les ordres* garnered the prize for Best Director (tied with Costa-Gavras) at the 1975 Cannes International Film Festival and four awards at the 1975 Canadian Film Awards (Best Feature Film, Film of the Year, Best Director, and Best Screenplay).

BIBLIOGRAPHY: Pierre Vallières, "An Account by a Privileged Hostage of *Les ordres*: Brault Has Missed His Shot," trans. John Van Burek, in Feldman and Nelson, 264–68;

Gilles Marsolais, *"Les ordres*: Repousser les faux maîtres . . . ," *24 Images*, no. 81 (Spring 1996): 17–19.

Donato Totaro

LÉO-ERNEST OUIMET. Born 1877, Saint-Martin-de-Laval, Quebec; died 1972, Montreal. The importance of Léo-Ernest Ouimet in the history of Quebec cinema is outstanding, since he is a pioneer in more than one area—most notably, in the establishing of theaters, in distribution, and in the production and directing of films. Ouimet opened his first "Ouimetoscope" in 1906, in a former concert-café on Sainte-Catherine Street in Montreal, where he presented *La vie et la Passion de Jésus-Christ* with much success. In 1907 he opened a second "Oui-metoscope," which has been called the "first deluxe theatre constructed expressly for the cinema in North America" (Yves Lever). His interest in the cinema extended beyond the areas of exhibition and distribution: his theaters also presented *actualités* which he and his operators filmed throughout the large cities of Quebec—films such as *L'incendie de Trois-Rivières* or *Le congrès euchar-istique de Montréal*. However, Ouimet's work ran into two major obstacles: the authority of the Catholic Church, which considered the cinema immoral, and competition from Toronto, which wanted to control the distribution and exhi-bition of films throughout Canada. Ouimet's successful years were quickly fol-lowed by a more difficult period. In 1908 Ouimet found himself forced to sell his business responsible for the distribution of American films. His activities in the domain of the exhibition, distribution, and production of films continued willy-nilly over the course of the next decade. Ouimet even tried his luck in the United States, moving to California, where he produced an unsuccessful fiction film, *Why Get Married?* (1922). In 1923 he sold his distribution company, Spe-cialty Film Import, to the American firm Famous Players. In California and Toronto, he continued to work as a film distributor until his return to Quebec in 1933. Although he always remained interested in the cinema, Léo-Ernest Ouimet worked as a liquor-store manager in Quebec until the age of eighty.

BIBLIOGRAPHY: Léon-H. Bélanger; Germain Lacasse (1985).

Louis Goyette

OUR NORTHERN NEIGHBOUR. Stuart Legg, (Ottawa) NFB, "World in Ac-tion" series, 1944, 21 min., b+w. Incorrectly listed in official publications of the NFB as being directed by TOM DALY, *Our Northern Neighbour* nevertheless was the film that producer/director STUART LEGG gave his assistant Daly the major responsibilities of research and editing—selecting the found footage, and putting it together—virtually constituting the director's role on a compilation film where no new footage was being shot. So controversial, in trying to per-suade Canadians that their Soviet fighting partners in World War II were true allies, *Our Northern Neighbour* required a supplementary didactic five-minute documentary to be made, entitled, *Getting the Most Out of a Film* (the first in a series), where Ottawa union members asked questions of Drummond Wren, the general secretary of the Workers' Educational Association. Interestingly, much of the footage in *Northern* was taken from fictionalized Soviet docudramas, including a fairly long section of Eisenstein's *October* (1927) which brilliantly reconstructed the storming of the Winter Palace. Legg and Daly also employed the services of NORMAN MCLAREN to animate a map of Europe that dramatically represents Nazi Germany's menace as an expanding, rampaging, three-dimensional black mass. Reseen today, the film's support for Stalin, "man of steel," seems problematic at best. But at the time little was known of his dark side, and Daly stands by *Northern*'s view of the Soviet Union as a whole. Indeed, it is no more declamatory than other films in the NFB wartime series. The high visibility of *Our Northern Neighbour*, though, added to the impression of NFB commissioner JOHN GRIERSON being a communist—he fought hard to get it made—which led partially to his resignation in 1945.

BIBLIOGRAPHY: D. B. Jones (1996).

Peter Rist

OUTRAGEOUS! Richard Benner, Toronto, 1977, 96 min., color, 16mm. A low budget feature ($165,000) made with the help of the CFDC ($99,000), *Outrageous!* was a surprise box office hit, especially in New York City, where much of it was set, and where it grossed $18,000 in one August 1977 week alone. Primarily, *Outrageous!* showcases the brilliant female impersonating talents of Craig Russell: he does Karen Black, Tallulah Bankhead, Bette Davis, Joan Crawford, Barbra Streisand, Carole Channing, Bette Midler, and Judy Garland, among others. His character, Robin Turner, is a gay Toronto hairdresser who is the only real friend to a young schizophrenic woman, Liza Conners (Helen McLaren). He rescues her from the insensitive care of her family and medical professionals, after she has lost her illegitimate child, and takes her with him to New York, where he has become a star on the drag queen circuit. Thus, secondarily, the film works well in championing marginalized characters and their off-beat lifestyles. In this way, the film was very much of its time, the mid-1970s, and place, northeastern North American cities (Toronto, New York, and Montreal), where drag shows and drug taking were far more popular than mere "underground culture" elements. Many of Robin's lines remain memorable; for example, when he tells Liza that she's "alive and sick and living in New York like eight million other people" and his endorsement of her being "special" rather than "normal" and being "mad as a hatter, darling." Benner, who was American born, directed an American-produced feature in Toronto in 1980, *Happy Birthday, Gemini,* and in 1987 he reunited with Russell to make their disappointing sequel, *Too Outrageous.* Tragically, both men succumbed to AIDS-related illnesses not long after.

BIBLIOGRAPHY: Jim Kelly, "Seen from Behind the Camera," *Cinema Canada*, no. 41 (October 1977): 19–21; John W. Locke, "A Healthy Case of Craziness: *Outrageous,*" *Cinema Canada*, no. 41 (October 1977): 17–18.

                                                                                         Peter Rist

DON(ALD) OWEN. Born 1935, Toronto. Director, writer, cinematographer. Best known for the groundbreaking NFB feature, *NOBODY WAVED GOODBYE*, Don Owen was the person most responsible for bringing "realism" to the Canadian tradition of fiction filmmaking. He studied anthropology at the University of Toronto and worked as a writer of documentary narration and as a stagehand in television before joining the NFB in 1960. There, he first worked as a cine-matographer (*LA LUTTE*), then directed two interesting short observational doc-umentaries, *Runner*, on middle-distance runner Bruce Kidd, with a "poetic" commentary by W. H. Auden, and *Toronto Jazz*. The innovative strategies he and his crew employed on *Nobody Waved Goodbye*—including the use of light-weight equipment and encouraging the actors to improvise their dialogue—had a wide-ranging influence on fiction filmmaking both inside and outside Canada, especially in film schools. He himself continued to work in this mode on the underrated and virtually unseen *Notes for a Film About Donna & Gail*, and on his second (and last) fiction feature at the NFB, *The Ernie Game*, which won the Etrog in 1968 for Best Canadian Film. During this period he continued to direct short documentaries and remained innovative, but his work began to de-cline in the 1970s, and by the time he made an embarrassingly bland sequel to *Nobody* in 1983, entitled *Unfinished Business* (released in 1984), he was almost a forgotten figure in Canadian cinema.

FILMS AS DIRECTOR INCLUDE: *Runner*, 1962; *Toronto Jazz; Nobody Waved Goodbye* (feature), 1964; *High Steel; Ladies and Gentlemen: Mr. Leonard Cohen* (co-dir. with Donald Brittain), 1965; *Notes for a Film About Donna & Gail*, 1966; *The Ernie Game* (feature); *Gallery, a View of Time*, 1967; *Snow in Venice; Graham Coughtry in Ibiza*, 1971; *Cowboy and Indian*, 1972; *Not Far from Home*, 1973; *Partners* (feature) 1976; *Holstein*, 1978; *Spread Your Wings*, 1981; *Unfinished Business* (feature), 1984.

BIBLIOGRAPHY: Natalie Edwards, "Who's Don Owen? What's He Done, and What's He Doing Now?," *Cinema Canada*, no. 8 (June/July 1973), reprinted in Feldman and Nelson, 160–78.

                                                                                         Peter Rist

P

PARALLAX: TEN CENTS A DANCE. Midi Onodera, Toronto, 1985, 30 min., color, 16mm. *Parallax: Ten Cents a Dance* is a remarkable example of a new kind of Canadian experimental film that combines textural concerns—it is what P. Adams Sitney would call a "structural film"—with textual ones—being "about" gender and sexuality. It also marks a breakthrough for Canadian multiculturalism: Midi Onodera, the film's director, is Japanese Canadian. *Parallax* is divided into three sections, equal in length, which depict three different relationships, where each individual is represented in a separate frame. In fact, the film, like Andy Warhol's *Chelsea Girls* (1973), was initially projected by two separate projectors (but, unlike its predecessor, with synchronous sound). The first part depicts two women in a restaurant, facing each other across the frame breaks, reaching out their arms and touching through the medium of a red rose. The second shows a man in each frame in an adjoining toilet cubicle. Each camera looks down on its subject in vertical high angle. One man performs (unseen) fellatio on the other across the frame boundaries. As with the first segment there is no dialogue, only ambient sound. The final part depicts heterosexual phone sex. At the time when *Parallax* was made, Ontario was embroiled in censorship struggles. Experimental film and other arts communities throughout the province challenged the police to close down screenings, seize films, and arrest filmmakers, and Onodera cleverly made a provocative film containing no explicit sex or nudity, which was probably sent to the censors on separate reels, so that they couldn't clearly divulge its message. Onodera's choice of split-screen format is suggestive of communication problems, and the three narratives cover the range of homo- and heterosexual couples. It could be argued that *Parallax* is anti-gay with its ostensibly negative second part, but Onodera presumably wished to question contemporary alienation in the sexual arena, while challenging the Ontario censors to comprehend vanguard filmmaking. Onodera has since moved into more conventional (but still controversial) arenas with a documentary on the internment of Japanese Canadians during World War II, *The Displaced View* (1988), and a fiction feature on the pleasure/ pain of tattooing, *Skin Deep* (1995).

Peter Rist

PAS DE DEUX. Norman McLaren, (Montreal) ONF, 1967, 13 min., b+w, no dialogue. Rarely has the expression "poetry in motion" found such a literal and numinous incarnation as in *Pas de deux*. This beautiful short film by NORMAN MCLAREN shows a couple of dancers engaged in a hypnotic ballet, where the human eye is given an opportunity to linger on movement and its dissection through the fascinating combination of slow-motion cinematography and optically multiplied images. The result is a technical tour de force, enhanced by highly contrasted lighting, which at first outlines the dancers' moving bodies against a dark background, and ultimately reduces them to skeleton shapes that become increasingly abstract as the image reproduction process intensifies. The opening moments of *Pas de deux* follow Margaret Mercier as she dances alone. A few minutes into the film, when the spectator is already captivated by the music and drawn in by the controlled slowness of the spectacle, the camera tracks back to reveal, at the bottom left corner of the image, a man (Vincent Warren) looking at the female dancer, as we are. Such a direct confrontation of the viewer's voyeuristic activity is partly redeemed by the fact that Warren eagerly joins Mercier in the dance, almost inviting us along. Beyond that invitation, it is the sheer nature of cinema and its spectatorship that McLaren invokes. With his blend of lights, shadows, and motion, the filmmaker could be said to analyze and deconstruct film itself, thus transforming *Pas de deux* into a vibrant metaphor of the art he so rigorously and brilliantly extended. *Pas de deux* has won seventeen awards throughout the world (Toronto, London, New York, Melbourne), as well as an Oscar nomination in Hollywood.

Alain Dubeau

YVAN PATRY. Born 1948, Iroquois Falls, Ontario. Director, producer. It was the programming of his short film, *Octobre 68*, dealing with student demonstrations, by SRC's public events television series "Les temps changent" that gave Yvan Patry his first chance in cinema. In 1969 he directed his first fiction feature for the ONF, *Ainsi soient-ils*, on the new cultural mentality that emerged from 1968. During the 1970s he worked as a professor/film director at Montmorency College, where he made a number of educational audiovisual documents. In 1974, he collaborated with Bernard Lalonde, Roger Frappier, Guy Bergeron, and André Gagnon, and oversaw the direction of the collective effort, *On a raison de se révolter*, on workers' conflicts. He carried this theme into his video work for Vidéographe. Beginning in 1980 he made several trips to Nicaragua, where he filmed under difficult conditions. In 1982 Patry founded Alter-Ciné, which brought together filmmakers, journalists, and technicians specializing in the documentary and international reporting and who worked with Third World organizations for educational and production projects. It is then that he turned himself toward "direct" style political cinema as a consciousness-raising tool and interested himself particularly in Central American questions. In 1983 he co-directed with Danièle Lacourse (and J. Reiter) *Nicaragua/Honduras: Entre deux guerres*, and then *Nicaragua: La guerre sale* (1985), providing a significant portrait of the war fought by the Contras against the population of Nicaragua. Two years later, he retraced the conflict between Eritrea and Ethiopia in a series of three documentaries entitled *Eritrea and the Horn of Africa*. Since 1982, Patry and Lacourse have covered all of the regions of the world at war and in conflict, and have increasingly directed films for television, including *L'histoire muselée*, which allowed them to introduce the general public to the assassination of the majority of the 1,000 inhabitants of the Salvadoran village of El Mozote, a fact which had been hidden from the world's press since the massacre had occurred in 1981, and *Hand of God, Hand of the Devil*, which centered on the unexpected assassination (following the genocide in 1994) of Father Claude Simard, who had been a missionary in Rwanda for twenty-nine years. With such work, Yvan Patry has been able to revolt against the injustices to which he has been witness, and, always under difficult conditions, has attempted to expose the truth.

FILMS AS DIRECTOR INCLUDE: *Octobre 68* (TV, short); *Ainsi soient-ils*, 1969; *On a raison de se révolter*, 1974; *Nicaragua/Honduras: Entre deux guerres* (co-dir.), 1984; *Nicaragua: La guerre sale* (co-dir.), 1985; *Chants de la terre prochaine; La blessure et l'espoir; La guerre oubliée*, 1986; *Erythrée* (series of 3 films), 1987; *Nuit et silence* (short, co-dir.), 1990; *L'histoire muselée* (TV, co-dir.), 1994; *Hand of God, Hand of the Devil* (TV); *Chronicle of a Genocide Foretold*, 1996.

BIBLIOGRAPHY: Jean Saint-Arnaud, " 'Je crois qu'un cinéaste doit aller plus loin que de constater l'impasse: il doit lancer des cris': Entretien avec Yvan Patry," *Ciné-Bulles* (April–May 1985): 25–28.

Isabelle Morissette

PAUL TOMKOWICZ: STREET-RAILWAY SWITCHMAN. Roman Kroitor, NFB, "Faces of Canada" series, 1954, 9 min., b+w. *Paul Tomkowicz: Street-Railway Switchman* is a clear example of a "documentary" film that has almost as many controlled elements as a fiction film. Although it was shot on location, in Winnipeg, Manitoba, without yet-to-be-developed lightweight, synchronized camera and sound equipment, and although it featured the sixty-four-year-old title character enacting his working life, most of the wintry action was staged for the camera, the sound was post-synched, and the heavily accented, scripted narration was spoken by an Anglo-Canadian. Yet, for most observers, the film works exceptionally well as an honest slice-of-life, depicting the Polish immigrant "face of Canada" experience. Lorne C. Batchelor's expressive cinematography, key lighting Tomkowicz in high and low angle, while he reattaches the trolley to the electric wire, and sweeps the rail switch points, at night, in a snowstorm, is enhanced by Joan Edward's sound effects, with winter wind adding an even harsher aspect to the man's arduous tasks. The strong sense of coldness is elegantly balanced by a scene of Tomkowicz eating a huge breakfast, including steaming hot coffee, in the friendly confines of a diner, and of exterior images of steam and electrical sparks. *Street-Railway Switchman* also provides an early example of TOM DALY as creative producer playing the role of editor and delivering a tightly constructed work. It was also Roman Kroitor's first film as a director. Although not itself a true example of "direct cinema," *Street-Railway Switchman*, with its emphasis on quotidian, ordinary experience, looked forward to Unit B's "Candid Eye" series, and in finding a matter-of-fact heroism in arduous yet menial work, it stands as a quintessentially Canadian film.

BIBLIOGRAPHY: Gary Evans (1991), 75.

Peter Rist

PETER PEARSON. Born 1938, Toronto. Director, writer, producer. *THE BEST DAMN FIDDLER FROM CALABOGIE TO KALADAR* and *Paperback Hero* (1973) have secured Peter Pearson's place as a major figure in Canadian cinema. These vigorous works depict dangerously inflated male egotism chafing against working-class privations. Oddly, Pearson (second cousin to former Canadian Prime Minister Lester B. Pearson) has recalled having little interest in film at the start of his career. He studied political science at the University of Toronto prior to becoming a newspaper reporter. He soon entered television current affairs programming, which sparked his ambition to make films. In 1963 he enrolled in the Centro Sperimentale di Cinematographia in Rome for formal filmmaking training. Pearson then wrote and directed documentaries for the CBC series "Document" and "This Hour Has Seven Days" before joining the National Film Board of Canada in 1966. Two years of intense activity there culminated in *Fiddler*, which brought him a Best Director Etrog among the many awards it received in Canada and abroad. *Paperback Hero*, his first theatrical feature, raised his reputation further. Pointedly unsatisfying, *Hero* has an enduring freshness because of its ambivalence—its protagonist, "Marshal" Rick Dillon, is at once a comically anachronistic blowhard and a pitiable victim of a waning male image ideal. The film had moderate financial success. *Only God Knows*, Pearson's second feature, received poor reviews and failed commercially. He worked prolifically in television afterward. His topical dramas shown on CBC's "For the Record" series drew considerable attention, particularly *Snowbirds*, scripted by Margaret Atwood, and the hotly controversial *The Tar Sands* (1977). He contributed to the Etrog winning screenplay for Robin Spry's feature *One Man*. Telefilm Canada appointed him director of broadcast funds in 1983, recognizing his stature as a filmmaker and his extensive promotion of Canadian cinema as writer and spokesperson. As executive director there (1985 to 1987), he participated in the development of *Bethune: The Making of a Hero* (PHILLIP BORSOS, 1990).

FILMS AS DIRECTOR INCLUDE: *Queen in Charlottetown*, 1964; *Mastroianni* (also scr., prod.), 1965; *This Blooming Business of Bilingualism* (also scr.), 1966; *Whatever Happened to Them All?* (also scr., prod.), 1967; *Saul Alinsky Went to War* (co-dir., Donald Brittain); *The Best Damn Fiddler from Calabogie to Kaladar*, 1969; *Seasons in the Mind* (IMAX short; co-dir., Michael Milne), 1971; *Paperback Hero*, 1973; *A Thousand Miles of Holidays* (short; also scr.); *Only God Knows*, 1974; *The Insurance Man from Ingersoll* (also co-scr., Norman Hartley), 1976; *The Tar Sands* (TV; also co-scr., Peter Rowe, Ralph L. Thomas), 1977; *"The Chairman": A Portrait of Paul Desmarais* (TV; also scr., prod.), 1980; *Snowbirds* (TV; also story), 1981; *Quebec: Economy in Crisis* (also prod.), 1982.

Ian Elliot

PERFECTLY NORMAL. Yves Simoneau, Canada (Ontario)/UK, 1990, 108 min., color. It says a great deal about Canadians that their two most cherished institutions are beer, a working-class drink, and hockey, a game that periodically interrupts brawls on skating rinks across the country. While advertisers have always recognized the link between these two stereotypically Canadian concerns, Yves Simoneau's *Perfectly Normal* manages to connect the national beverage and the national sport to opera and Italian cuisine in a surprisingly charming and engaging film. After the apparent suicide of his aged mother, Renzo (Michael Riley), an employee at a small brewery and goalie for the factory's hockey team, spends his evenings driving around town in his late father's taxi in an effort to save enough money to build his dream home in the country. Renzo picks up Alonso (Scottish comedian Robbie Coltrane), who convinces him to use his inheritance to open a restaurant, La Traviata, which will feature waiters and waitresses performing the roles of various operatic figures. The film works to negate the dichotomy which Alonso insists exists between what he considers to be the drab routine of Renzo's life and the high passion of opera. In fact, throughout the film the everyday is revealed to be more than just dull and drab: Renzo sings opera in the shower; his lover Denise (Deborah Duchene), who works at the concession stand at the hockey rink, is an accomplished photographer; the hockey games are shot in elaborate slow-motion tracking shots and accompanied by an operatic score. The result is a compassionately humorous portrayal of the mundane, which recognizes the potential greatness of all lives and the small but significant accomplishments that make ordinary people extraordinary.

Mitch Parry

PIERRE PERRAULT. Born 1927, Montreal. Director. It is difficult to discuss Pierre Perrault's work without referring to Robert Flaherty. The similiarities between the two directors are quite stunning, if only because of the recurring themes present in their films—specifically a fascination with people, wide-open spaces, and cultural traditions. Perrault began his career in law, studying in Montreal (where he was nearly expelled for protesting against the teaching of law!), Paris, and Toronto. He abandoned the profession in 1956, opting instead for radio broadcasting. Already interested in poetry, Perrault's radio work established one of his most important concerns, that of language. Traveling throughout Quebec with French singer Jacques Douai, the future filmmaker chronicled rural traditions mostly through language, the people's voice becoming his vehicle. This experience led to a collaboration with René Bonnière, working on *Au pays de Neuve-France*, a series of thirteen documentaries produced for Crawley Films (*see* FRANK "BUDGE" CRAWLEY and JUDITH CRAWLEY). The ONF offered Perrault the chance to co-direct a documentary on fishing at l'Île-aux-Coudres, which became *POUR LA SUITE DU MONDE* (1963), the first French-NFB/ONF feature, as well as the first Canadian film in competition at Cannes. By recreating an abandoned fishing tradition (shades of Flaherty), Perrault placed himself at the forefront of the *direct* movement. The three aforementioned themes are already clearly established in this first film, and remain a constant throughout the director's oeuvre. This body of work can be roughly divided into four cycles: L'Île-aux-Coudres (a trilogy), four films on the Abitibi region of Quebec, a Native American component (two films), and finally two films that retrace Jacques Cartier's travels. The subject matter changes, but the approach, a lyrical anthropological view of language and nature (which has sometimes been criticized for "fictionalizing" the documentary form) consistently reflects Perrault's philosophy: "I love film, but above all I love mankind."

FILMS AS DIRECTOR: *Pour la suite du monde* (co-dir., Michel Brault), 1963; *La règne du jour*, 1966; *Les voitures d'eau; Le beau plaisir* (short; co-dir., Brault and Bernard Gosselin), 1968; *Un pays sans bon sens!*, 1970; *L'Acadie, l'Acadie?!?* (co-dir., Brault), 1971; *Tickets, S.V.P.* (short), 1973; *Un royaume vous attend* (co-dir., Gosselin), 1976; *Le goût de la farine* (co-dir., Gosselin); *C'était un québécois en Bretagne, Madame* (short); *Le retour de la terre* (short), 1977; *Gens d'Abitibi* (co-dir., Gosselin); *Le pays de la terre sans arbre ou le Mouchouânipi*, 1980; *La bête lumineuse*, 1982; *Les voiles bas et en travers* (short), 1983; *La grande allure*, 1985; *L'Oumigmatique*, 1993.

BIBLIOGRAPHY: Louis Marcorelles, 65–83; Stéphane-Albert Boulais.

Judes Dickey

LA PETITE AURORE L'ENFANT MARTYRE Little Aurore's Tragedy. Jean-Yves Bigras, Quebec, 1951, 102 min., b+w. The most important popular success of Quebecois cinema in the 1950s, and produced during the first wave of fiction films (1944–53), *La petite Aurore l'enfant martyre* is a somber melodrama retelling the martyrdom of Aurore, who, living in the memory of her mother Delphine, suffers the worst humiliations and is beaten to death by her stepmother, Marie Louise, who herself had poisoned Delphine in order to take her place at the side of Théodore, the girl's father. Strongly anchored in the values of the Duplessis Quebec, Bigras' film nevertheless proposes—not necessarily intentionally—a very pessimistic vision of the era of the "great darkness." The rural milieu is contaminated by ignorance and the mistreatment of children, whereas religion no longer functions as a place of refuge for anyone. One finds in this film several characteristics of melodrama, but carried to an extreme: excessive accumulation of dramatic situations, stereotypical characters, actors' performances without nuance, and nondiegetic music heavily underlining the drama. On the other hand, whereas the film's cinematographic techniques lack competence (the film contains a number of "bad" cuts), *La petite Aurore* definitely merits its place in the history of Quebecois cinema, especially for its strong contribution to the "collective imaginary." Throughout her career, the actress Lucie Mitchell was associated with her character of the unkind stepmother. In addition, the expression "petite Aurore" is still used to describe a mistreated child. Notably, the film continued to be programmed in several Quebec film theaters in the early 1970s.

BIBLIOGRAPHY: Christiane Tremblay-Daviault (1981).

Louis Goyette

DONALD PILON. Born 1938, Montreal, Quebec. Actor. Donald Pilon never sought to be an actor; rather his career found him. In 1967, while employed at the Expo in Montreal, he was discovered by GILLES CARLE, who cast him, along with his brother Daniel Pilon, as one of the youths who kidnap and rape a teenage girl in the miscalculated black comedy *Le viol d'une jeune fille douce*. Although the role itself was not inherently memorable, it did launch a successful long-term collaboration between Pilon and Carle which led to a further seven films together. Pilon offered an earthy realism in his early roles, something to which the emerging Quebecois filmmakers were drawn. In 1970, he starred in his first huge box office success, the sex farce *DEUX FEMMES EN OR*. Pilon was fast becoming one of the most successful leading men in Quebec. In 1971 he won the best actor Etrog for his performance as the rebellious Thomas Carufel in his fourth collaboration with Gilles Carle, *LE VRAIE NATURE DE BERNADETTE*. Pilon's complex performance matches MICHELINE LANCTÔT's (as Bernadette) charm and screen presence, scene for scene. On the wave of his success in Quebec, Pilon deftly turned his hand to English Canadian production by appearing as Christopher Plummer's sidekick in the police thriller *The Pyx* (1973), as well as starring in the CBC TV series "The Collaborators." In the 1980s he gradually moved away from leading roles, to character parts in ensemble pieces, as illustrated by his work as the coarse and manipulative Stan Labrie in both *Les Plouffe* (1981) and *Le crime d'Ovide Plouffe*. Although the 1970s may represent the peak of Pilon's career both in terms of performance and exposure, he remains a strong presence within the Canadian film industry. Adept at both comedy and drama, he exhibits the strength and presence of a star, albeit only attained in Quebec.

THEATRICAL FILMS AS ACTOR: *Le viol d'une jeune fille douce*, 1968; *Red; Deux femmes en or*, 1970; *Les mâles; Les chats bottés*, 1971; *Les smattes; La vraie nature de Bernadette*, 1972; *The Pyx; Les corps célestes* (Can/Fr), 1973; *Bulldozer*, 1971–74; *Child*

Under a Leaf, 1974; *Gina*, 1975; *The Uncanny* (Can/UK), 1977; *I Miss You, Hugs and Kisses*, 1978; *City on Fire; A Man Called Intrepid*, 1979; *Fantastica* (Can/Fr), 1980; *Les Plouffe*, 1981; *Le crime d'Ovide Plouffe*, 1984; *Keeping Track; La guêpe*, 1986; *Les tisserands du pouvoir*, 1988; *Une histoire inventée*, 1990; *Le vent du Wyoming*, 1994; *Angelo, Fredo et Romeo*, 1996.

BIBLIOGRAPHY: Gilles Carle, "Donald Pilon," *Cinéma Québec* 1, no. 6 (December 1971); Stephen Chesley and A'Ibranyi-kiss, "Pilon," *Cinéma Canada*, no. 17 (December–January 1976).

Stacey Abbott

GORDON PINSENT. Born 1930, Grand Falls, Newfoundland. Actor, writer, director. The revered star of two popular CBC television series and of the well-received Newfoundland-based feature *The Rowdyman* (1971), Pinsent is widely regarded as the quintessential Canadian actor. After gradually entering prominence over ten years of acting, on stage and on television, he played the terminally ill romantic lead of his first film, shot in Greece, *Lydia* (1964). In the title role of the CBC series "Quentin Durgens, M.P." (1966–69, thirty episodes), Pinsent became a major Canadian entertainment figure, as much for the values he embodied as for his acting capabilities. The character, a selflessly dedicated, industrious public official, established the Pinsent image: the impassioned, forthright populist. Though Pinsent's energy and charisma have brought him enormous praise, his range as an actor has conspicuous limits; his superficiality as a rakish, corruptible television news cameraman makes *The Heatwave Lasted Four Days* a tepid thriller. Amid his work in Hollywood (1969–75), which included co-starring in the film *The Forbin Project* and several U.S. television appearances, Pinsent returned to Canada with his screenplay for *The Rowdyman*, which celebrates his Newfoundland working-class origins as a background to a comic yet melodramatic narrative focused on the boyish hell-raiser he plays. The film's favorable reception made him, for many, "Canada's leading writer and director" (Gerald Pratley). Pinsent maintained his stature with prolific Canadian theater and television work and with roles in films directed by Peter Pearson (*Only God Knows*, 1974) and ALLAN KING (*WHO HAS SEEN THE WIND; Silence of the North*). Creator and star of the CBC series "A Gift to Last" (1976–79), he wrote eighteen of its twenty-one episodes. He began directing with *A Far Cry from Home* (1980), an entry in the CBC "For the Record" series. *John and the Missus* (based on his 1976 play, derived from actual events of 1962), written and directed by Pinsent, showcases him as the weathered Newfoundland copper-miner who bucks an insensitive government resettlement program. Pinsent's bravura in the role resulted in his third Genie for acting (he won Best Actor for *The Rowdyman* and Best Supporting Actor for *Klondike Fever*). In the most recent of his many honors, he accepted the Earl Grey Award at the 1997 Genies as a tribute to his entire career.

THEATRICAL FILMS AS ACTOR: *Lydia*, 1964; *Don't Forget to Wipe the Blood Off*, 1966; *The Rowdyman* (also scr.), 1971; *The Heatwave Lasted Four Days*, 1973; *Only God Knows*, 1974; *Who Has Seen the Wind*, 1976; *Klondike Fever; Silence of the North*,

1979; *The Devil at Your Heels* (narr. only), 1980; *John and the Missus* (also dir., scr.), 1987; *Babar: The Movie* (Fr/Can, voice only), 1989; *Blood Clan,* 1990; *Pale Saints; Pippi Longstocking* (voice only), 1997.

BIBLIOGRAPHY: Rota Herzberg Lister, "Gordon Pinsent," in Eugene Benson and L. W. Conolly, 361–62; Gordon Pinsent.

Ian Elliot

CHRISTOPHER PLUMMER. Born Arthur Christopher Orme, 1927, Montreal. Actor. As a child, Plummer studied music with a view to becoming a pianist, before turning to acting at age eighteen. He made his professional stage debut in 1950 in Ottawa, and toured the United States, where he played many of the classic roles. After an early stint in Hollywood, Plummer returned to Stratford, Ontario, and then went on to the Royal Shakespeare Company in Britain, honing his craft and earning himself an international reputation as a stage actor. Hollywood beckoned again more successfully with *The Fall of the Roman Empire* (1964) and the mammoth hit *The Sound of Music* (1965). Plummer was every inch the leading man, handsome, charismatic, and charming, but he bowed off the screen in 1970 to work in Britain's Royal National Theatre. He returned to the cinema in 1973 in his first Canadian feature, *The Pyx* (HARVEY HART), as a world-weary detective, displaying a laconic humor. Previously he had narrated the NFB's documentary *Trans-Canada Journey,* made in 1962, and appeared in the NFB short *Thirty Minutes Mr. Plummer* in 1963. Plummer was back on the screen with a vengeance, returning to Canada frequently to appear in some of his most challenging and uncharacteristic roles. He played a psychotic bank robber in *THE SILENT PARTNER* (D. Duke, 1978), and the following year he gave one of his best ever performances as Sherlock Holmes in the Anglo/Canadian co-production *Murder by Decree* (BOB CLARK). Plummer's Holmes is shrewd, logical, and idiosyncratic, and ranks alongside the greatest screen Holmeses. With age, Plummer has increasingly appeared in darker roles, playing a shady character in charge of a hit-man organization in *The Disappearance* (S. Cooper), and the venal Colonel Knox in *The Boy in Blue* (C. Jarrott, 1984). Though always professional (Plummer researches obsessively for each role), these films were not well received, and perhaps his best work in Canada during this period was his involvement in two documentaries by Harry Rasky. In the first, *Arthur Miller on Home Ground,* Plummer and Faye Dunaway act out scenes from Miller's *After the Fall,* and in the second, *Being Different,* Plummer narrates this extraordinary, bold film about physical deformity. Still active on stage and screen, he recently returned to London, Ontario, to appear in a one-man show playing the legendary John Barrymore.

FILMS AS ACTOR: *Trans-Canada Journey* (narr. only), 1962; *Thirty Minutes Mr. Plummer* (short), 1963; *The Pyx,* 1973; *Happy Prince* (voice only), 1974; *The Disappearance,* 1977; *The Silent Partner,* 1978; *Riel; Murder by Decree* (Can/UK); *Arthur Miller: On Home Ground,* 1979; *Being Different* (Can/US); *The Amateur,* 1981; *Highpoint,* 1979– 84; *Rumplestiltskin* (narr. only), 1985; *The Boy in Blue* (Can/US); *Traveling Light,* 1986; *Gandahar* (voice only), 1987; *Kingsgate; Mindfield,* 1989; *Red Blooded American Girl,*

1990; *Money* (Fr/It/Can), 1991; *Harrison Bergeron* (TV), 1995; *We, the Jury* (TV); *The Conspiracy of Fear* (TV), 1996; *The Arrow* (TV), 1997.

Simon Brown

ANNE-CLAIRE POIRIER. Born 1932, Saint-Hyacinthe, Quebec. Director, editor, producer. From the beginning of the 1960s, as an assistant director and editor at the ONF, Anne-Claire Poirier played the very important role of leading the struggle for women to gain access to the key post of film director. In 1963 she directed her own first short film, on the actor CHRISTOPHER PLUMMER, *Thirty Minutes Mister Plummer*, and then made a short fiction film based on a screenplay by Hubert Aquin, *La fin des étés* (1964). In 1967 Poirier directed her first documentary feature, *De mère en fille*, on pregnancy and maternity. Henceforth, the feminine condition would be the major theme throughout the cineaste's work. With the help of Jeanne Morazin and Marthe Blackburn, Poirier brought an important text to the attention of the powers that be at the ONF, "En tant que femmes nous-mêmes," in which she expressed the need for women to be directing films about women. The ONF then created the program "En tant que femmes," for which would be made six films where the feminine question was quintessential, including two directed by Poirier, *Les filles du Roy* (1974) and *Le temps de l'avant*. It was at this moment that her own individual style appeared: a heterogeneous film "language" where fiction rubs elbows with traditional documentary mixed with archival material. This technique reached its apogee in *MOURIR À TUE-TÊTE*: in this film, the form of "collage" gives a striking power of persuasion to Poirier's discourse. After *La quarantaine* (1982), she retreated somewhat from view, returning to the fray in 1988 with a TV film on the friendship of two seniors, *Salut Victor!* In 1996 she directed without a doubt her most personal film. Shot in very high contrast black and white, *Tu as crié let me go* explored the problem of teenage drug addiction while recording the emotionally moving and disturbing trauma of Poirier reflecting on her own daughter's death a few years earlier. This painful yet brilliant film won the Prix L-E-Ouimet-Molson at the Rendez-vous du cinéma québécois for the Best Quebec Feature Film of 1997.

FILMS AS DIRECTOR INCLUDE: shorts: *Thirty Minutes Mister Plummer*, 1963; *La fin des étés*, 1964; *Les ludions*, 1965; features: *De mère en fille*, 1967; *Les filles du Roy*, 1974; *Le temps de l'avant*, 1975; *Mourir à tue-tête*, 1979; *La quarantaine*, 1982; *Salut Victor!*, 1988; *Il y a longtemps que je t'aime*, 1992; *Tu as crié let me go*, 1997.

BIBLIOGRAPHY: Pierre Jutras and Pierre Véronneau, eds., "Anne-Claire Poirier: Entretien, témoinages et points devue" *Copie Zéro*, no. 23 (February 1985).

Louis Goyette

LÉA POOL. Born 1950, Switzerland. Director, writer. Léa Pool immigrated to Quebec in 1978, and has since proven herself to be one of the most significant voices in French-language film in Canada. Pool attended Université du Québec, and after graduation began working for Radio-Québec, making documentaries. Her first feature film was *Strass Café*, in 1980, but it was 1984's LA FEMME DE L'HÔTEL that drew attention to her abilities as a filmmaker. She followed with ANNE TRISTER and the well-received but difficult *À corps perdu* (1988), which depicts the efforts of a photographer to deal with the loss of his lovers. Her contribution to the ONF's "Parler d'Amérique" series was the feature-length documentary *Hotel Chronicle* (1990), and the following year she contributed the sketch "Respondetemi" to the omnibus film *Montréal vu par. . . .* Pool has argued that her films are feminist, but points out that they are not political in any dogmatic or discursive way; rather, Pool works to establish characters who are at odds with their environment—characters who are, as she claims, "displaced." Her cinematic style is adapted to its subject matter, ranging from the visual austerity of *La demoiselle sauvage* to the more poetic style of *Anne Trister* and *À corps perdu*. The narratives of her films tend to be relatively loose, allowing her to devote more attention to the communication of emotions. In fact, Pool has argued that the purpose of her films is to create "a market for poetry; a market for strong and beautiful personal films."

FEATURE FILMS AS DIRECTOR: *Strass Café*, 1980; *La femme de l'hôtel*, 1984; *Anne Trister*, 1986; *À corps perdu*, 1988; *Hotel Chronicle*, 1990; *La demoiselle sauvage; Montréal vu par . . .* (sketch: "Respondetemi"), 1991; *Mouvements du désir*, 1994.

BIBLIOGRAPHY: Suzanne Gaulin, "Pool's Splash: An Interview with Léa Pool," *Cinéma Canada*, no. 111 (December 1984): 7–9.

Mitch Parry

PORKY'S. Bob Clark, Toronto, 1981, 99 min., color. *Porky's*, a teen sex-as-joke film, is Canada's all-time highest grossing film ($110 million). It features established actors (Susan Clark, Doug McGrath, Alex Karras, Art Hindle, Nancy Parsons) in the adult roles, and unknown actors in the young roles: a reason perhaps why young audiences identified so strongly with the film. Set in 1950 Florida, *Porky's* follows the high school shenanigans of a group of libido-driven teen males. Plot is an afterthought in a film structured almost entirely around a series of sex-related pranks. These pranks lead to some of the film's central set pieces: the scene with the prostitute "Cherry Forever" (Clark); the first visit to "Porky's," the saloon-whorehouse; and the Peeping Tom shower scene. An obsession with penises drives the film, evident in the character nicknames "Pee Wee" and "Meat." However, for all of its male sexual chutzpah, *Porky's* is anything but sexually liberating. Males (and their penises) are consistently objectified and ridiculed. Plans for sex are continually frustrated, to the point of masochism. This becomes physically obvious when Mickey (Roger Wilson) continually returns to the place where the group was emasculated, the saloon-whorehouse, for yet another beating at the hands of its grossly overweight owner, Porky (the "monster-penis"). *Porky's* is clearly modeled on Hollywood films such as *Animal House* (John Landis, 1978), *American Graffiti* (George

Lucas, 1973), and *Carrie* (Brian De Palma, 1976). However, in reducing the comic palette to such phallic single-mindedness and by introducing full frontal male nudity, *Porky's* has gone further (or more accurately "lower") than any other film in defining what William Paul has called the "animal comedy." *Porky's* has spawned two sequels, *Porky's 2: The Next Day* (Clark, 1983) and *Porky's Revenge* (James Komack, 1985).

BIBLIOGRAPHY: F. Dhont and J. MacTrevor, "Porky's," *Cine Revue*, no. 62 (August 12, 1982): 18–21; William Paul, 113–22.

Donato Totaro

LOUISE PORTAL. Born Louise Lapointe, 1950, Chicoutimi, Quebec. Actor. Louise Portal has had an erratic career, appearing in major roles in significant and acclaimed films, yet also interspersing these with smaller, less commercial projects, some well received, some not. After studying at the Conservatoire d'Art Dramatique in Montreal, her first film role came in 1971, with a small part in LA VIE REVÉE. She followed this with parts in *Taureau* (1973), *Les deux pieds dans la même bottine*, and *Vie d'ange* (both 1974), in which she appeared alongside her three sisters. She also appeared as the actress in ANNE-CLAIRE POIRIER's extraordinary MOURIR À TUE-TÊTE. Although her body of cinema work in the 1970s was small, she nevertheless continued to act in the theater and on television before making her mark in 1978 playing the title role in JEAN BEAUDIN's *Cordélia*, the follow-up to Beaudin's successful *J. A. MARTIN, PHOTOGRAPHE*. Inevitably to be compared to MONIQUE MERCURE's award-winning portrayal of Rose-Aimée Martin, Portal gives a strong performance as the free-spirited Cordélia, like Rose-Aimée following her own path and her own inner zest for life in the face of 19th century convention. Yet this is a tragedy. Portal allows Cordélia's free-spirited vitality to dominate while the tragedy flows from the oppression of that spirit. Less satisfactory than *J. A. Martin*, *Cordélia* was nonetheless a critical and commercial success, and made Portal a star. *Larose, Pierrot et la Luce* (1982) was less well received, and it was not until 1986 that Portal won another leading role in a hit film, this time opposite GABRIEL ARCAND in *LE DÉCLIN DE L'EMPIRE AMÉRICAIN*. Here she played Diane, a university professor embroiled in a sadomasochistic relationship with a man who may or may not be a drug dealer. Portal's character is the link between the verbose university professors and the laconic Arcand and is the only one who finds fulfillment. Despite an outstanding performance in 1994 in Johanne Pregent's *Les amoureuses*, Louise Portal has yet to achieve the status of a major star.

FILMS AS ACTOR: *La vie rêvée*, 1972; *Taureau*, 1973; *Les deux pieds dans la même bottine*; *Les beaux dimanches*, 1974; *Vie d'ange*, 1974–79; *Mourir à tue-tête*, 1979; *Cordélia*, 1978–80; *Larose, Pierrot, et La Luce*; *Gourou*, 1982; *On fait toutes de show business*, 1984; *Le déclin de l'empire américain*; *Exit*, 1986; *Tinamer*; *Histoire infâme* (short), 1987; *Les amoureuses*, 1994; *Sous-Sol*; *Lobby*, 1996.

Simon Brown

JOHN PORTER. Born 1945, Toronto. Director, cinematographer, performance artist. One of the principal members of Toronto's Funnel Film Co-operative in the 1970s and 1980s, John Porter also exemplified this group's propensity for extreme low-budget, independent, experimental, Super-8 filmmaking. Indeed, some of his films virtually define the limits of the lightweight medium, while providing a puzzle for the viewer in determining how they were made. *Cinefuge* (1979–81, 4.5 min.) presents a dizzying view of Porter strangely transfixed in the center of the frame while Toronto whirls by behind him. He attached a wire to his Super-8 camera, and then twirled it about his body, while turning on the spot, like a hammer thrower. For *Down on Me* (1980–81, 4 min.) he attached his camera to a fishing line, and, holding the rod erect, lowered and raised the camera with the reel. In the finished film, again, his body is center frame, here, alternately receding and approaching while the surrounding staircase twists and turns. The delirious movement renders the title an understatement. Without replicating the visceral dynamism of these two single-shot spectacles, *Scanning* (1981, 3 min.) shares an interest in camera movement and extends it to the projector. Reminiscent of the early years of cinema, Porter liked to travel with his films, and often asked the audience to pick which ones they would like to see. It is hard to imagine him not showing *Scanning*, and even harder to imagine it being shown without him. He literally scanned a building, a Toronto warehouse, tilting up the wall, then panning or walking alongside, right, then tilted down the wall, panned or tracked more right, and so on. At a screening he would actually hold the projector himself and move among the audience, repeating his camera movements as projector movements! Most of Porter's films are very short, and many contain only a single shot. They often glimpse their subject in pixillation. Unfortunately, this unique traveling showman seems to have virtually disappeared following the closing of the Funnel and with the demise of the Super-8 format. He has become a shadowy figure on the Toronto scene, and his remarkable films, most of which only exist in a single Super-8 copy, are in danger of being lost forever.

SUPER-8 FILMS INCLUDE: *Santa Claus Parade*, 1976; *Landscape*, 1977; *Ferries*, 1978; *Amusement Park*, 1978–79; *Angel Baby*, 1979; *Firefly*, 1980; *Cinefuge*, 1979–81; *Down on Me*, 1980–81; *Drive In Movies; Scanning*, 1981; *Tour of a Cat House; Scanning 2*; 1982; *Scanning 5*, 1983.

BIBLIOGRAPHY: Michaelle McLean, co-ordinator, *Funnel* catalogue (Toronto: The Funnel, 1984), 35–36; Peter Rist, "John Porter: Super-8 Idealist," *Vanguard* 15, no. 2 (April/May 1986): 30–33.

Peter Rist

LA POULETTE GRISE. Norman McLaren, ONF, series "Chansons de chez nous," 1947, 6 min., color. One of NORMAN McLAREN's favorites among his own films, *La poulette grise* is also one of the most beautiful films ever produced at the ONF/NFB. In illustrating an old French song about a chicken that changes color each time it nests, McLaren managed to create the impression of one long (5 min. 32 sec.), continuously changing shot. Assigned to supervise two new series of films on popular songs, McLaren began by co-directing *Alouette* in 1944 ("Let's All Sing Together [No. 1]"), using paper cut-outs of bird figures. Later in the same year he made a stylistic breakthrough with *C'est l'aviron* ("Chants populaires" no. 5), drawing on black card with (white) gouache, moving the camera down toward the artwork on the animation stand and overlapping multiplane backgrounds to create the illusion of depth, and dissolving the images to create an ever changing picture. With his next "chant populaire," *Là-haut sur ces montagnes*, he began working with pastels on card, and after developing this technique with *A Little Phantasy on a Nineteenth Century Painting* (1946) he made his masterpiece of the genre, *La poulette grise*. McLaren was obsessed with bird imagery, it seems, beginning with transforming variations on his beloved chicken in *Hen Hop* (1942). With *Grise* he would wipe off and reapply pastels and fade in and out with each change, delicately dissolving from nest to nest while regularly shifting from hen to egg and back again. With such subtle changes in color and McLaren's attention to detail, including blowing snow and stars in the sky, one could easily linger on each "painting," each frame of film. But we see the film at twenty-four frames per second, and observe a gently flowing, magical, charming visual accompaniment to the song. Indeed, the director has said of this film that he wished to put the audience's attention on "process rather than the end product." *La poulette grise* virtually defines "moving pictures" while actually containing no movement at all.

BIBLIOGRAPHY: Maynard Collins, 39, 74.

Peter Rist

POUR LA SUITE DU MONDE *Moontrap*/For Those Who Follow*. Pierre Perrault and Michel Brault, (Quebec) ONF, 1963, 105 min. (*85 min.), b+w. *Pour la suite du monde* is one of the finest works of filmic ethnography ever produced, and a landmark in Quebecois and Canadian cinema for introducing PIERRE PERRAULT's *cinéma vécu* (lived cinema) to complicate the documentary/fiction dichotomy. Working very closely with the great cinematographer of Quebecois *cinéma direct*, MICHEL BRAULT, and the person most responsible for recording the sound of Quebecois speech, Marcel Carrière, Perrault traveled to l'Île-aux-Coudres. Here they met up with the family and friends of Alexis Tremblay, the "star" of a seminal (anglophone) NFB documentary on rural Quebec, *Alexis Tremblay, Habitant* (1943, Jane Marsh Beveridge), to try to persuade the people to catch a beluga (whale) in the old way. The film crew, working very closely with their "social actors" (in Bill Nichols' words), would film whatever tran-

---

*Unfortunately, the English version of *Pour la suite du monde* is a travesty of the original. It is drastically cut, and even renamed *Moontrap*, and worse, has a voice-over added to explain the action of the film. When explanation is needed in Perrault and Brault's original film, the participants provide it themselves.

spired. Not strictly a documentary (because there would have been no film without the filmmakers' intervention), *Pour la suite du monde*, with its rhythmic oscillation between speech and action and its poetic evocation of everyday life, becomes a truly "lived cinema" experience. Unlike most "anthropological films," which are produced by outsiders, this one provides an intimate insider's portrait of a rural community for all Quebecois and a time capsule of a vanishing world for future generations (although some would argue that the college-educated filmmakers worked from an elitist, higher-class position). The men of the town initially debate whether or not they should try whalehunting again, and Pierre Harvey and Alexis' son Léopold lead the adventure. Alexis' voice is a dissenting one, and he continues to play devil's advocate, providing some conflict, but the overall mood of the film is extremely harmonious, and when the islanders do eventually catch a beluga, it is lovingly transported to an aquarium in New York City.

BIBLIOGRAPHY: Louis Marcorelles, "Pierre Perrault," in Marcorelles: 65–83; Peter Ohlin, "The Film as Word," *Ciné-Tracts* 1, no. 4 (Spring/Summer 1978): 63–70; Peter Harcourt, "Pierre Perrault and *le cinéma vécu*," in *The Human Elements*, Second Series (Ottawa: Oberon, 1981), reprinted in Feldman, 125–35; David Clandfield, "Ritual and Recital: The Perrault Project," revised version, in Feldman, 136–48.

Peter Rist

POUVOIR INTIME. Yves Simoneau, Montreal, 1986, 85 min., color. Worthy successor to Jean-Claude Lord, Yves Simoneau creates here an effective thriller, a sort of cross between the postmodern aesthetic of Jean-Jacques Beneix and the frenzy of Martin Scorcese. The intrigue of *Pouvoir intime* resides in the theft of an armored car by a gang of social misfits, a theft that rapidly transforms into a veritable fiasco. Although the film is not without a certain artificiality, Simoneau displays a good mastery of the genre, making brilliant use of camera movement, unusual camera angles, and a nervous montage. Equally important, there is no "dead time" in this pitiless descent into hell. But in addition to these formal considerations, one can equally find in *Pouvoir intime* an interesting sociopolitical reflection. Some have seen in Simoneau's film a metaphor for the defeat of the independence project of the Quebecois collective. In effect, there is no cohesion between the members who compose the criminal gang, and the couples we find in it are all in a state of rupture. Furthermore, the conclusion of the film proves revelatory of the collapse of moral values and the triumph of individualism. The two survivors of the gang divide the loot in a ruined church and separate, without any promise of seeing each other again.

Louis Goyette

PROLOGUE. Robin Spry, NFB (Montreal), 1969, 88 min., b+w. Robin Spry's *Prologue* encapsulates a few weeks in the lives of Jesse (John Robbe) and Karen (Elaine Malus), to whom we are introduced as "professional" agitators. The film is structured around a series of contrasts—between the establishment and protesters, between passive and active protesters, and finally between the type of "serious" protesting in which Jesse participates and the almost gleeful activism proposed by Abbie Hoffman during one of the film's key scenes. Karen embodies the questioning between passive and active demonstration, leaving Jesse—who is going to Chicago to participate in an anti–Vietnam War protest at the Democratic National Convention—to join a commune with an American draft-dodger, David (Gary Rader). The bridge between these two forms of demonstration is the common goal of peace and harmony, captured in one of the film's few beautiful moments. The scene in question has Allen Ginsberg, joined by Jesse and other Chicago protesters, chanting peacefully on a beach. This is intercut with Karen and David at the commune swimming and kissing by a waterfall. A later sequence contrasts these two forms of political expression more explicitly by intercutting antiwar protesters running from violent police intervention and commune dwellers running to clear their clothesline during a rainstorm. Although it is a fictional film, the use of hand-held camera, location shooting, mostly diegetic sound, found footage, and the appearance of personalities like Hoffman, Ginsberg, William S. Burroughs, and Jean Genêt contribute to the feeling of watching a "direct cinema" documentary. Because of this, the power and immediacy of Spry's film can still be felt years after its release.

BIBLIOGRAPHY: Jan Dawson, "Robin Spry: From Prologue to Action," *Cinema Papers*, no. 3 (June/July 1976): 42–43.

Sandra Gallant

MAURICE PROULX. Born 1902, Saint-Pierre-Montmagny, Quebec; died 1988, La Pocatière, Quebec. Along with Monseigneur ALBERT TESSIER and the Abbé Louis-Roger Lafleur, the Abbé Maurice Proulx was a pioneer in the domain of documentary in Quebec. It is an interesting paradox that at the moment when the Catholic Church severely condemned cinema and the dissolute morals its images presented (a condemnation that culminated in the burning of the Laurier Palace in 1927), three clergymen developed an interest in the documentary film. By restoring moral and religious virtues to the cinema, the work of the filmmaker-priests played a beneficial role in "reconciling" the Church with the cinema, the former "corrupter of souls." Taking orders in 1928, Maurice Proulx studied agronomy at Laval University in Quebec, and then at Cornell University in the United States. It was there that he discovered 16mm film and became aware of its didactic potential. Upon his return to Quebec in 1933, he taught agronomy at Saint-Anne de la Pocatière. The government then sent Proulx to Abitibi, and he filmed the evolution of the settlers' work, resulting in *EN PAYS NEUFS* (1934–37). *Sainte-Anne de Roquemaure* (1942), which followed *En pays neufs* and which was filmed in color, once again presented the rapid progress of colonization. Considered the "official" filmmaker of the government, Proulx proved faithful to Maurice Duplessis' Union Nationale, filming the party's political rallies and the fulfillment of its projects in education, roadway development, health, and so on. Proulx continued making films until the early 1960s. His frequently didactic films also emphasized his passion for agronomy and highlighted the tourist attractions of the regions he filmed.

FILMS AS DIRECTOR INCLUDE: *En pays neufs*, 1934–37; *La vache canadienne; Congrès eucharistique de Québec*, 1938; *En pays pittoresque*, 1939; *Sainte-Anne de Roquemaure; La betterave à sucre; Les couches chaudes; Le miel nectar; Une journée à l'Exposition provinciale de Québec*, 1942; *Le percheron; Défrichement motorisé*, 1946; *Le lin du Canada; Congrès marial Ottawa*, 1947; *La culture de la betterave à sucre; La chimie et la pomme de terre; Les ennemis de la pomme de terre*, 1949; *Les ailes sur la péninsule; Congrès marial Ottawa juin 1947; Ski à Québec; Sucre d'érable et coopération*, 1950; *Le cinquantenaire des caisses populaires; Le tabac jaune du Québec; Jeunesse rurale; Les routes du Québec*, 1951; *Marguerite Bourgeoys*, 1954; *Vers la compétence; Waconichi*, 1955; *Iles de la Madeleine*, 1956; *Au royaume de Saguenay; La Gaspésie pittoresque*, 1957; *Penser avant de dépenser*, 1958; *Le bas du Saint-Laurent; Médecine d'aujourd'hui*, 1959; *La béatification de Mère d'Youville; Film politique de Roméo Lorrain; La culture maraîchère en évolution*, 1961.

BIBLIOGRAPHY: Pierre Véronneau and Gisèle Côté; Antoine Pelletier.

Louis Goyette

Q

QUEST FOR FIRE/LA GUERRE DU FEU. Jean-Jacques Annaud, France/Canada (Montreal), 1981, 100 min., color, imaginary dialogue. *Quest for Fire* (simultaneously released to the French market in an identical version as *La guerre du feu*) is a rare early example of an international co-production which successfully matched various locations in Kenya, Scotland, and three Canadian provinces and cleverly mixed its multinational cast with imagined prehistoric gestural and verbal languages created for the film by Desmond Morris and Anthony Burgess, respectively. *Quest* follows the travels of three men from the Ulam tribe (Everett McGill, Ron Perlman, and Nameer El-Kadi) searching for fire after losing it through a raid by a group of wild Neanderthal ape men. On the way, they rescue a young woman, Ika (Rae Dawn Chong), from cannibalism. She belongs to a more developed tribe and teaches Naoh (McGill) how to make fire (and love, in the "missionary position"). The film is a triumph of location scouting, costume design (gaining John Hay a Genie in 1983), and makeup (winning an Oscar in 1982). Elephants were dressed as mammoths, aiding in the illusion of Africa being cold, while the muted color cinematography and the decision to shoot under predominantly cloudy skies helped bring Kenya closer to Scotland. Also, the various tribes were color-coded, with the drab, brown/black animal skin–covered Ulams and relatively attractive blueish gray and white mud and dust painted markings of Ika's tribe linking Alberta's badlands, British Columbia's Cathedral Grove, and Ontario's Bruce Peninsula to Kenya and Scotland. The last of these Canadian settings provided the film's opening cave dwellings (while their lookout over Georgian Bay was eliminated). *Quest for Fire* was a commercial success in North America, generating over $12 million in rentals for its distributor, 20th Century Fox, since its release in 1982, while in France it was also a critical success, winning the coveted industry-awarded César for Best Feature Film. Moreover, in Canada it won five Genies including Best Actress for Rae Dawn Chong. She was born in Vancouver, the daughter of Tommy Chong (also Canadian) of "Cheech and Chong" fame. She managed to escape the image of her nakedness in *Quest* to become a minor young star in Hollywood, for example, in *Beat Street* (1984) and *The Color Purple* (1985).

BIBLIOGRAPHY: *Cinema Canada*, no. 77 (September 1981): 35–36; Review, in *Cinema Canada*, no. 82 (March 1982): 30.

Peter Rist

R

THE RAILRODDER. Gerald Potterton, NFB, 1965, 21 min., b+w. In a varied career that includes live-action features (*The Rainbow Boy*, 1983; *The Awful Fate of Melpomenus Jones*, 1983), animated features (*HEAVY METAL*), and television productions (*Pinter People*, 1968; *George and the Star*, 1985; *The Smoggies*, 1986), *The Railrodder* is producer/director Gerald Potterton's best known work. This charming two-reeler reunites Buster Keaton with his great love of the outdoors and trains. Upon reading a newspaper ad stating "See Canada Now!" Keaton imagines a series of stock clichéd images of Canada, then excitedly jumps over a bridge (a stunt person in extreme long shot). Keaton reemerges from the ocean (a gag inspired by the end of *The Navigator*, 1924) and begins his cross-Canada tour on a CN motorized rail car. Potterton tries to capture the Keaton style by maintaining a constant sense of movement in the frame and constructing several gags in long and extreme-long shot. One of the funnier gags has the camera inside a teahouse framing a table of people in the foreground and a stoic Keaton cutting across the extreme background of the frame right to left. Naturally at Keaton's advanced age (seventy) the film lacks the acrobatic dynamism and abrupt changes in tempo so vital to classic Keaton. There is still a nice sense of déjà vu watching Keaton perform in *The Railrodder*, like recognizing the slowed down yet familiar movements of a once-great athlete. Compulsory viewing alongside *The Railrodder* is the excellent Canadian documentary on its making, *Buster Keaton Rides Again* (John Spotton, 1965). *The Railrodder* won an award in the "Travel and Recreation" category at the 1966 Canadian Film Awards.

BIBLIOGRAPHY: Jim Kline, 210–11.

Donato Totaro

LES RAQUETTEURS The Snowshoers. Michel Brault and Gilles Groulx, ONF, 1958, 17 min., b+w. Hailed as the first *cinéma direct* short to have come out of the NFB/ONF, it should be noted that this brilliant documentary, directed by maverick filmmakers MICHEL BRAULT and GILLES GROULX, was shot before the technological advances that made *cinéma direct* possible in the first place. In other words, even though the young directors did not yet have lightweight cameras and sync-sound recorders at their disposal, they nonetheless were so driven to revolutionize the ideology and aesthetics of documentary filmmaking that they willed *Les raquetteurs* into being, shooting MOS* and relying on editing and sound design to convey the spirit of the new documentary form. Even so, their film came very close to never seeing the light of day, having been refused by the NFB in the early post-production stages. The administrators were expecting a benign four-minute-long portrait of snowshoers, but what they were presented with was an elaborate, audacious, and subtly sarcastic critique of Quebec's retrograde society. The painfully funny shots of snowshoers running and falling on snowless streets underline the absurdity and "passéism" of folk-lore in the light of Quebec's urban reality. The insistent close-up on a vigorous handshake between Sherbrooke's mayor and a U.S. delegate brings to mind other similar but less innocent diplomatic exchanges between Quebec's premier, Maurice Duplessis, and American businessmen. Brault's wide-angle lens magnifies the grotesque appearances of some of the participants. Groulx's frantic editing, in the final celebration scene, captures the numbing abandon of the partyers—all in all, a rather classist portraiture but a liberating one, shot on the eve of Quebec's Quiet Revolution.

BIBLIOGRAPHY: Gilles Marsolais, (1972); Marsolais (1974).

Johanne Larue

RAT LIFE AND DIET IN NORTH AMERICA. Joyce Wieland, Toronto, 1968, 14 min., color, 16mm. Deliberately low-tech and humorously self-deprecating, *Rat Life and Diet in North America* is perhaps the quintessential Canadian independent film. As a way of commenting on the lack of funding in Canada for independent filmmaking, JOYCE WIELAND decided to make a film in 16mm without synchronized sound, and to use gerbils (as the "rats" in the film's title) and cats (as police) instead of actors, who cost money. *Rat Life and Diet*'s minimal story is told as much through silent film-style intertitles as through its imagery: gerbils running in a treadmill (as political prisoners), searching through a maze (as escaping to Canada), eating flowers and cherries (as hippies at a cherry festival). The soundtrack consists of an avant-garde, free-form musical score, complete with saxophone honks and beeps matching the gerbils' antics, and sparse sound effects: for example, explosions and machine guns marking the presence of the American military. Like other key Canadian experimental films, *Rat Life and Diet* resists categorization and works on a number of levels. The filmstock's graininess and rich color saturation together with the loose, episodic narrative construction and jagged editing are modernist, reflexive elements

*Literally "mit-out" (without) sound.

which mark the film as a Super 8–like "home movie." But Wieland's film also functions as a postmodernist allegory of the Vietnam War on the homefront, with the gerbils/rats representing oppressed American draft dodgers who escape to ecologically conscious Canada.

BIBLIOGRAPHY: Lianne McLarty, "The Experimental Films of Joyce Wieland," *Ciné-Tracts*, no. 17 (Summer/Fall 1982): 51–62.

Peter Rist

LA RÉGION CENTRALE. Michael Snow, Quebec, 1971, 180 min., color, 16mm. *La Région Centrale* is arguably the most spectacular experimental film made anywhere in the world, and for John W. Locke, writing in *Artforum* in 1973, it was "as fine and important a film as I have ever seen." Following *WAVELENGTH*, MICHAEL SNOW continued to explore camera/frame movement and its relationships with space and time. But with *La Région Centrale*, Snow managed to create moving images that heretofore couldn't possibly be observed by the human eye. For this project he enlisted the help of Pierre Abaloos to design and build a machine which would allow the camera to move smoothly about a number of different axes at various speeds, while supported by a short column, where the lens of the camera could pass within inches of the ground and zoom into the infinity of the sky. Snow placed his device on a peak near Sept Îsles in Quebec's région centrale and programmed it to provide a series of continuously changing views of the landscape. Initially, the camera pans through 360° passes which map out the terrain, and then it begins to provide progressively stranger views (on its side, upside down) through circular and back-and-forth motions. The weird soundtrack was constructed from the electronic sounds of the programmed controls, which are sometimes in sync with the changing framing on screen and sometimes not. Here, allusions to other films occur, especially science fiction works like Stanley Kubrick's *2001: A Space Odyssey* (1968), which similarly reveals a barren, human-less primal landscape (with odd sounds) and spatially disorients the spectator. In *La Région Centrale*'s second hour, the world is inverted for so long that when the camera swings vertically through a full circle to restore the horizon line to its rightful position, above the earth, it looks wrong. It is impossible not to notice camera movement in this film, and, as Locke notes, one is inclined to observe the frame edge leading the movement (rather than the center) much of the time. The last hour offers up an incredible experience, with unbelievably high-speed twisting and swirling motions rendering dynamic color and line abstractions. Finally, by rephotography—of the film jumping out of the gate—and flaring out of the image to red and yellow colors, and, closing with the camera apparently motionless on the sun, Snow presents a reflexive impression of the camera as the ultimate transformative, creative apparatus, capable of any magic. *La Région Centrale* presents a definitive "metaphor on vision."

BIBLIOGRAPHY: John W. Locke, "Michael Snow's *La Région Centrale*: How You Should Watch the Best Ever Film I Ever Saw," *Artforum* 12, no. 3 (November 1973): 66–71; J. Hoberman, "Secrets of the Hand-Held Camera: Films Hollywood Won't Allow," *Village Voice* (April 5, 1976): 77–78; Annette Michelson, "About Snow," *October*, no. 8 (Spring 1979): 111–24; Bill Simon, "A Completely Open Space: Michael Snow's *La Région Centrale*," *Millennium Film Journal*, nos. 4–5 (Summer-Fall 1979): 93–100.

Peter Rist

KATE REID. Born 1930, London, England; died 1993, Stratford, Ontario. Actor. Kate Reid, born Daphne Kate, grew up in Oakville, Ontario. At fifteen she commenced acting studies at the Toronto Conservatory of Music, and later trained in New York. She came to prominence, after several years of performing in summer stock, in the 1956 Canadian and British productions of *The Rainmaker*. Director Sidney J. Furie, then a bravely enterprising Toronto-based novice filmmaker, cast her in his first feature, *A Dangerous Age*. She joined the Stratford Festival Company in 1959, there consolidating her renown, particularly with her enthusiastically received Lady Macbeth. In 1961 she played the lead in an episode of a Canadian-American co-production, writer-director Arch Oboler's mildly exploitative omnibus film *1 + 1: Exploring the Kinsey Reports*. Over the next few years Reid became a mainstay of theater and television in both Canada and the United States, highly regarded for her resonant "cello-toned" voice and warmly powerful acting. She brought her welcome salty humanity to several American films, notably *This Property Is Condemned* (1966) and *The Andromeda Strain* (1971). In Canadian films, she delivered three memorable performances. As one of a trio of flaky modern-day prospectors in Gerald Potterton's *The Rainbow Boys*, she is colorfully wry. In her Genie-winning portrayal of Grace, the hilariously surly layabout of Louis Malle's *Atlantic City* (Canada/France, 1980), she has her best moments on film—raucous and mean, but soulful. On screen only fleetingly in ANNE WHEELER'S *BYE BYE BLUES*, her conviction and venerable presence fortify the film's emotional pull. Recipient of an honorary Ph.D. (from York University, 1970) and inductee into the Order of Canada (1974), she worked prodigiously until her death from cancer.

THEATRICAL FILMS AS ACTOR: *A Dangerous Age*, 1957; *1 + 1: Exploring the Kinsey Reports*, 1961; *The Best Damn Fiddler from Calabogie to Kaladar*, 1969; *The Rainbow Boys*, 1972; *Shoot*, 1975; *Plague*, 1977; *Crossbar*, 1978; *Double Negative; Death Ship; Highpoint; Circle of Two*, 1979; *Atlantic City*, 1980; *The Blood of Others*, 1983; *No Sad Songs* (narr. only), 1985; *Bye Bye Blues*, 1989.

Ian Elliot

IVAN REITMAN. Born 1946, Komarmo, Czechoslovakia. Producer, director. Ivan Reitman was born in post–World War II Czechoslovakia, to parents who had survived the Holocaust in a concentration camp. Leaving the torn European continent, his family immigrated to Canada, where he was raised. At university Reitman majored in music, but became interested in filmmaking while taking a course with the NFB. Here he completed several short subjects and went on to direct his first feature, *My Secret Life* (1970), based on the Victorian erotic novel of the same name. Reitman stayed in the "exploitation" genre with his next two films, *Foxy Lady* and *Cannibal Girls*. The latter teamed him up with Second City, a group of Canadian comedians based in Toronto, many of whom later achieved stateside fame along with Reitman. During this era of Canadian filmmaking, Reitman, Bob Fothergill, Ian Ewing, and DAVID CRONENBERG came together to form the Toronto Film Co-op. Reitman then produced Cronenberg's controversial first two (theatrically released) feature films, *SHIVERS* and *Rabid* (1976), which brought the two notoriety if not fame. Cronenberg would later say that Reitman "was nothing but astonishing, and always knew what he wanted. . . . He knew entertainment, commercial filmmaking." Reitman continued producing low budget films, turning in huge profits and making huge stars. In 1979 he directed *MEATBALLS* starring Bill Murray. Continuing to push boundaries, Reitman produced a film adaptation of the fantasy comic *HEAVY METAL* (1981); this was his second-to-last Canadian production. Reitman was drawn to Hollywood, and in 1984, reuniting with members of Second City, directed the blockbuster *Ghostbusters*. Reitman still produces and directs studio films, staying "hip" and controversial with *Beavis and Butt-head Do America* (1996).

FILMS AS DIRECTOR AND PRODUCER: *My Secret Life*, 1970; *Foxy Lady*, 1971; *Cannibal Girls*, 1973; *Meatballs*, 1979; *Stripes*, 1981.

FILMS AS PRODUCER: *Shivers*, 1975; *Rabid; House by the Lake*, 1977; *Blackout; National Lampoon's Animal House*, 1978; *Heavy Metal*, 1981; *Spacehunter: Adventures in the Forbidden Zone*, 1983.

Rob Cotterill

RÉJEANNE PADOVANI. Denys Arcand, Montreal, 1973, 94 min., color. After the *ON EST AU COTON* affair (see entry for the film), DENYS ARCAND took leave from the ONF and turned toward fiction and private industry. If it was no longer possible for him to treat reality in the form of the documentary, he might as well use the cover of the fiction film. This decision would finally allow him to train his critical gaze on Quebec society with complete freedom. While remaining a fictional story, *Réjeanne Padovani* at the same time abounds with characters and situations inspired by the reality of the era. Vincent Padovani, a contractor in public works, celebrates the construction of a section of the highway in his neighborhood with great ceremony. The return of his ex-wife Réjeanne, as well as the organization of a demonstration against the highway project, casts a shadow over the events of the party. There follow machinations, betrayals, and settlings of accounts which finally liberate Padovani from all constraints. Arcand confides that he wished to demonstrate that we are "governed by fools." Mission accomplished. The filmmaker presents one of the most unforgiving depictions of political corruption ever directed in Quebec. Arcand depicts a perverse universe to the spectator, who is pounded from beginning to end with a profoundly cynical and pessimistic vision. Throughout the film, he opts for cinematography in cold colors and distanced performances from the actors. As well as being well received in Quebec, the film also made a strong impression in France.

BIBLIOGRAPHY: Louis Goyette, *"Réjeanne Padovani* et *Au pays de Zom* ou l'opéra revisité," *Copie Zéro*, no. 37 (October 1988); 27–30.

Louis Goyette

REQUIEM POUR UN BEAU SANS-COEUR Requiem for a Ruthless Killer/ Requiem for a Tough Guy. Robert Morin, Quebec, 1992, 92 min., color. Voted Best Canadian Film of its year at the Toronto Film Festival, *Requiem pour un beau sans-coeur* is one of the most unapologetically original and unrelentingly challenging fiction films to have come out of mainstream Quebec cinema in a very long time. First, it is a genre film, specifically a crime and gangster thriller, something extremely rare in the Quebec corpus, which is almost entirely composed of documentaries, realist social dramas, and vaudevillian comedies. Second, and more important, it is entirely filmed in subjective POVs, not those of one hero, as is the case in Robert Montgomery's prototypical *Lady in the Lake* (United States, 1947), but those of a multitude of characters who come into contact with the protagonist, Régis Savoie. An escaped convict, he is performed with boundless nervous energy and vernacular glee by Gildor Roy. The intricacies of the film's narrative include violent juxtapositions of contradictory visual testimonies—no one remembers events in the same manner, *à la Rashomon* (Japan, 1950)—which make it possible for Morin to experiment with film form: the style of each segment echoes the different personalities of the narrators. The first visual testimonies are rather impersonal: a police station identikit shows us Savoie's likeness, his estranged son witnesses his escape from prison, and a young detective investigates his whereabouts . . . until his superior gets a cryptic phone call leading them to Savoie, who is then shot and killed. After the viewer is let in on the resolution of the story, after just a few minutes have elapsed in the plot, Morin cuts back in time to fill in the temporal gaps, treating us to more intimate testimonies of Savoie's last days. The structure resembles that of a target (a geometrical figure Savoie wears as a tattoo on his chest), each circular ring representing one more ocular narration, narrowing and intensifying in nature until we reach the core, Savoie himself. *Requiem* is a mind-boggling and yet immensely entertaining film whose experimentations Morin was to take up again in his next film, *Windigo* (1994).

BIBLIOGRAPHY: Geoff Bowie, *"Requiem pour un beau sans-coeur," P.O.V.: Point-of-View*, no. 20 (Winter 1992): 16–18; Maurie Alioff, *"Requiem pour un beau sans-coeur," Take One*, no. 2 (Winter 1993): 27–29.

Johanne Larue

RHAPSODY IN TWO LANGUAGES. Gordon Sparling, Montreal, 1934, 11 min., b+w. Perhaps the most accomplished Canadian film made during the

1930s, *Rhapsody in Two Languages* represents GORDON SPARLING's most creative use of limited resources while heading up the Associated Screen Studios' "Canadian Cameo" series. Tracing a day in the life of Montreal, *Rhapsody* is structured like *Berlin, Symphony of a City* (Germany, 1927), which Sparling claimed not to have seen. The film begins on a partially masked high angle framing of legs walking at the camera as it tracks back, with credits over, followed by a shot of narrator Corey Thomson, wearing a hat marked "conducteur," encouraging us to step out on a tour of Montreal, "city of contrasts." Walking feet become a motif of dynamic movement in the film, while the idea of "contrast" is carried through Eisensteinian montage juxtaposition of shots, and elements within shots, setting graphic elements like oblique angles in opposition and employing multiple superimpositions. Thomson's voice introduces shots of modern buildings—"the new"—followed by shots of Old Montreal, and the "comings and goings" of trains, then ships. Typical of Sparling's "Canadian Cameos," many of the film's apparent documentary shots were staged for the camera, and perhaps *Rhapsody*'s greatest strength is its efficiency in the composition of these mostly detail shots, where, for example, a bottle of milk and an approaching cat represent "morning." The most impressive (but derivative) part of *Rhapsody in Two Languages* is the final scene, which centers on risqué nightclub action, and where the atmosphere is partially created by dynamic movement and rhythmic editing. It has even been suggested that this sequence influenced Busby Berkeley's "Lullaby of Broadway" in *Gold Diggers of 1935*.

BIBLIOGRAPHY: Gordon Sparling, "The *Short* Way to Canadian Entertainment," in André Pâquet; Michie Mitchell.

Peter Rist

DAVID RIMMER. Born 1942, Vancouver, British Columbia. Filmmaker. After Michael Snow, David Rimmer is Canada's most acclaimed experimental filmmaker. Closely identified with "structural film," especially in his employing the optical printer for rephotography of individual film frames, Rimmer's work resists tight categorization, despite its apparent simplicity. He graduated from the University of British Columbia in 1967 and began a master's program in English at Simon Fraser University. After being introduced to film by Stan Fox, a producer at the CBC, he abandoned his studies, but continually returned to the university environment from 1977 as a film and video instructor, a profession that enabled him to continue making noncommercial films and videos. Rimmer is best known for the films he made over a short two-year period, 1969–70. A number of them have been classified as "landscape" films, including, of course, *Landscape*, which provides in its seven-minute running time a simple, stopmotion, fixed position view of a British Columbia ocean inlet from dawn to dusk. Bart Testa has argued that this film is especially "Canadian," following Northrop Frye's notion of a "garrison mentality" in literature and Gaile M. McGregor's extension of the concept to painting, whereby the spectator is safely contained within a frame looking out on an untameable wilderness. But it can also be appreciated as a minimalist, reflexive analysis of film time and space—a rapid montage of still photographs—and lead us to contemplate the wonder of nature's changing light (which affects cinematography), and ultimately, how we perceive things in the world. *Surfacing on the Thames* provides an even more intense exploration of cinema's frame-by-frame articulation, where Rimmer re-photographed and stretched forty-eight distinct frames from an old piece of World War I footage, and slowly dissolved the resultant "shots" together. The effect has been called pointillist and likened to Impressionist paintings, especially Turner's. In recognizing the complexity of *Surfacing*, Blaine Allan has noted a "tension" between realist and illusionist tendencies. Many observers point to the two *Canadian Pacific* (1974–75) films as major accomplishments in Canadian landscape filmmaking, and, like *Landscape* and *Blue Movie*, they were intended to be shown as part of an installation. Although outside the scope of this book, it is important to note that Rimmer has also worked in the medium of video since 1975. Indeed, the curator of Rimmer's major film retrospective at the Art Gallery of Ontario in 1993, Jim Sheddon, believes that no other Canadian artist has moved so smoothly between film and video, and Katie Russell shares with Sheddon the opinion that Rimmer's most creative period has been since 1984. In the first book-length study of Rimmer, Russell argues that in recent films such as *Black Cat White Cat* and *Local Knowledge*, he has made significant explorations in filmic ethnography and gender representation, as well as landscape.

FILMS (ALL 16MM, SOUND, SHORTS, EXCEPT WHERE NOTED): *Head/End; Knowplace*, 1967; *Square Inch Field*, 1968; *Migration; Landscape* (silent), 1969; *Blue Movie* (silent); *Treefall* (silent); *Variations on a Cellophane Wrapper; Surfacing on the Thames* (silent); *The Dance*, 1970; *Real Italian Pizza; Seashore* (silent), 1971; *Fracture* (silent); *Watching for the Queen* (silent), 1973; *Canadian Pacific* (silent), 1974; *Canadian Pacific II* (silent), 1975; *Shades of Red*, 1977; *Al Neil: A Portrait* (40 min.), 1979; *Narrows Inlet* (silent), 1967–80; *Bricolage*, 1984; *Along the Road to Altamira; As Seen on TV* (also on video), 1986; *Divine Mannequin*, 1988; *Black Cat White Cat It's a Good Cat if It Catches the Mouse*, 1989; *Beaubourg Boogie Woogie*, 1991; *Local Knowledge*, 1992.

BIBLIOGRAPHY: Blaine Allan, "David Rimmer's *Surfacing on the Thames*," *Ciné-Tracts*, no. 9 (Winter 1980): 56–60; Bart Testa (1989); Jim Sheddon, Preface to *David Rimmer: Films and Tapes, 1967–1993*, 9–10; Catherine Russell, "Twilight in the Image Bank," in *David Rimmer*, 17–58.

Peter Rist

ROADKILL. Bruce McDonald, Ontario, 1989, 80 min., b+w. Bruce Mc-Donald's quirky, low budget, and reflexive *Roadkill* foregrounds cinematic technique through its references to the documentary (the long take) and music video forms. Several of these elements are established in an early scene, beginning with the lead character Ramona (Valerie Buhagiar) seated outside a roadside diner in front of a white wall. Abruptly, we hear the offscreen words "lights, camera, action," as a floodlight is turned on and Ramona is interviewed. The scene is played from a static, single camera set-up, but is fragmented with frequent jump cuts. Soon into the scene, a soundman enters the frame, followed by a second man who introduces himself to Ramona as documentary filmmaker Bruce Shack (played by McDonald). *Roadkill* and its film-within-a-film share plot elements (both are films about "women and rock and roadkill"), though *Roadkill*'s central thematic is the search for personal identity. While this is a common theme in Canadian cinema, *Roadkill* is unconventional in the context of Canadian narrative cinema because of its frequent disregard for coherent plot progression. McDonald also draws on the rich road movie tradition to underscore Ramona's internal journey of introspection and transition. McDonald continues this metaphor of physical/emotional journey by equating Ramona's growth as a character with her learning how to drive. Ramona succeeds in all her goals, but realizes the words of the fictional director Shack, "if you wanna drive, you gotta kill," when the band she was searching for are shot and killed during a concert she organized. Nevertheless, she is able to drive off happily into the North Ontario wilderness, having attained the self-assurance and confidence that she set out to find.

BIBLIOGRAPHY: Colin Brunton, "Roadkill," *Cinema Canada*, no. 165 (July/August 1989): 5–6; Deborah Knight, "Metafiction, pararealism and the canon of Canadian cinema," *Cinémas* 3, no. 1 (Autumn 1992): 125–146.

Sandra Gallant

PATRICIA ROZEMA. Born 1958, Kingston, Ontario. Director, writer. Raised in Southern Ontario by strict Calvinists, Patricia Rozema saw her first film when she was sixteen years old and directed her first feature, the short *Passion, a Letter in 16mm* (1986), after a five-week night course in film production. Beforehand, she had worked in television, notably in Chicago and New York, and been a producer for the CBC in Toronto, but once she caught the movie bug, there was no holding her back. Her first feature, *I'VE HEARD THE MERMAIDS SINGING* (1987), won the Young Filmmaker prize at Cannes. Echoing the last images of the film, which show Sheila McCarthy flying through the sky, the film was received as "a breath of fresh air," a welcome change from the often morose and repressive "Canadian" film. And no one turned a blind eye to Rozema's joyously subversive inclusion of lesbian themes and characters, something that takes center stage in her latest feature, *When Night Is Falling* (1995). Sadly, this film suffers from superficial character development and a certain heaviness in the mise-en-scène, but Rozema's uncanny cinematographic talent remains apparent in *White Room* (1990) and her segment of *Montréal vu par . . .* ("Desperanto [Let Sleeping Girls Lie]," 1991). In many ways, the latter can be viewed as an appendix to her first feature. In it, McCarthy plays a shy but nonetheless bubbly Toronto tourist who, like Polly in *Mermaids*, gets to fly through the air (this time with DENYS ARCAND, no less) in a lovely and heart-warming homage to a city and a culture possibly closer in spirit to Rozema's artistic vision than the one in which she evolved. But it is *White Room* which impresses the most because of the complexity of its discourse. Though not advertised and rarely discussed as such, the feature can be seen as a remake of Alfred Hitchcock's *Vertigo*, with elements of *Rear Window* thrown in to round out the director's contemporary reworking of the Master's exposé on the sexual politics of Romanticism and voyeurism.

FILMS, AS DIRECTOR: *Passion, a Letter in 16mm* (short), 1986; *I've Heard the Mermaids Singing*, 1987; *White Room*, 1990; "Desperanto (Let Sleeping Girls Lie)" in *Montréal vu par . . .* , 1991; *When Night Is Falling*, 1995.

BIBLIOGRAPHY: M. Elia, "Patricia Rozema," *Séquences*, no. 132 (January 1988): 24–27.

Johanne Larue

THE RUBBER GUN. Allan Moyle, Montreal, 1974–77, 86 min., color, 16mm. The sequel to MONTREAL MAIN, featuring many of the same characters playing themselves, *The Rubber Gun* is one of the most remarkable Canadian documentary/fiction hybrid features ever made. Allan Moyle, who was born in Arvida, Quebec, became friends with film and video maker Frank Vitale in Montreal and acted as himself in *Montreal Main* (from which he received his nickname, "Bozo"). After acting in Vitale's second feature, *East End Hustle* (1975), DAVID CRONENBERG's *Rabid* (1976), and Ron Benner's OUTRAGEOUS!, as well as starring in *The Mourning Suit* (1974), Moyle directed his own first feature, *The Rubber Gun*. Here Moyle plays the part of a McGill University sociology student who believes that drugs have a positive effect on group dynamics. He becomes involved with the (clearly) gay artist/drug dealer Steve (Lack), who is also a father figure/guru to a street community. The film is narratively driven by having the Montreal police watching over a Windsor Station locker containing a cache of drugs, which Steve and his group are looking to retrieve. Meanwhile, group members Peter (Brawley) and Pierre (Robert) have turned from cocaine to heroin and are caught trying to clandestinely nab the shipment, leaving Pierre's family (played by real-life wife Pam and daughter Rainbow) stranded and abandoned. "Bozo" completes his written thesis on Lack while the film's audience is left with a very strong (and negative) impression of the drug culture having lost the direction of the 1960s (an impression which is compounded by Steve's art shown to be inferior, "under the influence"). Amazingly, Moyle managed to make *Gun*'s story coherent, while shooting over a two-year period with a greatly varied number of helpers*, but the film's strength is in the dynamics of the participants/actors during each individual scene, recalling the best work of *la nouvelle vague* and American original John

---

*In the credits, Moyle listed fifteen people as assistants to the producers, four as "assistant camera," two for "additional photography," and even an assistant to the director. Clearly it was very much a cooperative venture.

Cassavetes. *The Rubber Gun* was finally premiered at La cinémathèque québécoise on September 28, 1977. Like Vitale, Moyle left Canada for the United States at the end of the decade, where he became a very successful director. *Pump Up the Volume* (1990), in particular, with its positive treatment of rebellious young DJ (Christian Slater), is reminiscent of his Canadian work.

BIBLIOGRAPHY: P. M. Massé-Connolly, "How to Shoot a Rubber Gun," *Cinema Canada*, no. 46 (April–May 1978): 23–27; J. Paul Constabile, "Allan Moyle's *Rubber Gun*," *Cinema Canada*, no. 57 (August 1979): 39–40.

Peter Rist

JAN RUBES. Born Czechoslovakia. Actor, presenter, singer. Jan Rubes' career can best be described as a multidisciplinary one. A leading tennis champion at sixteen, he has since earned fame as an actor, TV presenter, and opera singer. His musical career began at the State Conservatory of Prague, where his musical studies were interrupted by the outbreak of World War II. Following the liberation of Czechoslovakia Rubes resumed his opera career at the Prague Operahouse, where he stayed until 1949, when he immigrated to Canada. Although most famous as an opera singer (he has sung in over a thousand performances with the Canadian Opera Company), he has also made a significant contribution to Canadian film. His first role on the big screen came immediately in the political thriller *Forbidden Journey* (1950), where he drew upon his own cultural background to play a European émigré attempting to smuggle important information out of the Eastern bloc. The film was met with a lukewarm response from both the public and critics, but Rubes himself did receive several positive reviews. Since that first film, Rubes has, with films like 1988's *Something About Love* and *The Outside Chance of Maximilian Glick*, contributed to the presence of a European immigrant community in Canadian cinema. Throughout his career, he has portrayed a diverse selection of characters struggling to convey the cultural and personal concerns of a community trying to reconcile their own traditions with their new cultural surroundings, such as in *Something About Love*, in which he plays a Ukrainian Canadian Cape Breton man, trying to resolve a troubled relationship with his L.A.-based son. Although experienced at playing both heroes and villains, Rubes will probably be best remembered for his sympathetic father figures, such as in the acclaimed CBC film *Charlie Grant's War* or in "The Day Granddad Died," for which he won an ACTRA. He received an honorary degree of doctor of letters from the University of Guelph in 1983 and has been awarded the Canadian Centennial Medal.

FILMS AS ACTOR: *Forbidden Journey*, 1950; *Lions for Breakfast*, 1975; *Deadly Harvest*, 1977; *Utilities*, 1980; *Your Ticket Is No Longer Valid; Mr Patman; The Amateur*, 1981; *One Magic Christmas; Charlie Grant's War* (TV), 1985; *Marriage Bed*, 1986; *Blood Relations; Long Dark Night; The Outside Chance of Maximilian Glick; Something About Love; Two Men* (TV), 1988; *Blind Fear; The Experts* (Can/US); *Cold Front* (Can/

US), 1989; *The Amityville Curse*, 1990; *On My Own*, 1991; *Colour Grey*, 1995; *The Marriage Bed* (TV), 1996; *Bach Cello Suite #4* (TV); *Never Too Late*, 1997.

Stacey Abbott

SAUL RUBINEK. Born 1948, Fohrenwold, Germany. Actor. Saul Rubinek was born in a displaced persons' camp in Germany, but he and his parents soon immigrated to Canada. By the age of eight he was already appearing on radio and with a theater group in Toronto, and was also an accomplished musician, performing both classical and modern compositions. He also started writing and singing his own songs. Equally adept at both drama and comedy, his early supporting roles were in the horror film *Death Ship* and the thriller *Agency* (both 1980), on the topical subject of subliminal advertising. Although he garnered some good reviews for this last project, he made much more of an impact in a fifty-two-minute TV movie, *Clown White*, a sensitive look at the subject of deafness, in which, for the first time, he received top billing. His first real breaks in the cinema, however, came crucially in supporting roles. In CLAUDE JUTRA's first English-language film, *By Design*, he co-starred as the vaguely uncomprehending but nonetheless willing assistant to a lesbian couple who wish to conceive. Rubinek was nominated for a Best Actor Genie. In TICKET TO HEAVEN, Rubinek played Larry, best friends with David (played by NICK MANCUSO), who is brainwashed by an evangelical sect. For this role he won the Genie for Best Supporting Actor. Rubinek has subsequently played a number of leading roles, such as Private Investigator Benny Cooper in *Suicide Murders*. In *Obsessed*, he played an American driver in Canada who gets lost, and accidentally hits and kills a young child. Rubinek's sympathetic playing allows for an interpretation of the film that digs deeply into the issues of the U.S./Canadian divide. This basic situation was the springboard for the far less successful *The Bonfire of the Vanities* (United States, 1990), in which Rubinek also appeared. Rubinek has had the opportunity to explore his Jewish ancestry in *Oakmount High, The Quarrel*, and *The Outside Chance of Maximilian Glick*, in which he plays a Hasidic rabbi who really wants to be a stand-up comic. The story of his parents' life in their native Poland and of the reunion forty years later with those that helped them escape the Nazis is the subject of a documentary based on his book *So Many Miracles*, which he also co-produced. Rubinek is a supremely gifted and versatile character actor who has managed to play sinister, Machiavellian characters with the same ease with which he has played down-to-earth, hardworking individuals or even weak and agonized characters who are not in command of their own lives.

FILMS AS ACTOR: *Love on the Nose* (TV), 1978; *The Wordsmith* (TV), 1979; *Death Ship; Agency* (1980); *Ticket to Heaven*, 1981; *By Design*, 1982; *The Terry Fox Story*, 1983; *Highpoint*, 1984; *Oakmount High*, 1985; *The Suicide Murders*, 1986; *Hitting Home; Murder Sees the Light; Prescription for Murder*, 1987; *The Outside Chance of*

Maximilian Glick, 1988; *Falling Over Backwards*, 1990; *The Quarrel*, 1991; *Hiroshima* (TV), 1995; *Pale Saints; Hostile Intent*, 1997.

Sergio Angelini

RUDE. Clement Virgo, Toronto, 1995, 89 min., color. Remarkably, after no Canadian feature film had ever been directed by a person of African descent, 1995 saw two, both of which were commercially released: SOUL SURVIVOR, directed by Steven Williams, and *Rude*, directed by Clement Virgo. *Rude* is also strikingly ambitious in combining African diasporic thematics with the recent tendency for Canadian fiction features to incorporate experimental strategies. Virgo's route to becoming a Canadian feature film director was meteoric. Emigrating with his parents from Jamaica, he worked in the fashion industry following high school. After taking a single film course at night school he worked with Virginia Rankin on her Canadian Film Centre project, *A Small Dick Fleshy Ass Thang*. The success of this film on the festival circuit led to Virgo's being included in the Centre's first Summer Lab in 1991, and then the full-time program. His own Centre project, *Save My Lost Nigga' Soul*, was even more successful than Rankin's, and a feature-length script that he had been working on while employed as a window display designer was one of the first three to be produced by the Canadian Film Centre's Feature Film Project. *Rude* interweaves three stories and their three troubled African Canadian central characters: "General" (Maurice Dean Wint), an ex-convict who refuses to be dragged back into crime by his brother Reese (Clark Johnson); Maxine (played by supermodel Rachael Crawford), a model struggling with narcissism and a failed relationship; and Jordan (Richard Chevolleau), a boxer struggling with homophobia and his own sexuality. While none of the characters in the different episodes are connected narratively, they are enmeshed both thematically—through the concept of young people of African descent searching and fighting for their own identity and society's respect—and stylistically. Here Virgo and his creative team brilliantly link episodes through the sexy, rapping, cigar-smoking female DJ, Rude (Sharon M. Lewis), who seems to orchestrate the nighttime cathartic confrontations. She talks in biblical terms, and we see religious icons (including murals painted by General). She speaks of the Lion of Judah, and we see an actual lion, associated closely with General, but also linking all three episodes. And the camera continually moves to connect the dark, troubled spaces, breaking through their entrapment, powered by the fiery magnetism of the oneiric mise-en-scène and the pulsating music. Remarkably, *Rude* was voted the Best Canadian Film of 1995 in *Take One*'s first Toronto Film Critics' poll.

BIBLIOGRAPHY: Marc Glassman, "Where Zulus Meet Mohawks: Clement Virgo's *Rude*," *Take One*, no. 9 (Fall 1995): 16–21.

Peter Rist

S

MARCEL SABOURIN. Born 1938, Montreal. Actor, writer. After spending time in the Parisian theater, Marcel Sabourin returned to Canada to study at the Théâtre du Nouvel Monde. A writer as well as an actor, his break in films came in 1966 when he co-wrote and starred in JEAN PIERRE LEFEBVRE's *Il ne faut pas mourir pour ça*. Here he played Abel, a gentle, tender, naive character to whom he returned ten years later in *LE VIEUX PAYS OÙ RIMBAUD EST MORT*. Often cast in such film roles, while prone to playing more aggressive characters in the theater, Sabourin is considered to be one of the most versatile actors in Quebec. He has worked with some of Quebec's best known directors and actors, including GILLES CARLE and CAROLE LAURE (*La mort d'un bûcheron*) and DENYS ARCAND (*La maudite galette*). He also cultivated a fruitful relationship with Lefebvre, appearing in six of his films including *Les maudits sauvages* (1971) and as the traumatized salesman in *Le Jour "S..."*. A career highlight came in 1976 as co-writer and star of *J. A. MARTIN, PHOTOGRAPHE*. With *Le vieux pays* also showing, Sabourin found himself in the enviable position of being the co-writer of one film and star of two others at the Cannes International Film Festival, a unique achievement for a French Canadian actor. His performance as J. A. is subtle and strong, short on dialogue but conveying the character's own conflicting emotions about his rebellious wife. Since then he has worked with director Jean Beaudin again in *Cordélia* and *Mario*, as well as with MICHELINE LANCTÔT (*L'homme à tout faire*), and MARC-ANDRÉ FORCIER (*Le vent du Wyoming*), and continues to be much in demand. In addition to being an actor and screenwriter, he is also a songwriter whose work has been recorded by, among others, Robert Charlebois, Yvon Deschamps, and Louise Forestier. On screen his delicate and finely detailed performances, searching for and displaying every nuance of his character's inner life, are magnetic, whether in the lead or in supporting roles. His versatility has provided him with one of the most impressive filmographies in Quebec.

FILMS AS ACTOR INCLUDE: *Côté cour, côté jardin* (short), 1953; *Le festin des morts*, 1966; *Il ne faut pas mourir pour ça* (also scr.), 1967; *La chambre blanche*, 1969; *Deux femmes en or; Mon bout du monde* (as dir. only), 1970; *Le martien de Noël; On est loin du soleil; Les maudits sauvages*, 1971; *La maudite galette; Les smattes; Le temps d'une chasse*, 1972; *La mort d'un bûcheron; Taureau; Ah! si mon moine voulait . . . ; Les dernières fiancailles*, 1973; *Bingo; Par une belle nuit d'hiver*, 1974; *Eliza's Horoscope* (1970–75); *Gina; Mustang*, 1975; *J. A. Martin, photographe*; 1976; *Ti-mine, Bernie pis la gang; Le vieux pays où Rimbaud est mort; Riel*, 1977; *Cordélia; L'homme à tout faire; Le château de cartes*, 1980; *Salut! J. W*, 1981; *Doux aveux*, 1982; *Mario; Le jour "S . . ."*, 1984; *Équinoxe*, 1986; *Alfred Laliberté, sculpteur*, 1987; *La fille du Maquignon*, 1990; *Chainstore Massacre*, 1991; *Le vent du Wyoming*, 1994; *L'oreille d'un sourd; Été des abeilles* (as dir. only); *Lilies*, 1996; *L'homme perché*, 1997.

Simon Brown

SAD SONG OF YELLOW SKIN. Michael Rubbo, NFB, 1970, 58 min., color. *Sad Song of Yellow Skin* remains, to this day, one of the finest films ever made on the war in Vietnam, and was, for a long time, the only significant film document relating the effects of the war on the South Vietnamese people (rather than focusing on the war itself). Mike Rubbo, who was born and educated in Australia, moved to the United States to study film. Admiring films made by Canada's NFB, he traveled to Montreal specifically to get a job at the board. After being hired in 1966, he directed eight short films (mostly for children) before making his breakthrough with *Sad Song* under TOM DALY's guidance. According to the producer, he had a large hand in structuring the material, away from a focus on three young American journalists working for peace in Saigon and toward the personality of Rubbo as investigator. *Sad Song* became a kind of personal essay on the filmmaker's discovery of the problems facing the citizens of Saigon in wartime. The film weaves action in three principal locations via the work of the Americans: a refugee "slum" built on a cemetery, a home for orphaned shoeshine boys, and a Buddhist monastery on a nearby island in the Mekong Delta. Rubbo's struggle to understand the marginalized lifestyles of his Saigon subjects becomes the viewer's struggle, and to his (and Daly's) credit far more questions are raised by *Sad Song of Yellow Skin* than answers given.

BIBLIOGRAPHY: Piers Handling, "The Diary Films of Mike Rubbo," *Cinema Canada*, no. 41 (October 1977): 34–39.

Peter Rist

SAM AND ME. Deepa Mehta, Toronto, 1990, 94 min., color. In *Sam and Me*, her second feature film, Deepa Mehta uses comedy and complex characterizations to provide a fresh take on Canadian multiculturalism. In the film, Nikhil (Ranjit Chowdhry) is a newly arrived immigrant from India whose family has sent him to live with his ambitious uncle, Chetan (Om Puri), in the hopes that he will become a financial success. Through his uncle's influence, Nikhil is given a job as caretaker for the elderly and irascible Sam Cohen (Peter Boretski), the Jewish immigrant founder of Cohen Medical Supplies, who is an embarrassment to his son Morris (Heath Lamberts). Neither Nikhil nor Sam is initially happy with the arrangement, but they overcome the barriers of age and culture to unite against the family members who seek to control them, and set off on a spirited exploration of Toronto's cityscape. Particularly memorable is the film's depiction of a boarding house inhabited by male Indian immigrants, each of whom has his own dreams and rationale for leaving home. While Sam dreams of returning to his land of birth (Israel), Nikhil dreams of making good in his new country, as compensation for failing to succeed in India. In less capable hands, the developing bond between Sam and Nikhil could seem clichéd, but in *Sam and Me* the relationship between two "strangers in a strange land" is moving and believable in its depiction of cultural marginality.

BIBLIOGRAPHY: Craig MacInnis, *"Sam and Me* Sees a Different Toronto," *Toronto Star* (September 20, 1991): D13; Elizabeth Aird, "Feel-Good Film Is a Triumph of Authenticity," *Vancouver Sun* (October 12, 1991): E10.

Helen and Paul Salmon

SCREAMERS. Christian Duguay, Canada (Montreal)/United States/Japan, 1995, 108 min., color. The second major science fiction film to be made in Canada in less than a year, *Screamers* was much more of a critical success and less of a box office success in 1996 than its cyberpunk predecessor, *Johnny Mnemonic*, in 1995. It is the most accomplished work produced by the prolific, fledgling Montreal-based company, Allegro Films, founded by Concordia University cinema graduates Tom Berry and Franco Battista. Director Christian Duguay (also a former Concordia student) had made two sequels to DAVID CRONENBERG'S *Scanners* with Allegro and the acclaimed television mini-series on the Dionne quintuplets, "Million Dollar Babies," after gaining a reputation as being perhaps the best steadicam operator in North America. The late Philip K. Dick's 1953 story, "Second Variety," provides the premise of mechanical cutters which turn and tunnel underground, programmed to cut up the enemy. Renamed "screamers" by Dan O'Bannon (who wrote *Alien*, and co-wrote *Total Recall* from a Dick story) and Miguel Tejada-Flores, these subterranean whirling killers, run amok, provide the title for Duguay's film. *Screamers* is set on an imaginary planet, Sirius 6B, in 2078, where Colonel Hendrickson (Peter Weller) of the Alliance forces has been sent from Earth to quell the NEB (New Economic Bloc) forces. The apocalyptic narrative kills off everyone but Hendrickson, while he discovers more and more sophisticated "screamers," including his love interest, Jessica (Jennifer Rubin). Quebec TV heartthrob Roy Dupuis, sporting an unusual accent, is featured as another NEB robot who quotes Shakespeare, but the real achievements of the film are visual. Perri Garrara's production design brilliantly combines dingy Montreal warehouse and abandoned cement factory interiors with a stylish use of the "Big O" Olympic Stadium, while Ernest Farino managed to coordinate various stop-motion, CGI, and mechanical special visual effects. Three local companies were involved—Richard Ostiguay oversaw some 150 effects shots and 20 matte shots for Buzz Image, Ryal Cosgove handled the on-set mechanical and pyrotechnic sequences for Cineffects Productions, and Adrien Morot coordinated the makeup effects—while the Chiodo Brothers in Los Angeles created the mechanical screamers and their stop-motion sequences. And Duguay's great energy as director and camera operator helped transform deep winter conditions in Montreal and Joliette into a dystopic futuristic wasteland, more unified in its grim, gray/brownish specter than almost any film since the *Alien* cycle, all on a $13 million budget.

BIBLIOGRAPHY: John Thonen, *"Screamers*: Peter Weller Stars in a Philip K. Dick Story Adapted by Way of Dan O'Bannon;" and "Screamers EFX: Coordinating Stop Motion, CGI and Mechanicals," *Cinefantastique* 27, no. 2 (November 1995): 40–43.

Peter Rist

SEEING IN THE RAIN. Chris Gallagher, British Columbia, 1981, 10 min., color. This film, from Chris Gallagher's "structural" period, features the deconstruction of a bus ride down Granville Street in Vancouver. The fixed frame of the front windshield of a bus offers the viewer a knowable frame of reference for the journey, but our certainty of the events of the journey ends there as Gallagher edits the film on the rhythm of the windshield wiper, destabilizing both time and space. As with other films of this period, Gallagher plays with the narrative expectation of the viewer, forcing her/him to recognize the ephemeral nature of cinema. The film remains one of Gallagher's best known, and was selected as an official Canadian entry for the Paris Biennale of 1982. Gallagher's structural film period extended from the mid-1970s, with works that foregrounded his Vancouver locale, such as *Plastic Surgery* (1975), through the early 1980s, with films such as *The Nine O'Clock Gun* (1980) and *Terminal City* (1982). These highly regarded projects culminated in Gallagher's tour de force feature-length structural film, *Undivided Attention* (1983–87). Since then, Gallagher has continued to make experimental films in Vancouver, all the while teaching at the University of British Columbia. He has also developed an interest in documentary cinema.

BIBLIOGRAPHY: R. Bruce Elder (1989b).

Dave Douglas

AL SENS. Born 1933, Vancouver, British Columbia. Animator, writer. Aguably Vancouver's most famous contribution to the pantheon of Canadian animators, Al Sens opened his animation studio in Vancouver in 1958. Without the benefit of professional or academic training in animation or generous funding (such as that enjoyed by animators at the NFB), Sens approached the art in a free-form manner, making use of his satiric wit as well as his family (his wife inked and painted most of his personal films that required cel animation). Sens' anarchic

The See Hear Talk Think Dream and Act Film featured a series of vignettes, drawn "live" under the camera by what Sens termed "the spit technique." The stream of consciousness flow of the film is punctuated by Sens' voice-over commentary. Further recognition came in the form of short stories and cartoons which Sens contributed to various publications in Canada and the United States. Two of his cartoons, *Men and Machine* and *The First Canadian in Space*, were purchased by "The Smothers Brothers" television show. Sens did make a couple of films through the NFB (*Pacific Connection* and *The Twitch*), but for the most part remained independent. As a result of this, a portion of his work was commissioned by various private and public groups. Sens further supplemented his filmmaking by teaching animation in the Vancouver area, as well as renting out his studio, Al Sens Animation, to other Vancouver filmmakers.

FILMS INCLUDE: *The Puppet's Dream*, 1958–59; *The Pedlar of Poesy*, 1959; *The Sorcerer*, 1960–61; *The See Hear Talk Think Dream and Act Film*, 1961–65; *The Peripatetic Patient*, 1964–65; *First Canadian in Space*, 1965; *Progress Medicine*, 1966; *The Brotherhood; An Unidentified Man*, 1967; *Henry*, 1967–68; *Men and Machine*, 1969; *New World*, 1970; *Diacritical Materialisms*, 1970–71; *La vache histoire*, 1973; *The Twitch*, 1973–74; *Cartoon Characters in Search of a Director*, 1977; *Logger*, 1978; *Portrait of a Musician*, 1978–79; *Physical Fitness*, 1979; *Brotherhood*, 1980; *The Funny Cow*, 1981; *Pacific Connection*, 1982–83; *Backstage at a Nursery Rhyme*, 1983; *Landlord and Tenant*, 1991; *Political Animals*, 1991–92; *Characters in Colour; A Galactic Chance*; 1993.

BIBLIOGRAPHY: N'eema Lakin, "Animation in Vancouver," *Cinema Canada*, no. 30 (August 1976): 34–37.

Dave Douglas

KATHLEEN SHANNON. Born 1935, Vancouver, British Columbia. Executive producer, producer, director, editor. Founder of the special Women's Unit at the NFB in 1974, later becoming its executive producer, Kathleen Shannon is the key figure in Canadian feminist filmmaking, who helped make it an important national tradition. She began her work in film by assisting the music director at Crawley Films (*see* FRANK "BUDGE" CRAWLEY and JUDITH CRAWLEY) in 1952, and she joined the NFB in 1956. She progressed from sound editor to film editor and first became a director in 1970. Her breakthrough came in 1974 when she founded Studio D, and produced a series of eleven films on working mothers in the context of "Challenge for Change" (and directed or co-directed ten of them). These short films, between five and sixteen minutes long, consist mainly of interviews, where mothers from all walks of Canadian life tell their tales of struggle directly to the camera. This proud and confrontational directness, as well as a solidarity with women, characterized Shannon's work throughout her career at the film board. Among her other most notable achievements as a director was *Dream of a Free Country: A Message from Nicaraguan Women* (co-dir., Ginny Stikeman), which showed revolutionary women engaged in building a new society and telling their own stories (carrying on the spirit of "Challenge for Change"). But Kathleen Shannon is best known for her work as executive producer of the Women's Unit, where she oversaw the making of some of the strongest feminist documentaries made anywhere in the world, including *I'll Find a Way* (Beverly Shaffer, 1977) for which she won an Oscar; *NOT A LOVE STORY (A FILM ABOUT PORNOGRAPHY)* (Bonnie Sherr-Klein, 1981); *Abortion: Stories from North and South* (Gail Singer, 1984), and *Behind the Veil: Nuns* (Margaret Wescott, 1984). In all, she executive produced ninety films from 1975 to 1989. Although Unit D has been criticized for being very white and middle class in the component of its workforce, Shannon clearly fought against racial and class prejudice with the films she supported, and she handed over the reins as executive producer to Rina Fraticelli, who encouraged independent production by younger and minority women filmmakers. However, the charges against Shannon's work for being formally conservative and lacking theoretical feminist rigor have gone unchallenged. Indeed, after the unfortunate closing of the studio in 1996, Shannon claimed that she wasn't particularly interested in making "experimental films"; she deliberately made political films, because she "wanted to change the world." When she retired from the NFB in 1992 she returned to British Columbia to run a guest house and a counseling service.

FILMS AS DIRECTOR: *"I Don't Think It's Meant for Us . . . ,"* 1971; *Goldwood*; "Working Mothers" series: *Extensions of the Family; It's Not Enough; Like the Trees; Luckily I Need Little Sleep; Mothers Are People; They Appreciate You More; Tiger on a Tight Leash; Would I Ever Like to Work,* 1974; "Working Mothers" series: *". . . and They Lived Happily Ever After"; Our Dear Sisters,* 1975; *Dream of a Free Country: A Message for Nicaraguan Women* (co-dir., Ginny Stikeman), 1983.

BIBLIOGRAPHY: Kay Armatage, "Kathleen Shannon," in Kuhn and Radstone, 363; Matthew Hays, "Lament for Studio D: A Conversation with Kathleen Shannon," *Point of View,* no. 29 (Spring 1996): 16–19.

Peter Rist

HELEN SHAVER. Born 1951, St. Thomas, Ontario. Actor. Helen Shaver is one of Canada's most recognizable character actresses. Although stardom has consistently eluded her, she has been working in Canadian films since the early 1970s. She first got a taste for acting while in high school when her drama teacher encouraged her to audition for a role in a school production of *Not Enough Rope.* She won the role, which led to numerous amateur acting awards and a scholarship to attend the Banff School of Fine Arts. She later appeared in small theatrical productions of *The Tender Trap* and *Hostage.* Spurred on by her success, Shaver moved to Los Angeles in an attempt to launch a Hollywood career but, unable to obtain the proper work papers, she was forced to return to Canada. In Toronto, however, she finally managed to achieve moderate screen success by taking small roles in films such as *The Supreme Kid* (1974), *Shoot,* and *OUTRAGEOUS!* Shaver was nominated for a Canadian Film Award as best supporting actress for her performance in the film adaptation of the classic Canadian coming of age story *WHO HAS SEEN THE WIND.* She gave an energetic performance as Pickup, the free-spirited truck driver, opposite Peter Fonda, in the road movie/action thriller *High Ballin'*. Her status as a strong character actress was, however, cemented by her eccentric performance as Ann MacDonald, a student who seduces her philosophy lecturer in the controversial film *In Praise of Older Women*. Although the film itself received mixed reviews, the stellar cast of leading actresses, including Karen Black, Alexandra Stewart, and Susan Strasberg, was highly regarded by critics, and Shaver walked away with the Best Actress Genie for her performance. Shaver consistently brings depth and personality to the smallest of roles but has rarely been given the opportunity to exhibit the full range of her talent. Finally, in the 1980s she successfully made the move to Hollywood, appearing in a series of films. More recently, however, she has returned to playing small character roles in mainstream films both in Canada and the United States.

FILMS AS ACTOR: *Christina; Wolfpen Principle*, 1974; *The Supreme Kid; Shoot* (Can/US), 1976; *Who Has Seen the Wind; Outrageous!; Starship Invasions*, 1977; *In Praise of Older Women; High-Ballin'* (Can/US), 1978; *Gas*, 1981; *Off Your Rocker*, 1979–82; *Harry Tracy*, 1982; *The War Boy*, 1984; *The Park Is Mine* (TV); *Lost!*, 1986; *No Blame* (Can/Fr, TV); *Walking After Midnight*, 1988; *Bethune: The Making of a Hero*, 1990; *Change of Heart*, 1991; *Falling for You*, 1995; *Rowing Through* (Can/Jap), 1996.

Stacey Abbott

DON(ALD) SHEBIB. Born 1938, Toronto. Director, writer, producer, editor, cinematographer. Along with a handful of Canadian and Quebecois directors in the late 1960s and early 1970s, Don Shebib was seen as a promising representative of the future of Canadian film. While studying at university in Toronto, Shebib was encouraged to attend film school at UCLA. On the strength of student films such as *The Duel* and *Joey* (both 1962) he was hired to work for producer/director Roger Corman, eventually serving as assistant editor on Corman's own *The Terror* (1963). His thesis film *Revival* (1963) led to work writing and directing for the CBC with *Surfin'* (1964). In 1965 he directed the NFB film *Satan's Choice*, a documentary about the motorcycle gang of the same name; in 1967 he shot a short sequel for the CBC, also entitled *Satan's Choice*, detailing the criminal trial against some of the people who had appeared in the NFB documentary. Shebib continued in television, and directed the theatrical feature *Good Times Bad Times* in 1969. He began working on an hour-long CBC documentary about Maritimers who head west to seek their fortunes in Toronto; when the CBC pulled out, Shebib continued the project, resulting in the groundbreaking film *GOIN' DOWN THE ROAD* (1970). This sensitive film brought Shebib national attention. However, his next film, *Rip-Off*, concerning a group of teenage boys leaving high school, failed, and Shebib returned to television for the next few years, directing only *BETWEEN FRIENDS* for theatrical release. Hopes were high for *Second Wind*, a drama about a dissatisfied Toronto stockbroker and runner who is forced to reassess his values; like *Rip-Off*, the film failed. Shebib was called in as replacement director for *Fish Hawk* and in

1981 directed *Heartaches* with MARGOT KIDDER and American actress Annie Potts; both films went largely unnoticed. Since then, Shebib has worked mostly in television, although he continues his work in cinema with occasional releases such as *The Ascent* and *The Pathfinder*.

FILMS AS DIRECTOR INCLUDE: *Good Times Bad Times*, 1969; *Goin' Down the Road*, 1970; *Rip-Off*, 1971; *Between Friends*, 1973; *Second Wind*, 1976; *Fish Hawk*, 1979; *Heartaches*, 1981; *Running Brave*, 1983; *The Climb*, 1986; *The Little Kidnappers* (TV), 1990; *Change of Heart*, 1993; *The Ascent*, 1994; *The Pathfinder* (TV), 1996.

BIBLIOGRAPHY: Piers Handling (1978).

Mitch Parry

ERNIE SHIPMAN. Born 1871, Ottawa, Ontario; died 1931, New York City. Producer, entrepreneur. Born Ernest George Montague Shipman, "Ten Percent Ernie" was one of the first promoters of Canadian cinema. A colorful character who acquired two fortunes and four wives during his lifetime, Shipman has often been described as the founding father of the Canadian feature film industry. In the short span of four years, from 1919 to 1922, Shipman established five film companies and produced seven feature films in Canada. Educated in Hamilton and at Ryerson Polytechnical Institute in Toronto, Shipman began his business career as a partner in his father's real estate firm until 1895, when he joined the show business world. By 1897 he had become the general manager of the theatrical management company Sweely, Shipman & Co. In 1900, he met Helen Foster-Barham (NELL SHIPMAN). They married and settled in Pasadena, California, where their only son Barry was born. The failing theater business inspired Shipman to stake his future on motion pictures. A great schemer, Shipman came up with countless ideas for moneymaking ventures that were never realized, including a floating studio which would travel to exotic locales and a studio nestled in the foothills of the Canadian Rockies. In early 1919, the Shipmans' association with author James Curwood was cemented by the incorporation of the Canadian Photoplay Company in Alberta and the production of the film BACK TO GOD'S COUNTRY. Shortly after the shooting ended, Nell and Ernie separated, and divorced on April 18, 1920. The year 1922 was one of frenetic activity for Ernie Shipman. While Ottawa Film Productions was responsible for bringing Ralph Conner's popular stories to the screen in *The Man from Glengarry* and *Glengarry School Days*, Shipman was simultaneously producing *The Rapids* in Sault Ste. Marie with David Hartford, the director of *Back to God's Country*. In the summer of 1922, Shipman began his final Canadian productions, both to be set in the Maritime Provinces; *The Viking Blood* in Halifax, Nova Scotia, and *Blue Water* in St. John, New Brunswick. Shipman had developed a sure-fire formula that brought him considerable success: he based each film on a Canadian story and raised the funds in the location where the story was set in an effort to excite community participation. He believed that the Canadian distributor must export his product to create a viable national industry. His insistence on using natural locations over high-cost studio filmmaking had considerable effect on other independent productions in Canada during this period. At a point when he was dividing his time between New York and Canada, it was the failure of *Blue Water* that signaled the end of his role as a truly Canadian film producer. He traveled to Florida hoping to duplicate the system of independent filmmaking he pioneered in Canada, but was eventually overshadowed by the stronghold of the major studios over U.S. exhibitors. He died in New York City at the age of fifty-nine.

FILMS AS PRODUCER: *Back to God's Country* (Calgary), 1919; *God's Crucible* (Winnipeg); *Cameron of the Royal Mounted* (Winnipeg), 1920; *The Man from Glengarry* (Ottawa); *Glengarry School Days* (Ottawa); *The Rapids* (Sault Ste. Marie); *Blue Water* (New Brunswick), 1922.

BIBLIOGRAPHY: Peter Morris (1978); D. J. Turner, "Ernest Shipman: Some Notes," in *Griffithiana* Anno XV—no. 44/45 (1992): 147–76.

Alice Black

NELL SHIPMAN. Born 1892, Victoria, British Columbia; died 1970, Los Angeles, California. Producer, director, writer, actor. Born to English immigrants as Helen Foster-Barham, Nell Shipman was a true pioneer: a feminist auteur filmmaker. Although her family moved to the United States when she was only ten, and although she never returned to live in Canada, she remained deeply attached to the country of her birth. Hating school in the States, she attended the Egan Dramatic School in Seattle, and was allowed to join a traveling acting troupe when she was only thirteen. At eighteen she met and married ERNIE SHIPMAN, who obtained her first writing and acting assignments in film in 1912: *Outwitted by Billy* and *The Ball of Yarn*, respectively. In 1915 she wrote, acted in, and allegedly co-directed *God's Country and the Woman*, based on James Oliver Curwood's novel of the same name. Produced by Vitagraph, it was shot in Big Bear Valley and gave Nell the epithet "Girl from God's Country," which she would never lose. She was hired for this project because she was athletic and a good swimmer, and, in her own words, she "was to drive a team of sled dogs, paddle a canoe, travel on snowshoes." After her next Vitagraph Curwood, *Baree, Son of Kazan* (1918), she signed an exclusive contract with the author, leading to her only Canadian-made film, *BACK TO GOD'S COUNTRY* (1919), also her last with Ernie. Then, for four years after divorcing her husband, she became a truly independent auteur filmmaker, working closely with co-director Bert Van Tuyle and cinematographer Joseph Walker and producing many of her own films, including the extant *The Grub Stake* (1923). Most of these featured Nell in harmony with the wilderness and her menagerie of animals whom she claimed to love more than people. In Canadian film historian Peter Morris' view, she became a victim of Hollywood's vertical integration and move toward factory-style production. After a series of two-reelers in 1923–24 entitled "Little Dramas of the Big Places" she ceased acting and directing. One of her scripts became a Paramount feature in 1935, *Wings in the Dark*, and she produced one more film in 1946, *The Clam Digger's Daughter*.

BIBLIOGRAPHY: Joseph B. Walker and Juanita Walker; Nell Shipman; William K. Everson, "Rediscovery," *Films in Review* 40, no. 4 (April 1989): 228–31.

Peter Rist

SHIVERS *The Parasite Murders* (Quebec rel. title) [*They Came from Within* (United States)]. David Cronenberg, Montreal, 1975, 87 min., color. *Shivers*, DAVID CRONENBERG's first feature film to be released,* was produced in 1974 on a small budget of $185,000. Surprisingly, it launched both the director and the distribution company, Cinepix, into the big leagues both critically and financially by its success at the 1975 Cannes Film Festival and by grossing over $5 million in thirty-five countries. Set in an antiseptic, isolated apartment complex on Nun's Island outside Montreal, the film begins with an aborted experiment as a mad scientist brutally murders a young girl he has implanted with a genetically engineered parasite, part aphrodisiac/part venereal disease, designed to liberate the sexual spirit of humanity. Unbeknownst to him, however, the girl has already passed the parasite on to several men in the complex, and the disease, manifested as violent sexual behavior, begins to spread. Dismissed by many critics as a conservative reaction to sexual liberation, the film actually represents a more subtle critique of repression by proposing that extreme repression leads to an extremely hostile release of all that is repressed. The inhabitants of the Starlighter Towers live such a sterile pretense of humanity, blankly going through the motions of real life, that when infected by the disease they turn into automatons of another kind, mindlessly wandering the corridors in search of sexual release. When Betts (Barbara Steele), a character who stands in contrast to the rest of the building's inhabitants because of her exotic sexuality, is infected she does not, however, become a mindless monster. Instead she warmly seduces Janine (Susan Petrie) in the film's only nonviolent love scene. In this case, the parasite simply brings their barely hidden feelings for each other to the foreground. For Cronenberg, monstrosity does not lie in the body but rather in society's constraints upon the body.

BIBLIOGRAPHY: Michael J. Collins, "Medicine, Surrealism, Lust, Anger and Death: Three Early Films," *Post Script* 15, no. 2 (Winter/Spring 1996).

Stacey Abbott

GILBERT SICOTTE. Born 1948, Montreal. Actor. After dropping out of l'École Nationale de Théâtre in 1968 along with PAULE BAILLARGEON and PIERRE CURZI, Gilbert Sicotte joined the Grand Cirque Ordinaire, gaining his first film role in 1971 in the Cirque production *Montréal Blues*. In 1974, Sicotte starred in his breakthrough film, *Les vautours*, playing Louis Pelletier, a young man

---

*It was released initially in Montreal as *The Parasite Murders* in English, and as *Frissons* in French, and later in the rest of Canada and the UK as *Shivers*.

who, after the death of his mother, is dispossessed of everything by his three sisters. Intended as a political allegory, the film is filled with unlikeable characters, and Louis, as played by Sicotte, is lazy, passive, and weak. He played similar roles of disaffected youths in *Ti-cul Tougas* (J.-G. Noël) and *Les grands enfants* (PAUL TANA). These are unsympathetic characters, but Sicotte's subtle performances go beyond the individuals concerned to reach out and reflect the frustrations of a generation. During this time he also took smaller roles, offering superb supporting performances in films such as *Cordélia* (JEAN BEAUDIN) and *Maria Chapdelaine* (GILLES CARLE), which developed his versatility. In 1980 he gave a beautiful performance as the would-be consort of MARIE TIFO in FRANCIS MANKIEWICZ's moving and tragic tale *LES BONS DÉBARRAS*. Here there is no sense of passivity, more a pervading sense of futility and of people coping with situations beyond their control, an idea to which he returned in 1985 in JEAN-CLAUDE LABRECQUE's sequel to *Les vautours, Les années de rêves*. Sicotte is excellent in the center of this epic production, ably supported by the reunited cast of *Les vautours*. A veteran of over twenty features, Sicotte has often appeared in films in which the characters function as parts of a larger political message. Yet he always imbues his roles with warmth and humanity, endowing them with a life beyond the message. A great talent, he finally gained true stardom with his humorous portrayal of the seducer Jean-Paul in the TV series "Les dames de coeur" in 1986.

FILMS AS ACTOR: *Montréal blues*, 1972; *Les allées de la terre*, 1973; *Les vautours*, 1975; *Ti-cul Tougas; Je suis loin de toi mignonne; La p'tite violence*, 1976; *Anastasie, oh ma cherie*, 1977; *Au revoir . . . à lundi* (Can/Fr); *L'affaire Coffin*, 1979; *Cordélia; Les grands enfants; Fantastica* (Can/Fr); *Le château de carte*, 1980; *Une journée en taxi*, 1982; *Contrecoeur*, 1979–83; *Maria Chapdelaine* (Can/Fr), 1983; *Les années de rêves*, 1984; *L'hiver les blés*, 1984; *Visage pâle* (Can/Jap); *Le million tout puissant*, 1985; *Anne Trister*, 1986; *Lamento pour un homme de lettres*, 1988; *Le marchand de jouets; Les noces de papier*, 1989; *La Sarrasine*, 1991; *Léolo* (narr. only), 1992; *Cap Tourmente*, 1993; *Mon ami Max; La vie d'un héros*, 1994; *L'enfant d'eau*, 1995.

Simon Brown

SIFTED EVIDENCE. Patricia Gruben, Toronto, 1982, 42 min., color. *Sifted Evidence*, the second film by American Patricia Gruben (born 1947), resident in Canada since the early 1970s, gained her an international reputation as a practitioner of the feminist avant-garde, and led to her being called "clearly the most intelligent and complex" filmmaker in Canada by film scholar and programmer Kay Armatage. Ostensibly about a woman's quest for signs of an ancient matriarchal Mayan society in Mexico, *Evidence* is a central work of neo-narrative, or "new talkie," cinema which explores gender relations as inextricably tied to sound/image relations. Informed by contemporary feminist/psychoanalytic theory, Gruben presents the journey to Mexico in fragmented images—mostly studio filmed foreground action against painted or projected backdrops—accompanied by a variety of mostly female, first and third person voices. Initially, we see text on a scroll which is doubled by a woman's voice, introducing us to the concepts of image- and film-making linked to the spatial and temporal journey. A slide show gives way to the artificial recreation of Maggi's (Maggi Jones) ill-fated quest. In only one of the film's scenes is there synchronized dialogue, where Maggi's self-appointed guide, Jim (Doug Innis), a former major league baseball player, molests her in a hotel room. His over-attentiveness is posed as the main reason for her inability to find the ruins of Tlatlico. But the dominance of female voice and the variety of modes of its address—authorially directive, questioning, descriptive, analytical, commentative, direct to the audience—provide a feminine discourse as a counterbalance to the male-dominated narrative, while the disrupted image track and the generally reflexive nature of the piece call into question the entire spectrum of conventional (perhaps, patriarchal) narrative cinema. Although it may be accused of being potentially racist—the antagonist, Jim, is African American, and the protagonist is at his mercy in an exotic foreign land—its distancing and analytical narrative strategies mark *Sifted Evidence* as being one of the most important experimental films from the 1980s. Patricia Gruben moved into features, with the interesting, somewhat experimental *Low Visibility* in 1984, and, more recently, *Deep Sleep* (1989).

BIBLIOGRAPHY: Kay Armatage, "About to Speak: The Woman's Voice in Patricia Gruben's *Sifted Evidence*," in Wees and Dorland, 67–76.

Peter Rist

THE SILENT ENEMY. H. P. Carver, United States/Canada (Ontario), 1930, 84 min., silent, b + w. *The Silent Enemy*, filmed in the Timagami Provincial Forest of Northern Ontario, bears a generic resemblance to a unique group of American produced docudramas dealing with premodern cultures that thrilled urban audiences of the 1920s (*NANOOK OF THE NORTH*, 1922; *Grass*, 1925; *Primitive Love*, 1926; *Chang*, 1927; *White Shadows in the South Seas*, 1928; *Stampede*, 1928). *The Silent Enemy* recreates the pre-Columbian life and culture of the Ojibway Indians of the Hudson Bay area with great attention to authentic detail (dress, food, cooking, hunting, tool making). Though Richard Carver's script includes the required Hollywood quota of love interest and conflict, it does not detract from the many wonderfully staged adventure sequences or the film's pictorial beauty. The survivalist plot (its title referring to hunger) becomes the catalyst for many of the film's highlights: the fight for a deer carcass between a bear and a mountain lion; Baluk (Long Lance) hunting down a caribou; and the climactic caribou migration sequence (though co-editor W. Douglas Burden admitted to mixing in shots of deer with the authentic shots of migrating caribou). In some of the adventure sequences stylistic realism (long takes) is sacrificed for dynamism by having multiple camera setups that allow for varying camera angles (for example, the overhead shots during the mountain lion/bear fight). *The Silent Enemy* was released as a silent film at a time when sound film was the norm in North America. This largely explains why the film, though it attained great critical success, was a box office failure.

BIBLIOGRAPHY: Peter Morris (1978), 200–204; Kevin Brownlow.

Donato Totaro

THE SILENT PARTNER. Daryl Duke, Toronto, 1978, 105 min., color. Miles Cullen (Elliott Gould), a milquetoast bank teller, pieces together evidence suggesting that a bank heist is being planned by a shopping mall Santa Claus (CHRISTOPHER PLUMMER). Miles is correct, but rather than informing the police he thwarts the thief by switching most of the $48,350 into a bag under the till and keeping it for himself. What ensues is an effective cat and mouse game between an angry murderer-thief and a surprisingly resourceful bank teller. The sadistic and misogynist Reikle (Plummer) is the seasoned criminal, but the novice Miles continually frustrates and outsmarts him. In the end Miles defeats Reikle, cheats big business (banking), and wins the woman of his dreams, Julie (Susannah York). The story has the classic appeal of the social lamb turned wolf, but Gould's low-key performance fails to exploit the role's emotional potential. Plummer, who spends a fair amount of time in disguise (Santa Claus in the beginning, in drag at the end), fares better as the villain. York is unfortunately wasted as Gould's love interest. Céline Lomez (Elaine) is given slightly more range as the seductive accomplice who switches her allegiance from Reikle to Miles. Lomez also appears in the film's most notorious scene: her death by decapitation on a broken aquarium tank glass. *The Silent Partner* was one of the first films to take advantage of the Canadian government's "Capital Cost Allowance" plan. The film did extremely well financially and critically, winning seven Canadian Film Academy Awards, including Best Film and Best Director.

BIBLIOGRAPHY: Mark Irwin, "A Softlight Man: Billy Williams b.s.c.," *Cinema Canada*, no. 43 (December 1977/January 1978): 18–22; Will Aitken, "The Silent Partner: An Incipient Fassbinder?," *Take One*, no. 7 (1979): 10–11.

Donato Totaro

SKIP TRACER. Zale R. Dalen, British Columbia, 1977, 94 min., 16mm, color. One of the earliest Canadian films to have been made in British Columbia which gained some prominence outside its own province as an "independent" feature, *Skip Tracer* also has the distinction of being one of the very first Canadian films to be screened at the New York Film Festival. Prior to making his first feature, director Zale R. Dalen had made a number of short films after attending a Simon Fraser University film workshop in 1969. This film chronicles the transformation of a "skip tracer," a credit collector for a Vancouver loan company, named John Collins (David Petersen). He is attempting to win the company's "Man of the Year" award for the fourth year in a row by repossessing cars. One of his "clients," George Pettigrew (Al Rose), is also harassed by Collins' mentor (Rudy Szabo), causing Pettigrew's suicide. Collins, whose ruthlessness had begun to cause self-doubt, instantly reforms, and wipes the files of all his other potential victims from the computer. *Skip Tracer* is significant in producing a new kind of "private eye" anti-hero in an urban world dominated by new technologies, and is scored to a cleverly mixed soundtrack of electronic rock and noisy, grating effects. The character is still a Bogart-style, slick loner, but his approach is extremely cold, and his only friend is an unfeeling, electronic calculator. Dalen's second feature, *The Hounds of Notre Dame* (1980), was well received, but he was unable to make another until the end of the decade. He now works mainly in television.

BIBLIOGRAPHY: Peter Morris (1984), 78, 274.

Peter Rist

MICHAEL SNOW. Born 1929, Toronto. Filmmaker, musician, visual artist, composer, writer. Canada's best-known living artist is also one of the world's two most highly acclaimed experimental filmmakers (the other being Stan Brakhage of the United States). Although Michael Snow practiced as a visual artist in Toronto in the 1950s, Canadian art critics as a whole only began to champion his work after he moved to New York City with his wife, JOYCE WIELAND, in 1962. In the 1960s, he developed a reputation for being an important innovator in the fields of Pop and Minimalist art, with his "Walking Women" series, and with his film work. Retrospectively, his second film, *New York Eye and Ear Control* (1964), is now viewed as being a key to the important contrapuntal complexities of Snow's oeuvre. In it, the improvised, spontaneous, "expressionist" and "emotional" music of avant-garde jazz musicians Albert Ayler, Don Cherry, John Tchicai, Roswell Rudd, Gary Peacock, and Sonny Murray "coexists" with the "classical," measured, "composed," and "intellectual" filmed images (in Snow's own words). The year 1967 saw the appearance of Snow's first real "structural" film, *Standard Time*, in which the main subject appears to be the camera's panning movements, and, perhaps the most discussed and admired experimental film ever made, the "45 minute zoom," WAVELENGTH. Prominent art and film historians/scholars P. Adams Sitney and Annette Michelson make claims for its cinematic processes being analogous to "philosophical thought" and "consciousness" itself, respectively. At the very least, *Wavelength* extends the artist's exploration of temporality linked inexorably with space. He continued in this "movement" mode with *(Back and Forth)* and his epic "metaphor on vision," LA RÉGION CENTRALE, but earlier, in 1969's *One Second in Montreal*, he combined a concern for duration with a cross-media exploration of the boundary conditions of film and photography. Snow made a comic parody of *Wavelength* in the early 1970s with the Dada-esque *Breakfast (Table Top Dolly)*, where the camera itself, tracking forward, destroys the contents of an overstuffed breakfast table. He continued in the comic vein with *SO IS THIS*, a semiological deconstruction of the English language. The term "Renaissance man" is greatly overused, but is an apt moniker for Michael Snow, who is an accomplished writer, with significant things to say about visual art and film and an important figure on the avant-garde, improvisational music scene. He also has a great sense of community, being a principal supporter over the years of Toronto's nonprofit cultural institutions, including the Music Gallery and the Funnel Film Cooperative, and especially the Canadian Filmmakers Distribution Centre, which he has helped keep operational by depositing all his films in their care. In 1994 the Power Plant and the Art Gallery of Ontario collaborated on "The Michael Snow Project," an extensive retrospective of the artist's work from 1951 to 1993, through four separate exhibitions, and the publication of four books.

FILMS (SOUND, 16MM SHORTS, EXCEPT WHERE NOTED): *A to Z* (silent), 1956; *New York Eye and Ear Control*, 1964; *Short Shave* (silent), 1965; *Standard Time; Wavelength*, 1967; *(Back and Forth)*, 1968–69; *One Second in Montreal* (silent); *Dripping Water* (co-dir., Joyce Wieland), 1969; *Slide Seat Paintings Slides Sound Film*, 1970; *La Région Centrale* (feature), 1971; *Rameau's Nephew by Diderot (Thanx to Dennis Young) by Wilma Schoen* (feature), 1974; *Breakfast (Table Top Dolly)*, 1972–76; *Presents* (feature), 1980–81; *So Is This* (silent), 1982; *Funnel Piano* (Super-8), 1984; *Seated Figures*, 1988; *See You Later (Au Revoir)*, 1990; *To Lavoisier, Who Died in the Reign of Terror*, 1991.

BIBLIOGRAPHY: P. Adams Sitney, "Michael Snow's Cinema," in Sitney (1970): 79–84; Annette Michelson, "Toward Snow: Part 1," *Artforum* 9, no. 19 (June 1971): 30–37; Michael Snow (1993); Jim Sheddon.

Peter Rist

SO IS THIS. Michael Snow, Toronto, 1982, 43 min., color and b+w. What might at first appear to be a simplistic cinematic joke (in fact, the film is sometimes considered an avant-garde comedy) is actually a complex response to the question of whether or not one can talk about a film language. *So Is This* is an experiment unique in the history of cinema: as the film itself makes clear, *So Is This* "consist[s] of single words presented one after another to construct sentences." In theory, the concept would seem quite obvious, but the spectator (reader?) quickly realizes that the concerns the film raises extend beyond its apparent "one-liner" quality. For example, the rhythm of the editing is often consistent with the rhythm of speech; at other times, however, single words are presented in shots whose duration confounds logical expectations. What we are presented with are words *as* images; further, we come to recognize that what we are seeing are photographically recorded representations of words, and that these words are functioning simultaneously as both text and image. The film also raises questions about the spectator's role in the creation of meaning, claiming that "hopefully (this is where you come in) words convey meaning." And yet, the spectator, who has been presented with, perhaps, the most elemental "narrative" ever filmed, is unable to rely on his or her ability to link the words in order to create meaning—after a point, the sheer accumulation of words becomes too much for us. MICHAEL SNOW manages to include some comments about the Ontario Censor Board's obscenity policies in the early 1980s, and to briefly mention the issue of bilingualism (especially ironic in a film made up exclusively of words) while at the same time maintaining the playful quality that has earned him the reputation of the *enfant terrible* of Canadian avant-garde cinema.

Mitch Parry

SONATINE. Micheline Lanctôt, Montreal, 1982–84, 91 min., color. After a highly favorable critical response in Quebec, MICHELINE LANCTÔT's *Sonatine* was released and almost immediately withdrawn from theaters because of its poor performance at the box office. Recipient of the Lion d'Argent at Venice in 1984, the film was released in the hope that this prestigious prize would give it a second life. The Quebecois public still would not attend, and the film remained in theaters for scarcely a week. The failure of the film was certainly not deserved: *Sonatine* contains numerous aesthetic attributes, above all a striking dramatic impact on account of its narrative sobriety. With a subject as morose as the suicide of two adolescent women facing an adult world that is totally indifferent to their actions, one can understand in part why the Quebecois audience responded so negatively to such a depressing social statement, especially if handled with an experimental treatment. Composed of three distinct movements, Lanctôt's film avoids the superfluous in order to go to the essence of things and relies on numerous narrative ellipses. As well, the film displays a genuine economy of dialogue, privileging the expressiveness of a look, of lighting, and of an elaborate use of the soundtrack to signify the distress of the two protagonists and their withdrawal from the adult world. The final scene, in which the two assist each other in their suicide in a metro-car, is a model of visual and sound abstraction. *Sonatine* was, perhaps, a cursed film but, like many cursed films, deserves a great deal of admiration.

BIBLIOGRAPHY: Gilles Blain, "*Sonatine*: Un film à recherche d'un public," in Claude Chabot et al.

Louis Goyette

SOUL SURVIVOR. Steven Williams, Toronto, 1995, 89 min., color. Developed and released around the same time, Stephen Williams' *Soul Survivor* and Clement Virgo's *RUDE* both stand as striking testimony to a bright, young, and intelligent cinema emerging from Toronto's Jamaican community. A socially relevant and engaging effort, Williams' film follows the meanderings of Tyrone, a relatively poor young man who is pulled into the local Mafia after he vows to help his cousin pay off a debt. Similar to Boaz Yakin's excellent *Fresh* (United States, 1994), and evocative of African American Spike Lee's universe and Paul Schrader's explorations of tormented souls on the road to redemption, the director's first feature still stands out and deserves our respect, if only for the surprising mastery of mise-en-scène displayed by such a young artist (Williams was only twenty-seven when he worked on the film). For the viewer, this translates into the impression that a strong personality is at work behind the camera, a quality not to be dismissed in today's faceless industry. Williams' ability to create a mounting tension and a strong story line is well supported by his choices as a director and as a writer. At times, the use of slow motion combined with the warm orangey sheen of the cinematography produces a feeling of oozing sensuality, in line with the warm depiction of most characters. The various camera movements and angles subtly emphasize the protagonist's progressive entrapment. Moreover, *Soul Survivor* contains explicitly pertinent references to social and racial prejudices that are commonly accepted and reinstated, or adapted to fit the ever-evolving practice of cultural plundering which can be observed in new urban trends and fads. From that standpoint, Williams' feature not only renders a believable and sensitive portrait of a community, but also reclaims ownership of cultural freedom.

Alain Dubeau

GORDON SPARLING. Born 1900, Toronto; died 1994. Producer, director, and writer. Gordon Sparling was virtually the only creative filmmaker working in English Canada through the 1930s. After graduating from the University of Toronto he was hired by the Ontario Motion Picture Bureau in 1924 as a title artist. At the Trenton, Ontario, studios he worked on the big budget feature CARRY ON, SERGEANT! in 1927, then spent some time at the Canadian Government Motion Picture Bureau before moving to New York City and the Paramount Astoria studio. This important sojourn gave him expertise in the new sound technology, which stood him in good stead with his new employer in 1931, Associated Screen News (ASN) in Montreal. ASN made newsreels and was the principal lab for theatrical prints for Canada and the northeastern United States. Here Sparling persuaded founder and general manager Bernard E. Norrish to allow him to produce and direct a series of theatrical "novelty" shorts as a condition of Sparling being the new production manager of Associated Screen Studios. This series, "Canadian Cameos," was the longest running (1932–54) and most successful series of Canadian films until the heyday of the NFB. Eighty-five one-reel (approximately ten-minute) "Canadian Cameo" vignettes on various aspects of Canadian life were made, almost exclusively written and directed by Sparling. He also helped in the construction of Canada's first sound studio for ASN in Montreal in 1935, where he directed a feature-length docudrama for Shell Oil in both English and French versions, *House in Order/La maison en ordre*. During World War II he worked in England but returned to ASN in 1946, where he stayed until the company ceased operations in 1957. Television had taken over their role. Sparling joined the NFB in 1958 and left in 1966, after which he continued to be active, researching and writing on cinema. He emerged from retirement in 1982 to finish a film he had begun in 1936, *Fencer's Art*.

FILMS AS DIRECTOR INCLUDE: *When Kappa Kappa Gamma Visited Ontario*, 1924; *Spare Time*, 1927; *Forward Canada!*, 1931; *The Breadwinner;* "Canadian Cameos"

(CCs): *She Climbs to Conquer; Grey Owl's Little Brother; The Pathfinder*, 1932; (CCs): *Carnival on Skates*, 1933; (CCs): *Grey Owl's Strange Guests; Rhapsody in Two Languages; Did You Know That?*, 1934; *Acadian Spring Song* (CC), 1935; *House in Order/ La maison en ordre* (feature), 1936; *Crystal Ballet* (CC); *Wings over the Atlantic* (2 reels), 1937; *Music from the Stars* (CC); *Ballet of the Mermaids* (CC); *The Kinsmen* (5 reels), 1938; *Royal Banners over Ottawa* (CC, 2 reels, color); *The Bright Path* (3 reels), 1939; *Peoples of Canada* (30 min.), 1940; *Those Other Days*, 1941; *The Thousand Days* (CC, 2 reels) 1942; *The Antwerp Story*, 1945; *The Mapleville Story*, 1946; *Sitzmarks the Spot* (CC), 1948; *Design for Swimming* (CC, color), 1949; *The Beloved Fish* (last CC, color), 1954; *Fraser's River*, 1958; *Royal River*, 1959; *The Water Dwellers*, 1963; *Landfall Asia* (28 min.), 1964; *Better Housing for the Atlantic Provinces*, 1965; *Fencer's Art*, 1936–82.

BIBLIOGRAPHY: Peter Morris (1978), 155–57, 225–31.

Peter Rist

THE STREET. Caroline Leaf, (Montreal) NFB, 1976, 10 min., color. A winner of multiple international awards, *The Street* remarkably captures the childhood angst lying at the core of Mordecai Richler's witty and bittersweet tale about a Jewish boy waiting impatiently for his grandmother to die in order to finally get her bedroom. An example of unassuming childish cruelty hiding a deeper and more poignant philosophical quest, it is conveyed by Caroline Leaf with great visual poetry, humor, and narrative economy. Especially striking is her ability to evoke the urban and cultural landscape inhabited by the characters: the famous outdoor staircases of Montreal, its clothesline-cluttered alleyways, the faded wallpaper inside typical tenement apartments, the lingo of the neighborhood. The technique she employs to give life to this social fresco is gouache on glass mixed with glycerine with which she can simulate live action film movements and transitions. With an astounding agility and ease she tricks us into believing that we are indeed seeing optical fades, dissolves, and tricked wipes when we are not. The same is true of the apparent, but nonexistent, camera movements, wide angle distortions, and telephoto fuzziness with which she expressively and impressionistically illustrates her hero's journey—a design worthy of the best and most visionary experimental films.

BIBLIOGRAPHY: John Canemaker.

Johanne Larue

DONALD SUTHERLAND. Born 1934, St. John, New Brunswick. Actor, narrator. Tall, thin, and pale, it is not surprising that Donald Sutherland's earliest roles were in horror films. What is surprising is that from this most inauspicious of starts, Sutherland has grown into one of Canada's most talented and respected actors. His interest in performance began as a child when he ran his own puppet theater and worked as a DJ. While at university, he joined the drama club. Uncertain of a career in acting, it was only when he received positive reviews for his performance as Stefano in *The Tempest* that he finally decided to make acting his profession. He spent two summers performing in summer stock while completing a literature degree. He then left for England to broaden his classical training. After appearing in various forgettable European horror films in the mid-1960s, Sutherland leapt to stardom in a series of successful American films. In 1969, he made his first Canadian film, appearing opposite GENEVIÈVE BUJOLD in PAUL ALMOND's *Act of the Heart*. Although the film belongs to Bujold, Sutherland does imbue his supporting role with a breath of humanity as he plays a monk confronting his own desires for the young choir singer in his parish. This was followed three years later by a starring role in Claude Fournier's *Alien Thunder*, a Canadian Western, where Sutherland brings strength and dignity to his role as a Mountie. Sutherland has twice portrayed a role quite close to his heart, that of Dr. Norman Bethune. He first played him in 1977 in the CBC production *Bethune* and reprised the role in 1990 in the long awaited epic Canadian/Chinese/French co-production *Bethune: The Making of a Hero*, a project that Sutherland had supported from its original conception in the early eighties. Sutherland portrays the noble doctor as vivacious, colorful, and inherently human, a man made into a hero by good intentions and circumstances beyond his control. It is a charismatic performance that, due to a series of production and distribution problems, has been seen by far too few people. A supporter of the Canadian film industry, Sutherland often lends his services to small, quality projects with little consideration for the size of his role. In 1981 he provided the narration for ANNE WHEELER's personal documentary, *A War Story*, based on her father's experiences during World War II. Sutherland's voice, reading the commentary taken from Dr. Wheeler's diaries, is personable and familiar, bringing the people and events described in the film to life. More recently, he provided the narration to Frédérick Back's Oscar-nominated animated short *The Mighty River*, celebrating the history of the St. Lawrence River. An incredibly skilled actor, Sutherland consistently brings intelligence and wit to his performance, making each role, whether hero or villain, eccentric or madman, more than what it appears on the surface.

FILMS AS ACTOR: *The Act of the Heart*, 1970; *Alien Thunder*, 1974; *The Disappearance; Bethune* (TV), 1977; *Blood Relatives* (Can/France), 1978; *Murder by Decree; Bear Island* (Can/UK); *A Man, a Woman and a Bank*, 1979; *North China Commune* (narr. only); *Nothing Personal*, 1979; *A War Story* (narr. only); *Gas; Threshold*, 1981; *Give Me Your Answer True*, 1988; *Bethune: The Making of a Hero; Eminent Domain*, 1990; *Scream of Stone; Buster's Bedroom*, 1991; *Agaguk; Shadow of the Wolf*, 1993; *Mighty River* (short, narr. only), 1994; *Lifeforce Experiment* (TV); *Hollow Point*, 1995; *Natural Enemy* (TV, Can/US); *The Assignment*, 1997.

BIBLIOGRAPHY: David Pirie, "Reflections of a Star: Donald Sutherland," in Pirie; Barbara Graustark, "Donald Sutherland's Seventh Inning Stretch," *American Film* 9, no. 6 (April 1984).

Stacey Abbott

THE SWEET HEREAFTER. Atom Egoyan, Ontario/British Columbia, 1997, 112 min., color. With its three major awards at the 1997 Cannes International Film Festival—Grand Prix, International Film Critics Prize, and Ecumenical Jury Prize—its two prestigious Oscar nominations for ATOM EGOYAN—Best Director and Best Adapted Screenplay—and eight Genie Awards, including Best Film and Best Director, *The Sweet Hereafter* has become the most acclaimed Canadian feature film of all time. After the success of *EXOTICA*, its director, Egoyan, received a number of offers from Hollywood. But after struggling to get a project he liked off the ground, he returned to Canada to work on his first adaptation of another's work, Russell Banks' *The Sweet Hereafter*. Ironically, given the tendency for Canadians to head south, and for Canadian film projects to become Americanized, Egoyan changed the setting and place of U.S. writer Banks' novel from post–Vietnam War upstate New York to contemporary British Columbia. The casting of British actor Ian Holm in the central role, and the sensitive treatment of a difficult subject, the fatal crash of a school bus, helped gain *The Sweet Hereafter* a wider audience than any of Egoyan's previous films, but perhaps the film's principal interest lies in the ways in which the director adapted the novel and made the story his own. The novel follows the tragic event and the effects it has on a small town, chronologically, but through the eyes of successive characters, ending with a chapter from the perspective of the female bus driver, who is unfairly accused by the only other survivor of driving too fast. Egoyan focuses on the insurance agent, Mitchell (Holm), who tries to persuade the victims' parents to pursue a joint lawsuit, but as a way of comparing Mitchell's relationship (at a distance) with his drug addicted daughter to that between an apparently incestuous father and daughter: the (above) survivor, the teenaged Nicole (Sarah Polley). Egoyan also fragments the narrative in time and space, forcing the audience to figure out the tense interpersonal relationships, and, mercifully, he stages the scene of the bus crashing through the surface of a frozen lake in extreme-long shot and very briefly. (Contrast the other disaster film of 1997 directed by a Canadian, *The Titanic*, which builds to the tragedy as climax.)

Peter Rist

T

TALES FROM THE GIMLI HOSPITAL. Guy Maddin, Manitoba, 1988, 68 min., b+w. One of the most daring and innovative of all Canadian first features, Guy Maddin's *Tales from the Gimli Hospital* confounded its critics when it premiered at the Winnipeg Film Group in April 1988. Prior to making *Gimli* Maddin had made only one short film, *The Dead Father* (1985), and outside a small circle at the Winnipeg Film Group, he was virtually unknown. With a budget of $5,000 for promotion, executive producer Greg Klymkiw approached film festivals in Montreal and Toronto to launch the film. Montreal accepted, but Toronto refused. The film was later screened at festivals around the world, including Mannheim and Berlin. From its Montreal premiere the film was picked up by Andre Bennett's Cinephile, and has gone on to attain cult status across North America. Ironically, with a script of only eight pages, Maddin found himself receiving a Genie nomination for Best Original Script. The story recounts a chance encounter of two strangers, Gunnar (Kyle McCulloch) and Einar (Michael Gottli), who are brought together when quarantined in a Manitoba fishing village during a smallpox epidemic. The two develop a friendship that is soured when a nurse favors one over the other. Maddin created a world that resembles a dreamscape; a delirious, nightmarish setting that at times eschews any sense of narrative causality. The dark, surreal quality of the images, combined with the absurd elements of the story, ensured the film's success as a "midnight movie" across the United States.

BIBLIOGRAPHY: Geoff Pevere, "Greenland Revisited: The Winnipeg Film Group During the 1980's," in Hébert.

Dave Douglas

PAUL TANA. Born 1947, Ancona, Italy. Director, writer. Paul Tana is one of the growing number of immigrant Quebecois filmmakers who have made ethnicity and cultural identity an integral part of their films (Tahani Rached, Marilú Mallet, German Guiterrez). Tana immigrated to Montreal in 1958. He graduated from the Université de Québec in literature, where he would later teach film production. After working on the French Radio-Québec television show "Planète," he made his first feature film, *Les grands enfants*. This film featured a young immigrant Italian woman as a central character, a harbinger of future Tana script dynamics. Tana's two major feature films, *Caffé Italia* and *La Sarrasine*, deal directly and honestly with the Italian immigrant experience. Tana co-scripted both films with historian Bruno Ramirez, which partially accounts for their wonderful sense of authenticity. *Caffé Italia* is an engaging documentary on the generations of Italians (11 million strong) who have been immigrating to Canada since the turn of the 20th century. Tana's chosen style, far removed from conventional documentary form, is an eclectic blend of talking heads, archival footage, and dramatizations. The film also stirred controversy with such issues as the fascist presence in Montreal and the internment of Italians during World War II. Tana interviews a cross-section of the Montreal Italian community, including actors PIERRE CURZI, Tony Nardi (who plays the lead in *La Sarrasine*), and rock star Aldo Nova. Nova aptly expresses the cultural fragmentation felt by younger generation Italians when he says, "I am the son of an Italian, who speaks French and sings in English." *La Sarrasine*, based on a real incident, is a moving account of French-Italian relations in turn of the century Montreal. It is stately in style, and reminiscent at times of Gordon Willis' low-key lighting and color palette for *The Godfather* (United States, 1972).

THEATRICAL FEATURE FILMS AS DIRECTOR: *Les grands enfants*, 1980; *Caffé Italia*, 1985; *Le rêve de Joe Aiello*, 1986; *Marchand de jouets*, 1988 (short feature); *La Sarrasine*, 1992.

BIBLIOGRAPHY: Michael Dorland, "Caffe Italia," *Cinema Canada*, no. 125 (December 1985): 30–31.

Donato Totaro

ALBERT TESSIER. Born 1895, Sainte-Anne-de-la-Pérade, Quebec; died 1976, Trois-Rivières, Quebec. Director, cinematographer. Monseigneur Albert Tessier was the first clergyman to use the cinema as a pedagogical device. Between 1924 and 1956 he made approximately seventy films that primarily functioned didactically to promote the beauty of nature (*Arbres et bêtes* and *Le forêt bienfaisante*, both 1943), education (*Écoles et écoliers*, 1940), and the all-encompassing power of God (*Cantique de la création*, 1942). Tessier was born into an agricultural family. After completing a classical education in Trois-Rivières, he was ordained a priest in 1920. Passionately concerned with history, which he taught at Laval University (among other institutions), Tessier also worked as both a journalist and an editor. From his classical studies, he developed a passion for photography that is echoed in his cinematography. Indeed,

Tessier showed a particular interest in shot composition and depth of field. But his style is weakened by a lack of concern for montage and rhythm. As Yves Lever noted in his *Histoire générale du cinéma au Québec*, "Autodidact of the camera and montage alike, Tessier paid little attention to the rules of cinematography or the harmony of connections." Although several of his films had sound added by the Service de cinématographie du Québec, Tessier liked to provide his own commentary, in person, everywhere he traveled with his films. In 1980, the Quebec government created the Prix Albert Tessier to be awarded to a filmmaker or administrator who had contributed to the promotion of Quebec cinema.

BIBLIOGRAPHY: René Bouchard.

Louis Goyette

THE THINGS I CANNOT CHANGE. Tanya Ballantyne, (Montreal) NFB, 1966, 58 min., b+w. *The Things I Cannot Change* was conceived as a pilot project for the "Challenge for Change" program (1967–1980), an NFB series that had as its mandate the goal of promoting social change. Tanya Ballantyne brings her camera into the lives of a downtrodden welfare family living in a low-rent Montreal apartment. The Baileys, headed by an unemployed father, have nine mouths to feed and a tenth on the way. They are the archetypical poor Catholic family, though never sentimentalized or "ennobled." With its close-up zoom shots and liberated camera style, the film sensitively captures the anguished expressions on the faces of the parents, and succeeds in winning our sympathy. However, the film provides little optimism, and is structured as a series of setbacks heading in a downward social spiral. The spiral hits rock bottom in the scene where the father suffers a pathetic beating at the hands of a bigger man. As an ethical issue, it is unlikely that the father, prone to moments of on-camera social martyrdom, would have behaved as "valiantly" (i.e., stupidly) had the camera not been there. Moments such as these continue until a freeze frame protracts the final moment of destitution (no money, no food, and a newborn baby). The film does not provide a full-fledged criticism on the ravages of capitalism, but it succeeds in its principal goal of exposing the problem of urban poverty. Heated reactions to the film, coupled with the embarrassment it caused for the family after it aired on CBC television, led the producers to rethink "The Challenge for Change" series. As a result, it was decided that subjects would have more input into editorial decisions. Ballantyne revisited the Bailey family some twenty years later in the documentary *Courage to Change* (1985).

BIBLIOGRAPHY: Patrick Watson, "Challenge for Change," in Feldman and Nelson, 112–19; D. B. Jones (1981), 157–75.

Donato Totaro

THIRTY-TWO SHORT FILMS ABOUT GLENN GOULD. François Girard, Ontario, 1993, 90 min., color. Confronted with the difficult task of treating the life and career of the eccentric and intensely private Toronto pianist Glenn Gould, François Girard and DON MCKELLAR chose instead to eschew the traditional documentary form in favor of a fragmented depiction of Gould's various passions. *Thirty-Two Short Films About Glenn Gould* combines interviews with friends and critics, dramatic performances by Stratford (Ontario) actor Colm Feore, and writings by Gould, whose definitive treatment of Bach's *Goldberg Variations* provides the structure for the film. An opening "Aria" (a long take of a barren snowscape in which Gould walks toward the camera, moving from extreme long shot to long shot) is followed by thirty "Variations" depicting Gould's love of the north, his radio work, his isolation and death; the film concludes with a reprise, in reverse, of the opening shot. True to Gould's own refusal to perform live, Girard avoids showing Feore performing the music; instead, we see the actor responding to recorded versions of the pieces. The film's structure allows for some truly insightful and innovative scenes. In what are perhaps the most amusing sections of the film, Gould's chronic abuse of prescription medications is depicted through a series of shots of the various drugs with a voice-over (by Feore) reading the side-effects and warnings by which the drugs are described. Elsewhere, the film image is replaced by the optical soundtrack as it recreates the music. *Thirty-Two Short Films About Glenn Gould* won four Genie Awards, including Best Film, Best Director, Best Cinematographer, and Best Editing.

Mitch Parry

R. H. THOMSON. Born 1947, Richmond Hill, Ontario. Actor, writer. R. H. Thomson, the man whom Canadian film historian Gerald Pratley, in 1986, called "easily the most distinguished and versatile actor on stage, screen and television," is probably best known for his role in the popular, long running CBC TV series, "Road to Avonlea." Thomson made his amateur stage debut at age four, and first consciously wanted to be an actor at eight, but he studied mathematics and physics at the University of Toronto before turning to theater school, first in Canada, then England. He was already a well-established stage actor when he took his first film role, which was also a starring one, in Ralph Thomas' made-for-TV *Tyler*. In 1980, while working on *If You Could See What I Hear* (Eric Till), he took a week off to appear in Ralph Thomas' TICKET TO HEAVEN (which was released in 1981). He received Genie nominations as Best Supporting Actor for each role, in successive years, winning in 1983 for playing the eccentric but very supportive foil to Marc Singer's rendition of real-life blind singer Tom Sutherland. Thomson's quirky, comic turn—at the film's opening he enters the shower, fully dressed complete with pipe, to join his friend—is far superior to anything else in *If You Could*. In looking back on this period, Thomson has expressed surprise that such a small amount of work in *Ticket to Heaven* could have had so much impact, and he has followed this example by appearing in films and on television as support for his first acting love, the theater. Nevertheless, he always brings seriousness of purpose to his television and theatrical film roles. For example, in *Heaven and Earth* (Allan Kroeker), he manages to run the gamut of emotions—from despair and depression following his young wife's death to delight in the presence of the "home children" from Wales—while always understating them. Indeed, he is probably the most "Canadian" and self-effacing of great actors and is something of a philosopher/theorist on the subject, opining that there is perhaps a Canadian style of acting: "communal," "rough-edged," with "an indirect quality," "more or less dependent on each moment" and with "a kind of introversion to it," where the actor, most importantly, draws "strength from within, rather than from without." A perennial Genie nominee, most recently for *The Lotus Eaters* (Paul Shapiro, 1993), he is also an accomplished writer and theater director.

FILMS AS ACTOR: *Tyler* (TV), 1977; *L'homme en colère; An American Christmas Carol* (US/Can), 1979; *A Population of One* (TV), 1980; *Surfacing; Ticket to Heaven; Les beaux souvenirs; Escape from Iran: The Canadian Caper* (TV), 1981; *If You Could See What I Hear*, 1982; *The Terry Fox Story*, 1983; *Charlie Grant's War* (TV), 1984; *Samuel Lount; Canada's Sweetheart: The Saga of Hal C. Banks* (TV), 1985; *Heaven on Earth* (TV), 1986; *And Then You Die* (TV); *The First Season; Glory Enough for All*, 1988; *Love and Hate: The Story of Colin and Joanne Thatcher* (TV), 1989; *Defy Gravity*, 1990; *The Lotus Eaters; The Quarrel*, 1993; *Max*, 1994; *Net Worth* (TV), 1995; *The Marriage Bed* (TV), 1996; *Silent Cradle; Twilight of the Ice Nymphs*, 1997.

BIBLIOGRAPHY: Douglas Abel, "Drawing Strength from Within" (interview with R. H. Thomson), *Canadian Theatre Review*, no. 62 (Spring 1990): 42–49; Gerald Pratley, "R. H. Thomson: Acting Like a Canadian" (interview), *Performing Arts* (Spring 1991): 26–28.

Peter Rist

TICKET TO HEAVEN. R. L. Thomas, Ontario, 1981, 107 min., color. *Ticket to Heaven* was a critical and commercial success south of the border; in Canada, the film won four Genie Awards, including Best Film (1982). The film is based on the book *Moonwebs*, which documents the true story of a Montreal man who became entangled in Sun Myung Moon's Unification Church. NICK MANCUSO plays David, a Canadian who goes to California to visit his friend Karl and recover from the recent breakup of his relationship with Sarah (Dixie Seatle). Once he arrives, however, David is quickly absorbed into the cult to which Karl belongs. His best friend Larry (SAUL RUBINEK) and his family (including Sarah) kidnap and eventually "deprogram" him, and the group returns to Canada. Although the film's stylistic qualities are competent and the story itself is engaging, as Marshall Delaney points out, the film "fails to rise above its material." At no point does the film address the problematic issue of deprogramming, but instead presents it exclusively as a healing experience for David and his family. In the end, when the ordeal is over, David is simply welcomed back into the embrace of his family and his—previously unsuccessful—relationship with Sarah. *Ticket to Heaven* was cause for much optimism in the early 1980s, and proved that

Canada could produce narrative films that could successfully compete with their Hollywood counterparts.

BIBLIOGRAPHY: Marshall Delaney, "Ticket to Nowhere," in Feldman, 11–13.

Mitch Parry

MARIE TIFO. Born 1949, Chicoutimi, Quebec. Actor. The release of *LES BONS-DÉBARRAS* in 1980 brought Marie Tifo to prominence in Quebecois cinema. Her Hugo and Genie winning performance as a single mother caught in a complex relationship with her daughter cemented her reputation as a leading actor of the 1980s. Tifo graduated with top honors from Quebec's Conservatoire de Théâtre in 1971, and immediately traveled, spending a year perfecting her craft in Europe. Upon her return, she quickly established her name in the theater before turning to occasional film work (*Stop*, JEAN BEAUDIN, 1971), opening the door to *Les bons débarras*. The short film *Dernier voyage* marked the beginning of a six-year working relationship with director Yves Simoneau that would result in five films. It is during this period that Tifo's style, characterized by restraint and nuance, comes into its own. The evolution of Tifo's on-screen persona reflects the versatility that came through practice. Described as a tomboy in critical reaction to her early work, her roles seem almost angelic by *Les pots cassés* (F. Bouvier, 1993). This versatility reaches its apex in *Le jour "S . . ."* (JEAN PIERRE LEFEBVRE, 1984), in which Tifo plays several characters who appear in Jean-Baptiste's life. The late 1980s brought more recognition through TV appearances ("T'es belle Jeanne," 1988) and occasional theater appearances, yet it appears that Tifo, with only two films in the past seven years, seems content working in her garden with husband actor PIERRE CURZI rather than maintaining her grueling schedule of the eighties.

FILMS AS ACTOR: *Stop*, 1971; *La conquète*, 1973; *Les bons débarras*, 1980; *Dernier voyage* (short), 1981; *Lucien Brouillard; Les yeux rouges*, 1982; *Maria Chapdelaine; Rien qu'un jeu*, 1983; *Le jour "S . . . ,"* 1984; *Pouvoir intime; Les fous de bassan*, 1986; *Charles et François*, 1987; *Kalamazoo; Le marchand de jouets; Popofnikov ou comment se débarrasser d'un Goslave encombrant*, 1988; *Dans le ventre du dragon*, 1989; *Babylone; T'es belle Jeanne*, 1990; *Les pots cassés*, 1993.

Judes Dickey

TIT-COQ Lil' Rooster. René Delacroix and Gratien Gélinas, Montreal, 1953, 101 min., b+w. The best of the early Quebec fiction films, *Tit-Coq* is the brainchild of actor, administrator, and popular playwright Gratien Gélinas, who was coaxed into adapting for the big screen his hugely successful play about the return of a conscripted soldier. The strategy paid off immensely, both at the box office and in reviews. What people in the know responded to were not necessarily the film's formal qualities, because although the rhythm of the editing and the acting are certainly better than those found in other Quebec productions of the time, the quality of the overall direction still suffers from a lack of filmic expertise. Rather, the true value of *Tit-Coq* lies in its courageous attempts at portraying the French Canadian as an urban, modern man with contemporary concerns and a quick tongue for criticism. It is a far cry from the clergy-approved masculine role model to be found in pre-Révolution tranquille fiction films: usually that of a God-fearing farmer and father, content in the hardships of rural life and living in a narrative which excludes all references to the outside world [see LA PETITE AURORE L'ENFANT MARTYRE]; in effect, perpetuating the Duplessis ghettoization of the Quebecois and the "folklorization" of his culture. The latter was something Gélinas fought against vigorously, as attested to by his official complaints to the NFB, which he accused of this particular sin during his stint on its board of directors in 1950. *Tit-Coq* is a testament to Gratien Gélinas' visionary stance. It foreshadows the important role realistic social dramas would play in the cinematographic landscape of Quebec films from the 1960s onward.

BIBLIOGRAPHY: Christiane Tremblay-Daviault (1979); Heinz Weinmann (1992), 267–79.

Johanne Larue

TRANSITIONS. Barbara Sternberg, Ontario, 1982, 10 min., color, 16mm. This early work of Barbara Sternberg reimagines the traditional avant-garde trance film. The psychological state of being/nonbeing is at the center of *Transitions*, which features a woman caught between being awake and asleep. Time and space dissolve into one another. Images of a room are juxtaposed with scenes of a snowy exterior and events suggesting familial relations which may or may not have occurred. The soundtrack offers a complex layering of voices, all of which contribute to the metaphysical terror of being and not being. The critical recognition accorded *Transitions* (awards at the Atlantic Film Festival, 1982, and the Athens Film Festival, 1983) helped establish Sternberg as an important artist among her peers. She has subsequently gone on to produce a prodigious body of experimental work, including *A Trilogy* (1985), *At Present* (1990), and *Through and Through* (1991).

Dave Douglas

V

JOHN VERNON. Born Adolphus Vernon Agopsowicz, 1932, Montreal. Actor. After beginning his acting career in local parlor plays, John Vernon won a scholarship to the Royal Academy of Dramatic Arts (RADA) in London, where he studied alongside Albert Finney, Alan Bates, and Peter O'Toole. He graduated in 1953, and soon after was heard as the voice of Big Brother in the first big screen adaptation of George Orwell's *1984* (M. Anderson, 1954). He returned to Canada, working in the theater before achieving stardom as the coroner Dr. Steve Wojeck in the hit CBS series "Wojeck." He made his on-screen feature film debut in 1963 in *John Cabot—Man of the Renaissance* (M. Parker) and then took a small but memorable role in the NFB's classic story of growing up, *NOBODY WAVED GOODBYE*. Three years later, his screen career took off when he was invited to America to appear opposite Lee Marvin in John Boorman's first American film, *Point Blank* (1967). Vernon has had an international career, working in Europe and the United States as well as in his native Canada. A character actor, his heavy features have often led him to be cast in villainous roles. Regrettably, his Canadian films have been undistinguished. He played the vengeful Ben Kincaid, out to get Sophia Loren as the wife who put him in jail in *Angela* (B. Sagal, 1976). He followed this with the Amicus-style anthology, *The Uncanny*, before appearing in the stalk and slash thriller *Curtains* (R. Ciupka). Though not an impressive film, Vernon takes the plum role of the tyrannical film director Jonathan Stryker (who is credited as director in the film). Vernon's performance goes beyond the limits of the script, relishing every sadistic impulse of his dominating character, bringing much-needed power to the lightweight project. Misused on the screen, yet effortlessly rising above the material, Vernon's most impressive work in Canada has been in television dramas such as *Rat Tales* (P. Campbell, 1987) and *Two Men* (G. Pinsent, 1988). Here he proves that, given the right material, he is more than the equal of his RADA contemporaries.

FILMS AS ACTOR: *Nobody Waved Goodbye,* 1964; *Face Off,* 1971; *Journey,* 1972; *Sweet Movie* (Can/Fr/Ger), 1974; *More Joy in Heaven,* 1975; *A Special Day* (Can/Italy); *The Uncanny* (Can/UK), 1977; *Angela* (Can/US), 1976–78; *It Rained All Night the Day I Left* (Can/Fr/Isr); *Fantastica* (Can/Fr), 1980; *Crunch* (Can/US); *Heavy Metal* (voice only), 1981; *Curtains,* 1983; *Blood of Others* (Can/Fr), 1984; *Coast of Dreams; Louisiane,* 1984; *Mob Story; Rat Tails* (TV); *Time Pilot,* 1987; *Two Men* (TV), 1988; *Wojeck—Out of the Fire* (TV), 1990; *Paris or Somewhere* (TV); *Sodbusters* (TV), 1994.

Simon Brown

VIDEODROME. David Cronenberg, Toronto, 1983, 87* min., color. Arguably the finest amalgam of science fiction/horror made since the heyday of the 1950s, *Videodrome* is also quintessentially Canadian in presenting a flawed yet sympathetic central male character who fails to triumph over adversity while representing a dystopic McLuhanesque world of dominating communications technology, where "the medium is the [lethal] message." It is also director DAVID CRONENBERG's most complex work, based on the last original script he would write for himself. Max Renn (James Woods), part-owner of a Toronto television station, Civic TV, searches for "tough" pornography and finds scenes of torture allegedly transmitted through satellite from Malaysia. But this "videodrome" show (which he learns is taped, possibly in Pittsburgh) contains a signal which gives the viewer a brain tumor, causing hallucinations and enabling the victim to be controlled by the functionaries of Spectacular Optical (who make "glasses for the 3rd World" and "nuclear warheads"). Renn is literally programmed by inserting a video cassette in his stomach. Along the way he is seduced by the image of Nicki Brand (Deborah Harry), but in the end becomes the pawn of the Cathode Ray Mission, led by Bianca O'Blivion (Sonia Smits) with the rallying cry "death to Videodrome, long live the 'new flesh.' " Although the camera mostly observes Max objectively, *Videodrome* is intentionally constructed as a first-person film: he is in every single scene in the film; occasionally we get perceptually subjective, point-of-view shots, as seen through Renn's eyes, but always we experience the world as he does, including his hallucinations. The difficulty of the film is experienced here, in its structure. As viewers, we are unaccustomed to seeing visions, dreams, or hallucinations unless they are marked as such. In *Videodrome,* we can never be sure of the "reality" of the image. According to Bianca's father, Professor O'Blivion, "there is nothing real outside our perception of reality," and the film represents this view while progressively confusing the veracity of earlier narrative events. For example, toward the end it is revealed that Nicki had possibly been killed on "Videodrome" before Max had even met her on a TV talk show! Like the best horror films, *Videodrome* simultaneously attracts and repulses the viewer, seducing one to go

*Another version, released outside North America, and which may be the latest "director's cut," is listed at eighty-nine minutes, while a censored version for American television, which contains additional footage—much of which extends Deborah Harry's role—runs six minutes longer. The film was shot in 1981, but not released in Canada and the United States until January 1983.

where one would rather not go, while brilliantly pulling one outside of the action to reflect on the powers and manipulations of media technology under corporate control. The special Cronenberg touch here is in giving tangible, physical form to the workings of the mind, the "new flesh," where television sets and video-tapes become living, organic entities, and by merging humans and machines, where Max can be "played" like a VCR.

BIBLIOGRAPHY: Tim Lucas, "The Image as Virus: The Filming of *Videodrome*," in Handling (1983), 149–58; Chris Rodley, 93–108.

Peter Rist

LA VIE HEUREUSE DE LÉOPOLD Z. The Merry World of Léopold Z. Gilles Carle, ONF (Montreal), 1963–65, 69 min., b+w. Somewhat in the manner of GILLES GROULX (*LE CHAT DANS LE SAC*, 1964), GILLES CARLE transformed a short documentary project in order to direct his first feature-length fiction film. Sensing that he was too restricted by the documentary form, Carle found in *La vie heureuse de Léopold Z*. the opportunity to demonstrate his undeniable talent for storytelling. Suffused with a contagious good humor, the film presents a gallery of characters, each one more colorful than the last, and contains some of the most savory dialogue Quebec cinema has produced. *Léopold* recounts the working day of a snow remover who not only must satisfy the demands of his boss and his wife but must also finish his work in time to hear his son singing at Midnight Mass. While he sheds light on Léopold's submissive nature, Carle never looks down on his character, and shows sympathy for his plight until the end of the film. In any event, Léopold (GUY L'ÉCUYER) is not completely ignorant about his condition. He doesn't pass up the opportunity, when the time comes, to make fun of his boss, and imagines himself to be on-track to having an affair with another woman. Like many Quebecois films, *La vie heureuse de Léopold Z*. presents a very skillful articulation of the techniques of *cinéma direct* in a fictional context. Carle even allows himself to thumb his nose at the documentary through the use of a self-mocking voice-over narration. The film won the Grand Prix for the best feature film at the Festival du cinéma canadien (1965).

BIBLIOGRAPHY: Carol Faucher and Michel Houle.

Louis Goyette

LA VIE RÊVÉE Dream Life. Mireille Dansereau, Quebec, 1972, 85 min., color. Produced by ACPAV (of which Mireille Dansereau was one of the founding members), *La vie rêvée* occupies a special place in the history of Quebecois cinematography, since it was the first fiction feature made in the private sector to have been directed by a woman. The film relates the friendship between two free and happy young women, working in the world of advertising. Virginie (Véronique Le Flaguais) is direct and pragmatic, whereas Isabelle (Liliane Lemaître-Auger) is very much a dreamer and naive. The object of her dreams is Jean-Jacques (Jean-François Guité), married and father of an excessive family. With Virginie's help (she lends her apartment), Isabelle spends a night with Jean-Jacques, only to discover in the morning that he is nothing more than a petit-bourgeois type, and much too stuck-up for her. More than being a criticism of a consumer society (the other "dream life" of the film's title), Dansereau's film seduces by its portrait of two women discovering each other in a friendship more sincere than one that they could find with a man. Le Flaguais and Lemaître-Auger were excellent in the two principal roles. *La vie rêvée* also marked the film debuts of the actors Marc Messier and LOUISE PORTAL.

BIBLIOGRAPHY: Louise Carrière, "À propos des films fait par des femmes au Québec," *Copie Zéro*, no. 11 (1981): 44–51.

Louis Goyette

LE VIEUX PAYS OÙ RIMBAUD EST MORT The Old Country Where Rimbaud Died. Jean Pierre Lefebvre, Canada (Montreal)/France, 1977, 113 min., color. Typical of the kind of limited exposure that JEAN PIERRE LEFEBVRE's films receive outside their own country, *Le vieux pays où Rimbaud est mort* was shown for two days only at the Thalia Repertory Cinema in New York City, in November 1984, on a double bill with his later *LES FLEURS SAUVAGES*. Yet both films had received their world premieres at the Cannes International Film Festival, with *Le vieux pays* being in competition. *Le vieux pays* was, atypically for Lefebvre, a relatively expensive film, costing slightly over $350,000, mainly because it was a co-production with France. The director's chief co-worker was Mireille Amiel, who helped write the screenplay. Basically, she wrote for the French characters and Lefebvre wrote for the Quebecois Abel (MARCEL SABOURIN), a visitor to the "old country." The film's narrative is episodic in keeping with the picaresque nature of Abel's wandering journey to observe and listen. Many people that he meets are puzzled by his French accent, thinking him to be Belgian, Algerian, or even Cambodian, and at one point he claims to have visited France "to see if there were still Frenchmen in France—to see if they resembled me." Early in the film, in the Parisian Chez Charles bar, a shooting and editing style is adopted which becomes a pattern for the film as a whole. Abel is composing, aloud, a letter to his father. He is seated at a table and facing the camera, which is angled to the rear wall at 90°. It is as if he is responding to an invisible interviewer. Intercut shots of other characters in the bar provide illustrations for Abel's letter which together present mostly a comical and negative image of French culture. In one shot, three soldiers raise their glasses. The first toasts France, the second himself, and the third utters an obscenity. By contrast, the scene ends with a cut to an art gallery, an altogether more positive image of French culture. It is clear that stylistic decisions made in the film were very deliberate. Somewhat like Godard in its anti-illusionism, *Le vieux pays'* long take style more pertinently alludes to Bertolt Brecht's theory of "epic theater" where the characters directly address the audience, but where the intended audience response is still emotionally charged. The film begins and ends on an aerial view, apparently of ice floes, merging white and blue. Throughout the film, the color white has been associated with Quebec (a frozen expanse and a clean slate), and Abel's final visit to Cassis ends on the Mediterranean Sea bleached out by the sun—in Rimbaud's words: "swallowed" by it—momentarily linking the two "nations" which for Abel have come to seem so distinct.

BIBLIOGRAPHY: Susan Barrowclough; Peter Harcourt (1981), 77–87, 138–49; Peter Rist, "*The Old Country Where Rimbaud Died*," in Magill (1985), 2260–65.

                                                                    Peter Rist

THE VIKING. George Melford, United States/Newfoundland, 1931, 71 min., b+w. *The Viking* is not, strictly speaking, a Canadian film: it was produced by a company incorporated in Delaware, and many of the principals involved were American. (Also, at the time it was made, Newfoundland was a separate country, not becoming part of the Dominion until 1949.) But the producer and prime mover of the project, American-born explorer Varick Frissell, had already made short films in Labrador (*The Lure of Labrador*, 1925) and Newfoundland (*The Swilin' Racket*, 1927–28), places he had come to love. The latter film gave him his interest in the seal hunt, and he determined to return to make a full-length film, entitled *Vikings of the Ice Fields*. Paramount, who had put up $100,000 in financing for the project, insisted that it be a dramatic film utilizing Hollywood personnel. Frissell hired a director, George Melford, who had experience with Canadian subjects (*Behold My Wife*, 1920; *A Wise Fool*, 1921; *The Flame of the Yukon*, 1926) and who was educated at McGill University in Montreal. He had also directed many action dramas including some set at sea (*The Sea Wolf*, 1920; *Moran of the Lady Letty*, 1922), but despite these experiences, he was unable to make the performances or the script convincing. Only the ship's captain, Bob Bartlett, and his men, and the documentary-like sequences on the ice floes saved the project. The latter, shot by Alexander Penrod, who had filmed the excellent whale-hunting scenes of *Down to the Sea in Ships* (1922), were remarkable. Accompanied by the sounds of howling wind, breaking ice, and the creaking timbers of the *Viking*, the images of ice-breaking, with men rushing from one side of the ship to the other, and men (who couldn't swim) jumping from one block of ice to another on huge waves are frighteningly memorable. Frissell and Penrod were even able to get the film's audience to sympathize with the object of the hunt: the seals. We hear the cries of a pup for its mother as it escapes a rifle shot. But the bravery of the men overwhelms the film's forward-looking ecological aspect. *The Viking* stands as a testament to the spirit of exploration and man's attempt to conquer the wilderness. But, ironically, after Frissell was able to convince Paramount that the documentary nature of the film should dominate, with the company financing a second voyage in March 1931, he, Penrod, and twenty-six others, mostly crew, were killed in an explosion on the *Viking*. A prologue, read by Sir Wilfred Grenfell, was added to the film in tribute to the victims of the tragedy, especially Frissell.

BIBLIOGRAPHY: Peter Morris (1978), 206–15; Kevin Brownlow, 541–45.

Peter Rist

24 HEURES OU PLUS . . . 24 Hours or More. Gilles Groulx, (Montreal) ONF, 1971–72 (rel. 1977), 113 min., color and b+w. During the politically troubled years at the turn of the seventies, it seems that the ONF was prone to give with one hand and take away with the other. *24 heures ou plus* . . . , GILLES GROULX's most ambitious and controversial film, was one of several casualties of state censorship. After having made the post-production of Groulx's Marxist social fresco excruciatingly difficult, then-film commissioner Sydney Newman shelved the documentary upon its completion, saying, "It would be inexcusable for the NFB to distribute a film which advocates the complete rejection of the social and political system now in place in Canada" (my translation of J. Lacoursière and H.-A. Huguet, *Québec 72–73: Bilan* [Montreal: Fidès, 1973]). We can measure Newman's overreaction and lack of respect for artistic freedom by comparing his position to that of his 1975 replacement, André Lamy, who lifted the ban in 1976 after Groulx agreed to cut out two words from one sentence, "democracy" and "capitalism." Although the public was finally allowed to view his opus, so much time had elapsed since its creation that the film simply did not resonate the way it was meant to. The fight had been fought and the state of things in Quebec had changed, not as radically as the filmmakers would have hoped for but enough to satisfy the discontent. As with *ON EST AU COTON*, the long wait had somewhat diffused the potency of the work without rendering Groulx's discourse obsolete. It was and remains an enlightening film on Quebec's social mores, the tensions between labor and management, economic and cultural stress, and the ever present question of national identity. The structure of the film is built on the principle of stream-of-consciousness, but Eisensteinian intellectual montage is used to link the many disparate segments. The film might look and feel like a free-styling exposé, but its mechanisms are maniacally precise.

BIBLIOGRAPHY: Jean-Pierre Bastien; Christine Noël, "Gilles Groulx et les médias," *24 Images*, no. 75 (December 1994-January 1995): 20–25.

Johanne Larue

VOLCANO: AN INQUIRY INTO THE LIFE AND DEATH OF MALCOLM LOWRY. Donald Brittain, NFB, 1976, 99 min., color. For fourteen years, during the writing of *Under the Volcano*, Malcolm Lowry lived in Vancouver (which he described as "the most hopeless of all cities of the lost") and Dollarton, then a rural squatters' community ten miles outside Vancouver. Of his stay in Dollarton, Lowry would later say that it was the only time he had been truly happy during an otherwise chaotic life. *Volcano: An Inquiry into the Life and Death of Malcolm Lowry* traces that life, from Lowry's traumatic childhood in England, to New York, Mexico, Los Angeles, British Columbia, and, finally, back to England, where the writer died an apparent suicide. The film uses old photographs and interviews with people who knew Lowry—especially his wife Margerie, to whom *Volcano* is dedicated—and intersperses these with contemporary location footage (often slightly out of focus, as though to recreate Lowry's drunkenness), accompanied by the voice of Richard Burton reading from Lowry's letters and from *Under the Volcano*. The film is, one could argue, perhaps the most personal of DONALD BRITTAIN's films; it is certainly the one in which his voice-over narration, with its world-weary, slightly sardonic tone, is most convincing, most appropriate. *Volcano* is a compelling and moving documentary, and was nominated for the best documentary Oscar in 1977.

Mitch Parry

LA VRAIE NATURE DE BERNADETTE The True Nature of Bernadette. Gilles Carle, Quebec, 1972, 96 min., color. The cherished child of many Quebecois *cinéphiles, La vraie nature de Bernadette* also marks "the first spectacular breakthrough of a Quebecois film in France" (Pierre Véronneau). Bernadette Brown, disenchanted with her role as spouse and housewife, leaves her husband as well as the pollution of Montreal in order to relocate in the countryside with her son Yannick; she is convinced that life in the country will be much more peaceful. She soon finds out that the country is far from being the paradise she imagined it to be, as she falls victim to exploitation and the mistrust of the villagers. Once again, GILLES CARLE demonstrates his skills as a storyteller. But beyond its purely comic aspects, *La vraie nature* is equally a virulent satire of Quebec manners of the time. Carle displays an implacable lucidity in taking as his target the myth of the return to the land and in exploring the eccentricities of Quebec society. Avoiding a nostalgic evocation of the rural environment, Carle chooses instead to depict a world in perpetual conflict, which the arrival of a woman from the city further disrupts. In effect, the liberal morals of Bernadette are rather badly seen in an area where the Catholic religion has always had a solid foundation. Nevertheless, when she succeeds in making water flow from a dry well, the villagers, convinced that she has performed a miracle, begin to pray in front of her house, making Bernadette into a saint. It is all rural Catholic bigotry which Carle ridicules here. As well as the quality of the film's dialogue, one can also find in *La vraie nature* the luminous performance of MICHELINE LANCTÔT as Bernadette, her first role in the cinema.

BIBLIOGRAPHY: Gilles Carle, "*La vraie nature de Bernadette*: Un western religieux?," *Cinéma Québec*, no. 9 (1972); Carle and Jean-Pierre Tadros, "Rejoindre le mythe par le quotidien," *Cinéma Québec*, no. 9 (1972).

Louis Goyette

W

WAITING FOR FIDEL. Michael Rubbo, NFB, 1974, 58 min., color. Michael Rubbo's *Waiting for Fidel* is an often hilarious documentary with an intriguing premise. Having been told that he will be granted an interview with Fidel Castro, Rubbo makes his way to Cuba with Joey Smallwood (the socialist former premier of Newfoundland) and Geoff Stirling (a conservative entrepreneur who owns a chain of radio and television stations), who also expect an audience with Castro. This unlikely trio waits in vain for an interview that never occurs, and the film documents their exploration of Cuba while they wait. Like many Rubbo documentaries, *Waiting for Fidel* features the director onscreen as an inquiring, self-doubting investigator, and calls into question the purpose and veracity of the documentary form itself. For example, one hilarious episode features an onscreen argument between Stirling, who has money invested in Rubbo's film, and Rubbo himself, who is forced to defend his own time-consuming and apparently aimless methods of filmmaking. Equally charming are the many encounters in the film between Smallwood, the old-style socialist, and numerous Cubans who extoll the virtues of the new communism. As a film diarist, Rubbo invigorates the documentary form by combining insightful observation with a humorous critique of the limits of that form—the impossibility of avoiding the influence of the filmmaker on his subject and of presenting a truly objective view of reality.

BIBLIOGRAPHY: David Denby, "How to Make a Castro Movie Without Castro," *New York Times* (November 16, 1975): D15; Jay Cocks, "Havana Bound" *Time* (March 15, 1976).

Helen and Paul Salmon

WALKING. Ryan Larkin, (Montreal) NFB, 1968, 5 min., color. *Walking* is a good representative film of its director Ryan Larkin's style, but also of the tendency of the NFB to continue NORMAN MCLAREN's legacy in producing experimental animated films far from the Disneyesque realist norm. Larkin, who studied painting and sculpture at Montreal's École du Musée des Beaux-Arts, was encouraged to be a film animator after attending a workshop with McLaren. On his first films, *Cityscape* and *Syrinx* (1965), Larkin worked in charcoal. In the second of these, strangely beautiful expressionist, grotesque figures transform to the music of Debussy. In his third film, *Walking*, Larkin seems simply to be playing with the animated representation of human figures running and walking, and yet his "sketches" richly evoke a dynamic changing, youthful world. In its use of psychedelic flashing from one animation technique to another (e.g., charcoal drawing, color wash), its use of rock music, and the appearance of its flamboyantly dressed and coiffured characters, *Walking* is very much of its period, the 1960s. Surprisingly, as a film with no story, it was even one of only three films nominated for the 1969 Oscar for Best Short Subject: Cartoon. As such it was the seventh NFB animated short so honored, beginning in 1952 with *The Romance of Transportation*, a tradition that may have helped to inspire the category change from "Cartoon" to "Animated Film" in 1971; for NFB films were rarely "cartoons." While working on his next film, *Street Music* (1972), Larkin began teaching in British Columbia. He stopped making animated films in the mid-1970s and turned more and more to painting and the other arts.

Peter Rist

WARRENDALE. Allan King, Toronto, 1967, 100 min, b+w. ALLAN KING's award-winning documentary embodies both the promise and the pitfalls of "direct cinema" in its purest form. The subject of the film is an experimental home for emotionally disturbed youths in Ontario. The home attempted to replace drug therapy by close personal contact with the children, and with "holding sessions" (physically containing the children with the body of the therapist) during periods of emotional duress. The film follows an episodic structure, which culminates in a scene where the children are informed of the death of the Warrendale cook. Here, an extended scene features some of the children we have come to know in a period of extreme duress. Longtime Fred Wiseman cinematographer William Brayne's camera work rivets the viewer by remaining in close-up for the majority of the film. The testing of the emotional commitment of the therapists is evident throughout the day's activities. The absence of any voice-over or subtitles to identify the participants in the film forces viewers to immerse themselves in the moment, but also denies an explanatory potential. We can only speculate on the various conditions afflicting the children, and the value of the treatment remains questionable. Beyond such questions of the film's experiential power one is left with the ethical question, "Does the film violate the privacy of the individual children?" The film, originally intended for presentation on television, was pulled from broadcast by the CBC (due to bad language and the film's controversial content). King persevered and released the film commercially, winning both critical acclaim (two awards at Cannes, CFA Film of the

Year Award) and a respectable box office. Thirty years after the fact the film aired on public television in Ontario.

BIBLIOGRAPHY: Peter Harcourt, "Allan King: Filmmaker," in Feldman, 69–79.

Dave Douglas

WATCHING FOR THE QUEEN. David Rimmer, British Columbia, 1973, 11 min., b+w, silent. *Watching for the Queen* is, perhaps, the quintessential DAVID RIMMER film. On the one hand, it is determinedly image-based, and, in being structured around the principle of rephotography with the single frame as the basic unit of film (rather than the shot), it fits P. Adams Sitney's formula for "structural film." On the other hand, the film's subject, a crowd watching something off screen—presumably, Queen Elizabeth II—leads us to cultural analysis, opening the film's context much wider. Rimmer took a short section of unidentified found footage and step printed it, initially to so slow a f.p.s. rate that movement is imperceptible, gradually increasing the rate until it is projected at normal speed (24 f.p.s.). Eventually, we can clearly observe a large group of men and women, filling the frame (and tiered as if standing on terraces), lifting their heads to view something happening slightly to the right of the camera. We are never shown anything else, so that, knowing only the film's title, we surmise that the devoted Canadian subjects have been waiting to see the Queen of England. If one is not totally alienated from the beginning in having to view an apparently still photograph over a long duration, one begins to marvel at how much there is to see in such a short piece of "movie." We start to scan the image and pick up on individuals in the crowd, noticing their attire and varied movements. While questioning Canadians' apparent keen interest in British royalty, we reflect on the magic of the cinema.

Peter Rist

WAVELENGTH. Michael Snow, United States (New York City)/Ontario, 1967, 45 min., color. Screenings of *Wavelength* have probably generated more mixed emotions—frustration, boredom, exhilaration, and awe (sometimes in the same spectator)—than any other Canadian film. *Wavelength* has also been a challenge for film critics, who have all too often incorrectly described it as a "continuous" zoom taken from a single fixed camera position. The film begins at the widest setting of the zoom lens and concludes at its shortest, but this trajectory is neither continuous (but rather intermittent), nor taken from a fixed position (but rather from slightly altered camera positions). On the soundtrack we hear (among many other things) an aural equivalent to the zoom lens shot(s), a sine wave which goes from its lowest note (50 cycles per second) to its highest note (12,000 cycles per second). The events that occur in between (too complex to adequately describe here), both formal and "narrative," give *Wavelength* its varied philosophical and cinematic meanings. There are four linked human events in the film: (1) A woman enters, followed by two men carrying a bookcase. (2) Two women enter the loft; one turns the radio on, then off; the other shuts the window. (3) A man staggers into the frame and falls onto the floor. (4) A woman enters and makes a phone call to report the fallen man. The events trigger a pretense of "narrative," but our concentration soon changes from an interest in the meaning of the events to an interest in the teleological purpose of the zoom: where is it heading? In *Wavelength* cinematic interpretations (as an examination of filmic narrative; as an ontology of filmic time/space) coexist alongside non-filmic philosophical interpretations. The philosophical meaning most often ascribed is to read *Wavelength* as a metaphor for consciousness. John Belton notes that "every zoom makes an epistemological statement, contemplating man's relationship not with the world itself but with his idea or consciousness of it." In addition, the many textural changes in the course of the film—subtle and radical color changes, exposure changes, black and white shots, clear images, negative images, light flares, day to night changes, visible splices, and different film stocks—recall David Hume's belief that the mind is but a "bundle of perceptions." Snow's own description of the film as a "summation of . . . religious inklings" supports a reading of the zoom's trajectory, from a view of the loft to a full frame view of the ocean wave in the wall photo, as a transcendental journey where the spectator is "carried" from one space/time to another. *Wavelength* has a rich critical legacy, but is best understood through a phenomenological, sensuous, "Sontagian" viewing experience. *Wavelength* won the top prize at the Fourth International Experimental Film Exposition at Knokke-le-Zoute, 1967.

BIBLIOGRAPHY: Bruce Elder, "Michael Snow's *Wavelength*," in Feldman and Nelson, 308–323; Regina Cornwall, 60–79.

Donato Totaro

AL(BERT) WAXMAN. Born 1935, Toronto. Actor, director. Al Waxman has had a long and prolific career. With his instantly recognizable ubiquitous visage it is sometimes hard to remember his exact roles. Waxman has enjoyed much success as an actor in both film and television. He began his long journey into the cinematic arts with a role in *The Last Gunfighter* (1959) and has continued acting in film to this day. In the late 1960s Waxman began his directing career with his short film *Tviggy*, a story about the life of a Jewish model. In 1974 he directed a soft-core porn movie, *My Pleasure Is My Business*, which met with limited success. However, the seventies were good to Waxman, who hit it big with his role as Larry King on CBC television's long running (111 episodes) situation comedy series "King of Kensington," about a community-minded, avuncular working-class guy and his neigborhood. Waxman's most memorable role came in 1980 in Louis Malle's *Atlantic City*, where he played Alfie, a pumped-up, always smiling cocaine dealer. In 1982 he had U.S. television success with his role as Lt. Bert Samuels on the hit female cop show "Cagney and Lacey," which ran for six years. Waxman continues to direct and act in many

B films for both theatrical and television release, hitting a questionable low point with his role in *Iron Eagle IV* (1995).

THEATRICAL FILMS AS ACTOR: *The Last Gunfighter*, 1959; *Isabel*, 1968; *The Last Act of Martin Weston* (Can/Czech), 1970; *A Star Is Lost!*, 1973; *Child Under a Leaf; Sunday in the Country*, 1974; *The Heatwave Lasted Four Days*, 1973–75; *The Clown Murders*, 1975; *Wild Horse Hank*, 1978; *Atlantic City* (Can/Fr); *Double Negative*, 1980; *Heavy Metal* (voice only), 1981; *Class of 1984; Spasms*, 1982; *Meatballs III*, 1987; *Malarek; The Return of Ben Casey; Switching Channels*, 1988; *Mob Story*, 1990; *Operation Golden Phoenix* (Can/Lebanon), 1994; *Iron Eagle IV*, 1995; *The Assignment*, 1997.

FILMS AS DIRECTOR: *Tviggy*, 1969; *The Crowd Inside* (also scr., act., prod.), 1971; *My Pleasure Is My Business*, 1974; *The Abortion Issue*, 1980; *Cop; Tulips* (also act.), 1981; *White Light*, 1991; *The Great Diamond Robbery*, 1992.

Rob Cotterill

ANNE WHEELER. Born 1946, Edmonton, Alberta. Director, writer. Anne Wheeler graduated from the University of Alberta with a mathematics degree and held a variety of jobs, traveling the world before she started working in the film industry. Hired by Filmwest she wrote and directed her first project, *Grandmother*, in 1975. This documentary about the history of prairie women won nine Alberta Motion Picture Industry Awards. She produced a number of films at the NFB's North West studio, including *Augusta, Priory: The Only Home I've Got*, winner of the 1979 Genie for best short film; *Teach Me to Dance*, a docudrama which won a diploma of honor at the Milano Film Festival; and *A War Story*, based on her father's World War II diaries as a POW in a Japanese camp. Wheeler's first feature-length film, *Loyalties*, co-written by Sharon Riis, explores a friendship between two women of different cultural and economic backgrounds. Similarly, *Cowboys Don't Cry* focuses on a father-son relationship decimated by personal tragedy. While Wheeler's most recent works explore the family as the locus of personal struggle, they also capture specific moments in Canadian history. *BYE BYE BLUES* was inspired by the experiences of Wheeler's mother in the prairies during World War II, and *The War Between Us* chronicles a Japanese family's internment by the Canadian government. Although Wheeler's films often focus on an individual woman's struggle for survival in the world, her work is integrally a reflection of her native province, Alberta. This explains why her characters and narratives are informed by both the physical landscape and the social climate that surrounds them. Anne Wheeler, who has been given the Order of Canada and is an honorary member of Women in Film in Los Angeles, Toronto, and Vancouver, continues to live and work in her hometown, Edmonton.

FILMS AS DIRECTOR: *Great Grandmother* (also cinematography), 1975; *Augusta*, 1976; *Happily Unmarried*, 1977; *Teach Me to Dance*, 1978; *A War Story*, 1981; *Change of Heart* (TV), 1984; *One's a Heifer* (TV); *To Set Our House in Order* (TV); *Loyalties*

(also scr.), 1985; *Cowboys Don't Cry*, 1988; *Bye Bye Blues* (also scr., prod.), 1989; *Angel-Square* (also writer), 1991; *Other Women's Children* (TV); *The Diviners*, 1993; *The War Between Us* (also scr.), 1995; *The Diana Kilmury Story* (also scr., prod.), 1996.
Alice Black

WHISPERING CITY. See LA FORTERESSE/WHISPERING CITY

WHO HAS SEEN THE WIND. Allan King, Saskatchewan, 1977, 103 min., color. ALLAN KING combined with Patricia Watson to adapt W. O. Mitchell's 1947 novel for the screen. The story centers on the world as seen by a young boy growing up in Saskatchewan. Young Brian O'Connal (Brian Painchaud) learns about life as he witnesses the daily life of his community. Brian befriends a local boy who is the son of the "Old" Ben (Jose Ferrer), a town drunk, who is himself a truant. He witnesses the pious posturing of the town's upstanding citizen watchdog, Mrs. Abercrombie, and is abused by the town's repressive schoolteacher, Miss Macdonald (Patricia Hamilton). With the death of his father (GORDON PINSENT), who had been his confidant, Brian spends a night out on the prairie amid a violent storm in a sod hut with the Young Ben (Douglas Junor) and a farmer. Emerging after the storm, Brian returns home with a growing understanding of the world around him. The strong performance of Painchaud, along with the talented production staff, many of whom had worked with King on numerous documentary productions, results in a triumphant adaptation of Mitchell's novel. Critically well received, the film went on to be the largest Canadian box office success in 1977–78.

BIBLIOGRAPHY: Peter Harcourt, "Allan King: Filmmaker," in Feldman, 69–79.
Dave Douglas

JOYCE WIELAND. Born 1931, Toronto. In April 1987 the Art Gallery of Ontario mounted their very first exhibition of work by a living female Canadian artist, Joyce Wieland. More than ten years after she had virtually stopped making films, her art would finally emerge out of the shadow cast by her former husband, MICHAEL SNOW. Both of Wieland's English immigrant parents died when she was young, a trauma which probably contributed to strong memories of childhood and childlike images in her adult work. At Toronto's Central Technical School in the mid-1940s Wieland was able to concentrate her studies in art, and was influenced by teacher Doris McArthy as a role model. In the 1950s, through her membership in the Toronto Film Society, she became increasingly involved in the medium, especially animation. In 1956 she married Snow, and in the late 1950s and early 1960s her painting and drawing developed strong sexual connotations. Her bold, sometimes explicit, often comical depictions of male sexuality horrified Toronto's (predominantly male) art establishment, but her work received more favorable, open responses after she moved to New York with her husband in 1962. Her filmmaking then began to dominate her interests, but here, the experimental film establishment tended to underappreciate her work, especially in relation to the formal rigor of Snow's. Retrospectively, her films of the 1960s are now viewed as importantly "pre-feminist" (Kay Armatage), and in producing "culturally constructed ways of seeing," following Shirley Clarke's earlier New York example of experimental filmmaking (Lauren Rabinovitz). The years 1967 through 1969 were a key period of Wieland's filmmaking. *Hand Tinting* provides a good example of her use of repetitious ritual to draw visual attention to the restrictions on women in society, while the playful *Catfood* is both charming and sinister in its depiction of her subject, cats' relationship with dead fish. Political and naive, intellectual and childlike attitudes and structures were somehow combined in RAT LIFE AND DIET IN NORTH AMERICA. The period also saw the production of her first feature, *Reason over Passion*, a kind of political travelogue, which makes the audience vividly aware of time and space—the temporality of the film medium and the vastness of Canada—through simultaneously attending to form and content. In July 1971 Wieland was honored by Canada's National Gallery with its very first one-woman show, "True Patriot Love." Typically for a Canadian artist in only being recognized in her own country after acclaim elsewhere, Wieland returned to live in Toronto in the same year. Her work became less humorous and ironic and more politically engaged as she became a leader of feminist art. In one of the most unusual films imaginable, *Pierre Vallières*, we see only the Quebec radical's mustachioed mouth for thirty-three minutes speaking separatist and feminist platitudes, inviting the viewer to collapse male and female (bodies and ideas). Unfortunately, the failure of her second feature film, THE FAR SHORE, to enjoy either popular or critical success when it was first released in 1976 seemed to lead Wieland to abandon filmmaking. But this film and her work as a whole are now regarded more positively than ever before.

FILMS AS DIRECTOR (16MM SHORTS, UNLESS NOTED): *Tea in the Garden*, 1958; *A Salt in the Park*, 1959; *Larry's Recent Behaviour* (8mm), 1963; *Patriotism, Part I; Patriotism, Part II; Peggy's Blue Skylight* (8mm), 1964; *Water Sark*, 1964–65; *Sailboat; 1933*, 1967; *Hand Tinting; Catfood*, 1967–68; *Reason over Passion/La raison avant la passion* (feature), 1967–69; *Dripping Water* (co-dir., Michael Snow), 1969; *Pierre Vallières*, 1972; *Rat Life and Diet in North America*, 1968–73; *Solidarity*, 1973; *The Far Shore* (feature), 1976; *A & B in Ontario* (co-dir., Hollis Frampton), 1967–84; *Birds at Sunrise*, 1972–85.

BIBLIOGRAPHY: Lauren Rabinovitz, "The Films of Joyce Wieland," in Rabinovitz (1987), 117–79; Kay Armatage, "Joyce Wieland," in Kuhn and Radstone, 425–26.

Peter Rist

A WINTER TAN. Jackie Burroughs, Louise Clark, John Frizzell, John Walker, and Aerlyn Weissman, Toronto, 1987, 91 min., color. During the anti-censorship struggles in the province of Ontario in 1984, the prominent Canadian actor JACKIE BURROUGHS read excerpts of graphic, sexually descriptive letters written from Mexico by Maryse Holder, a New York feminist. Louise Clark and John

Frizzell, who were present at the readings, began discussions with Burroughs and film directors John Walker and Aerlyn Weissman with a view to collectively making a filmed version of Holder's posthumously published book, *Give Sorrow Words*. They filmed in Mexico during the early winter months of 1987, while unusually deciding to share the directing credit. The resulting film, *A Winter Tan*, like the one-woman show it was originally planned to be, finds Jackie Burroughs, playing Maryse Holder, on screen virtually nonstop. Often she talks directly to the camera as a privileged witness, and sometimes she speaks to an on-screen observer, usually her fellow American "tourist" Pam (Anita Olanick), who remains totally silent. Periodically we hear Burroughs' voice, off-screen, but always, we assume that we are listening to Holder's letters. The film is framed with her friend Edith (Diane D'Aquila), a Toronto resident, talking off-right, as if in a documentary film responding to an interviewer. She begins the tale of Holder's passionate self-destructive journey through young Mexican men, by way of liquor and cigarettes. Her mood swings from euphoric love of all things Mexican to despair and self-hatred in seconds, as she struggles to be an independent, mature woman and find ecstatic love in a foreign land. *A Winter Tan* is a tour de force for Burroughs, and one of the most critically divisive Canadian films ever made. In the same way that Jonathan Demme's *Silence of the Lambs* (1991) could be simultaneously praised for its feminism and condemned for homophobia, *Tan* was admired as feminist investigation and criticized for its potentially racist and ethnocentric approach. And whereas film critic Robin Wood found Burroughs' performance to be embarrassing to watch, the *Village Voice*'s J. Hoberman found it enthralling—"she's less a bird of prey than some pterodactyl of paradise"—and put the film on his 1988 ten-best list.

BIBLIOGRAPHY: J. Hoberman, "Bad Girls," *Village Voice* (October 18, 1988): 57; Robin Wood, "Towards a Canadian International Cinema," *CineACTION!*, no. 16 (May 1989): 59–63.

Peter Rist

***WOMAN AGAINST THE WORLD*.** David Selman, British Columbia, 1937, 65 min., b+w. *Woman Against the World* is one of the most remarkable very low budget (sub-B) films made anywhere in the 1930s, evidence of which suggests that Kenneth J. Bishop's "quota quickies" made for the British market are worthy of reappraisal. Edgar Edwards' script packs all kinds of drama into the film's short running time, especially the first half, in which Anna (Alice Moore) and Johnny (Edgar Edwards) fall in love and get married secretly, angering her miserable father (George Hallet), who kicks him out; Johnny is shot and killed by thieves while working as a night watchman in the anonymous "city"; cut to Anna with (equally miserable) Aunt Freida (Ethel Reese-Burns) wondering what to do about her pregnancy; after learning that Freida has sent the child away for anonymous adoption, Anna accidentally kills her aunt and is jailed for manslaughter. David Selman's direction of these scenes and the transitions between them is remarkably efficient: eliding action (e.g., Johnny going to the city and getting a job), using letters and newspaper headlines to convey information, making good use of limited sets and locations (which could be anywhere in North America). *Woman* slows down sufficiently in its second half to concentrate on Anna's building strength of character—searching for her child, Betty Jane, forging a friendship with another woman, Patsy (Collette Lyons)—while the film's ending is truly remarkable. After gaining parole and finding Betty Jane, she inadvertently kidnaps her, and following another trial where she is acquitted, Betty Jane rejects her birth mother for her adopted mother, leaving the audience to wonder about the future. Apart from being readily comparable in style and action to gritty Warner Brothers' melodramas of the period, *Woman Against the World* was ahead of its time in positing woman as intelligent action hero, asking serious social questions, and leaving the ending open, requiring audiences to think. Selman, who has heretofore been known only for making some competent B Westerns at Columbia starring Tim McCoy and Charles Starrett, is also due some revaluation. He directed two other good little films for Bishop at the Willows Park (Victoria) studio and environs in 1936: *Tugboat Princess*, another proto-feminist work, and *Secret Patrol* with Starrett as a Mountie.

BIBLIOGRAPHY: Colin Browne, 23–28.

Peter Rist

WOMEN ARE WARRIORS. Jane Marsh (Beveridge), NFB, "Canada Carries On" series, 1942, 14 min., b+w. In retrospect, *Women Are Warriors, Wings on Her Shoulders*, and *Proudly She Marches* (both 1943), all directed by Jane Marsh, can be considered the first intentionally feminist Canadian films. Marsh, who was married to James Beveridge, one of JOHN GRIERSON's first hires at the NFB, was assigned the job of making compilation documentaries aimed at Canadian women, to encourage them to get involved in the war effort. The first one, *Women Are Warriors*, is arguably the best directed of all the "Canada Carries On" films, especially in its exciting conclusion, where cuts are made on action, from a fast tracking camera scanning numerous women at work on machines, to a pan of women leaving the workplace, and, later, from a shot of two proximous women framed in heroic low angle, looking up to the sky, to a shot of aircraft. The fortuitous nature of these images fitting together so well as a tribute to female factory workers helping to build up the Canadian Air Force suggests that Marsh may have been allowed to shoot footage just for this film. Earlier, *Women Are Warriors* depicted British women working in various jobs followed by similar images of Soviet women, leading to the narrator's surprised reaction to Canadian women doing the same. While Grierson was forward-thinking enough to pioneer the hiring of women in key roles at the NFB, he was also responsible for demanding that the familiar, comforting voice of LORNE GREENE dominate the soundtrack of these films for women. Ultimately, his condescending words—such as "what would she have been doing before?"—undercut the notion that women can do the same jobs as men, and inadvertently prefigure men reclaiming their positions at war's end. But nothing can detract from Marsh's dynamic, forthright directing of images, and her work with actresses in *Proudly She Marches* has led feminist film scholar Marilyn Burgess to argue that the construction of the spectator's "gaze" or "look" can be interpreted as being lesbian. Jane Marsh directed the important three-reel Quebec documentary, *Alexis Tremblay: Habitant* in 1943 and one more film in the "Canada Carries On" series, *Air Cadets* (1944) before leaving the NFB. She worked for a while as a scriptwriter and editor for the British Information Service in New York before abandoning filmmaking altogether in 1948.

BIBLIOGRAPHY: Barbara Halpern Martineau, "Before the Guerillières: Women's Films at the NFB During World War II," in Feldman and Nelson, 58–67; Marilyn Burgess, "*Proudly She Marches*: Wartime Propaganda and the Lesbian Spectator," *CineACTION!*, no. 23 (Winter 1990–91): 22–27.

Peter Rist

Y

YOU TAKE CARE NOW. Ann-Marie Fleming, British Columbia, 1989, 12 min., color. This early film of Ann-Marie Fleming's, made while she was a student at Emily Carr College, recounts two stories, told in second-person voice-over. The first describes the sexual harassment and rape of a woman traveling in Brindisi, Italy, the second the accident of being hit by a car while crossing the road in Vancouver. The voice-over sums up the experiences by asking, "What did you ever do to get raped and run over in one lifetime? And you realize there is only one." Visually the film displays a catalogue of images from diverse sources: stills, video clips of boxing, a woman wrapped in a shroud. Fleming manipulates the images further onscreen with animation techniques. Stencil and gouache are employed to highlight images. The combined effect of image and voice-over evokes the sense of a stream of consciousness, of a figure struggling to place meaning into a sequence of horrible events. The voice-over, done by Fleming herself, carries the film to the individual viewer, allowing Fleming to compress a considerable amount of detail into a relatively short film. The style used here would subsequently be employed with equal effectiveness in Fleming's contribution to the NFB's *Five Feminist Minutes*, entitled *New Shoes*. Fleming's penchant for doing her own voice-over and taking stories from every-day events prompted critic/filmmaker MIKE HOOLBOOM to dub her "the queen of disaster." On the basis of the success of her early films, Fleming achieved considerable recognition, which enabled her to expand *New Shoes* into a dramatic feature-length film in 1990. Fleming further pursued the possibilities of mainstream cinema with a residency at the Canadian Film Centre. From this she directed the short film *Buckingham Palace*. Since this time Fleming has worked on music videos and various short film projects.

BIBLIOGRAPHY: Scott MacDonald, "Ann Marie Fleming," in MacDonald.

Dave Douglas

Z

ZIGRAIL. André Turpin, Quebec, 1995, 78 min., b+w. André Turpin is at the forefront of Quebec's new wave of young and aggressively talented filmmakers, the likes of which have not been seen since the coming of age of MICHEL BRAULT, GILLES GROULX, and the other leaders of *cinéma direct* in the late fifties. Like these better known "angry young men" did before him, Turpin is making a name for himself by breaking established rules, brandishing his right to experiment, and making very few compromises just to get ahead, both as a cinematographer and a director. In *Zigrail*, he shuns the "high-standard" glossy look of big budgeted pictures as he does that of the lackluster realist drama inherited from the documentary tradition. In reaction, Turpin offers a disjointed and highly kinetic look, one that openly borrows from the visual language of rock videos while transcending its superficiality and commercial raison d'être by anchoring its formalist flights of fancy in the characters' drive and their imagination. Certain scenes in *Zigrail* function as allegorical mental projections of its young hero's psyche as he comes to grips with the facts of life and the uncertainty of his future. Upon learning, over the phone, that his girlfriend is pregnant, the hyperactive hero freezes, but the film goes into overdrive: quick abstract shots in movement and explosive flashbacks zoom by, accompanied by thunderous noises, until everything becomes silent over a vertigo-inducing and yet graceful shot of the young man falling through the air, one foot attached to a bungee cord, like some airborne fetus. It is a visionary shot linking the father to his unborn child and translates without words the life-altering aspects of the news he's just received. In *Zigrail*, the originality of Turpin's style also extends to his extensive use of nonprofessional actors who, surprisingly, perform with unaffected ease and to the genre; a road movie stretched to international loca-tions. By challenging the sedentarism of the prototypical Quebec hero, Turpin breaks down the barriers that keep him prisoner of a geographically and socially constricted state he cannot call his own and the stagnancy of a sometimes hopeless state of mind.

BIBLIOGRAPHY: Martin Girard, *"Zigrail*: Renaissance," *Séquences*, no. 178 (May/June 1995): 25; Bernard Perron, "Tourner, oui. Mais tourner librement," *Ciné-bulles* (Winter-Spring 1995): 48–51.

Johanne Larue

UN ZOO LA NUIT Night Zoo. Jean-Claude Lauzon, Quebec, 1987, 116 min., color. JEAN-CLAUDE LAUZON's debut feature drew considerable attention when first released. Co-produced with the ONF, the film is a dark and often disturbing treatment of male bonding in general and father/son relationships in particular. Marcel (Gilles Maheu), a musician, is released from prison, where he has been serving time on a cocaine charge. Back in Montreal, Marcel stops for a coffee at an old hangout, where he sees his former lover Julie (Lynne Adams) and her new lover. Returning to his loft, Marcel is confronted by Charlie (GERMAIN HOUDE), a corrupt cop, and his partner George (Lorne Brass). The two men demand the unrecovered cocaine, which Marcel has stashed away at his father's apartment, and a large sum of money; they claim that they will kill Julie and Albert (Roger Le Bel), Marcel's father, if Marcel doesn't deliver the goods. Marcel's main concern, however, is the continuation of the life he left behind when incarcerated. His efforts to reclaim his relationship with Julie fail, and so he concentrates his attentions on Albert, a lifelong hunter who, he learns, is dying. After he and his prison lover, The American (Jerry Snell), kill George and Charlie, Marcel takes his father to the zoo (hence the film's title) in order to take part in one last hunt; the two men are reconciled, and Albert dies peacefully, in bed. The film is problematic in some ways: female characters fare very poorly in this film (Julie, for example, plays only a marginal role in the narrative), and the film's emphasis on cars, motorcycles, and guns—all the trappings of machismo—often assumes too prominent a place; it is also difficult for non-hunters to derive much satisfaction from a resolution that involves the shooting of a caged elephant. However, the film is stylistically rich, with a highly baroque use of lighting, camera movement, and mise-en-scène. Of particular interest, in light of Lauzon's next film, *LÉOLO*, is the sound design by Marcel Pothier. *Un zoo la nuit* virtually swept the Genies, winning more Canadian Film Awards, thirteen, than any other film, before or since.

Mitch Parry

APPENDIX A: 100 OTHER NOTABLE CANADIAN FILMMAKERS AND ACTORS

Names marked with an asterisk indicate individuals who were either raised in Canada or became Canadian.

Pamela ANDERSON LEE	pin-up (*Playboy* centerfold), then TV star ("Baywatch")
Dan AYKROYD	New York television and Hollywood film comedian (*Ghostbusters*)
Robert BEATTY	television and film actor, mostly in Great Britain (*49th Parallel*)
Hart BOCHNER	television and film actor (*Die Hard*) and director (*High School High*)
Raymond BURR	Hollywood villain, then TV star (Perry Mason)
James CAMERON	Oscar winning director of biggest box office smash of all time, *Titanic*
Jim CARREY	comedian, especially popular with teenagers; the world's highest paid film star
Jack CARSON	Hollywood supporting actor in 1940s and 1950s, usually as obnoxious villains
Kim CATTRAL*	British-born, U.S. trained actor in Canadian and U.S. films, also TV ("Wild Palms")
Rae Dawn CHONG	film and television actor; Tommy Chong's daughter
Tommy CHONG	half of "hippie" comic improv duo Cheech and Chong
Al(bert) CHRISTIE	silent film actor, director, and then producer of "Al Christie" comedies
Susan CLARK	child actor on stage, then Hollywood actor 1960s on; won Emmy for "Babe"
Susan CLOUTIER	model, then screen actor, notably as Desdemona in Orson Welles' *Othello*

Bill CODY	Hollywood stuntman, then Western star
Hume CRONYN	Broadway and Hollywood actor, married to Jessica Tandy from 1942
Jack CUMMINGS	MGM producer, especially of musicals (*Seven Brides for Seven Brothers*)
Lolita DAVIDOVICH	young Hollywood actor, notably in *Blaze* and *The Inner Circle*
Richard DAY	six time Oscar-winning Hollywood art director, notably for *Dodsworth* and *How Green Was My Valley*
Yvonne DE CARLO	dancer, then actor, especially as exotic temptress and in Hollywood films noir
Joseph DE GRASSE	director of Hollywood silent films in 1910s and 1920s; brother of Sam (below)
Sam DE GRASSE	silent film villain, notably as Prince John in Fairbanks' *Robin Hood*
Katherine DE MILLE	Hollywood actor of 1930s; adopted at age nine by Cecil B. De Mille
Edward DMYTRYK	Hollywood director (*Crossfire; Murder, My Sweet*); one of "Hollywood Ten" found guilty of communist affiliations who "named names" for House Un-American Activities Committee
Fifi D'ORSAY	vaudeville performer, then Hollywood actor, often typecast as sexy Parisian
Marie DRESSLER	comic star of vaudeville and Hollywood films; Oscar winner (*Min and Bill*)
Douglas DUMBRILLE	Broadway actor, then Hollywood character actor (in over 200 films)
George DUNNING	director and animator, mostly in England (*Yellow Submarine*)
Deanna DURBIN	teenage star (*Three Smart Girls* rescued the Universal studio) and Hollywood's #1 box office draw of early 1940s, who suddenly retired in 1948
Allan DWAN	Hollywood director from 1911 to 1958, especially of Westerns
Harry EDWARDS	silent comedy director, notably of Harry Langdon films (*Tramp Tramp Tramp*)
J. Gordon EDWARDS	silent film director, notably of Theda Bara and William Farnum vehicles
Glenn FORD	Hollywood star, notably in Westerns and Fritz Lang thrillers (*The Big Heat*)
Rosemary FORSYTH	model, then television, now film actor
Michael J. FOX	TV sitcom star ("Family Ties"), then film star (*Back to the Future*)

Sidney J. FURIE	Canadian TV producer/director, then director of British (*The Leather Boys*) and American (*Lady Sings the Blues*) films
Corey HAIM	child actor, then teen star of Hollywood films (*Thee Lost Boys*)
Dell HENDERSON	early silent film actor and director, especially for D. W. Griffith
Natasha HENSTRIDGE	supermodel, then movie star (*Species*)
Arthur HILLER	TV, then Hollywood film director (*Love Story*); current president of the U.S. Academy of Motion Picture Arts and Sciences
Victoria HOPPER	popular leading actor in British films of the 1930s
Kathleen HOWARD	opera singer, then fashion editor and character actor in 1930s Hollywood films
Walter HUSTON	engineer, then award-winning actor (including Oscar for *Treasure of the Sierra Madre*); father of director John Huston
John IRELAND	Oscar-nominated actor (*All the King's Men*)
May IRWIN	comic Broadway star involved in the first screen kiss (*The Kiss*, Edison, 1896)
Norman JEWISON	TV, then acclaimed Hollywood film director (*In the Heat of the Night; Moonstruck*); founder of Canadian Centre for Advanced Film Studies
Robert JOY	actor in Canadian and U.S. films (*Radio Days, Desperately Seeking Susan*)
Ruby KEELER	dancing and singing star of 1930s Warners' musicals (*42nd Street*)
Barbara KENT	Hollywood actor in late 1920s and early 1930s, often opposite Reginald Denny
Mia KIRSCHNER	intense young Canadian film actor (*Exotica*), now in United States (*Mad City*)
Alexander KNOX	stage and screen actor in United States and UK; Oscar nomination for *Wilson*
Elias KOTEAS	actor, notably in Atom Egoyan's films, but also Hollywood (*The Prophesy*)
Matheson LANG	actor in British silent films
Florence LAWRENCE	the first real star of American films: known as "The Biograph Girl"
Eugene LEVY	comic star of film and TV ("Second City"), in Canada and the United States
Bea(trice) LILLIE	comic star of London and Broadway stage, radio, and occasional films
Gene LOCKHART	stage actor and writer who also appeared in over 100 films

Wilfred LUCAS	early silent film actor and director, notably with D. W. Griffith (at Biograph)
David MANNERS	writer and actor, esp. in Universal horror films (*Dracula, The Black Cat*)
Raymond MASSEY	highly acclaimed actor in British, then Hollywood films; often played Lincoln
Lois MAXWELL	actor in U.S., British, and Italian films; Miss Moneypenny to James Bond
Sheila McCARTHY	double Genie-winning actor (*I've Heard the Mermaids Singing, The Lotus Eaters*) who now also works in Hollywood (*Die Hard 2*)
Rick MORANIS	TV ("Second City") comedian (Bob McKenzie), then film, also director
Barry MORSE*	British-born stage and screen actor, best known as TV detective ("The Fugitive")
Silvio NARIZZANO	TV director, then film director in Britain (*Georgy Girl*), United States, and Canada
Leslie NIELSEN	Hollywood actor; career resurrected as comedian (*Naked Gun*)
Catherine O'HARA	TV comedian ("SCTV"), then Hollywood actor (*After Hours, Beetlejuice*)
Sidney OLCOTT	important pioneer; director of the first U.S. feature film, *From the Manger to the Cross*
Michael ONTKEAN	child actor whose adult career took off in the United States with *Slapshot*
Anna PAQUIN	young Oscar-winning actor (*The Piano*)
Daniel PETRIE	TV and film director, mainly in the United States (*A Raisin in the Sun*); his only Canadian feature, *The Bay Boy*, won the Genie for Best Film
Jack PICKFORD	silent actor whose career was greatly helped along by his sister, Mary (below)
Mary PICKFORD	"America's sweetheart" was Canadian! One of the biggest film stars of all time, she won an Oscar for her first talkie, *Coquette*, and a special Academy Award in 1975; before she died she regained her Canadian citizenship
Walter PIDGEON	twice Oscar-nominated actor who played doctors and other responsible adults in 1930s and 1940s Hollywood films
Marie PREVOST	silent star, from Sennett bathing beauty to sophisticated Lubitsch comedian
John QUALEN	Hollywood character actor from 1931 to 1960s, often as Scandinavian immigrant
Alvin RAKOFF	film and television director in England and United States

Keanu REEVES*	glamorous Hollywood star of the 1990s (*Speed, Bram Stoker's Dracula*)
John S. ROBERTSON	Hollywood's "most liked filmmaker" in the 1920s
Mark ROBSON	Hollywood editor and director, most notably for Val Lewton at RKO
Harold RUSSELL	World War II veteran who won two Oscars for his supporting role in *Best Years of Our Lives*; a casualty, both his hands had been amputated
Ann RUTHERFORD	Hollywood actor; Polly Benedict to Mickey Rooney's Andy Hardy
Harry SALTZMAN	film producer in UK (James Bond series) and Hollywood
Michael SARRAZIN	actor; came to prominence in the late sixties (*They Shoot Horses, Don't They?*)
Mack SENNETT	important American film pioneer; director and producer of silent "slapstick" comedies (Keystone Kops); winner of Special Oscar in 1937 as "master of fun"
William SHATNER	"Star Trek" perennial; formerly stage and film actor in Canada and United States
Douglas SHEARER	12 time Oscar winner for Sound Recording; brother of Norma (below)
Norma SHEARER	elegant MGM star after marrying Irving Thalberg; Oscar winner for *The Divorcee*
Martin SHORT	TV comedian ("Saturday Night Live"), then Hollywood film star
Jay SILVERHEELS	native actor, played native roles in film and TV: "The Lone Ranger's" Tonto
Alexis SMITH	Warner Bros. actor in the 1940s and 1950s
John N. SMITH	director of Canadian film and TV (notably, *The Boys of St. Vincent*), now in Hollywood (*Dangerous Minds*)
Alexandra STEWART	model, then actor in Europe (*Day for Night*), United States, (*Exodus*), and Canada
Kiefer SUTHERLAND	young actor, member of Hollywood "Brat Pack," son of Donald Sutherland
Meg TILLY*	young Hollywood actor of 1980s and 1990s, beginning with *Fame*
Jack L. WARNER	Hollywood studio mogul (Warner Bros.)
Lucille WATSON	matronly Hollywood actor of the 1930s and 1940s
Richard WILLIAMS	animator in UK, opening his own studio, then Hollywood; multiple Oscars
Joseph WISEMAN	stage actor from 1930s and in films from 1950; often plays "thinking" villains
Fay WRAY	Hollywood actor; became star with von Stroheim's sensational *The Wedding March*, but best known as *King Kong's* love interest

APPENDIX B: ACADEMY OF CANADIAN CINEMA AND TELEVISION, CANADIAN FILM AWARDS

GENIES

Year	Date of awards	Best Film	Best Director
1997	Dec. 15	*The Sweet Hereafter* (8 awards)	Atom Egoyan
1996	Nov. 27	*Lilies* (4 awards)	David Cronenberg, for *Crash* (5 awards)
1995	Jan. 14, '96	*Le confessional* (3 awards)	Robert Lepage
1994	Dec. 7	*Exotica* (8 awards)	Atom Egoyan
1993	Dec. 12	*32 Short Films About Glenn Gould* (4 awards)	François Girard
1992	Nov. 22	*Naked Lunch* (8 awards)	David Cronenberg
1990–91	Nov. 26	*Black Robe* (6 awards)	Bruce Beresford
1989	Mar. 20, '90	*Jésus de Montréal* (12 awards)	Denys Arcand
1988	Mar. 22, '89	*Dead Ringers* (10 awards)	David Cronenberg
1987	Mar. 22, '88	*Un zoo la nuit* (13 awards)	Jean-Claude Lauzon
1986	Mar. 18, '87	*Le déclin de l'empire américain*	Denys Arcand
1985	Mar. 20, '86	*My American Cousin* (6 awards)	Sandy Wilson
1984	Feb. 18, '85	*The Bay Boy* (6 awards)	Micheline Lanctôt, for *Sonatine*

1983	Mar. 21, '84	*The Terry Fox Story* (5 awards)	shared: David Cronenberg, for *Videodrome*/Bob Clark, for *A Christmas Story*
1982	Mar 23, '83	*The Grey Fox* (7 awards)	Phillip Borsos
1981	Mar. 3, '82	*Ticket to Heaven* (4 awards)	Gilles Carle, for *Les Plouffe* (7 awards)
1980	Mar. 12 '81	*Les bons débarras* (8 awards)	Francis Mankiewicz
1979	Mar. 20 '80	*The Changeling* (8 awards)	Bob Clark, for *Murder by Decree*

ETROGS:

Year	Date of Awards	Best Feature Film	Best Film (if other)
1978	Sep. 28	*The Silent Partner* (6 awards)	
1977	Nov. 20	*J. A. Martin, photographe* (7 awards)	
1976	Oct. 24	*Lies My Father Told Me* (6 awards)	
1974–75	Oct. 12	"1975 Film" *Les ordres* (4 awards); "1974 Film" *The Apprenticeship of Duddy Kravitz* (2 awards)	
1973	Oct. 12	*Slipstream* (3 awards)	no award
1972	Oct. 13	*Wedding in White* (3 awards)	no award
1971	Oct. 1	*Mon oncle Antoine* (8 awards)	no award
1970	Oct. 3	*Goin' Down the Road* (3 awards)	*Psychotratie* (also Animated Film)
1969	Oct. 4	no features entered	*The Best Damn Fiddler from Calabogie to Kaladar* (8 awards)
1968	Oct. 4	*The Ernie Game* (2 awards)	*A Place to Stand* (3 awards)
1967	Sep. 23	*Warrendale* (3 awards)	
1966	May 6	*Le festin des morts* (2 awards)	*The Mills of the Gods: Viet Nam* (2 awards)

1965	May 15	*The Luck of Ginger Coffey*	no award
1964	May 8	*À tout prendre*	*Pour la suite du monde* (2 awards)
1963	May 10	no features entered	*Lonely Boy* (2 awards)
1962		no features entered	no award
1961	May 13	no features entered	*Universe* (2 awards)
1959–60		no Best Feature Film or Best Film awards given	
1958	June 21	no features entered	*City of Gold* (2 awards)
1956–57		no Best Feature Film or Best Film awards given	
1955	no presentation	*The Stratford Adventure*	
1954	May 10	*The Seasons*	
1953	Apr. 30	*Tit-Coq*	
1952	Apr. 27	*Royal Journey* (2 awards)	*Newfoundland Scene* (2 awards)
1950–51		no Film of the Year	
1949	Apr. 27	*The Loon's Necklace*	

APPENDIX C: CANADA'S TEN BEST

The following are the results of two polls conducted by Toronto's Festival of Festivals in 1984 and 1993, where over 100 critics, professors, and industry people around the world with a concern for Canadian film were asked to name the "10 Best Canadian Films" of all time. The results of the first poll accompanied the programming of the 1984 Toronto festival, which was followed by a Canadian tour of the "ten best" films. The results of the second poll were published in the Fall 1994 issue of *Take One*, along with ninety-six individual lists (some people wished their choices to remain secret). I have appended my own list as I sent it to the organizers, which is slightly different from the one published. It goes without saying that my choices would be different now; even then I found it impossible to keep it down to less than thirteen titles.

1984

1. *Mon oncle Antoine* (1971)
2. *Goin' Down the Road* (1970)
3. *Les bons débarras* (1979)
4. *The Apprenticeship of Duddy Kravitz* (1974)
5. *The Grey Fox* (1982)
   Les ordres (1974)
7. *J. A. Martin, photographe* (1976)
   Pour le suite du monde (1963)
9. *Nobody Waved Goodbye* (1964)
   Le vrai nature de Bernadette (1972)

1993

1. *Mon oncle Antoine* (1971)
2. *Jésus de Montréal* (1988)

3. *Goin' Down the Road* (1970)

4. *Le déclin de l'empire américain* (1986)

5. *Les bons débarras* (1979)

6. *Les ordres* (1974)

7. *The Apprenticeship of Duddy Kravitz* (1974)

8. *The Grey Fox* (1982)

9. *I've Heard the Mermaids Singing* (1987)

10. *The Adjuster* (1991)

MY 1993 LIST

The first two titles are placed jointly at the top, slightly above the others, which are listed chronologically. Unlike most participants, I didn't confine my list to feature films.

1. *La région centrale* (1971)
   Pour la suite du monde (1963)

3. *Back to God's Country* (1919)

4. *Begone Dull Care* (1949)

5. *Les raquetteurs* (1958)

6. *Lonely Boy* (1962)

7. *Rat Life and Diet in North America* (1968)

8. *Watching for the Queen* (1973)

9. *Le vieux pays où Rimbaud est mort* (1977)

10. *Mourir à tue-tête* (1979)

11. *Videodrome* (1983)

12. *Parallax: Ten Cents a Dance* (1985)

13. *Masala* (1991)

Peter Rist

SELECTED BIBLIOGRAPHY

Abel, Marie-Christine. *Le cinéma québécois à l'heure internationale*. Montreal: Stanké, 1990.

Backhouse, Charles F. *Canadian Government Motion Picture Bureau, 1917–1941*. Ottawa: Canadian Film Institute, 1974.

Baril, Gérald. *Les Amérindiens du Québec dans le cinéma documentaire, 1960–1980*. 1984.

Barrowclough, Susan, ed. *Jean-Pierre Lefebvre: The Quebec Connection* BFI Dossier Number 13. London: British Film Institute, 1981.

Bastien, Jean-Pierre. *Gilles Groulx: Rétrospective, février 1978*. Montreal: Cinémathèque québécoise Presses, 1978.

Bastien, Jean-Pierre, and Pierre Véronneau. *Jacques Leduc/Essais de travail d'equipe*. Cinéastes du Québec, No. 12. Montreal: Conseil québécois pour la diffusion du cinéma, 1974.

Beattie, Eleanor. *The Handbook of Canadian Film*. 2nd ed. Toronto: Peter Martin Associates, 1977.

Bélanger, Léon-H. *Les Ouimetoscopes: Léo-Ernest Ouimet et les débuts du cinéma québécois*. Montreal: VLB Éditeurs, 1978.

Bendazzi, Giannalberto. *Cartoons: One Hundred Years of Cinema Animation*. Trans. Anna Taraboletti-Segre. Bloomington: Indiana University Press, 1994.

Benson, Eugene, and L .W. Conolly, eds. *The Oxford Companion to Canadian Theatre*. Toronto: Oxford University Press, 1989.

Berton, Pierre. *Hollywood's Canada: The Americanization of Our National Image*. Toronto: McClelland and Stewart, 1975.

Bérubé, Ronald, and Yves Patry, eds. *Jean-Pierre Lefebvre*. Montreal: Les Presses de l'Université du Québec, 1971.

Beveridge, James, *John Grierson: Film Master*. London: Collier Macmillan, 1978.

Bidd, Donald W., ed. *Le répertoire des films de l'ONF: La production de l'Office national du film du Canada de 1939 à 1989 (Productions en français)*. Montreal: L'Office national du film du Canada, 1991a.

————. *The NFB Film Guide: The Productions of the National Film Board of Canada from 1939 to 1989 (English Language Productions)*. Montreal: National Film Board of Canada, 1991b.

Bonneville, Léo. *Dossier de cinéma: Jour après jour*. Montreal: Fidès, 1968.

Bouchard, René. *Filmographie d'Albert Tessier*. Montreal: Éditions du Boréal Express, 1973.

Boulais, Stéphane-Albert. *Le cinéma vécu de l'intérieur: Mon expérience avec Pierre Perrault*. Hull: Éditions de Lorraine, 1988.

Browne, Colin. *Motion Picture Production in British Columbia, 1898–1940*. Heritage Record No. 6. Victoria: British Columbia Provincial Museum, 1979.

Brownlow, Kevin. *The War, the West, and the Wilderness*. New York: Alfred A. Knopf, 1979.

Canemaker, John. *Storytelling in Animation: The Art of the Animated Image. An Anthology*. Los Angeles: American Film Institute Presses, 1998.

Carrière, Louise, et al. *Femmes et cinéma québécoise*. Montreal: Boréal Express, 1983.

Chabot, Claude, Michel Larouche, Denise Pérusse, and Pierre Véronneau. *Le cinéma québécois des années 80*. Montreal: Cinémathèque québécoise/Musée du cinéma, 1989.

Chabot, Jean. *Claude Jutra*. Cinéastes du Québec, No. 4. Montreal: Conseil québécois pour la diffusion du cinéma, 1970.

Changing Focus: The Future for Women in the Canadian Film and Television Industry. Toronto: Toronto Women in Film and Television, 1991.

Clandfield, David. *Canadian Film*. Toronto: Oxford University Press, 1987.

Collective. *Silencing the Workers: Censorship in the NFB*. Montreal: Cinémathèque québécoise archives, 1973.

Collins, Maynard. *Norman McLaren*. Ottawa: Canadian Film Institute, 1976.

Cornwall, Regina. *Snow Seen: The Films and Photographs of Michael Snow*. Toronto: PMA Books, 1980.

Coulombe, Michel. *Denys Arcand: La vraie nature du cinéaste*. Montreal: Éditions Boréal, 1993.

———. *Entretiens avec Gilles Carle: Le chemin secret du cinéma*. Montreal: Éditions Liber, 1995.

Coulombe, Michel, and Marcel Jean. *Le dictionnaire du cinéma québécois*. Montreal: Boréal, 1988.

Daudelin, Robert. *Gilles Groulx*. Cinéastes du Québec, No. 1. Montreal: Conseil québécois pour la diffusion du cinéma, 1969.

David Rimmer: Films and Tapes, 1967–1993. Toronto: Art Gallery of Ontario, 1993.

Desbarats, Carole, Daniele Riviere, Jacinto Lageira, and Paul Virilio. *Atom Egoyan*. Trans. by Brian Holmes. Paris: Éditions Dis Voir, 1993.

Donohoe, Joseph I., Jr., ed. *Essays on Quebec Cinema*. East Lansing: Michigan State University Press, 1991.

Easterbrook, Ian K., and Susan Waterman MacLean, with Bernard M.L. Katz, Kathleen E. Scott, and Paul W. Salmon, comp. *Canada and Canadians in Feature Films: A Filmography, 1928–1990*. Guelph, Ontario: University of Guelph, 1996.

Edsforth, Janet. *Paul Almond: The Flame Within*. Ottawa: Canadian Film Institute, 1972.

Egoyan, Atom, *Speaking Parts*. Toronto: Coach House Press, 1993.

Elder, R. Bruce. *The Body in Film*. Toronto: Art Gallery of Ontario, 1989a.

———. *Image and Identity: Reflections on Canadian Film and Culture*. Waterloo: Wilfred Laurier Press, 1989b.

Evans, Gary. *John Grierson and the National Film Board: The Politics of Wartime Propaganda*. Toronto: University of Toronto Press, 1984.

————. *In the National Interest: A Chronicle of the National Film Board of Canada from 1949 to 1989*. Toronto: University of Toronto Press, 1991.

Falardeau, Pierre. *La liberté n'est pas une marque de yogourt*. Montreal: Stanké, 1995.

Faucher, Carol. *La production française à l'ONF: 25 ans en perspectives*. Montreal: Cinémathèque québécoise/Musée du Cinéma, 1984.

Faucher, Carol, and Michel Houle. *Gilles Carle*. Cinéastes du Québec, No. 2. Montreal: Conseil québecois pour la diffusion du cinéma, 1976.

Feldman, Seth, ed. *Take Two: A Tribute to Film in Canada*. Toronto: Irwin Publishing, 1984.

Feldman, Seth, and Joyce Nelson, eds. *Canadian Film Reader*. Toronto: Peter Martin Associates, 1977.

Fetherling, Douglas, ed. *Documents in Canadian Film*. Peterborough: Broadview Press, 1988.

Fischer, Dennis. *Horror Film Directors, 1931–1990*. Jefferson, NC: McFarland and Co., 1991.

Fulford, Robert. *Marshall Delaney at the Movies: The Contemporary World as Seen on Film*. Toronto: Peter Martin Associates, 1974.

Garebian, Keith, ed. *William Hutt: Masks and Faces*. Oakville, Ontario: Mosaic Press, 1995.

Garel, Sylvain, and André Pâquet, eds. *Les cinémas du Canada: Québec, Ontario, Prairies, côte Ouest, Atlantique*. Paris: Centre Georges Pompidou, 1992.

Glover, Guy. *McLaren*. Montreal: National Film Board of Canada, 1980.

Gobeil, Charlotte, ed. *Terence Macartney-Filgate: The Candid Eye*. Ottawa: Canadian Film Institute, 1966.

Graff, Tom, ed. *Jack Chambers Films. The Capilano Review*, no. 33 (1984).

Green, Mary Jean. "Lea Pool's *La femme de l'hôtel* and Women's Films in Quebec." *Quebec Studies*, no. 9 (Fall-Winter 1990): 48–62.

The John Grierson Project: McGill University. *John Grierson and the NFB*. Papers presented at a conference held at McGill University, Montreal, Quebec, October 29–31, 1981. Toronto: ECW Press, 1984.

Guilet, M. *Cours d'histoire du cinéma canadien*. Montreal: Cinémathèque québécoise archives.

Hancox, Rick, and Catherine Jonasson. *Richard Hancox*. Toronto: Art Gallery of Ontario, 1990.

Handling, Piers. *The Films of Don Shebib*. Ottawa: Canadian Film Institute, 1978.

————, ed. *The Shape of Rage: The Films of David Cronenberg*. Toronto: General Publishing Co., 1983.

Harcourt, Peter. *A Canadian Journey: Conversations with Time*. Canada: Oberon Press, 1994.

————. *Jean Pierre Lefebvre*. Ottawa: Canadian Film Institute, 1981.

————. *Movies and Mythologies: Towards a National Cinema*. Toronto: CBC Publications, 1977.

Hardy, Forsyth. *John Grierson: A Documentary Biography*. London: Faber and Faber, 1979.

————, ed. and comp. *Grierson on Documentary*. London: Faber and Faber, 1966; New York: Praeger, 1971.

Hayes, R. M. *3-D Movies: A History and Filmography of Stereoscopic Cinema.* Jefferson, N.C.: McFarland & Co., 1989.

"Heavy Metal." Film Review Annual, 1982. Englewood, NJ: Film Review Publications, 1983.

Hébert, Gilles. Introduction to *Dislocations.* Winnipeg, Manitoba: Winnipeg Art Gallery, 1995.

Hofsess, John, *Inner Views: Ten Canadian Filmmakers.* Toronto: McGraw-Hill Ryerson, 1975.

Hoolboom, Mike, *Inside the Pleasure Dome: Fringe Film in Canada.* Toronto: Gutter Press, 1997.

Houle, Michel, and Alain Julien. *Dictionnaire du cinéma québécois.* Montreal: Éditions Fidès, 1978.

Jean, Marcel. *Le cinéma québécois.* Montreal: Boréal Express, 1991.

Jonasson, Catherine, and Jim Shedden, eds. *Recent Work from the Canadian Avant-Garde* (catalogue). Toronto: Art Gallery of Ontario, 1988.

Jones, D. B. *The Best Butler in the Business: Tom Daly of the National Film Board of Canada.* Toronto: University of Toronto Press, 1996.

———. *Movies and Memoranda: An Interpretive History of the Film Board of Canada.* Ottawa: Canadian Film Institute and Deneau Publishing, 1981.

Kline, Jim. *The Complete Films of Buster Keaton.* New York: Citadel Press, 1993.

Knelman, Martin. *Home Movies.* Toronto: Key Porter, 1987.

———. *A Stratford Tempest.* Toronto: McClelland and Stewart, 1982.

———. *This Is Where We Came In: The Career and Character of Canadian Film.* Toronto: McClelland and Stewart, 1977.

Kolomeychuk, Terry, ed. *Donald Brittain: Never The Ordinary Way.* Winnipeg, Manitoba: National Film Board of Canada, 1991.

Kuhn, Annette, and Susannah Radstone, eds. *Women in Film: An International Guide.* New York: Fawcett Columbine, 1990.

LaBruce, Bruce. *The Reluctant Pornographer.* Toronto: Gutter Press, 1997.

Lacasse, Germain. *Histoire de scopes: Le cinéma muet au Québec.* Montreal: Cinémathèque québecoise/Musée du Cinéma, 1988.

———. *L'historiographe (Les débuts du spectacle cinématographie au Québec).* Montreal: Cinémathèque québécoise/Musée du Cinéma, 1985.

Larochelle, Réal. *Jean-Claude Labrecque.* Cinéastes du Québec, No. 7. Montreal: Conseil québécois pour la diffusion du cinéma, 1971.

———. *Québec/Canada: L'enseignement du cinéma et de l'audiovisuel/The Study of Film and Video.* Condé-sur-Noireau, France: CinémAction-Corlet, 1991.

Lerner, Loren R. *Canadian Film and Video/Film et vidéo canadiens: A Bibliography and Guide to the Literature/Bibliographie analytique sur le cinéma et la vidéo.* 2 vols. Toronto: University of Toronto Press, 1997.

Lever, Yves. *Les 100 films québécois qu'il faut voir.* Quebec: Nuit Blanche Éditeur, 1995.

———. *Histoire générale du cinéma au Québec.* Montreal: Boréal, 1988.

Loiselle, André, and Brian McIlroy. *Auteur-Provocateur: The Films of Denys Arcand.* Westport, CT: Greenwood Press, 1995.

Lowder, Rose, ed. *The Visual Aspect: Recent Canadian Experimental Film.* Avignon, France: Éditions des Archives du film expérimental d'Avignon, 1991.

MacDonald, Scott. *Screen Writings: Scripts and Texts by Independent Filmmakers.* Berkeley: University of California Press, 1995.

Macek, Carl. *The Art of Heavy Metal, the Movie: Animation for the Eighties.* New York: New York Zoetrope, 1981.

Magder, Ted. *Canada's Hollywood: The Canadian State and Feature Films.* Toronto: University of Toronto Press, 1993.

Magill, Frank N., ed. *Magill's Survey of Cinema: Foreign Language Films, Vol. 5.* Englewood Cliffs, NJ: Salem Press, 1985.

————, ed. *Magill's Cinema Annual: A Survey of the Films of 1986.* Englewood Cliffs, NJ: Salem Press, 1987.

Major, Ginette. *Le cinéma québécois à la recherche d'un public, bilan d'une décennie.* Montreal: Presses de l'Université de Montréal, 1982.

Marcorelles, Louis. *Living Cinema.* New York: Praeger, 1973.

Marsolais, Gilles. *L'aventure du cinéma direct.* Paris: Cinéma club Seghers, 1974.

————. *Michel Brault* Cinéastes du Québec, No. 11. Montreal: Conseil québécois pour la diffusion du cinéma, 1972.

McCrohan, Donna. *The Second City: A Backstage History of Comedy's Hottest Troupe.* New York: Perigee Books, 1987.

McLean, Michaelle, coordinator. *Funnel* (catalogue). Toronto: The Funnel, 1984.

McWilliams, Donald, comp. and ed. *Norman McLaren on the Creative Process.* Montreal: National Film Board of Canada, 1991.

Meigs, Mary. *In the Company of Strangers.* Vancouver: Talonbooks, 1991.

Mitchell, Michie. *A Canadian Film Pioneer: Gordon Sparling.* Ottawa: National Film, Television and Sound Archives, 1980.

Morris, Peter. *David Cronenberg: A Delicate Balance.* Toronto: ECW Press, 1994.

————. *Embattled Shadows: A History of Canadian Cinema, 1895–1939.* Montreal: McGill-Queen's University Press, 1978.

————. *The Film Companion.* Toronto: Irwin Publishing, 1984.

Nelson, Joyce. *The Colonized Eye: Rethinking the Grierson Legend.* Toronto: Between the Lines, 1988.

Noguez, Dominique. *Essais sur le cinéma québécois.* Montreal: Éditions du Jour, 1971.

Pâquet, André, ed. *How to Make or Not to Make a Canadian Film.* Montreal: Cinémathèque canadienne, 1967.

Patry, Yvan, and Robert Daudelin. *Arthur Lamothe.* Cinéastes du Québec, No. 6. Montreal: Conseil québécois pour la diffusion du cinéma, 1971.

Paul, William. *Laughing Screaming.* New York: Columbia University Press, 1994.

Pelletier, Antoine. *Collection Maurice Proulx.* Catalogue: Direction générale du cinéma et de l'audiovisuel. Quebec: Éditeur officiel du Québec, 1978.

Pendakur, Manjunath. *Canadian Dreams and American Control: The Political Economy of the Canadian Film Industry.* Toronto: Garamond Press, 1990.

Pérusse, Denise. *La conquête d'un nouvel espace dans les films "féministes" québécois.* Montreal: Cinémathèque québécoise Presses, 1989.

Pevere, Geoff, and Greig Dymond. *Mondo Canuck: A Canadian Pop Culture Odyssey.* Scarborough, Ontario: Prentice-Hall Canada, 1996.

Pinsent, Gordon. *By the Way.* Toronto: Stoddart, 1992.

Pirie, David, ed. *Anatomy of the Movies.* London: WHS Distributors, 1981.

Pitschen, Salome, and Annette Schönholzer, eds. *Peter Mettler: Making the Invisible Visible.* Germany: Reihe Andreas Züst Im Verlag Ricco Bilger, 1995.

Poirier, Raynald. *Cinéma québécois: dossier: le cinéma d'animation sociale, document de travail.* Montreal: Cinémathèque québécoise archives, 1971.

Posner, Michael. *Canadian Dreams: The Making and Marketing of Independent Films.* Vancouver: Douglas & McIntyre, 1993.

Postscript 15, no. 1 (Fall 1995) (Special Cronenberg Issue).

Rabinovitz, Lauren. *Joyce Wieland* (exhibition catalogue). Toronto: Art Gallery of Ontario and Key Porter Books, 1987.

———. *Points of Resistance: Women, Power and Politics in the New York Avant-garde Cinema, 1943–71.* Chicago: University of Chicago Press, 1991.

Raffan, James. *Bill Mason and the Canadian Canoeing Tradition.* Toronto: Harper-Collins, 1996.

Rasselet, Christian. *Jean-Pierre Lefebvre.* Cinéastes du Québec, No. 3. Montreal: Conseil québécois pour la diffusion du cinéma, 1970.

Reid, Alison, ed. *Allan King: An Interview with Bruce Martin and a Filmography.* Ottawa: Canadian Film Institute, 1970 (revised and reprinted, 1971).

Richler, Mordecai. "Making a Movie." In *Home Sweet Home: My Canadian Album.* Toronto: McClelland and Stewart, 1984.

Richmond, Cindy, curator. *Richard Kerr: Overlapping Entries.* Regina, Saskatchewan: Mackenzie Art Gallery, 1994.

Rodley, Chris, ed. *Cronenberg on Cronenberg.* Toronto: Alfred A. Knopf Canada, 1992.

Roffman, Peter. *The Story of "Carry on Sergeant!"* Don Mills, Ontario: Ontario Film Institute, 1979.

Rombout, Luke, director. *Vancouver: Art and Artists, 1931–93.* Vancouver: Vancouver Art Gallery, 1983.

Rosenthal, Alan. *The Documentary Conscience.* Berkeley: University of California Press, 1980.

———. *The New Documentary in Action.* Berkeley: University of California Press, 1971.

Russell, Catherine, and Pierre Véronneau, eds. *Le cinéma muet au Québec et au Canada: Nouveau regards sur une practique culturelle.* CiNéMAS 6, no. 1 (Fall 1995).

Sheddon, Jim, ed. *Presence and Absence: The Films of Michael Snow, 1956–1991, The Michael Snow Project.* Toronto: Art Gallery of Ontario, Alfred A. Knopf Canada, 1995.

Shipman, Nell. *The Silent Screen and My Talking Heart.* Boise, Idaho: Boise State University, 1987; 2nd ed., designed and edited by Tom Trusky, 1988.

Sitney, P. Adams. "Michael Snow's Cinema." In *Michael Snow/A Survey.* Toronto: Art Gallery of Ontario in collaboration with the Isaacs Gallery, 1970, 79–84.

———. *Visionary Film: The American Avant-Garde.* New York: Oxford University Press, 1974.

Snow, Michael. *The Michael Snow Project: The Collected Writings of Michael Snow.* Foreword by Louise Dompierre. Waterloo, Ontario: Wilfred Laurier University Press, 1994.

———. ed. *1948–1993: Music/Sound, The Michael Snow Project.* Toronto: Art Gallery of Ontario, The Power Plant, Alfred A. Knopf Canada, 1993.

Steven, Peter. *New Canadian Documentary Film and Video.* Toronto: Between the Lines, 1973.

Tajibnapis, Marjah. "Foregrounding Women: An Annotated Index of 52 Canadian Women Filmmakers." *Resources for Feminist Research* 8, no. 4 (1979): 25–26.

Testa, Bart. *Spirit in the Landscape.* Toronto: Art Gallery of Ontario, 1989.

Tremblay-Daviault, Christiane. *Un cinéma orphelin: Structures mentales et sociales du cinéma québécois: 1942–1953.* Montreal: Éditions québec/amérique, 1981.

———. *Structures sociales et idéologie dans la pré-histoire du cinéma québécois: Longs métrages de fiction de 1942 à 1953.* Montreal: Université de Montréal Presses, 1979.

Turner, D. J. *Canada's Recovery and Restoration of "Back to God's Country."* Boise, Idaho: Boise State University Canadian Studies Program, 1987.

Turner, D. J., and Micheline Morisset. *Canadian Feature Film Index/Index des films canadiens de long métrage.* Ottawa: Public Archives Canada, 1987.

Turner, Michael. *Hard Core Logo.* Vancouver: Arsenal Pulp Press, 1993.

Véronneau, Pierre. *Cinéma de l'époque duplessiste: Histoire du cinéma au Québec II.* Montreal: Cinémathèque québécoise, 1979a.

———. *Le succès est au film parlant français: Histoire du cinéma au Québec I.* Montreal: Cinémathèque québécoise, 1979b.

———, ed. *À la recherche d'une identité: Renaissance du cinéma d'auteur canadien-anglais.* Montreal: Cinémathèque québécoise/Musée du Cinéma, 1991.

Véronneau, Pierre, and Gisèle Côté. *Rapport de l'expertise de la "collection Proulx."* Montreal: Cinémathèque québécoise, 1977.

Véronneau, Pierre, Michael Dorland, and Seth Feldman, eds. *Dialogue: Cinéma canadien et québécois/Canadian and Quebec Cinema.* Montreal: Médiatexte Publications/Cinémathèque québécoise, 1987.

Véronneau, Pierre, and Piers Handling, eds. *Self Portrait: Essays on the Canadian and Quebec Cinemas.* Ottawa: Canadian Film Institute, 1980.

Walker, Joseph B., and Juanita Walker. *The Light on Her Face.* Hollywood: ASC Press, 1984.

Walz, Gene, ed. *Flashback: People and Institutions in Canadian Film History.* Montreal: Médiatexte Publications, 1986.

Wees, William C., and Michael Dorland, eds. *Words and Moving Images: Essays on Verbal and Visual Expression in Film and Television.* Montreal: Médiatexte Publications, 1984.

Weinmann, Heinz. *Cinéma de l'imaginaire québécoise: De "La petite Aurore" à "Jésus de Montréal."* Montreal: L'Hexagone, 1990.

———. *Cinéma et imaginaire collectif: Le Québec ou la "naissance d'une nation."* Sainte-Foy, Quebec: Université Laval Presses, 1992.

York, Karen. *Great Scott! The Best of Jay Scott's Movie Reviews.* Toronto: McClelland and Stewart, 1994.

INDEX

Page numbers in **bold** indicate main entries.

ABOUT THE EDITOR AND CONTRIBUTORS

STACEY ABBOTT is undertaking a Ph.D. on the modern American vampire for the University of London. She is employed as an Education Officer for the British Film Institute and also works as a part-time lecturer in film studies at the University of North London.

SERGIO ANGELINI gained his degree in law from London School of Economics and his masters in film studies and film archiving from the University of East Anglia. He has worked in education and documentary film footage sales and is currently working as a Cataloguer at the British Film Institute.

ALICE BLACK received a BFA (Film Studies) from Concordia University, an MPhil (Media & Culture) from the University of Glasgow and an MA (Cinema Studies) from New York University. She worked as a researcher on Ian Easterbrook's book *Canada and Canadians in Feature Films* and she wrote two collection guides for the MoMA Film Library. At present, she is working as the administrator for the Federation of Irish Film Societies.

SIMON BROWN gained his master's degree in film studies and film archiving at the University of East Anglia. He is currently Footage Sales Officer at the British Film Institute and has lectured on the work of Nell Shipman and the history of the *Titanic* on film.

MARK CARPENTER is a budding Toronto screenwriter. Recently he received his MFA in film from York University in Ontario, where he focused his attention on the "Godfather" trilogy. Prior to this he received a BFA in Film Studies from Concordia University.

ROB COTTERILL is currently working as an "assistant" on a feature film production in New Brunswick. Since graduating from Concordia University with a

BFA he has worked as a teacher, a freelance writer and in various capacities on New Brunswick film and television productions.

JUDES DICKEY graduated from the Concordia University Film Studies Program sometime in the last decade. He currently writes content for websites while worrying about things (past, present and future) that really shouldn't concern him.

DAVE DOUGLAS studied film at Queen's University and received his M.A. and Ph.D. from Northwestern University. He has lectured in numerous cinema courses at both McGill University and Concordia University.

ALAIN DUBEAU is a freelance film critic living in Montreal who contributed for many years to the magazine *Séquences* and the webzine *Hors-Champ*. He also taught cinema at Cégep François-Xavier-Garneau and Université de Montréal. He is currently working on his Masters in Film Studies at Concordia University.

IAN ELLIOT is a lifelong film enthusiast and collector, knowledgeable in silent and early sound cinema. He has an Honors B.A. in English language and literature from the University of Western Ontario, and is a longtime employee of A Different Drummer Books in Burlington, Ontario, one of Canada's oldest and most respected independent bookstores.

SANDRA GALLANT received a B.F.A. in film studies from Concordia University and has maintained her interest in the field. She is currently working in the telecommunications industry.

LOUIS GOYETTE completed an undergraduate degree in film studies at Concordia University. He obtained his master's degree from Université de Montréal, writing his thesis on Japanese film director Mizoguchi Kenji. His interests also include Quebec cinema and experimental film. He's currently teaching film studies at Concordia University and Université de Montréal, and collaborated on *Le dictionnaire du cinéma québécois* (Boréal, 1999).

JOHANNE LARUE received a bachelor of fine arts, with distinction, specialization in film studies and a major in film production (1985) from Concordia University, where she has taught film studies ever since. She has given numerous cinema workshops and conferences in Montreal, Quebec, New Orleans, and Blois (France). An awarded film critic and editor for *Séquence* film magazine (1987–1997) and the press agency Médiafilm (since 1989), she has had many essays and articles published elsewhere. She is a screenwriting and editing consultant and has been awarded grants for her screenwriting work. She is presently pursuing doctoral studies in the humanities at Concordia University.

ISABELLE MORISSETTE is a Ph.D. student (in a special independent fine arts program) at Concordia University. She is particularly interested in silent cinema and will be preparing her thesis on self-reflexivity during this era. She has contributed to the work of research groups such as GRAFICS and "Cinéma et Réception" at Université de Montréal, where she completed her master's thesis on Antonioni's trilogy. She has written for *IRIS* on sound and has recently conducted research for André Roy's *Dictionnaire du film*. She is now working on a documentary about composer and silent film accompanist Gabriel Thibaudeau.

MITCH PARRY is a creative writer and professor living in Montreal. His work has appeared in *Grain, Event, Pottersfield Portfolio*, and *The Malahat Review*. In 1994 he published a novella with Anvil Press. He currently teaches film studies at Concordia University.

PETER HARRY RIST has been the chair of the Mel Hoppenheim School of Cinema at Concordia University, Montreal, Quebec, Canada, for six years. He teaches courses in film history and aesthetics, while specializing in Third World cinemas. He co-edited the book *South American Cinema: A Critical Filmography, 1915–1994* with Timothy Barnard and has had articles published on various aspects of film studies, including Canadian, Korean, and Chinese cinemas.

SANDRA SABATHY was born and raised just outside London, Ontario. She graduated in 1987 from the University of Western Ontario with an honors B.A. in English and dramatic arts, minor in film studies. She spent ten years living in the United States working in the film industry and publishing. She is now living in Oxford, England.

HELEN SALMON is a librarian, and is head of Social Sciences and Arts Information Services at the University of Guelph Library. Her research interests and prior publications are in the subject areas of film studies, theater bibliography, and reference publications in the social sciences.

PAUL SALMON teaches English and film courses in the School of Literatures and Performance Studies in English at the University of Guelph. His primary areas of research interest include Canadian cinema, British cinema, African American cinema, and the connections between fiction and film. His publications include entries for the *Dictionary of Literary Biography*, an article on Hanif Kureishi, and film reviews of works by such directors as Spike Lee, Federico Fellini, Stephen Frears, and Denys Arcand. He was an entry compiler and author of the introduction for *Canada and Canadians in Feature Films: A Filmography*.

DONATO TOTARO is presently writing his doctoral dissertation on time and the long take at the University of Warwick, UK. He has been a part-time film studies lecturer at Concordia University since 1990, and is editor of the online film journal "Offscreen" (www.offscreen.com). He has published on recent Asian cinema, the cinema of Andrei Tarkovsky, and the horror genre.